Cataloging
Cultural
Objects

Cataloging Cultural Objects: A Guide to Describing Cultural Works and Their Images

Editors

Murtha Baca
Head, Getty Vocabulary Program and Digital Resource Management, Getty Research Institute, Los Angeles, California

Patricia Harpring
Managing Editor, Getty Vocabulary Program, Getty Research Institute, Los Angeles, California

Elisa Lanzi
Director, Imaging Center, Department of Art, Smith College, Northampton, Massachusetts

Linda McRae
Director, College of Visual and Performing Arts, Visual Resources Library, University of South Florida, Tampa, Florida

Ann Whiteside
Head, Rotch Library of Architecture and Planning, Massachusetts Institute of Technology, Cambridge, Massachusetts

Project Manager

Diane M. Zorich
Information Management Consultant for Cultural Organizations, Princeton, New Jersey

Advisory Committee

Matthew Beacom
Metadata Librarian, Yale University Library, New Haven, Connecticut

Erin Coburn
Manager, Collections Information, J. Paul Getty Museum, Los Angeles, California

Janice Eklund
Curator of Visual Resources, Department of History of Art, University of California, Berkeley, California

Mary Elings
Archivist for Digital Collections, The Bancroft Library, University of California, Berkeley, California

Ardys Kozbial
Digital Projects Librarian, University of California, San Diego, La Jolla, California

Elizabeth O'Keefe
Director of Collection Information Systems, Pierpont Morgan Library, New York, New York

Trish Rose
Metadata Librarian, University of California, San Diego, La Jolla, California

Layna White
Head of Collections Information and Access, San Francisco Museum of Modern Art, San Francisco, California

Acknowledgements

MAJOR FUNDING

The Getty Foundation, Los Angeles, California

Digital Library Federation, Washington, DC

ADDITIONAL ASSISTANCE

Andrew W. Mellon Foundation
New York, New York

Donald J. Waters, Program Officer, Scholarly Communications

Getty Research Institute
Los Angeles, California

Murtha Baca, Head, Getty Vocabulary Program and Digital Resource Management

J. Paul Getty Trust, Los Angeles, California
Kenneth Hamma, Executive Director, Digital Policy and Initiatives

Rice University, Houston, Texas
Chuck Henry, Chief Information Officer
Mark Pompelia, Director of Visual Resources, Department of Art History
Gaylon Denney, Budget Director, Department of Art History

Union Catalog of Art Images, University of California, San Diego, La Jolla, California
Linda Barnhart, UCAI Project Coordinator
Brad Westbrook, formerly UCAI Design Librarian

University of South Florida
College of Visual and Performing Arts, Tampa, Florida, Faculty Research Council

Visual Resources Association

EXECUTIVE BOARD 2005

Kathe Hicks Albrecht
Visual Resources Curator, American University, Washington, DC

Virginia (Macie) Hall
Senior Information Technology Specialist, Johns Hopkins University, Baltimore, Maryland

Jeanne M. Keefe
Visual Resources Librarian, Rensselaer Polytechnic Institute, Troy, New York

Betha Whitlow
Curator of Visual Resources, Washington University in Saint Louis, Saint Louis, Missouri

Linda Reynolds
Visual Resources Curator, Williams College, Williamstown, Massachusetts

Ann M. Thomas
Slide Curator, Union College, Schenectady, New York

Christine E. Hilker
Director, Smart Media Center, University of Arkansas, Fayetteville, Arkansas

PROJECT TREASURER

Loy Zimmerman
Arts Curator, Visual Resources Collection, University of California, Irvine, Irvine, California

Project Web Designers

PHASE I DESIGN

Mark Pompelia
Director, Visual Resources Center, Department of Art History, Rice University, Houston, Texas

Phase I Web site images courtesy of Allan T. Kohl and the Art Images for College Teaching Web site, a free-use image resource for the educational community.

Cataloging Cultural Objects: A Guide to Describing Cultural Works and Their Images

PHASE II DESIGN AND CCO LOGO

Kalika Yap
CEO, Citrus Studios,
Santa Monica, California

CCO Listserv Coordinator

Benjamin Kessler
Chicago, Illinois

CCO Reviewers

Randal Brandt
Principal Cataloger,
Bancroft Library, University of California,
Berkeley, California

Carole Campbell
Registrar, J. Paul Getty Museum,
Los Angeles, California

Jennie Choi
Collections Management Coordinator,
Metropolitan Museum of Art, New York, New York

Sherman Clarke
Head of Original Cataloging,
Bobst Library, New York University,
New York, New York

Claudine Dixon
Curatorial Associate,
Grunwald Center for the Graphic Arts, Hammer
Museum, UCLA, Los Angeles, California

Heather Dunn
Heritage Information Analyst, Standards,
Canadian Heritage Information Network,
Gatineau, Quebec

James Eason
Archivist for Pictorial Collections,
The Bancroft Library, University of California,
Berkeley, Berkeley, California

Eileen Fry
Fine Arts Slide Librarian and DIDO Administrator,
Indiana University, Bloomington, Indiana

Jonathan Furner
Associate Professor, Department of Information
Studies, University of California, Los Angeles,
Los Angeles, California

Jocelyn Gibbs
Head of Special Collections Cataloging,
Getty Research Institute, Los Angeles, California

Virginia (Macie) Hall
Senior Information Technology Specialist,
Johns Hopkins University, Baltimore, Maryland

Benjamin Kessler, Chicago, Illinois

Brian Mains
Art Information Manager,
The Huntington Library, Art Collections, and
Botanical Gardens, San Marino, California

Marla Misunas
Collections Information Manager,
San Francisco Museum of Modern Art,
San Francisco, California

Lina Nagel Vega
Project Director, Tesauro de Arte & Arquitectura,
Centro de Documentación de Bienes Patrimoniales,
Santiago, Chile

Maria Oldal
Head of Cataloging and Database Maintenance,
Pierpont Morgan Library, New York, New York

Jane Bassett Rosario
Principal Processing Archivist,
The Bancroft Library, University of California,
Berkeley, Berkeley, California

Judy Silverman
Head of Cataloguing, Canadian Centre
for Architecture, Library,
Montréal, Québec

Erin Stalberg
Head, Cataloging Services, University of Virginia
Library, Charlottesville, Virginia

Kay Teel
Cataloging Librarian, Stanford University,
Stanford, California

Special Thanks

To Joan Weinstein, Associate Director, and Jack
Meyers (formerly Deputy Director) of the Getty
Foundation, and David Seaman, Executive Direc-
tor, and Daniel Greenstein (formerly Executive
Director) of the Digital Library Federation, for
their vision and advocacy.

To Madeleine Lafaille, Canadian Info-Muse
Network, for providing copies of the Canadian
Info-Muse Network cataloging guide, *Documenting Your Collections: Info-Muse Network Documentation Guide*; Elizabeth O'Donnell for the
translations of *Méthode d'inventaire informatique
des objects beaux-arts et arts décoratifs*, the
French museum documentation guide.

To members of the VRA Data Standards
Committee who were actively involved in the ini-
tial planning stages: Jane Ferger, Margaret
Webster, Benjamin Kessler, Eileen Fry, Janice
Eklund, and Elizabeth O'Donnell. The following
individuals contributed unpublished cataloging
manuals used at their institutions: Sheryl Fisch
(California State University cataloging manual);
Gregory Most (Manual for Cataloging and
Classifying Slides, National Gallery of Art Slide
Library); Linda Bien (ARTSI—Automated
ReTrieval of Slide Information Cataloging Man-
ual, Concordia University); and Sheila Hannah
(VIRCONA Data Dictionary, Bainbridge Bunting
Memorial Slide Library, University of New
Mexico).

To Patrick Hogan, Editorial Director, and Jenni
Fry, Acquisitions Editor, of ALA Editions, and to
Helen Glenn Court of Formandsubstance.com.

Last, but not least, to the many catalogers
across the cultural heritage community who
have contributed their valuable expertise and
point of view.

Cataloging Cultural Objects

A Guide to Describing Cultural Works and Their Images

Murtha Baca • Patricia Harpring

Elisa Lanzi • Linda McRae • Ann Whiteside

On behalf of the Visual Resources Association

AMERICAN LIBRARY ASSOCIATION
Chicago   2006

CCO Logo Design: Citrus Studios

Cover image courtesy of Allan T. Kohl, Art Images for College Teaching

Design and composition by ALA Editions in Bookman and Helvetica Condensed typefaces using QuarkXPress 5.0 on a PC platform.

Printed on 50-pound white offset, a pH-neutral stock, and bound in 10-point cover stock by Victor Graphics.

The paper used in this publication meets the minimum requirements of American National Standard for Information Sciences—Permanence of Paper for Printed Library Materials, ANSI Z39.48-1992. ∞

Library of Congress Cataloging-in-Publication Data

Cataloging cultural objects : a guide to describing cultural works and
    their images / editors, Murtha Baca ... [et al.].
        p.   cm.
    Includes bibliographical references and index.
    ISBN 0-8389-3564-8
    1. Cultural property—Documentation—Standards. 2. Antiquities—
Documentation—Standards. 3. Architecture—Documentation—
Standards. 4. Art—Documentation—Standards. 5. Cataloging—
Handbooks, manuals, etc. 6. Cataloging of art—Handbooks, manuals,
etc. 7. Cataloging of pictures—Handbooks, manuals, etc. I. Baca,
Murtha.
CC135.C37 2006
363.6'9—dc22   2006013342

ISBN-10: 0-8389-3564-8
ISBN-13: 978-0-8389-3564-4

Printed in the United States of America

10   09   08   07   5   4   3   2

Contents

Introduction

PURPOSE

Over the last decade, many organizations and agencies have been working toward developing data standards for creating descriptions of and retrieving information about cultural objects. Data standards not only promote the recording of information consistently but are also fundamental to retrieving it efficiently. They promote data sharing, improve content management, and reduce redundant efforts. In time, the accumulation of consistently documented records across multiple repositories will increase access to content by maximizing research results. Ultimately, uniform documentation will promote the development of a body of cultural heritage information that will greatly enhance research and teaching in the arts and humanities.

Standards that guide data structure, data values, and data content form the basis for a set of tools that can lead to good descriptive cataloging, consistent documentation, shared records, and increased end-user access. In the art and cultural heritage communities, the most fully developed type of data standards are those that enumerate a set of categories or metadata elements that can be used to create a structure for a fielded format in a database. *Categories for the Description of Works of Art* (CDWA) is an example of a metadata element set. The *CDWA Lite* XML schema and the *VRA Core Categories, Version 4.0* schema are examples of metadata element sets expressed within an XML structure. Although a data structure is the logical first step in the development of standards, a structure alone will achieve neither a high rate of descriptive consistency on the part of catalogers, nor a high rate of retrieval on the part of end users.

Standards that govern the words (data values), and their selection, organization, and formatting (data content) are two other types of standards that must be used in conjunction with an agreed-upon data structure. Far more work has been done in developing standards for data values than for data content, typically in the form of thesauri and controlled vocabularies such as the *Thesaurus for Graphic Materials* (TGM), the *Art & Architecture Thesaurus* (AAT), the *Union List of Artist*

Names (ULAN), and the *Getty Thesaurus of Geographic Names* (TGN). Along with the Library of Congress Name and Subject Authorities, the Getty vocabularies and other thesauri bring us to the second step on the road to documentation standards and the potential for shared cataloging.

Cataloging Cultural Objects (CCO) takes us to the third step by providing standards for data content. Until now, little published documentation on data content standards has applied to cultural works—standards that guide the choice of terms and define the order, syntax, and form in which data values should be entered into a data structure. The library and archival communities have well-established rules for data content in the form of the *Anglo-American Cataloguing Rules* (AACR) and, more recently, *Describing Archives: A Content Standard* (DACS). The cultural heritage community in the United States, on the other hand, has never had any similar published guidelines that meet the unique and often idiosyncratic descriptive requirements of one-of-a-kind cultural objects. *Cataloging Cultural Objects* has been developed to fill this gap. Building on existing standards, *Cataloging Cultural Objects* provides guidelines for selecting, ordering, and formatting data used to populate metadata elements in a catalog record; this manual is designed to promote good descriptive cataloging, shared documentation, and enhanced end-user access. It is also intended to inform the decision-making processes of catalogers and builders of cultural heritage systems. In CCO, the emphasis is on principles of good cataloging and documentation, rather than on rigid rules that do not allow catalogers and system implementers to make informed judgments about the information they create and how it will be presented to their users. We hope that, whether used locally as an aid in developing training manuals or in-house cataloging rules, or more broadly in a shared environment as a guide to building consistent cultural heritage documentation, this manual will advance the increasing move toward shared cataloging and contribute to improved documentation and access to cultural heritage information.

AUDIENCE

Cataloging Cultural Objects was designed specifically for members of the communities engaged in describing and documenting works of art, architecture, cultural artifacts, and images of these things—museum documentation specialists, visual resources curators, archivists, librarians, or anyone who documents cultural objects and their images. Although the guide is not about system design, it may also be useful to system designers who need to understand the nature and form of cultural object information.

The guide attempts to balance the needs of various audiences but recognizes that each institution will have its own local requirements. Additionally, it is understood that those who describe original objects rather than analog or digital images of objects may require some additional, specialized guidelines. Museum registrars, for example, may require more detailed procedures for measuring an object or describing its condition or conservation. In addition to the bibliography that accompanies this manual, recommendations within the chapters include additional specialized sources for cataloging museum collections.

SCOPE AND METHODOLOGY

Cataloging Cultural Objects focuses on data content standards for descriptive cataloging—standards that guide the choice of terms, and that define the order, syntax, and form in which those terms, phrases, values, and narrative descriptions are recorded. Other types of data standards (for example, data structure, data value, and interchange standards) are excluded, except where relevant to a discussion of data content standards. For example, each chapter references standard tools appropriate to specific elements. Controlled vocabularies and various thesauri are recommended for building local authority files.

The primary emphasis of CCO is descriptive metadata and authority control—data intended to describe a cultural work, data used to create catalog records for that work and images of it. Administrative metadata (data used in managing and administering information resources) and technical metadata (for example, data to record digital image file properties) are excluded except where relevant to a discussion of descriptive metadata. For example, the guide often makes the distinction between controlled fields and fields used for display. Although the guide is system independent, it sometimes recommends using one or both types of fields within a local database based upon the needs of the cataloging institution. CCO includes elements used to describe both works and images, but does not include elements that involve administrative metadata. For example, Chapter 3: Physical Characteristics covers the physical characteristics of the work but not of the image, because physical characteristics of the image such as its size and format fall within the realm of technical metadata.

CCO covers many types of cultural works, including architecture, paintings, sculpture, prints, manuscripts, photographs and other visual media, performance art, archaeological sites and artifacts, and various functional objects from the realm of material culture. CCO is designed for museum collections, visual resources collections, archives, and libraries with a primary emphasis on art and architecture. CCO is not intended for natural history or scientific collections.

The research for CCO began with a review of the literature, emphasizing cataloging applications and best practice. Critical elements from the *VRA Core 3.0* and from *Categories for the Description of Works of Art* (CDWA) were included. A summary of practice related to each element was compiled from the sources under review. Whenever possible, recommendations were based on common practice. The survey of literature produced a short list of published sources consisting of data dictionaries, museum documentation manuals, and standard library and archival sources. To obtain unpublished manuals, a call went out to various electronic discussion lists requesting local manuals and guidelines; these were also used in the initial evaluation of materials.

Some elements were eventually rejected on the grounds that they dealt more with administrative, technical, or structural metadata relating to assets than with descriptive metadata relating to works and their images. The elements that were retained were grouped according to purpose and formed the basis for the nine chapters that comprise Part 2 of this manual.

Both the form and content for the guide underwent rigorous editorial review, as well as the critique of an advisory committee representing all of the various target communities, including library, archival, museum, and visual resources professionals.

Part ONE

General Guidelines

I. HOW TO USE THIS GUIDE

The Cataloging Cultural Objects (CCO) guide is not a metadata element set per se. The elements it covers refer to areas of information in a cataloging record that may be mapped to various metadata element sets such as VRA Core, CDWA, and CDWA Lite (and, by extension, to MARC and Dublin Core, and the like, because those element sets can be mapped to VRA and CDWA.[1] CCO is a broad document that includes rules for formatting data, suggestions for required information, controlled vocabulary requirements, and display issues.

CCO is organized in three parts. Part 1 contains guiding principles for basic cataloging issues such as minimal descriptions, Work and Image Records, complex works, item-level cataloging and collection-level cataloging, controlled vocabularies, and authority control. Part 2 is divided into nine chapters. Each chapter discusses one or more metadata elements and begins by describing the relationships between the elements contained in the chapter. Chapters are subdivided into sections representing the various elements. Each element is defined and includes information such as whether it is controlled, repeatable, or required, its uses, and examples. Part 3 discusses the authorities, including recommended elements and rules for building authorities. The appendices include a glossary, bibliography, and an index. In addition, the CCO Web site provides additional examples and ancillary materials.

The CCO guide is intended to advise in planning, implementing, and using databases and local cataloging rules. It is also intended to be a reference during cataloging, not necessarily to be read from cover to cover. The content and layout of the chapters in Part 2 and of the authorities in Part 3 are intended to facilitate the use of the manual as a reference work. As far as is possible, the structure of each chapter in these sections is the same. Repetition of selected information from chapter to chapter is intended to aid the cataloger so that repeatedly turning back and forth between chapters is not necessary. However, to avoid repeating large blocks of information, the text occasionally refers the user to a pertinent section or chapter elsewhere in the guide.

In the cataloging rules sections, the tone of the text is prescriptive. Many issues are complex, however, and variation in the requirements and capabilities of different institutions is unavoidable. Therefore, in the discussion and presentation of data sections, the guide is less prescriptive and instead makes recommendations, explaining the ramifications of using one approach over another. In all cases, **CCO recommends that each institution analyze, make, and enforce local rules to allow information to be retrieved, repurposed, and exchanged effectively and efficiently.**

CCO and AACR

The *Anglo-American Cataloguing Rules* (AACR) were originally intended primarily for describing books; adaptations have been made for graphic materials and archival collections. Occasionally, AACR has been applied to works of art, but the rules fall short of the specific and idiosyncratic needs for describing works of art, architecture, cultural objects, and their images. Although CCO acknowledges AACR rules, it does not seek to conform to them, because it is a different standard for a different audience and different materials. For those who use AACR, CCO can be a complement or partner to AACR, supplementing established AACR rules.

Ten Key Principles of CCO

The following ten important principles of CCO form the foundation of this guide:

1. Establish the logical focus of each Work Record, whether it is a single item, a work made up of several parts, or a physical group or collection of works. Clearly distinguish between Work Records and Image Records.

2. Include all the required CCO elements.

3. Follow the CCO rules. Make and enforce additional local rules to allow information to be retrieved, repurposed, and exchanged effectively.

4. Use controlled vocabularies, such as the Getty vocabularies and the Library of Congress authorities.

5. Create local authorities that are populated with terminology from standard published controlled vocabularies as well as with local terms and names. Structure local authorities as thesauri whenever possible. Record and document decisions about local authorities.

6. Use established metadata standards, such as the *VRA Core Categories* or *Categories for the Description of Works of Art*.

7. Understand that cataloging, classification, indexing, and display are different but related functions.

8. Be consistent in establishing relationships between works and images, between a group or collection and works, among works, and among images.

9. Be consistent regarding capitalization, punctuation, and syntax. Avoid abbreviations, but when necessary, use standard codes and lists for abbreviations (for example, the ISO abbreviations for countries).

10. For English-language information systems and users, use English-language data values whenever possible.

II. WHAT ARE YOU CATALOGING?

To catalog a work is to describe what it is, who made it, where it was made, how it was made, the materials of which it was made, and what it is about. A related task is classifying the work; Chapter 7: Class discusses classification. Display and indexing are related to cataloging; these issues are discussed at the end of every chapter and in general terms here in Part 1, under Database Design and Relationships: Display and Indexing.

Before beginning the task of descriptive cataloging, a cataloger must ask a basic but potentially complex question: What am I cataloging? This question refers to the relationship between a work and its parts, and between a work and the images that represent it.

To make a coherent record, the cataloger must clearly understand the parameters of the work in question. Is the catalog record about a single painted canvas or an altarpiece made up of many panels? Is it about a monolithic sculpture or an installation of various works? Is it about a single built structure or a building composed of various parts that were constructed at significantly different times? Is it about a single drawing on one piece of paper, a volume of drawings in an album or sketchbook, or a group of archival materials comprising drawings, computer diskettes, videotapes, and photographs?

Works may be complex, consisting of multiple parts, or they may be created in series. Are you cataloging a part of a work that belongs to a larger whole? For example, a museum may own only one panel of a triptych or one page from a manuscript. An institution may own one engraving that comes from a published series of engravings. Does the cataloger create a record for the series or the whole, even if the museum only owns a part? When cataloging numerous works in a collection or a series of archival objects belonging to a group, can a record for the entire collection suffice, or should some objects in the collection be cataloged individually? See Related Works for a detailed discussion.

Perhaps you are cataloging images and the works represented in them. In the simplest of cases, the work is no longer in hand, but has been captured in a photograph. For example, imagine a photograph intended to document an original two-dimensional painting (that is, a photograph that contains the entire work and nothing more). Such images may take form in any number of media, be it a slide, a digital image, or, in this case, a photograph. Now imagine that the photographer had stepped back fifteen feet, expanded the perspective, and instead of a photograph of a painting, it becomes a photograph of a painting on a wall of a building with a sculpture in the foreground. The photograph is no longer a simple image of a single work; the photograph now represents a complex layer of information open to subjective interpretation.

A photographic image, particularly of three-dimensional works, can shift or obscure the emphasis by adding other works in the picture frame or by changing the perspective captured in the view. The lighting of the work in the image may alter its appearance. An especially knotty but not uncommon example can be found in the archives of the Institute of Fine Arts at New York University. The institute owns a 35-mm slide copied from a lantern slide of a photograph by Erwin Panofsky, a distinguished 20th-century art historian. The photograph is of a 15th-century Dutch manuscript page that depicts a 2nd-century Roman sarcophagus. What is the work? What is the subject? Who is the artist?

In this example, a cataloger might be tempted to consider Panofsky the creator because the original photograph was taken by an identifiable and well-known individual, albeit not an individual known as a photographer. But the question of authorship depends on the larger question with which the cataloger must begin: What am I cataloging? The photograph has the potential to be both an art work in itself worthy of cataloging and a documentary image depicting a separate work of art. If the cataloger chooses to catalog the photograph by Panofsky, the work is the photograph, the creator is Panofsky, and the subject is the manuscript. If the cataloger chooses to catalog the manuscript, the work is the manuscript, the creator is unknown, and the subject is the Roman sarcophagus. Panofsky is the creator of the image and could be recorded as such in a creator field in the Image Record. The answer to the question "What am I cataloging?" sets in motion the rest of the choices made in the cataloging process and helps to distinguish data about the work from data about the image.

III. WORKS AND IMAGES

CCO recommends making a clear distinction between the work and the image. It is important to make a distinction at the outset of cataloging because many of the same types of data elements used to document the work are also used to document the image. If the distinction is not clearly drawn, the results of a search can produce inaccuracies and confusion for the end user. It can also make it difficult to migrate or export the data to another system.

What Is a Work?

In CCO, a work is a distinct intellectual or artistic creation limited primarily to objects and structures made by humans, including built works, visual art works, and cultural artifacts. Built works are architecture, other structures, or a man-made environment, typically large enough for humans to enter, usually serving a practical purpose, being relatively permanent and stable, and usually considered to have aesthetic value. Visual arts are physical objects meant to be perceived primarily through the sense of sight, created by the use of skill and imagination, and exhibit an aesthetic of a quality and type that would be collected by art museums or private collectors. A contemporary form such as performance art is considered a visual art, but the performing arts and literature are not. Cultural artifacts are physical objects produced or shaped by human craft, especially tools, weapons, ornaments, or other items that inherently give cultural clues about the person (and culture) who made or used them, and are further characterized by being of archaeological or historical interest and of the type collected by museums or private collectors.[2]

Works may be monumental, attached to other works, collected by art museums, held by ethnographic, anthropological, or other museums, or owned by private collectors. Works include architecture, landscape architecture, other built works, objects such as paintings, sculptures, murals, drawings, prints, photographs, furniture, ceramics, tools, costume, textiles, other decorative or utilitarian objects, or any other of thousands of types of artistic creations and other cultural remains. Performance art, installations, and site-specific works are included. Excluded are literary works, music, performing arts, language arts, culinary arts, science, religion, philosophy, and other intangible culture.

A work may be a single item or made up of many physical parts. Also note that a Work Record may be made for a physical or virtual collection of individual items.

What Is an Image?

An image is a visual representation of a work. It typically exists in photomechanical, photographic, or digital format. In a typical visual resources collection, an image is a slide, photograph, or digital file. A visual resources collection may own several images of a given work. Images do not include three-dimensional physical models, drawings, paintings, or sculptures, which are works in their own right.

If one work is depicted in another work (for example, if a cathedral is depicted in a painting), the cathedral is the subject of the painting (the painting is not an image of the cathedral); if a separate Work Record is made for the cathedral, it may be linked to the record for the painting as a Related Work (not as Work-Image). Likewise, if one work is a study for another work, records for the two works may be linked as Related Works, not as Work-Images.

A photograph of a work may also be treated as either a work of art or an image, depending on the stature of the photographer and the aesthetic or historical value of the photograph. For example, the photograph *La Tour Eiffel* by the well-known French photographer Brassaï depicts the Eiffel Tower at night. This photograph would typically be treated as a work of art, not simply as an image documenting the Eiffel Tower. In contrast, another photograph purchased from a commercial source depicting the same structure would probably be treated as a photographic documentation of the Eiffel Tower, recorded in an Image Record and linked to the Work Record for the Eiffel Tower as an architectural work.

Further considerations in distinguishing between work and image may involve the element of time. Note that the designation of an item as an image (that is, a surrogate for a work) versus a work may change over time. Consider an example at the Victoria and Albert Museum. The museum may have a digital image of a 19th-century photograph; in the photograph is depicted a plaster cast of the ancient Roman work, the *Column of Trajan*. Such plaster casts were originally made to serve as surrogates for the original works for the purpose of teaching, although they are now regarded by the museum as works in their own right. The 19th-century photograph was originally intended to be a surrogate for the plaster cast (and by extension, for the *Column of Trajan*), but that photograph is also now considered a work in its own right. What are the relationships between images and works in this example? In the most straightforward solution, the digital image is an image (surrogate) for the photograph, which is a work; the subject of the photograph is the plaster cast, which is a work; the subject of the plaster cast is the *Column of Trajan*, which is also a work.

Relationships between Work and Image Records

In a relational database structure, a record for the image would be linked to a record for the work and therefore would be linked to information about the work. The work may be linked to multiple images (for example, when there is more than one image of the work), and the image may be linked to multiple works (for example, when more than one work appears in the same image). The relational database model enables the cataloger to record work and image information in the appropriate places and clearly make the distinction between the work and the image. Although the Panofsky example is complicated by the fact that the photograph could be considered either a work or an image of a work, once the initial decision has been made, the cataloging is fairly straightforward. Today, most cataloging institutions use a relational database to catalog cultural works and their images; there are many software programs available for creating such an information system.

Cataloging Images of Complex Works

Cataloging images of complex works presents certain challenges. Consider the example of how to catalog a dozen images of Ghiberti's *Gates of Paradise*. This set of doors is on the east entrance to the Baptistery of San Giovanni in Florence, Italy. Taken as a whole, the work comprises ten large panels depicting various Old Testament scenes and numerous other, smaller panels and figures. The first decision involves whether to create a Work Record for the doors separate from the record for the Baptistery. In this case, the cataloger would probably create a separate Work Record for the doors because they have a different creator, different physical characteristics, different dates, and a different style than the Baptistery. The record for the doors should be linked in a part-whole relationship to the record for the Baptistery. The cataloger must next decide how to catalog the dozen images of the doors, including views of the door as a whole and details of the different panels of the doors. The panels are not physically separate from the door, but each depicts a different scene from the Old Testament. Each panel could be treated as a separate work; however, that may not be necessary, given that the panels have not been separated physically, are by the same artist, and are composed of the same materials. In this case, Image Records for each panel could be linked to the single Work Record for the doors, and each Image Record could include a view subject (see Chapter 9) that notes which particular scene is depicted in a given image.

Cataloging Images of Architecture

Current practice in visual resources collections admits several approaches to cataloging images of the built environment. The following three approaches may be combined as required in a single database, choosing one or another depending upon the situation at hand.

One approach creates a single Work Record for the building, to which Image Records for exterior views, interior views, details, and the like are linked. This method works well for fairly simple buildings or structures.

Another approach creates a Work Record for the building, to which Image Records for various views and details of the built work are linked. Separate Work Records for each plan, model, or other analytical or interpretive documents are created, and Image Records are linked to the various Work Records as appropriate (for example, images for the plan could be linked to the appropriate Work Record for the plan). This strategy works well when the documents about a building are themselves important.

A third approach virtually divides the building into pieces, making several Work Records for one building, including, for example, a Work Record for the building as a whole, and additional Work Records for each significant element, such as a chapel, portal, dome, and so on. This approach can be useful when cataloging large numbers of images of a complex built work.

Determining which approach to use in a given situation depends on the size of the building, how complex it is in structure, or how many components it contains on the one hand, and, on the other hand, how many images the cataloger has to describe. The goal is to determine how the user can best virtually "see" the building by using the various images of it in a collection. In the example of cataloging two hundred images of a large cathedral with many components, the cataloger might make separate Work Records for the exterior, the interior, the windows, and the frescoes, all linked as parts of the whole cathedral. If an individual chapel or room is architecturally important or designed by another architect or at a different date than the rest of the building, then a separate Work Record should be made for the room. In another example, if the cataloger has in hand only a few images of a particular building—for instance, of the Rotunda at the University of Virginia—a single Work Record for the Rotunda may suffice, and Image Records for views of exteriors, interiors, and details can be linked to the single Work Record. Note that this approach would not be as effective if the collection acquired more images of the Rotunda.

See also Related Works below.

IV. MINIMAL DESCRIPTIONS

Another basic question confronting the cataloger is "How much information should a catalog record contain?" The focus of cataloging should be twofold: promoting good access to the works and images coupled with clear, accurate descriptions that users will understand. This can be achieved with either a full cataloging record or a minimal cataloging record, so long as the cataloger follows standards and the descriptive cataloging is consistent from one record to another.

In determining how much information should be included, the answer depends upon several factors, including the types of materials being documented and the function, role, and purpose served by the documentation. Even among institutions with similar collections and similar objectives, practice may vary depending on the time, knowledge, and expertise of catalogers, the database structure and information system design, end-user needs and expectations, and long-established institutional practice.

Cataloging Depth: Specificity and Exhaustivity

Cataloging depth is often discussed in terms of specificity and exhaustivity, generally referring to the precision and quantity of terms applied to a particular element in the record. Specificity refers to the degree of precision or granularity used in description. For example, the cataloger would ideally choose the most specific term to describe an architectural work, such as *campanile* rather than the more general *tower*. Exhaustivity refers to the degree of depth and breadth that the cataloger uses in description. These are expressed by using a large number of terms or a more detailed description. For example, a cataloger might write "black-and-white photographs used to create a collage on graph paper, along with photocopies and typewritten texts," as opposed to "mixed media." In general, the greater the level of specificity and exhaustivity in catalog records, the more valuable the records will be for researchers. However, practical considerations often limit the ability of cataloging institutions to meet this goal. Cataloging institutions should establish local rules and guidelines regarding the level of specificity to be applied by catalogers for each element. See also Core Elements and Minimal Records below. **CCO recommends the following considerations to assist the cataloging institution in making decisions about minimal cataloging.**

Size and Requirements of the Collection

The size of the collection may play a role in limiting the levels of specificity and exhaustivity employed by any given institution. An institution that is cataloging a large collection may not have the need or resources to record extensive and specific information for every work. On the other hand, a small institution may be constrained by not having access to specific information; for example, a repository may not have a conservation laboratory to supply accurate analysis of measurements and materials. Even within a single collection, different levels of specificity and exhaustivity may be dictated by the works themselves. For example, one sculpture may have been cast of a single material, so simply stating the name of the material is sufficient (for example, *bronze*), and another may be composed of several materials applied with various processes that should be recorded (for example, *cast resin with oak veneer, gold leaf and paint applied, mounted on a carved wooden base*).

Focus of the Collection

The scope and focus of a given collection may dictate the types and specificity of required terminology. A collection that has a large variety of different types of works may have little need to record very specific information for each work. A specialized collection will require more specific information in order to distinguish one work from another. For example, an institution that holds three tapestries in a large general collection would probably need less specific information about those few than would a museum that specialized in tapestries and other textiles.

Expertise of the Catalogers and Availability of Information

The content of the records in any given information system will necessarily reflect the level of subject expertise of the catalogers. Catalogers may not be experts on the works being cataloged. Catalogers of visual resources collections may not have access to some information about the work. In any case, catalogers should never use a specific term unless they have the research, documentation, or expertise to support that use. It is better to use a broader term when there is uncertainty. For example, a cataloger should call a material *stone* rather than *banded slate* if he or she is unsure of the specific material. Local rules should be established regarding default values for required elements for which no information is available.

Expertise of the Users

The display information and the retrieval capability of the information should accommodate the expectations and knowledge of the intended users of the information system. Many institutions must satisfy a wide range of users, from the scholarly expert to the novice first-time visitor to the museum or Web site. Also consider whether or not your institution's information will be available in a larger pool of data along with records from other institutions. For example, consider if it will be contributed to one or more consortia or available for searching in a federated environment or union catalog. If so, your cataloging will need to be specific enough to allow your records to remain meaningful in the context of a larger information repository.

Technical Capabilities

Keep in mind that a good data structure and the data with which you populate the data elements are critical investments; your data will need to survive through a succession of computer systems over time. Ideally, the technical environment will not dictate cataloging practice. However, in the real world, technical concerns may limit or enhance cataloging in various ways. For example, if it is not possible to link to hierarchical authorities, it may be necessary for catalogers to enter both specific and general terms in each record to allow access, which may differ from traditional bibliographic practice. (In the context of CCO, linking refers to the process of establishing a relationship between two information objects, typically between two records or between values in an authority file and a field in a record.) That is, if the medium of a work is *etching* and *etching* is not linked to the broader term *print* in an authority, it may be necessary to explicitly enter both *etching* and *print* in the Work Record.

Core Elements and Minimal Records

Specificity and exhaustivity are also issues in another sense: when considering the depth and breadth of the record itself. Just as a museum or visual resource collection should set rules for a minimal number of terms to be assigned to each element in a catalog record, it should also mandate a minimal set of elements in the record, such as creator information, title of the work, and date of execution of the work. From the standpoint of end-user access, greater depth and breadth of cataloging are highly desirable; but from a practical point of view, this is not always possible because of the limitations of time, human resources, and the ability to locate and verify information.

Although the practice of employing both specificity and exhaustivity in creating a record is encouraged, consistency in the way the data is expressed is more important than the amount of data in the record. There can be no universal rule about the depth of cataloging as it pertains to either the number of terms used in a single element or the number of elements needed to construct a record; however, **CCO recommends using standard descriptive elements as outlined in the *VRA Core Categories* or the CDWA core categories as a basis for constructing a minimal record.** How these core metadata elements are used in building a cataloging database, and how the information is parsed for display in public access interfaces or printed labels, may require different local solutions than those presented in CCO.

How to Establish Core Elements

CCO discusses a subset of elements from the *VRA Core Categories*, which in turn are a subset of the CDWA metadata elements. The core elements in CCO comprise the most important descriptive information necessary to make a record for a work and an image. The chapters in Part 2 address cataloging issues related to all of the core elements for descriptive metadata (administrative metadata is not covered). Each chapter indicates which core elements are required and which are recommended (but not required). Minimal records contain the minimum amount of information in the minimum set of elements, as defined by the cataloging institution. **CCO recommends that a minimal record should include most if not all core metadata elements; a minimal record should contain data values for all of the required core elements whenever possible.** CCO does not prescribe cataloging depth and recognizes that not all institutions will require or have access to all of the data needed to complete a core record.

What should the cataloger do if core information is limited or not available? When an element is indicated as required, this means that the element is strongly recommended. However, it is recognized that occasionally data for any element may be missing during the cataloging process. It is then up to the cataloging institution to determine how to deal with missing data. Possibilities include using a value such as *unavailable, unknown,* or *not applicable*; making the value NULL on the database side; or leaving the field blank entirely and supplying data for missing values at the public access end. How these situations are implemented is a local decision and may vary from institution to institution.

The chapters in Part 2 describe what to do when core information for various elements is unavailable. In some cases, data may be supplied by the cataloger; for example, a cataloger might create a descriptive title if the title is not known. In other cases, the cataloger may use a broader term when more specific information is not known (for example, recording *metal* instead of *bronze* for the material). In yet other cases, no data of any kind is available, as described in the paragraph above.

On the other hand, what if the CCO core elements are insufficient to allow the cataloging institution to fully describe works in their collection? **CCO recommends beginning with the *VRA Core Categories* or CDWA core metadata elements as a basis for building a minimal record, to which additional elements of information from CDWA may be added as needed.** Although the CCO core elements map to the CDWA core categories, CDWA contains elements that are not included in CCO; some institutions may require elements that go beyond the scope of both. For example, a museum cataloger may have an abundance of information about the work, its provenance, or its conservation history that neither the *VRA Core Categories* nor the CDWA core metadata elements sufficiently cover. Institutions should add elements as needed for their requirements.

Elements for a Work Record

For a list of CCO elements, see the beginning of Part 2. Given the diversity of cultural works described by catalogers, no single set of minimal elements could suffice in all cases. For example, different information is needed to identify and describe works from various cultures and time periods. African tribal art will require different elements than Islamic manuscripts; ancient art will require different elements than performance art. CCO recommends the following types of information as essential for minimal records of all cultural works.

Creative Responsibility and Creation Contexts

Information about the creation of the work is required. Who created the work? If a creator is not named or identified, what is the culture of origin for the work? Where was the work created? When was it created?

Descriptive and Identifying Information

Catalogers should provide enough information to establish what the work is and to distinguish it from other works. What is it and what is it called? What is its work type and title? Where is it located? What is its subject? Of what materials is it made?

■ ■ ■

Chapters 1 through 8 in Part 2 list the recommended elements, and advise how to fill in values for those elements and what to do when minimal information for a given required core element is not known. See Part 2 for a full list of elements. A brief list of the elements in each chapter follows:

> *Chapter 1: Object Naming*
> > Work Type
> > Title
>
> *Chapter 2: Creator Information*
> > Creator
> > Creator Role

Elements for an Image Record

Most of the essential information about an image of a work will be documented in the administrative metadata (for example, repository information or identification numbers for digital or analog assets) and technical metadata (for example, image size, image format), which are outside the scope of this guide. CCO discusses descriptive metadata, including the following minimal information about the image that is essential to the end user:

View Information

View information is required for images. What is the description of this particular view of the work? A three-dimensional work, for example, might have several images representing multiple views.

■ ■ ■

Chapter 9 discusses required and recommended descriptive elements for the view represented in images: View Description, View Type, View Subject, and View Date.

Elements for a Group, Collection, or Series Record

The record for a group, collection, or series may have the same fields as a Work or Image Record, but a group, collection, or series record should be flagged (like Work and Image Records) with Record Type so that it is clear to the user that this is an aggregate record, not a record for a single work. Records for individual works or images can be hierarchically linked as part of the group, collection, or series record.

V. RECORD TYPE

CCO recommends using a Record Type element, although this is administrative rather than descriptive metadata and therefore outside of the scope of this manual.

Record Type indicates the level of cataloging, based on the physical form or intellectual content of the material. As a preliminary step in cataloging the work, determine the cataloging level that is appropriate to both the work and the goals of the cataloging institution. For visual resources catalogers, recommended Record Types are image, work, and collection. For catalogers of museum objects, see the definitions and discussion in *Categories for the Description for Works of Art: Object/ Work—Catalog Level*, where the terms *item*, *volume*, *group*, *subgroup*, *collection*, *series*, *set*, and *component* are suggested. Also consult *Describing Archives: A Content Standard* for terminology for archival groups.

VI. RELATED WORKS

In the context of CCO, Related Works are those having an important conceptual relationship with each other; records for Related Works are linked to each other in the database. Related Works may be relevant for works with parts (for example, a triptych), works of architecture, collections of works, and works in a series.

It is important to record works that have a direct relationship to the work of art or architecture being cataloged, particularly when the relationship may otherwise not be apparent. For example, works by the same artist or with the same subject need not be linked as Related Works on that basis alone; however, when one of these works is preparatory for another, this special relationship should be recorded, if possible. Whole-part relationships should always be recorded.

The following discussion focuses on intrinsic and extrinsic relationships between Work Records. Other records in a database may also be extrinsic to a Work Record, including records for images, bibliographic sources, and authorities. Note that, although authority files contain information that is extrinsic to the work at hand, information in authority files is considered essential to understanding the work being cataloged. See Works and Images above and Authority Files and Controlled Vocabularies below.

Intrinsic Relationships

In the context of CCO, an intrinsic relationship is a direct relationship between two works. **CCO recommends that catalogers distinguish between intrinsic and extrinsic relationships.** An intrinsic relationship is essential and must be recorded to enable effective searches. An extrinsic relationship, on the other hand, is not essential; although doing so may be informative, the cataloger need not identify the extrinsic relationship during the cataloging process.

Creating relationships between related works may be required when cataloging complex works, which are works that consist of several parts or that have complicated physical or conceptual relationships to other works. Complex works require special consideration. It may be necessary to make separate records for the parts of a work and the work as a whole, linked through hierarchical relationships (see Database Design and Relationships below).

Whole-Part Relationships between Works

Whole-part relationships, also known as larger entity-component or parent-child relationships, are intrinsic relationships. Complex works often require separate Work Records for the parts as well as for the whole. In this type of relationship, a part cannot be fully understood without its whole; the part inherits much of its information from the whole. Architectural complexes, manuscripts, and triptychs are examples of works requiring whole-part relationships.

CCO recommends creating separate Work Records for each part and for the whole when the information for the whole varies significantly from the information for the part. The purpose is to present the information clearly and distinctly, and to provide effective access to the parts as well as to the whole.

How does a cataloger know when to create separate records for the parts of a work? To some extent this depends on the type of work being cataloged and the policies of the cataloging institution, but **CCO recommends creating separate records when each part of a work contains enough unique information that it would be difficult to delineate the information in a single record.** Repositories will need to consider when separate records may be necessary to manage the works. Both museums and image collections will need to consider how separate records may aid in the retrieval of the information and its display to the end user. Criteria can include whether the artist, dates, style, media, or location differ between the whole and the parts of a work. For example, for an ancient Greek amphora with a lid, one Work Record may be sufficient to describe both components, because the artist, media, dates, and location are the same for both parts, although the dimensions are different for the vessel and its lid. In another example, a suite of furniture designed by Frank Lloyd Wright for a particular room may be described as a unit in a Work Record for the suite; however, individual Work Records for each chair and table may also be required if retrieval on the individual items is necessary—the cataloger must decide. For a 15th-century Korean landscape diptych in which each panel is a different size, has a different subject, was painted by a different artist in a different decade and in different media and later mounted together in a diptych, it would obviously be useful to create three separate records: for the diptych as a whole and for each panel as a part. Altarpieces, such as the *Isenheim Altarpiece* by Matthias Grünewald, are examples of works for which the parts may require individual, detailed, and complex treatment by the cataloger. This altarpiece is composed of several painted and carved panels arranged in two sets of folding wings, which can be displayed in three different views with complex iconographical subjects.

Decisions are not always self-evident. For example, in works where the creator is unknown, as is often the case with architectural decoration, determining whether the relationship between the decoration and the building is intrinsic or extrinsic can depend upon one's point of view; but access should be the primary consideration. Whether the decoration requires a separate record depends on whether essential elements of description such as the creator, title, and materials and techniques of the decoration differ significantly from the whole structure.

If the cataloging institution owns only a part of a work, or an image for a part of a work, it may still wish to make a record for the whole, because without a record for the whole, critical information may be lost to the end user (for example, the original location, ownership, overall dimensions, subject matter, and provenance of the whole). In addition, because the part can inherit information from the whole (for example, the title of the whole), making a record for the whole and linking it to the record for the part provides important context and improves access.

Group and Collection Relationships

When separate records are made for a group of works or a collection and its parts, the relationships between a group and its parts are intrinsic relationships. On the other hand, when it is impractical to make separate records for individual Related Works, a single record may be made for a group or collection of works. This same process may be used for a group or collection of related images as well.

Groups and collections may be cataloged similarly because they are both aggregates of items. Group- or collection-level records may be made for works or for images.

Group- or collection-level cataloging is often undertaken to gain initial control over a large body of works. For example, a museum or other collecting institution may make a collection record for a large, newly acquired collection of prints, drawings, rare books, or artifacts. In later cataloging phases, the institution may create more detailed, individual records for some or all of the works in the group or collection. Arranging Work Records into collections may also be useful when virtually reconstructing a historical arrangement of works, which may be physically dispersed in various geographic locations today. In a database, clustering Work Records or Image Records can be automatic when a search on a certain term in a given field brings together all the works or images indexed with that term. However, clustering can also be pre-determined by the cataloger by arranging items in groups, ensuring that a search yielding a large number of results may be displayed in a logical order.

If separate records are made for individual items and for the group or collection of which they are a part, the item records should be linked as part of the group or collection record. The same recommendation applies to collections of images.

Series Relationships

A relationship between an individual work and its series is intrinsic, because the work is best understood in the context of the series. Works done in series may require separate records for each part (the works) and for the whole (the series). Works done in series may include prints, photographs, paintings, sculptures, or installation art. Records for works in a series may require recording a particular chronological sequence.

CCO recommends making separate Work Records for each item in the series and for the entire series whenever possible. However, this may be impractical for large series, or for an institution that does not own all the works in the series. Practices vary among user groups. Museums may create a record for the series so that they will have access to all the necessary information for the series as well as for the work or works in their own collection (see also Group and Collection

Relationships above); visual resources repositories frequently do this as well. How the records are linked, searched, and displayed depends upon the needs and capabilities of the local information system, but a search on the whole series should retrieve the parts, just as the record for a part should also refer back to the whole. Some institutions do not have the resources to make separate records for the series and its parts; they typically make reference to the series by using a collective series title or otherwise referring to the series in the title in the Work Record rather than through separate, linked records for the series. See Chapter 1: Object Naming.

Components and Architectural Works

If multiple parts of an architectural work or any work with components are cataloged separately, the relationship between the whole and the parts is intrinsic.

Issues associated with cataloging complex works are particularly pronounced when cataloging the built environment and other works composed of components (multiple parts). Whether to conceptually subdivide an architectural structure or other work into multiple components for cataloging purposes is a subjective decision that the cataloger must make before cataloging begins. Some criteria that can help the cataloger with that decision include the relative importance of the various components, whether the components were designed by different creators, whether they were built in different periods, and whether users are likely to search for individual components.

Decisions about how to catalog works of architecture, other works with multiple parts, and images of these things are not always straightforward. Architectural structures may contain multiple rooms or components within a single building as well as multiple buildings within a single complex. Several different architects may have built or modified a single structure over a long period. This information may be captured in a single image or in a series of images. There may also be analytical or interpretive documents for the building (for example, a plan or model) that are works in their own right with separate Work Records.

A building or other complex work may be considered to be a whole consisting of parts, and thus records for built works and other works with components may be related in a hierarchy. For example, the dome and façade of a basilica may be cataloged as parts of the whole basilica; the records for the dome and façade may be hierarchically linked to the record for the whole basilica. Furthermore, a building has interior and exterior spaces and may be part of a larger complex of buildings. In the examples below, whole-part relationships are expressed by indentation.

Example

[for a monastery complex in Bulgaria]

Rila Monastery
...... *Cloisters*
...... *Church of the Birth of the Blessed Virgin*
.... *Dome*
.... *Façade*
...... *Tower of Hrelio*

Former structures, designs that were never built, and architectural competitions may also be linked through whole-part relationships. For further discussion of these issues, see the Architectural Drawings Advisory Group's *Guide to the Description of Architectural Drawings*.[3]

Examples

[for the basilica in the Vatican, Italy]

Saint Peter's Basilica
...... *Old Saint Peter's* (original structure, 324-1451)
...... *New Saint Peter's* (current structure, 1451-present)
.... *Façade*
.... *Dome*
.... *Piazza*

[for a memorial in Washington, DC]

Lincoln Memorial
.... *Structure* (as built)
.... *Competition* (1908-1909)
.... *Competition* (1911-1912)

The built environment often involves architectural complexes in which each building is significant in itself, yet all are related in some manner. In these cases, individual Work Records should be made for each building and a separate record should be made for the complex, linking records together through whole-part relationships.

Analytical and interpretive documentation, such as plans, sketches, renderings, models, and historical photographs of buildings can be cataloged as individual works with their own Work Records. If an institution actually owns such materials, certainly it will make separate records for the plans, sketches, and so forth. If models, drawings of plans, and the like have known creators and other descriptive information, catalogers typically should treat them as separate individual works. An example would be the plan of Amiens Cathedral by Robert de Luzarches, the French architect, master builder, and military engineer. If the building is also being cataloged, the models, plans, sketches, and other related materials should be linked as extrinsic Related Works.

Extrinsic Relationships

An extrinsic relationship is defined as one in which two or more works have a relationship that is informative, but not essential. That is, the described work and the referenced work can stand independently. The relationship is not essential either physically or logically in identifying either of the works. Such a relationship can be equated with a *see also* reference in a bibliographic record. Examples of extrinsic relationships are a preparatory sketch for a later work, a work copied after another work, or a work referenced within another work. Whereas extrinsic relationships enhance information about a work, some institutions may find it unnecessary to identify them.

Extrinsic relationships are generally temporal, conceptual, or spatial. Temporal relationships often include preparatory works such as models, studies, or plans.

Peruguino's study for the *Adoration of the Magi* or Antonio da Sangallo the Younger's model for Saint Peter's are examples of such preparatory works. Conceptual relationships may have a temporal element, for example, with works done after rather than before the original work, such as works that clearly reference other works while not necessarily being copies of them. Examples include Rubens's copy of Titian's *Bacchanal*, Gauguin's self-portrait that includes his painting *The Yellow Christ* as part of the background, or Duchamp's *L.H.O.O.Q.*, which borrows another work, Leonardo da Vinci's *Mona Lisa*, and changes it. An extrinsic relationship can also be the result of a spatial association, such as two or more works intended to be seen together, the Gilbert Stuart portraits of George and Martha Washington being a prime example.

Displaying Relationships between Works

Relationships should be displayed in a way that is clear to the end user. Relationships may display differently depending upon the context, such as in hierarchical displays, in the record for the work, and in lists. See also *Categories for the Description of Works of Art: Related Works.*

Hierarchical Display

A hierarchical display, using indentation, may be used to display whole-part relationships. In the example below, the titles (see Chapter 1) of the works appear in a hierarchical display.

Examples

[for a Japanese tea set]

Old Kutani Porcelain Tea Set
..... *Jar with Strainer*
..... *Hot Water Coolant Boat*
..... *Tea Caddy*
..... *Tea Pot and Lid*
..... *Five Cups and Saucers*

[for a series of prints by Jacques Callot]

Small Miseries of War Series
..... *Camp Scene*
..... *Attack on the Highway*
..... *Destruction of a Convent*
..... *Plundering and Burning a Village*
..... *The Peasants Avenge Themselves*
..... *The Hospital*

[for a built work, Notre Dame, Paris]

Notre Dame
..... *Interior*
..... *Exterior*
..... *West Front and Towers*
..... *Transepts*

Display in a Work Record

In a Work Record, whole-part and other relationships are described as Related Works. When records for works are linked, data for these Related Works may be concatenated from one record to form a display in the other. In the examples below, in the Work Record, the preferred Title, Work Type, and Creator display elements of the Related Work are concatenated for display.

> *Examples*
>
> [for display in the record for an illumination of the *Flight into Egypt*]
>
> **Related Work**:
>
> > **Relationship Type**: part of
> > **Related Work** *[concatenated label]*:
> > *Ruskin Hours*; prayer book; unknown French; ca. 1300; J. Paul Getty Museum (Los Angeles, California, United States); MS. LUDWIG IX 3
>
> [for display in the record for the Camp Scene print by Jacques Callot]
>
> **Related Work**:
>
> > **Relationship Type**: part of
> > **Related Work** *[concatenated label]*:
> > *Small Miseries of War*; series; designed and etched by Jacques Callot (French, 1592-1635); 1632-1633, published 1635; Paris (France)
>
> [for display in the record for Notre Dame, Paris]
>
> **Related Work**:
>
> > **Relationship Type**: larger context for
> > **Related Work** *[concatenated label]*:
> > *Transepts*; transepts; architects Jean de Chelles (French, died ca. 1270) and Pierre de Montreuil (French, ca. 1200-ca. 1264); ca. 1250-1267; Notre Dame (Paris, France)
>
> [for display in the record for a 16th-century drawing by Giovanni Antonio Dosio; the Pantheon could also be recorded under the Subject element]
>
> **Related Works**:
>
> > **Relationship Type**: depicted in
> > **Related Work** *[concatenated label]*:
> > *Pantheon*; rotunda; unknown Roman architect for the emperor Hadrian; begun in 27 BCE, rebuilt 118/119-125/128; Rome (Italy)
> >
> > **Relationship Type**: preparatory for
> > **Related Work** *[concatenated label]*:
> > *Pantheon*; engraving; design by Giovanni Antonio Dosio (Italian, 1533-after 1609), printmaker Giovanni Battista de'Cavalieri (Italian, ca. 1525-1601); published 1569; in *Urbis Romae aedificiorum illustrium quae supersunt reliquiae*, Florence (Italy)

VII. DATABASE DESIGN AND RELATIONSHIPS

The CCO guidelines have been carefully crafted to be useful in a variety of database settings and designs. Keep in mind that the scope of CCO is limited for the most part to descriptive data (and the metadata elements that contain the data) about cultural objects and images of those objects. CCO does not discuss administrative and technical metadata, though clearly these must also be accommodated in a cataloging system.

Database Design

Because of the complexity of cultural information and the importance of Authority Records, CCO recommends using a relational database. A relational database provides a logical organization of interrelated information (for example, data about works and images, authority files, and so on) that is managed and stored as a single information system. A data structure should provide a means of relating works to each other, works to images, and works and images to authorities. When records of the same type are related, they have a reciprocal relationship. Hierarchical relationships between records of the same type should be possible. Referencing unique numeric identifiers is a common way to express relationships in an information system. The specifics of how records are linked and related is a local database design issue, which this guide does not explicitly discuss.

The simple entity relationship diagram in Figure 1 illustrates how works may be related to other works, and how works may be related to images, sources, and authorities. A given authority file may be used to control terminology in multiple elements (for example, the Concept Authority will control Work Type, Materials, and the like). Also, a given element may use controlled terms from multiple authorities (for example, the Subject element of a work may use terms from several authorities).

Figure 1
Entity Relationship Diagram for CCO

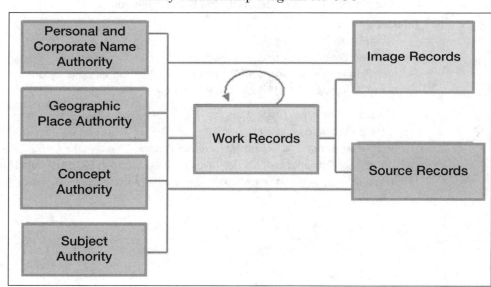

Types of Relationships

Whenever a relationship (called a *link* in CCO) is made between two Work Records, a Work and an Image Record, or a field in a Work Record and a term in an Authority Record, a relationship is being expressed. Relational databases can be designed to accommodate hierarchical and other relationships.

Hierarchical Relationships

Many relationships are hierarchical; they express broader or narrower (parent-child) contexts between two things; hierarchical relationships are typically whole-part or genus-species relationships between entities that are of the same type: hierarchical relationships may be made from works to works, images to images, or a record in one authority file to another record in the same authority file. A hierarchy imposes order and structure on description. As shown in the example of the *Gates of Paradise*, the doors are part of the Baptistery building. In the example of a related Authority Record for the materials of the bronze doors, *bronze* is a child or type of *metal*. When data is presented in a hierarchical display (using indentation, as in the examples just given), it helps users navigate the information space and understand the relationships between entities.

The information system should allow for the establishment of polyhierarchical relationships, meaning that each child in the hierarchy may have multiple parents. For example, in the Geographic Place Authority, the city of Siena may need to be linked as a child of its modern parent Italy as well as to a historical parent, Etruria.

Building the Relationships

Hierarchical and other relationships can exist in the same information system. Several distinctions need to be made when building such relationships into a database. First are the relationships between works and images of those works; then are relationships between works and other works; then come relationships between works and authority file records; and last are relationships between authority file records within the same authority file. For example, a database can be set up to have records for a whole work and a part of a work that have a hierarchical relationship; multiple images may have relationships to one or both of those entities. Figure 2 shows the relationships among the works and images for Lorenzo Ghiberti's *Gates of Paradise*. The *Gates* are part of the whole Baptistery, and the images of the *Gates* are linked to the Work Record for the *Gates*. Hierarchical relationships can be used in authority files to indicate broader and narrower contexts, thus facilitating consistency in cataloging and enhancing searching for end users, as in the example for Florence, Italy, from the Geographic Place Authority.

How do these various sets of relationships interact within a single information system? In the Figure 2 example, each box represents a record. Hierarchical relationships are indicated with indentation. Other relationships are indicated with connecting lines. The Work Record for the *Gates of Paradise* will include fields that convey to the user that the doors exist within the broader context of the building and in the geographical place, Florence. The Work Record for the doors is linked to the Work Record for the building, and both records can be linked to the record for

Figure 2

Links between Works, Authorities, Images

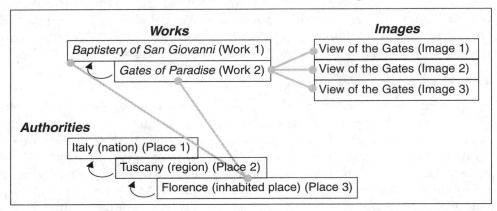

Florence from the geographic authority file. If the database employs a hierarchical model in the geographic authority file, the fact that Florence is in Tuscany and Italy can be carried into the Work Record. This type of functionality not only saves time for the cataloger (who won't have to type *Italy* every time he or she uses the term *Florence* in a Work Record), but also allows users to find everything in Italy or in Tuscany without having to specify Florence and every other town in Tuscany in a search. For a full explanation and examples, see Chapter 5: Location and Geography.

Relationship Type and Reciprocity

CCO recommends that relationships between entities be reciprocal. Relationships should be reciprocal so that a search on one entity can lead to the other. Reciprocity is most easily accomplished when reciprocal relationship capabilities have been built into the information system. The relationships between entities may be one-to-one, many-to-one, or many-to-many.

CCO recommends that the type of relationship between the work being cataloged and the related work be indicated. Whole-part hierarchical relationships may be made apparent by using indentation in displays. Other relationships may require explanation by noting the type of relationship between two entities. For example, a portrait of the master of a manor may be linked as a pendant of a matching companion portrait of the mistress of the manor. The Relationship Type may vary depending upon the point of view. For example, a drawing may be linked as a *study for* a particular tapestry. From the tapestry's record, the tapestry may be linked as being *based on* the drawing. A sculpture of Shiva and Parvati may be *part of* a Hindu temple; from the temple's record, the temple is the *larger context for* the sculpture. A relationship may be historical, as when a sculpture of a winged bull-lion was *formerly part of* the *Palace of Ashurnasirpal II*.

Figure 3 contains sample relationship types. To reduce redundancy in the illustration, reciprocal relationships are not listed twice (for example, *preparatory for—based on* is not listed again from the other point of view, *based on—preparatory for*, though the relationships would be reciprocal from both points of view in a real application).

Figure 3
Table of Relationship Types

RELATIONSHIP TYPE	RECIPROCAL RELATIONSHIP TYPE
<hierarchical - group - collection - series to parts>	
part of	larger context for
formerly part of	formerly larger context for
<general - default>	
related to	related to
<a work and its components>	
component of	component is
<works that are related as steps in the creation process>	
preparatory for	based on
study for	study is
model for	model is
plan for	plan is
printing plate for	printing plate is
prototype for	prototype is
others as required	
<works designed to be displayed together>	
pendant of	pendant of
mate of	mate of
partner in set with	partner in set with
others as required	
<works copied after or depicting other works>	
depicts	depicted in
copy after	copy is
facsimile of	facsimile is
derived from	source is
<work to image relationships>	
image of	depicted in

Repeatable Fields

CCO recommends that certain fields be repeatable. These refer, in the context of CCO, to categories of information for which there may be multiple data values. For example, there may be multiple media used to create a work, each of which should be recorded in a separate instance of the appropriate field, or related by multiple links to the authority file that controls the terminology for media. Related fields may be designated to repeat as a set.

Display and Indexing

Display issues refer to how the data looks to the end user in the database, on a Web site, on a wall or slide label, or in a publication. Information for display should be in a format that is easily read and understood by end users. In the context of this guide, indexing refers to how data is indexed (that is, what indexing terms are assigned to it), sorted, and retrieved. Such indexing should be a conscious activity performed by knowledgeable catalogers who consider the retrieval implications of their indexing terms, and not by an automated method that simply parses every word in a free-text field into indexes.

Controlled Fields vs. Free-Text Fields

CCO recommends that the database accommodate both controlled fields and free-text fields. Controlled fields contain indexing terms—that is, key data values drawn from standard vocabularies and formatted to allow for successful retrieval. Free-text fields communicate nuance, uncertainty, and ambiguity to end users.

The primary function of an indexed field is to facilitate end-user access. Access is improved when controlled vocabularies are used to populate database fields, because authorized terms have been checked against synonyms and broader and narrower terms and therefore are more likely to be used consistently throughout the database; consistency makes for more efficient retrieval. Ideally, the indexing terms will be linked to controlled vocabularies stored in controlled lists or authority files.

Consistency is less important for a free-text field than for a controlled field, but still desirable. Although free-text fields by definition contain uncontrolled terminology, the use of terminology that is consistent with the terms in controlled fields is recommended for the sake of clarity. Using a consistent style, grammar, and sentence structure is also recommended. To make the creation of free-text fields less labor-intensive, databases can be constructed so that values in related controlled fields may be passed into the free-text field, and then edited as necessary by the cataloger.

Display Issues

CCO recommends that data be recorded according to the various requirements of display and indexing. Display issues relate to the choice of fields or subfields appropriate for display to different end users, and to how the data looks to the end users.

Because a database may contain sensitive information that must be restricted or administrative information that is of no interest to most users, making decisions about which fields are appropriate for display to given user groups is necessary. The database design should allow for different displays of data depending on the needs of the user group. This is a matter to be settled at the local level, and is therefore not discussed at length in this guide.

Display usually refers to how the data appears to the end user in the database, on a Web site, on a wall or slide label, or in a publication. The information in controlled fields is not always user-friendly, because it may need to be structured in a way that facilitates retrieval or machine manipulation (required for sorting, arithmetic calculations, and the like). Information intended for display, however, should be in a format that is easy for the end user to read and understand.

Information for display may in some cases be expressed in a free-text field, and in other cases it may be concatenated or otherwise displayed from controlled fields. In many instances, the controlled terms are self-explanatory, and can be displayed as they are, or concatenated with other terms. For example, a preferred geographic place name and the broader hierarchical contexts for the place may be drawn from the Geographic Place Authority and concatenated for display in the linked Work Record's Creation Location element. It is recommended that indexing terms for a given data element display even when the data element also includes a free-text note. (Free-text notes will always display, because they explain the context of terms used in indexing.) Some systems allow moving by hyperlinks from the indexing terms to other Work Records indexed with the same terms. Even when the system lacks this functionality, displaying the indexing terms helps familiarize end users with the indexing vocabulary.

Do not let display or technical constraints drive the database design. **CCO recommends good and versatile database design and consistent cataloging rules.** When planning a database design and rules for data entry, do not allow immediate display demands to dictate database structure or data entry practice. For example, as a general rule, how information or images display in one context (for example, a slide label or a "light table" presentation tool) should be secondary to consistent and accurate cataloging. Consistent cataloging will facilitate dealing with display issues at the time and in the future. Allowing local display issues or the limitations of the current computer system to drive how the database is designed or how information is input may offer short-term solutions to some problems, but will make migrating and sharing data more difficult over the long term.

How to Decide on a Database Design

There are several key issues to keep in mind when designing and constructing a database for cultural objects and images: What is the purpose of the database? Who are the users it is intended to serve? Will it allow you to properly manage your data?

If a museum is cataloging works in its own collection, the primary focus is on documenting the object or work itself. Museum cataloging can also be used to generate descriptions for wall labels, publications, and Web pages. For example, a detailed physical description, including measurements to the nearest millimeter, may be critical for museum description. A museum record may require fields to describe inscriptions on works, fields that distinguish between the materials of different parts of the work, and fields that describe in detail the history and provenance of the work. Emphasis is on the work itself, not a particular image of the work. Of course, the museum will probably document the work through images (often called media in museum collection management systems), but the number and variety of images will differ from the number and variety in an image collection. The primary components in a database for cataloging museum works would include a Work Record, Authority Records, and in many cases one or more Image (or Media) Records.

In a visual resources collection, the primary focus of cataloging is to describe and provide access to image content. For example, subject description might be more important than a detailed physical description of the work depicted in a visual resources collection. Each Work Record may have many images linked to it. In addition, many images will be supplemental to the work—used to support access to some aspect of the work, set the work within a stylistic, geographical, or chronological context—but may not depict the work itself. In this type of collection, the image often serves a variety of purposes. A detailed description of the image may be important to the end user, and this should be reflected in the structure of the database. For example, it may be important to distinguish between the overall subject matter of the whole work and the detail of that subject in a specific image; consequently, there may be subject fields in both the Work and Image Records. The primary components in a database for cataloging images would include a Work Record, an Image Record, and one or more Authority Records.

These scenarios may vary from institution to institution, but they illustrate the importance of designing a database to accommodate the descriptive data point of view. Regardless of the information system or data model, CCO provides guidance for the choice of terms and how they are formatted. In doing this, CCO can help pave the way for sharing descriptive data among museums and image collections.

What Is the Purpose of the Database?

The term *database* is generic; a database can be built to accommodate any type of information. Within the context of cultural objects and images, databases constitute the basis of cataloging tools, collection management systems, presentation tools, and digital asset management tools. Any one of these can be built as a local or as a shared system. How these different databases work together is referred to as *interoperability*. In an ideal world, there would be one integrated database that provided all users with all functionalities. In reality, most organizations have several databases or software products that are used to fulfill a variety of needs, from collection management to digital asset management to presentation of high-resolution images, and so on.

CCO focuses on the types of data typically used in a cataloging tool—primarily the so-called descriptive metadata—that is, data used to describe and identify cultural works and images. Collection management systems and digital asset management systems also require other types of metadata—data that defines structure or assists in the administration of a resource, data about the way a work may be displayed, financial information about the work, data about the exhibition and loan history of a work, technical information about an image file, and so on.

The goal of the types of databases referred to in this manual is to facilitate indexing, identification, and discovery of the works or images in a particular collection or collections. Another goal is to facilitate the ongoing documentation of works (for example, to track the history of the titles of a work). Publishing data and presenting it to end users is often done by migrating it from the cataloging system to special presentation and public access databases before it is made available to end users. Typically, these kinds of systems focus on searching, browsing, and displaying the cataloged resources. For example, the presentation tool that faculty members use to show images in the classroom will probably be a separate database from the cataloging tool used to describe those images. To limit the public's access to sensitive data and to provide more nonspecialist language and access, a museum's collection on the Web typically has a public interface that is different from the staff's interface to the collection management system. Publishing and presenting data to end users involves a complex set of issues dealing with the user interface, search engines, and design, which are outside the scope of this guide; however, the CCO guidelines make exporting the descriptive metadata and repurposing it easier and more efficient.

Cataloging Tool

Until recently, many organizations relied on a simple cataloging tool to record the descriptive data for works and images. A cataloging tool focuses on content description and labeling output (for example, slide labels or wall labels). Today, a cataloging tool is often part of a more complex collection management system.

Collection Management System

For a database to manage a collection, be it a digital or a physical collection, a simple cataloging tool is inadequate. For example, in a museum setting, a museum collection management system (CMS) is appropriate. A CMS is a database system that allows a museum to track various aspects of its collections, including acquisitions, loans, and conservation. Nonetheless, a large part of a typical CMS is the cataloging module. CCO provides guidance for the cataloging component of the CMS (that is, regarding descriptive data about the works in the collection).

Digital Asset Management System

A digital asset management (DAM) system is a tool for organizing digital media assets for storage, preservation, and retrieval. Digital asset management tools sometimes incorporate a descriptive data cataloging component, but they tend to focus on managing workflow for creating digital assets (digital images and audio clips, for example) and managing rights and permissions.

Online Catalog

An online catalog allows end users to search for and view data and images. Many museums now make online catalogs containing part or all of their collections available to museum visitors or the general public. Such catalogs may also include consolidated collections from several institutions.

VIII. AUTHORITY FILES AND CONTROLLED VOCABULARIES

Authority control is critical in the online environment. Authority control is a system of procedures that ensures the consistent use and maintenance of information in database records. Procedures include recording and validating terminology using controlled vocabulary and authority files. The purpose of authority control is to ensure consistency at the cataloging level, and that the user searching a database can find material and relate it to other material in the database efficiently.

Details regarding how authorities are constructed and how they interact with each other and with Work and Image Records are critical issues that must be decided by the cataloging institution. There is no single answer that will serve all institutions. Each cataloging institution must devote sufficient time and resources to proper analysis and working out of solutions. The purpose of this discussion is to highlight issues, not to suggest a single solution that will work for every institution.

Authority Files

Authority files contain the terminology used in cataloging Work and Image Records. In the context of CCO, an authority file contains records for persons, places, things, and other concepts related to the works and images being cataloged. Such information is important for retrieval of the Work or Image Record, but it is more efficiently recorded in separate authority files rather than in the Work or Image Records themselves. The advantage of storing such ancillary (and frequently repeated) information in an authority file is that this information need be recorded only once, and it may then be linked to all appropriate Work and Image Records, rather than being repeated in each pertinent Work or Image Record. In a database with full authority control capability and functional links between records, another advantage is that changing or correcting a preferred name or heading in the Authority Record will automatically update the name or heading in the associated Work and Image Records. **CCO recommends using authority files for selected metadata elements to facilitate efficient cataloging and retrieval.**

In an authority file, records for persons, places, and other concepts may contain terms and names for the concept, with one term or name identified as the preferred term and the others considered variant terms. The record may contain other information as well; for example, in a personal and corporate name authority, the birth and death dates of a person would be included. The authority files described in this section are ideally structured as thesauri.

Controlled Vocabulary

A controlled vocabulary is an organized arrangement of words and phrases used to index content and to retrieve content by browsing or searching. It typically includes preferred and variant terms and has a limited scope or describes a specific domain. Controlled vocabulary is a broader concept than authority file, encompassing authority files as well as other controlled lists of terminology. For some elements or fields in the database, a controlled list may be sufficient to control terminology, particularly where the terminology for that field is limited and unlikely to have synonyms or ancillary information. Controlled vocabularies can be simple lists of unique preferred terms; they can be sets of equivalent terms for the same concept (synonym rings); they can include preferred and nonpreferred terms; they can identify hierarchies of terms (taxonomies); and they can include all of these characteristics in addition to having semantic relationships among terms and other concepts (thesauri). Various types of controlled vocabularies are defined below.

Controlled List

A controlled list is a simple list of terms used to control terminology. If well constructed, in such a list each term will be unique; terms will all be members of the same class; terms will not overlap in meaning; terms will be equal in granularity-specificity; and terms will be arranged either alphabetically or in some other logical order.

Synonym Ring File

A synonym ring file contains sets of terms that are considered equivalent.

Taxonomy

A taxonomy is an orderly classification for a defined domain.

Subject Headings

Subject headings are words or phrases used to indicate the content of something; pre-coordination of terminology is a characteristic of subject headings. That is, subject headings typically combine several unique concepts in a single string (for example, *medieval bronze vessels* combines a period, a material, and an object type in one heading).

Thesaurus

A thesaurus is a semantic network of unique concepts, including relationships between synonyms, broader and narrower contexts, and other related concepts. Thesauri may be monolingual or multilingual. Thesauri may have the following three relationships between terms:

EQUIVALENCE RELATIONSHIPS

Relationships between synonymous terms or names for the same concept, typically distinguishing preferred terms (descriptors) and nonpreferred terms (variants). For example, *Georgia O'Keeffe* and *Mrs. Alfred Stieglitz* refer to the same artist and the former name is preferred; *still life* and *nature morte* refer to the same concept and the former term is preferred in English; *Vienna* and *Vindobona* refer to the same city and the former name is the preferred current name in English (*Vindobona* is a historical name).

HIERARCHICAL RELATIONSHIPS

Broader and narrower (parent-child) relationships between concepts. Hierarchical relationships are generally either whole-part (*Nogales*, for example, is a part of *Veracruz*, which is part of *Mexico*) or genus-species (*bronze* is a type of *metal*). Relationships may be polyhierarchical, meaning that each child may be linked to multiple parents.

ASSOCIATIVE RELATIONSHIPS

Relationships between closely related concepts that are not hierarchical because they are not whole-part or genus-species. There may be many types of associative relationships. For example, in an associative relationship between artists,

Katsushika Hokusai was the teacher of *Katsushika Taito II*; their relationship is teacher-student.

Methodology for Creating a Controlled Vocabulary

Throughout this guide, we recommend which data elements need controlled vocabularies and which of those vocabularies should be authority files in the form of thesauri. Controlled vocabularies should be customized so that they work well with the specific situation and the specific collection or collections at hand. Each institution should develop a strategy for creating controlled vocabularies customized for its specific collection. On the other hand, if the collection is being queried in a consortial or federated environment, controlled vocabularies should be customized for retrieval across different collections; the requirements will be different and the terminology will be broader or narrower in scope depending on the particular situation.

Answering the following questions is crucial in creating controlled vocabularies to meet your institution's needs. What do you want your controlled vocabulary to do? Is it for use by a cataloger or by a search engine, or will the same vocabulary be used for both? In an ideal situation, a vocabulary for cataloging will contain expert terminology and at the same time will be designed to encourage the greatest possible consistency among catalogers by limiting choices of terminology according to the scope of the collection and the focus of the field being indexed. In contrast, a vocabulary for retrieval will typically be broader and will contain more nonexpert, and even "wrong," terminology, such as misspelled words or incorrect but commonly used terms. In a strictly structured vocabulary intended for cataloging, equivalence relationships should be made only between terms and names that have genuine synonymity or identical meanings. On the other hand, a vocabulary for retrieval may link terms and names that have near-synonymity or similar meanings in order to broaden results and improve retrieval. For practical reasons, many institutions will have to use the same vocabulary for both cataloging and retrieval, thus requiring a compromise between the two approaches. Will the vocabulary be used for navigation? Vocabularies that are intended to help end users browse collections online should be very simple and aimed at the nonexpert audience rather than at specialists.

Focus and Scope of the Terminology

What terms do you need in the vocabulary? A good strategy is to begin with published vocabularies, such as the Getty vocabularies or the Library of Congress authorities, and then customize them for local use to reflect your specific collection.[4] In addition, access by the cataloger to terminology should be customized for each particular field in the Work or Image Record. For example, when filling in values for the materials field, ideally catalogers should not have access to the styles and periods terms from the AAT, because excluding access to extraneous terms reduces the possibility for errors in indexing. However, note that access to terms should not be limited too narrowly. For example, a collage or other such work may be made of other works, so terminology generally reserved for Work Type, such as *photograph*, may also be a material in a collage. With what terms will your end users be familiar? These requirements must be accommodated as well.

Granularity in the Terminology

How much granularity or specificity should you use in customizing the vocabulary and in indexing with the vocabulary? The more similarity among items in your collection, the more specific your vocabulary will need to be and the more granularity should be used in indexing with that vocabulary. For example, if you are cataloging a specialized collection of furniture, the terminology used to index them will be much more specific than if you have only one or two pieces of furniture in a more general collection.

You should also keep in mind how your items will be retrieved in a consortial environment with other collections, and therefore include basic indexing terms appropriate to more general retrieval as well as specific terms that work well in your local environment. It is particularly important to include broader terms when a thesaurus will not be used in retrieval or when the general term in a thesaurus is not necessarily a parent of the more specific term. The general term *still life*, for example, will not be a broader term to the specific term *flowers* in a thesaurus, so both should be included in the Work Record.

Maintaining the Vocabulary

Terminology for art and material culture may change over time. Vocabularies need to be living, growing tools. What methodology will you use for keeping up with changing terminology? If it is possible to contribute terminology to a published vocabulary (such as the Getty vocabularies or the Library of Congress authority files), you should make a plan to submit new terms; this will of course have an impact on workflow, and must be taken into consideration.

Technical Considerations

What technology will you use and how will authority files, lists, and other controlled vocabularies be integrated into the rest of your system? These are critical questions that depend on local needs and resources.

How to Create Authority Records

Once you decide on the requirements and characteristics of the authority files required by your institution, the next step is to populate them with appropriate records. CCO recommends using standard, published authority information where possible, and then supplementing the authority file to make it collection specific, as determined by your institution's unique requirements. Throughout this guide, published sources of terminology are recommended for the given authority file or element. Such sources may include published vocabularies.

Where it is necessary to make new Authority Records, use standard, published sources for the terms or names and other information. Appropriate sources are suggested throughout this guide. Cite the sources for your information in the Authority Record. If the name or term does not exist in a published source, construct the names according to the *Anglo-American Cataloguing Rules* or other rules, as indicated throughout this guide. Among synonyms, flag one of the terms or names as preferred. This will be the term or name that can be automatically designated by algorithm in displays. It should be the one most commonly used in scholarly literature in the language of the catalog record, which in the United States is English. If sources disagree on the preferred form, go down the list of preferred sources (in the terminology section of each authority chapter) and use the name or term found in the source highest in the list of preferred sources.

Cataloging vs. Retrieval Issues

In building a database and in cataloging, you should ideally follow the best design theory and the best editorial practice. However, if either the cataloging or retrieval system is less than ideal, you will need to adjust your rules to accommodate the inadequacies of your information system or software, particularly concerning controlled vocabularies and authorities. A few of the issues surrounding the use of vocabularies in retrieval are discussed below.

Using Variant Terms and Names for Retrieval

Ideally, your controlled fields in the Work Record will be linked to authorities that include variant terms and names for the person, place, or things described in the Work Record, and you will also use the variants for retrieval. If this is not true, you should explicitly include the most important variants in the Work Record.

Using the Hierarchy for Retrieval

Ideally, your controlled fields will be linked to hierarchical authority files, and the hierarchies will also be used for retrieval. If this is not true, you should explicitly include broader contexts for your terms in the Work Record.

Case Insensitivity in Retrieval

Your retrieval system should accommodate end-user queries, no matter what case they use. For example, if an end user searches for *Bartolo Di Fredi* or *BARTOLO DI FREDI*, he or she should retrieve records containing the name *Bartolo di Fredi*. If your retrieval system does not accommodate such variations, you should add these variants to your Authority Record or to the Work Record (if you do not have an authority file).

Diacritics in Retrieval

Your retrieval system should accommodate both the end user's use of diacritics and punctuation and his or her omission of diacritics and punctuation. For example, if the end user searches for *Jean Simeon Chardin* without the hyphen and diacritic, he or she should retrieve records containing the name *Jean-Siméon Chardin*. If this is not the case, you should add these variants to your Authority Record, or to the Work Record if you do not have an authority file.

Singular and Plural in Retrieval

Your retrieval system should accommodate either the singular or plural form of the term or any other grammatical variant. For example, if an end user searches for plural *portals*, all records containing the term *portal* should be included in the results. Your retrieval system will ideally incorporate stemming, a feature that retrieves the term and all its grammatical variants: For example, stemming on *frame* would also retrieve *frames*, *framing*, and *framed*. If your system does not accommodate such variations, you should add the variants to your Authority Record or, if you do not have an authority file, to the Work Record.

Compound Terms and Names in Retrieval

Your retrieval system should accommodate compound terms and names spelled with or without a space. For example, an end user's search for *Le Duc* should retrieve records containing both *Charles Leduc* and *Johan le Duc*.[5] If your retrieval system does not accommodate such variations, you should add these variants to your Authority Record or to the Work Record (if you do not have an authority file).

Inverted or Natural Order in Retrieval

Your retrieval system should accommodate end users' use of terms and names in either natural or inverted order. For example, a search on *Arthur Wellesley, Duke of Wellington* should retrieve records containing *Wellesley, Arthur, Duke of Wellington*.[6] If your system does not accommodate such variations, you should add the variants to your Authority Record or to the Work Record (if you do not have an authority file).

Source Authority

A Source Authority is a bibliographic authority file. It is important to credit sources from which data in the Work, Image, and Authority Records is obtained, whether the source is a publication, a Web site, or the unpublished opinion of an expert. Using a Source Authority is strongly recommended. Use existing bibliographic records if possible. Alternatively, elements for a Source Authority file are described in CDWA. Whether or not a Source Authority is used, record citations consistently, using a free-text note if necessary (see Chapter 8: Description).

Elements for the Source Authority File

Elements in a Source Authority file could include title, author, publisher, place of publication, year of publication, and a variety of other fields for bibliographic information. In addition, Source Authority records could point to full bibliographic records in an online library catalog.

A simpler authority file for sources could include fewer elements, such as a full citation combining author, title, and publication information in a single field and a brief citation to be used for concise displays.

> *Example*
>
> [a simple Source Authority record, with two elements: Full Citation and Brief Citation]
>
> > **Full Citation**: Thieme, Ulrich, and Felix Becker, editors. *Allgemeines Lexikon der bildenden Künstler von der Antike bis zur Gegenwart.* 37 vols. Reprint, Leipzig: Veb E.A. Seemann Verlag, 1980-1986.
> > **Brief Citation**: Thieme-Becker, *Allgemeines Lexikon der Künstler* (1980-1986).

The brief citation may be used for display in the linked records. The page element would be in the record linked to the source, not in the Source Record itself. That is, each page reference is specific to the Work and Image Records, and to the Personal and Corporate Name, Subject, Geographic Place, and Concept Authorities, and so on, not to the source itself. As a result, Source Authority records can be used many times over.

Example

[a source reference and page number as it is displayed in a Personal and Corporate Name Authority record]

Sources:

Bolaffi, *Dizionario dei pittori italiani* (1972-1976) *[linked to Source Record]*
Union List of Artist Names (1988-) *[linked to Source Record]*
Thieme-Becker, *Allgemeines Lexikon der Künstler* (1980-1986) *[linked to Source Record]*

Page: 13:408 ff. *[field in the Personal and Corporate Name Authority record]*

Rules for the Source Authority

Record information in the Source Authority or in free-text source notes consistently, using the rules in CDWA, AACR, and the *Chicago Manual of Style*.

Other Authorities

See Part 3 for a discussion of the other four authorities, including recommended elements and rules:

A.1 Personal and Corporate Name Authority
A.2 Geographic Place Authority
A.3 Concept Authority
A.4 Subject Authority

IX. EXAMPLES OF WORK RECORDS

Examples of Work Records are included below. See additional examples at the end of each chapter in Part 2. In the examples, *controlled* refers to values controlled by an authority file, controlled list, or other rules (for example, rules for recording dates). *Link* refers to a relationship between a Work Record and an Authority Record, between two Work Records, or between Image and Work Records. All links are controlled fields. In the examples that follow, the Related Work Records are abbreviated for the sake of brevity. All Work Records should be as complete as possible. See the various chapters in Part 2 for discussions of the metadata elements and whether they should be controlled. In all examples in this manual, both within and at the end of each chapter, data values for repeatable fields are often separated by bullet characters.

Work Record

- ■ **Class** *[controlled]*: paintings • European art
- ■ ***Work Type** *[link to authority]*: painting
- ■ ***Title**: *Vase of Flowers* | **Title Type**: preferred
- ■ ***Creator display**: Jan van Huysum (Dutch, 1682-1749)
    ***Role** *[link]*: painter | * *[link]*: Huysem, Jan van
- ■ ***Creation Date**: 1722
    [controlled]: **Earliest**: 1722; **Latest**: 1722
- ■ ***Subject** *[links to authorities]*: still life • flowers • urn • ledge • crown of thorns plant • tulips • roses • bird's nest • insects • beauty • transience • life • death • senses • Vanitas • Passion of Christ
- ■ ***Current Location** *[link to authority]*: J. Paul Getty Museum (Los Angeles, California, United States) | **ID**: 82.PB.70
- ■ ***Measurements**: 79.4 x 60.9 cm (31 1/4 x 24 inches)
    [controlled]: **Value**: 79.4; **Unit**: cm; **Type**: height | **Value**: 60.9; **Unit**: cm; **Type**: width
- ■ ***Materials and Techniques**: oil on panel
    Material *[link]*: oil paint • panel (wood)
- ■ **Style** *[link to authority]*: Rococo
- ■ **Description**: The subject is a still life of flowers spilling onto a ledge, some decaying and being eaten by insects. It represents the senses of sight and smell; the decay and broken stems symbolize the transient nature of life, youth, and beauty; the ledge pushed up to the picture plane resembles the ledge seen in posthumous portraits, thus symbolizing death. The crown of thorns flower at the top symbolizes the Passion of Christ.
- ■ **Description Source** *[link]*: J. Paul Getty Museum. *Handbook of the Collections*. Los Angeles: J. Paul Getty Museum, 1991; **Page**: 115.

CREDIT: The J. Paul Getty Museum (Los Angeles, California, United States), Jan van Huysum (Dutch, 1682-1749). *Vase of Flowers*. 1722. Oil on panel, 31 1/4 x 24 inches (79.4 x 60.9 cm). 82.PB.70. © The J. Paul Getty Trust.

Figure 5

Work Record for a Collection of Works: Cartes-de-visite[8]

Required and recommended elements are marked with an asterisk.

Work Record

■ **Class** *[controlled]*: photographs • European art

■ ***Work Type** *[link to authority]*: cartes-de-visite

■ ***Title**: Peruvian Portrait Cartes-de-Visite | **Title Type**: preferred

■ ***Creator display**: Eugenio Courret (French, active ca. 1861-ca. 1900 in Peru) and Courret Hermanos (Peruvian, active 1863-ca. 1873)

   *Role *[link]*: photographer | *[link]*: Courret, Eugenio

   *Role *[link]*: studio | *[link]*: Courret Hermanos

■ ***Creation Date**: ca. 1870-ca. 1880 | *[controlled]*: **Earliest**: 1860; **Latest**: 1890

■ ***Subject** *[link to authorities]*: portraits • travel • Peru (South America) • veiled women • matador • Native Andean • soldier • camp follower • mother and child

■ ***Current Location** *[link to authority]*: Getty Research Institute, Research Library, Special Collections (Los Angeles, California, United States) | **ID**: 91-F46

■ ***Material and Techniques**: cartes-de-visite (photographs)

   Technique *[link]*: cartes-de-visite

■ ***Measurements**: 11 items, 9 x 8 cm each (3 1/2 x 3 1/8 inches)

   [controlled]: **Value**: 9; **Unit**: cm; **Type**: height | **Value**: 8; **Unit**: cm; **Type**: width || **Extent**: items; **Value**: 11; **Type**: count

■ **Inscriptions**: versos read: E. Courret, Fotográfo, 197 Calle de la Union (Mercaderes), 71 Calle del Palacio, Lima, República Peruana, Exposición 1869 Medalla de Honor, Exposición 1872 Medalla de Oro (9 items); Courret Hermanos, [same address], with monogram; E. Courret, Fotógrafo, Lima, República Peruana, Exposición.

■ **Description**: Studio portraits in cartes-de-visite format. 3 tapadas (veiled women); a matador; 9 images of indigenous Andeans, including a soldier and his rabona (camp follower), and a mother and child

■ **Related Work**:

   Relationship Type *[controlled]*: part of

   [link to related Work Record]: *Cities and Sites Cartes-de-visite*; collection; Eugenio Courret, Burton Brothers, Charles Leinack, and others; 1854-ca. 1905; Special Collections, Research Library, Getty Research Institute (Los Angeles, California, United States); no. ZCDV 2

Work Record

■ **Class** *[controlled]*: sculpture • costume • African art
■ *****Work Type** *[link to authority]*: mask
■ *****Title**: Pendant Mask: Iyoba I **Title Type**: preferred
■ *****Creator display**: unknown Nigerian, Court of Benin, for Oba Esigie (King of Benin, 1404-1550)
    *****Role** *[link]*: artist I *[link]*: unknown Nigerian
    Role *[link]*: patron I *[link]*: Oba Esigie
■ *****Creation Date**: early 16th century I *[controlled]*: **Earliest**: 1500; **Latest**: 1530
■ *****Subject** *[link]*: religion and mythology • apparel
    • human figure • female • face • ceremonial object
    • Iyoba (queen mother)
■ **Culture** *[link]*: Nigerian
■ *****Current Location** *[link to authority]*: Metropolitan Museum of Art (New York, New York, United States) I **ID**: 1978.412.323
■ *****Measurements**: 23.8 cm (height) (9 3/8 inches) I *[controlled]*: **Value**: 23.8; **Unit**: cm; **Type**: height
■ *****Materials and Techniques**: ivory, iron, copper **Material** *[link]*: ivory • iron • copper
■ **Style** *[link to authority]*: Edo (African)
■ **Description**: Believed to have been produced in the early 16th century for the Oba Esigie (1404-1550), the king of Benin, to honor his mother, Idia. The Oba may have worn it at rites commemorating his mother
■ **Description Sources** *[link]*:
    Metropolitan Museum of Art online. http://www.metmuseum.org (accessed February 1, 2004)
    British Museum online. http://www.thebritish museum.ac.uk (accessed February 9, 2005)
■ **Related Work**:
    Relationship Type *[controlled]*: pendant of
    [link to Work Record]: *Ivory Mask*; unknown Benin; probably 16th century; British Museum (London, England), Ethno 1910.5-13.1

Work Record

■ **Class** *[controlled]*: sculpture • costume • African art
■ *****Work Type** *[link to authority]*: mask
■ *****Title**: Ivory Mask
■ *****Creator display**: unknown Nigerian, Court of Benin, for Oba Esigie (King of Benin, 1404-1550)
    *****Role** *[link]*: artist I *[link]*: unknown Nigerian
    Role *[link]*: patron I *[link]*: Oba Esigie
■ *****Creation Date**: probably 16th century I *[controlled]*: **Earliest**: 1590; **Latest**: 1599
■ *****Subject** *[link]*: religion and mythology • apparel
    • human figure • female • face • ceremonial object
    • Iyoba (queen mother)
■ *****Current Location** *[link to authority]*: British Museum (London, England) I **ID**: Ethno 1910.5-13.1
■ *****Measurements**: 24.5 x 12.5 x 6 cm (9 3/4 x 4 7/8 x 2 3/8 inches)
    [controlled]: **Value**: 24.5; **Unit**: cm; **Type**: height I **Value**: 12.5; **Unit**: cm; **Type**: width I **Value**: 6; **Unit**: cm; **Type**: depth
■ *****Materials and Techniques**: ivory I **Material** *[link]*: ivory
■ **Source** *[link to authority]*: British Museum online (accessed February 17, 2004)
■ **Related Work**:
    Relationship Type *[controlled]*: pendant of
    [link to Work Record]: *Pendant Mask: Iyoba* Metropolitan Museum (New York, New York, United States); 1978.412.323

CREDIT: Pendant Mask: Iyoba, 16th century; Edo, court of Benin; Nigeria; ivory, iron, copper; H. 9 3/8 in. (23.8 cm) view #3; Metropolitan Museum of Art, Michael C. Rockefeller Memorial Collection, Gift of Nelson A. Rockefeller, 1972 (1978.412.323). Photograph © 1995 Metropolitan Museum of Art.

Figure 7
Work Records for Related Works: Whole/Part Relationships for Renaissance/Baroque Basilica
Required and recommended elements are marked with an asterisk.

Work Record

■ **Class** *[controlled]*: architecture • European art

■ ***Work Type** *[link]*: basilica

■ ***Title**: Saint Peter's Basilica I **Title Type**: preferred
Title: St. Peter's Basilica I **Title Type**: alternate
Title: New Saint Peter's I **Title Type**: alternate
Title: San Pietro in Vaticano I **Title Type**: alternate

■ ***Creator display**: designed and constructed by a long series of architects, including Donato Bramante (Italian, 1444-1514), Raphael Sanzio (Italian, 1483-1520), Antonio da Sangallo the Elder (Italian, ca. 1455-1534), Michelangelo Buonarroti (Italian, 1475-1564), Giacomo della Porta (Italian, 1532/1533-1602/1604), Carlo Maderno (Italian, ca. 1556-1629), and Gian Lorenzo Bernini (Italian, 1598-1680)
   *Role *[controlled]*: architect I *[link]*: Bernini, Gian Lorenzo
   *Role *[controlled]*: architect I *[link]*: Bramante, Donato
   *Role *[controlled]*: architect I *[link]*: Buonarroti, Michelangelo
   *Role *[controlled]*: architect I *[link]*: Fra Giocondo
   *Role *[controlled]*: architect I *[link]*: Ligorio, Pirro
   *Role *[controlled]*: architect I *[link]*: Maderno, Carlo
   *Role *[controlled]*: architect I *[link]*: Peruzzi, Baldassare
   *Role *[controlled]*: architect I *[link]*: Porta, Giacomo della
   *Role *[controlled]*: architect I *[link]*: Sangallo, Antonio da, the elder
   *Role *[controlled]*: architect I *[link]*: Sangallo, Giuliano da
   *Role *[controlled]*: architect I *[link]*: Sanzio, Raphael
   *Role *[controlled]*: architect I *[link]*: Sansovino, Andrea
   *Role *[controlled]*: architect I *[link]*: Vignola, Giacomo da

■ ***Creation Date**: designs begun 1451, constructed 1506-1615, piazza finished 1667
   [controlled]: **Qualifier**: design; **Earliest**: 1451; **Latest**: 1667 II **Qualifier**: construction; **Earliest**: 1506; **Latest**: 1615 II
   Qualifier: piazza; **Earliest**: 1667; **Latest**: 1667

■ ***Subject** *[links to authorities]*: architecture • religion and mythology • Saint Peter (Christian iconography) • cathedral • Papal power

■ ***Current Location** *[link]*: Vatican City (Rome, Italy)

■ ***Measurements**: height of dome: 138 m (452 feet); length of main structure: 187 m (615 feet)
   [controlled]: **Value**: 138; **Unit**: m; **Type**: height I **Value**: 187; **Unit**: m; **Type**: length

■ ***Materials and Techniques**: load-bearing masonry construction I **Material** *[link]*: masonry I **Technique** *[link]*: bearing walls

■ **Style** *[link to authority]*: Renaissance • Baroque

■ **Description**: A three-aisled Latin cross with a dome at the crossing. The basilica had a long building history and many architects: It was begun under Pope Julius II in 1506 to replace Old Saint Peter's, and completed in 1615 under Paul V. The original plan was a Greek cross by Donato Bramante; when he died in 1514, Leo X commissioned Raphael, Fra Giocondo, and Giuliano da Sangallo to continue the Work, changing the Greek-cross plan to a Latin cross with three aisles separated by pillars. Raphael died in 1520; Antonio da Sangallo the Elder, Baldassare Peruzzi, and Andrea Sansovino continued the Work. Sangallo died in 1546 and Paul III commissioned Michelangelo as chief architect. Michelangelo died in 1564, when the drum for the dome was nearly complete. Pirro Ligorio and Giacomo da Vignola continued the Work. Under Gregory XIII, Giacomo della Porta was put in charge of the Work. [and so on]

■ **Description Source** *[link]*: Millon, Henry A., and Craig Hugh Smyth. *Michelangelo architect*. Milan: Olivetti, 1988.

■ ***Related Work**:
   Relationship Type *[controlled]*: larger context for I *[link to Related Work]*: *Dome of Saint Peter's*; dome; Michelangelo Buonarroti (Italian, 1475-1564) and others; designed mid-1550s, constructed late 16th century; Saint Peter's Basilica (Vatican City, Rome, Italy)

Work Record

- **Class** *[controlled]*: architecture
- ***Work Type** [link]*: dome
- ***Title**: Dome of Saint Peter's | **Title Type**: preferred
- ***Creator display**: designed by Michelangelo Buonarroti (Italian, 1475-1564), design revised by Giacomo della Porta (Italian, born 1532 or 1533; died 1602)
    - ***Role** [controlled]*: architect | *[link to Personal and Corporate Name Authority]*: Buonarroti, Michelangelo
    - ***Role** [controlled]*: architect | **Extent**: revisions to design | *[link]*: Porta, Giacomo della
    - ***Role** [controlled]*: architect | **Extent**: revisions to design | *[link]*: Fontana, Domenico
- ***Creation Date**: designed mid-1550s, constructed late 16th century
    - *[controlled]*: **Extent**: design; **Earliest**: 1530; **Latest**: 1570 | **Extent**: construction; **Earliest**: 1451; **Latest**: 1600
- ***Subject** [link to authorities]*: architecture • dome
- ***Current Location** [link to authority]*: Saint Peter's Basilica (Vatican City, Rome, Italy)
- ***Measurements**: diameter: 42 m (138 feet); height of dome: 138 m (452 feet) above the street, 119 m (390 feet) above the floor
    - *[controlled]*: **Qualifier**: exterior; **Value**: 138; **Unit**: m; **Type**: height || **Qualifier**: interior; **Value**: 119; **Unit**: m; **Type**: height | **Value**: 42; **Unit**: m; **Type**: diameter
- ***Materials and Technique**: brick, with iron chain compression ring
    - **Material** *[link]*: brick | **Technique** *[link]*: compression reinforcement
- **Description**: The brick dome uses four iron chains for a compression ring; it is buttressed by the apses and supported internally by four massive piers more than 18 m thick. Bramante's original floor plan called for the dome over a Greek cross plan. Michelangelo designed the dome; after his death Giacomo della Porta and Domenico Fontana executed the dome, altering the shape to make it steeper and taller than Michelangelo's design. The dome was finally completed under Sixtus V; Gregory XIV ordered the erection of the lantern.
- ***Related Work**:
    - **Relationship Type** *[controlled]*: part of | *[link to Related Work]*: *Saint Peter's Basilica*; basilica; Donato Bramante (Italian, 1444-1514) and others; designs begun 1451, constructed 1506-1615; Vatican City (Rome, Italy)

CREDIT:
Saint Peter's Basilica—Dome,
Vatican City (Rome, Italy)
© 2005 Patricia Harpring.
All rights reserved.

Figure 8

Work Record for a Work and Related Images: 19th-Century Parliament Buildings

Required and recommended elements are marked with an asterisk.

Work Record

- **Class** *[controlled]*: architecture • European art
- ***Work Type** *[link to authority]*: parliament buildings
- ***Title**: Houses of Parliament | **Title Type**: preferred
  Title: Westminster Palace | **Title Type**: alternate
  Title: Westminster New Palace | **Title Type**: alternate
- ***Creator display**: architects: Charles Barry (English, 1795-1860), assisted by Augustus Welby Northmore Pugin (English, 1812-1852)
  *Role *[link]*: supervising architect | *[link]*: Barry, Charles
  *Role *[link]*: associated architect | *[link]*: Pugin, Welby Northmore
- ***Creation Date**: construction on current structure was begun in 1837, the cornerstone was laid in 1840, and work was finished in 1860
  [controlled]: **Earliest**: 1837; **Latest**: 1860
- ***Subject** *[link to authority]*: architecture • government • parliament
- **Style** *[link]*: Gothic Revival
- **Culture** *[link]*: British or English
- ***Current Location** *[link to authority]*: London (England)
- ***Measurements**: Victoria Tower: 102 m (height) (336 feet); Saint Stephen's Tower (Big Ben): 97.5 m (height) (320 feet) | *[controlled]*: **Extent**: greatest height; **Value**: 102; **Unit**: m; **Type**: height
- ***Materials and Techniques**: cut stone, bearing masonry | **Material** *[link]*: stone | **Technique** *[link]*: load-bearing walls • dimension stone
- **Description**: Possibly site of a royal palace of the Danish king of England, Canute. Site of the palace of Edward the Confessor in the 11th century, enlarged by William I the Conqueror. Badly damaged by fire in 1512; House of Commons met in Saint Stephen's Chapel by 1550, the Lords used another apartment of the palace. A fire in 1834 destroyed much of the palace. Construction on current structure dates 1837-1860. The Commons Chamber was destroyed in an air raid in World War II, reopened in 1950.
- **Related Images**:
  [links to Image Records]: 2345 (exterior view, facing west) • 2346 (exterior view, facing southwest)

Image Record

- **Image Number**: 2345
- ***View Description**: exterior view facing west with north end of House of Parliament, including Big Ben and view from Westminster Bridge
- ***View Type** *[link]*: exterior view, partial view
- ***View Subject**: clock tower • facade • Westminster Bridge (London, England) • Big Ben (Tower clock)
- ***View Date** *[controlled]*: 1980
- **Related Work** *[link to Work Record]*: *Houses of Parliament*; parliament buildings; Charles Berry (English, 1795-1860), assisted by Augustus Welby Northmore Pugin (English, 1812-1852); begun 1837, finished 1860; London (England)

Image Record

- **Image Number**: 2346
- ***View Description**: exterior view facing southwest with north end of Houses of Parliament
- ***View Type** *[link]*: exterior view • oblique view • partial view
- ***View Subject**: north facade • lamppost
- ***View Date** *[link]*: 1980
- **Related Work** *[link to Work Record]*: *Houses of Parliament*; parliament buildings; Charles Berry (English, 1795-1860), assisted by Augustus Welby Northmore Pugin (English, 1812-1852); begun 1837, finished 1860; London (England)

Notes

1. See *Metadata Standards Crosswalks* http:// www.getty.edu/research/conducting_research/ standards/intrometadata/3_crosswalks/ index.html.
2. *Work* in CCO is more concrete than *work* as defined in FRBR (Functional Requirements for Bibliographic Records), which is a bibliographical framework developed by a committee of the International Federation of Library Associations (IFLA) and published in 1998 (http://www.ifla .org/VII/s13/frbr/frbr.pdf). The work in CCO is usually a physical entity, whereas that in FRBR is an abstraction or intellectual entity, such as a literary work or a musical composition.
3. Porter, Vicki, and Robin Thornes. *Guide to the Description of Architectural Drawings.* New York: G.K. Hall, 1994 (updated version at http:// www.getty.edu/research/conducting_research/ standards/fda/). Architectural works are discussed as Authority Records in the built works authority chapter, though the same principles and examples apply to a work of architecture cataloged as a work in its own right.
4. Getty Vocabulary Program. *Art & Architecture Thesaurus* (AAT), *Union List of Artist Names* (ULAN), and *Getty Thesaurus of Geographic Names* (TGN). Los Angeles: J. Paul Getty Trust, 1988-. http://www.getty.edu/research/ conducting_research/vocabularies/. Library of Congress Authorities. *Library of Congress Name Authorities.* Washington, DC: Library of Congress. http://authorities.loc.gov/.
5. This and most of the other retrieval issues discussed in this section may be handled by normalizing (removing spaces, punctuation, diacritics, and case sensitivity) both the user's query string and the terms or names in the vocabulary being used for retrieval. This is, of course, a technical issue, but it has—or should have—an impact on cataloging practice.
6. These name variations could be created by establishing algorithms that use the comma as a pivot to create new variations of names and terms; this would be used behind the scenes in retrieval only, and would not be visible to the end user (because some of the variants thus created will be nonsense).
7. This example is intended to illustrate metadata elements discussed in this manual. Field names and data values in the example do not necessarily represent the record for this work in the Getty Museum's database.
8. This example is intended to illustrate metadata elements discussed in this manual. Field names and data values in the example do not necessarily represent the record for this Work in the database for the Getty Research Institute, Research Library, Special Collections.
9. This example is intended to illustrate metadata elements discussed in this manual. Field names and data values in the example do not necessarily represent the records for this work in the museums' databases.

Part TWO

Elements

I. CCO ELEMENTS

Below is a list of elements discussed in the CCO guide. Note that these are references to areas of a Work Record. They do not constitute data elements, though they may be mapped to various metadata element sets (see *Metadata Standards Crosswalks* at http://www.getty.edu/research/conducting_research/standards/intrometadata/3_crosswalks/index.html).

Required Elements

An element marked as *required* indicates that the element is strongly recommended. However, data for any element may occasionally be missing. It is then up to the cataloging institution to determine how to deal with missing data. Possibilities include using a value such as *not available*, *unknown*, or *not applicable*; using a NULL value on the database side; or leaving the field blank entirely.

Controlled Vocabulary

An element marked as *controlled* (link to <xxxx> authority) means that values in the element should be derived from controlled vocabulary and ideally will be linked to an appropriate authority. An element marked as *controlled list* means that the value should be derived from controlled vocabulary, but that a simple controlled list may suffice instead of a link to a full-blown authority. These are recommendations only. How values in various elements are controlled is a local decision. For a discussion of the differences between a controlled list and an authority, see Part 1: Authority Files and Controlled Vocabularies.

II. LIST OF ELEMENTS

Chapter 1

Work Type (required) (controlled) (link to Concept Authority)
Title (required)
Title Type (controlled list)
Language (controlled list)
Source (controlled) (link to Source Authority)

Chapter 2

Creator display (required)
Controlled Creator (required) (controlled) (link to Personal and
    Corporate Name Authority)
Role (required) (controlled) (link to Concept Authority)
Creator Extent (controlled list)
Attribution Qualifier (controlled list)

Chapter 3

Measurements display (required)
    Value (format controlled)
    Unit (controlled list)
    Type (controlled list)
    Extent (controlled list)
    Qualifier (controlled list)
    Shape (controlled list)
    Format (controlled list)
    Scale (controlled)
Materials and Techniques display (required)
    Material (controlled) (link to Concept Authority)
    Material Type
    Technique (controlled) (link to Concept Authority)
    Color (controlled) (link to Concept Authority)
    Mark (controlled list)
    Extent (controlled list)
    Qualifier (controlled list)
Edition display
    Impression Number (format controlled)
    Edition Size (format controlled)
    Edition Number (format controlled)
State display
    State Identification (format controlled)
    Known States (format controlled)
    Source of State (controlled) (link to Source Authority)
Inscriptions
    Inscription Type (controlled list)
    Inscription Location (controlled list)
    Inscription Author (controlled) (link to Personal and Corporate
        Name Authority)
Facture
Physical Description

View Display Date
    View Earliest Date (format controlled)
    View Latest Date (format controlled)

Personal and Corporate Name Authority
Names (required)
Display Biography (required)
Birth Date (required) (format controlled)
Death Date (required) (format controlled)
Nationality (required) (controlled) (link to Concept Authority)
Life Roles (required) (controlled) (link to Concept Authority)
Sources (required) (controlled) (link to Source Authority)
[Record Type (Person or Corporate Body) (controlled list)]
Date of Earliest Activity (format controlled)
Date of Latest Activity (format controlled)
Place/Location (controlled) (link to Geographic Place Authority)
Gender (controlled list)
Related People and Corporate Bodies (controlled) (link to another record
    in the Personal and Corporate Name Authority)
Relationship Type (controlled list)
Events (controlled list)
Note

Geographic Place Authority
Names (required)
Place Type (required) (controlled list)
Broader Context (required) (controlled) (link to another geographic place
    in this authority)
Sources (required) (controlled) (link to Source Authority)
[Record Type (controlled list)]
Coordinates (format controlled)
Dates (format controlled)
Related Places (controlled) (link to another geographic place in this
    authority)
Relationship Type (controlled list)
Note

Concept Authority
Terms (required)
Broader Context (required) (controlled) (link to another concept in this
    authority)
Note (required)
Sources (required) (controlled) (link to Source Authority)
Term Qualifier
[Record Type (controlled list)]
Dates (format controlled)
Related Concepts (controlled) (link to another concept in this authority)
Relationship Type (controlled list)

Subject Authority

Subject Names (required)

Sources (required) (controlled) (link to Source Authority)

Broader Context (required) (controlled) (link to another subject record in this authority)

Related Keywords (controlled list)

Related Subjects (controlled) (link to another subject record in this authority)

Related Geographic Places (controlled) (link to Geographic Place Authority)

Related People or Corporate Bodies (controlled) (link to Personal and Corporate Name Authority)

Related Concepts (controlled) (link to Concept Authority)

Relationship Type (controlled list)

[Record Type (controlled list)]

Dates (format controlled)

Note

Chapter 1

Object Naming

Work Type / Title

1.1 ABOUT OBJECT NAMING

1.1.1 Discussion

The Work Type and Title elements both provide fundamental ways to refer to a work. Determining how to refer to a work is part of the first critical decision in the cataloging process: defining what is being cataloged. See Part 1: What Are You Cataloging?

Work Type

The Work Type element identifies the kind of work or works being described. Work Type typically refers to a work's physical form, function, or medium (for example, *sculpture, altarpiece, cathedral, storage jar, painting, etching*). In this context, works are built works, visual art works, or cultural artifacts, including architecture, paintings, sculptures, drawings, prints, photographs, furniture, ceramics, costume, other decorative or utilitarian works, performance art, installations, or any other of thousands of types of artistic creations or cultural remains. See the definition in Part 1: Works and Images.

The Work Type establishes the logical focus of the catalog record, whether it is a single item, a work made up of several parts, or a physical group or collection of works. When a part of a work of art or architecture is important enough to require its own record, the Work Type should accurately describe the part being cataloged, and the cataloger should link the record for the part to a record for the whole work. For example, if you are cataloging a teacup that is part of a tea service, the Work Type element for the cup should be *teacup*; this record should be linked to a record for the whole tea set in which the Work Type could be *tea service*. It is often helpful to create separate records for the parts of a work when the parts have significantly different characteristics, including separate artists, dates of execution, styles, materials, or physical locations. For example, given that the dome of *Santa Maria del Fiore* in Florence was executed as a separate project from the church itself, the church could have Work Types of *basilica* and *cathedral*, and the dome could have a separate record with the Work Type *dome*. The focus of the record may also vary depending upon local practice and/or circumstances surrounding the history of the work. See Whole-Part Relationships and Components below and Part 1: Related Works for further discussion.

The Work Type element is often displayed with the Class element. The Work Type term is intended to identify the work that is the focus of the catalog record, whereas Class refers to broad categories or a classification scheme that groups works together on the basis of shared characteristics, including materials, form, shape, function, region of origin, cultural context, or historical or stylistic period. For further discussion of class, see Chapter 7: Class.

Title

The Title element records the titles, identifying phrases, or names given to a work of art or architecture. It may be used for various kinds of titles or names. Titles may be descriptive phrases that refer to the iconographical subject or theme of the art work, such as *Adoration of the Magi* or *Portrait of Thomas Jefferson*. They may also record the identifying phrases or names given to works that do not have a title per se. Such names may repeat information recorded elsewhere in the record, such as the Work Type (for example, *Ceramic Bowl*) or the dedication or name of a building (for example, *Mosque of Sultan Ahmed I*).

Works are given titles, names, or identifying phrases to identify and refer to them. One of the differences between a book or article title and a title for many works of art is that printed books and journal articles generally have an inscribed title as part of the thing itself. Catalogers transcribe the inscribed title and use it as a heading to facilitate access. For works of art and architecture, there is often nothing inherent in the work itself that tells the cataloger how to title the work.

Titles may come from various sources. Titles for works are typically assigned by artists, owning institutions, collectors, or scholars. Titles or names for architecture may come from the company that had the building constructed, the architect, or the owner or patron. Titles for well-known works commonly become authoritative through publications and scholarship (for example, *Mona Lisa*). However, many works, including utilitarian works, decorative art, cultural artifacts, maps, diagrams, archaeological works, ethnographic materials, and some buildings, do not have titles or names per se. For these works, a descriptive title should be constructed to facilitate identification by users. A visual resources collection may have to construct titles when there is no repository-supplied title for a work.

Construct titles when necessary. Titles may be derived from their subject content or iconography. For instance, a photograph that depicts a tree in a landscape might be titled *Landscape with Tree*. In composing a title or identifying phrase, it may be necessary to repeat terminology from other elements. Titles may include references to the owners of works or the places where they were used (for example, *Burghley Bowl*). Descriptive titles or identifying phrases may be simple descriptions of the work (for example, *Lidded Bowl on Stand*). Decorative works, non-Western art, archaeological works, or groups of works are often known by a name that includes or is identical to the Work Type (for example, *Chandelier, Rolltop Desk, Mask,* or *Portfolio of Sketches*). Work Type terminology may be used in combination with information from location or other elements to form a title (for example, *Reliquary Cross of Bishop Bernward*).

All significant titles or names by which a work is or has been known should be recorded. Works of art or architecture may be known by many different titles or names; titles may change throughout history. It is useful for researchers to know the alternate and former titles, names, or identifying phrases for the work.

Title Type

Including a Title Type provides a way to distinguish between the various types of titles (for example, *repository title, inscribed title, creator's title, descriptive title*).

Specificity

Work Type should be a term that most closely characterizes the work. Using the most specific, appropriate term is recommended. The focus of the collection and expertise of the users should be considered. For example, is the specific term *cassone* or the more general term *chest* appropriate? Should the cataloger use *canopic jar* or *container*? *Scroll painting* or *painting*? *Engraving* or *print*? Keep in mind that Work Type will often be displayed with Class, which is a broad term (for example, for a *cassone*, the Class could be *furniture*). See Chapter 7: Class. More than one Work Type may be recorded. For example, both *church* and *basilica* may be Work Types for a building, noting both its function and its form.

Titles should generally be concise and specific to the work. A preferred descriptive title should be concise (for example, from the National Gallery of Art in Washington, *Maiolica Plate with Profile Bust*), but an alternate title may include more details (for example, *Maiolica Plate with Running Plant Border, Geometric Panels, and Profile Bust of a Man in Armor*).

Organization of the Data

Work Type is required and should be recorded in a repeatable controlled field. If multiple Work Types are recorded, one should be flagged as preferred. Work Type terminology should be controlled by an authority file or controlled list. See Part 3: Concept Authority for discussion of an authority file that could control the Work Type terms.

Title is also required and should also be a repeatable free-text field. As with Work Type, if multiple Titles are recorded, one should be noted as preferred. If Title Type is used, it should be derived from controlled terminology.

Unique ID

For most institutions, Title and Work Type will not be adequate to uniquely identify a work. A unique numeric or alphanumeric code—for example, an accession number or identification number—is usually created for that purpose by the owner of the work. See Chapter 5 for a discussion of unique identification numbers.

Whole-Part Relationships and Components

Many works of art and architecture are complex works and comprise several parts. Examples include a page from a manuscript, a photograph from an album, a fresco from a cycle, a print in a series, or a church within a monastery. When parts and the whole are cataloged separately, they should be linked. That is, the parts of a work or group may have a hierarchical relationship to the whole. For example, a 16th-century illumination titled *Christ Led Before Pilate* may be part of the whole *Prayer Book of Cardinal Albrecht of Brandenburg*. The creation of whole-part relationships has implications regarding the assignment of Work Type and Title for the work. The Work Type and Title of the whole are important for the retrieval of the part; these data values for the whole should be visible in displays of the record for the part.

Figure 9
Whole-Part Relationships between Works

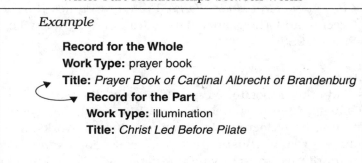

For further discussion of Work Type, how to catalog the components of a work, and item and group level catalog records, see Part 1: Related Works in this manual and *Categories for the Description of Works of Art: Object/Work*.

Recommended Elements

A list of the elements discussed in this chapter appears below. Required elements are noted.

> Work Type (required)
> Title (required)
>   Title Type
>   Language
>   Source

About the Examples

The examples throughout this chapter are for illustration only. Local practice may vary. The examples tend to show the fullest possible use of display and indexing fields, which may not be necessary for visual resources collections and some other institutions.

1.1.2 Terminology

1.1.2.1 *Sources for Terminology*

1.1.2.1.1 WORK TYPE

Work Type terminology should be controlled by using an authority file or controlled lists. Sources of terminology may include the following:

> Getty Vocabulary Program. *Art & Architecture Thesaurus* (AAT). Los Angeles: J. Paul Getty Trust, 1988-. (Especially the Objects Facet). http://www.getty.edu/research/conducting_research/vocabularies/aat/.

> Library of Congress. *Thesaurus for Graphic Materials 2, Genre and Physical Characteristics.* http://lcweb.loc.gov/rr/print/tgm2/.

> Chenhall, Robert G., *Revised Nomenclature for Museum Cataloging: A Revised and Expanded Version of Robert G. Chenhall's System for Classifying Man-Made Works.* Edited by James R. Blackaby, Patricia Greeno, and The Nomenclature Committee. Nashville, TN: AASLH Press, 1988.

1.1.2.1.2 TITLE

Museums and other repositories should assign Titles for their own works based on local guidelines, which may include consulting published scholarship or culling title information from documents accompanying the works, such as deeds of gift, dealer invoices, or labels. Visual resources collections should record Titles as found in authoritative sources when possible, which could include the following:

> Catalogs issued by the museum or other repository of the work.

> An inscription on the work, particularly if it is an integral part of the work (for example, a title inscribed in the plate of a print) or it was inscribed by the artist.

> Catalogues raisonnés, monographs, exhibition catalogs, and articles written about the artist and the work.

> *Grove Dictionary of Art Online.* New York: Grove's Dictionaries, 2003. http://www.groveart.com/.

> Standard textbooks in art history and architectural history.

> Online databases specializing in scholarly descriptions of cultural works.

> *BHA: Bibliography of the History of Art.* Los Angeles, California: J. Paul Getty Trust, 1991-. Published in French as *Bibliographie d'histoire de l'art.* Vandoeuvre-lès-Nancy, France: Centre national de la recherche scientifique, Institut de l'information scientifique et technique; 1991-. Also available online by subscription.

> Library of Congress Authorities. *Library of Congress Subject Headings.* Washington, DC: Library of Congress, 2005. http://authorities.loc.gov/.

Macmillan Encyclopedia of Architects. Edited by Adolf K. Placzek. New York: Free Press; London: Collier Macmillan, 1982.

Avery Architecture & Fine Arts Library, Columbia University. *Avery Index to Architectural Periodicals.* Los Angeles: J. Paul Getty Trust, 1994-. Online by subscription at http://www.getty.edu/research/conducting_research/avery_index/.

Fletcher, Banister. *Sir Banister Fletcher's History of Architecture.* 20th ed. Oxford; Boston: Architectural Press, 1996.

Thieme, Ulrich, and Felix Becker, eds. *Allgemeines Lexikon der bildenden Künstler von der Antike bis zur Gegenwart.* 37 vols. 1907. Reprint, Leipzig: Veb E.A. Seemann Verlag, 1980-1986.

Bénézit, Emmanuel, ed. *Dictionnaire critique et documentaire des peintres, sculpteurs, dessinateurs et graveurs.* 1911-1923. Reprint, Paris: Librairie Gründ, 1976.

If a cataloger cannot find the title in an authoritative source, he or she should construct a title using the recommendations in this chapter. Use guidelines in the Personal and Corporate Name Authority and the Geographic Place Authority to create personal and other names in titles.

1.1.2.2 *Choice of Terminology*

1.1.2.2.1 CONSISTENCY

Work Type

Using consistent terminology for Work Type enables efficient retrieval of records and is therefore strongly recommended.

Titles

If Titles are derived from authoritative sources, the style and use of terminology may vary. If Titles are constructed, consistent terminology is recommended. Although Title is a free-text field and not necessarily formatted with efficient retrieval in mind, consistency will make titles easier for end users to understand.

1.1.2.2.2 AUTHORITY RECORDS

If possible, Work Type terminology and definitions (for example, Scope Notes) should be stored in an authority file, which is linked to the work record. See Part 3: Concept Authority. If using an authority file is not possible, the data values in the Work Type element should be taken from a controlled list.

1.2 CATALOGING RULES

1.2.1 Rules for Work Type

1.2.1.1 *Brief Rules for Work Type*

Recording a Work Type is required. Record one or more terms that describe the type of work being cataloged, referring to the work's physical form, function, or media.

Use the most appropriate specific term, keeping in mind the focus and size of the collection and the intended users. Many institutions need to accommodate both expert users and the general public.

Singular vs. Plural

Generally, use the singular form of terms for Work Types.

> *Examples*
>
> **Work Type:** scroll painting
>
> **Work Type:** drawing
>
> **Work Type:** engraving
>
> **Work Type:** statue
>
> **Work Type:** canopic jar
>
> **Work Type:** monastery
>
> **Work Type:** performance

Use the plural form of the term where required; that is, use terminology that reflects the characteristics of the work being cataloged. For example, if a single drawing is being cataloged, use the singular term *drawing*. If a group of drawings is being cataloged, use the plural *drawings*. For groups of works, components, and whole-part relationships, see the introductory discussion to this chapter and Part 1: Related Works.

Capitalization and Abbreviation

Record the term in lowercase except where the term includes a proper noun or is otherwise capitalized in the controlled vocabulary. Avoid abbreviations.

> *Examples*
>
> **Work Type:** lithograph
>
> **Work Type:** altarpiece
>
> **Work Type:** basilica
>
> **Work Type:** découpages
>
> **Work Type:** Celtic cross
>
> **Work Type:** Brewster chair
>
> **Work Type:** A-frame house

Language of the Terms

Use terminology in the language of the catalog record (English in the United States), except in cases where no exact English-language equivalent exists. Use diacritics as required.

Examples

> **Work Type**: great chair
>
> **Work Type**: radiograph
>
> **Work Type**: skyscraper
>
> **Work Type**: point de neige
>
> **Work Type**: sinopia
>
> **Work Type**: lit à la duchesse
>
> **Work Type**: lyraflügel

1.2.1.2 *Additional Recommendations for Work Type*

1.2.1.2.1 SYNTAX

Record terms in natural word order, not inverted. Do not use punctuation, except hyphens as required.

1.2.1.2.2 VARIOUS TYPES OF WORKS

Choose terms that are appropriate to the work being cataloged, as outlined.

Referring to Form

For three-dimensional works, such as sculpture, decorative arts, furniture, and architecture, and for some textiles and two-dimensional works, include a Work Type that reflects the form of the work, if appropriate.

Examples

[for a small Chalcolithic female figure]
> **Work Type**: statuette

[for a Chinese painted scroll]
> **Work Type**: hanging scroll

[for a Japanese sash]
> **Work Type**: obi

[for the Empire State Building]
> **Work Type**: skyscraper

[for the Basilica of Maxentius]
> **Work Type**: basilica

Referring to Function

For decorative arts, costume, ethnographic materials, architectural drawings, and architecture, include a Work Type that refers to the function or purpose of the work, if appropriate. Works may have multiple Work Types, often including terms that refer to both form and function. A single term (for example, *mask* or *storage jar*) may refer to both form and function.

Examples

[for a stoneware vessel]
> **Work Type:** storage jar

[for a fragment from an Aztec shield]
> **Work Type:** shield strap

[for a Syrian lamp]
> **Work Type:** mosque lamp

[for an African carving]
> **Work Type:** diviner's figure

[for an architectural drawing]
> **Work Type:** presentation drawing

[for Notre-Dame, Paris]
> **Work Type:** cathedral

[for a 19th-century bowl]
> **Work Type:** bowl

Referring to Materials

For two-dimensional and some three-dimensional works, use Work Types that refer to the medium, support, or process by which the work was created, if appropriate. In such cases, the media should be repeated or recorded in more detail in the physical characteristics elements (see Chapter 3).

Examples

[for a print by Albrecht Dürer]
> **Work Type:** engraving

[for a work by J.M.W. Turner]
> **Work Type:** watercolor

[for a Romanesque apse decoration]
> **Work Type:** mosaic

Referring to Content

For architectural drawings, books, and some other works, you may include a Work Type that refers to the subject content of the work, if appropriate (for example, a

Work Type could be *elevation*). In such cases, the subject should be repeated or recorded in more detail in the subject element (see Chapter 6). Work Type may also include references to content in the sense of the style, period, or culture (for example, *Attic helmet*), which could be repeated in the appropriate Style, Period, or Culture elements (see Chapter 4).

> *Examples*
>
> [for an architectural drawing of a building's elevation]
>> **Work Type**: design drawing • elevation
>
> [for a medieval Islamic manuscript]
>> **Work Type**: manuscript
>
> [for an embroidered textile that illustrates a variety of stitches]
>> **Work Type**: sampler

Time-Based Works

Use appropriate terms for performances and other time-based works.

> *Examples*
>
> [for a performance in a museum gallery]
>> **Work Type**: performance art
>
> [for George Segal's life-size figures in an architectural setting]
>> **Work Type**: sculpture • environment (sculpture)

1.2.1.2.3 WHEN THE WORK TYPE HAS CHANGED

If the function or physical characteristics of a work have changed over time, record both the original and subsequent Work Types. List Work Types in reverse chronological order (the most recent first), or with the most important first. The changing use or characteristics of the work may be explained in the descriptive note (see Chapter 8: Description).

> *Examples*
>
> [for Hagia Sophia, Istanbul]
>> **Work Type**: cathedral • mosque • museum
>
> [for a sculpture that was originally the base of a table]
>> **Work Type**: sculpture • table base

When the Work Type has changed over time, visual resources collections may wish to note the form and function of the work as it appears in the specific image in their collection. See Chapter 9: View Information, particularly View Description and View Subject.

1.2.1.2.4 GROUPS OF WORKS

For groups of works, if the parts of the group are not going to be cataloged individually, record the Work Types for all of the works in the group.

Example

[for a box of items from an architectural project]

Work Type: measured drawings • presentation drawings • elevations • oblique projections • plans

1.2.1.2.5 RECORD TYPE

Including a Record Type element to distinguish between single works or images, or collections or from groups, collections, volumes, and the like is strongly recommended. Record Type is an administrative element outside the CCO scope of discussion. See the brief discussion in Part 1: Minimal Descriptions and Record Type and the full discussion in *Categories for the Description of Works of Art: Catalog Level.*

1.2.2   Rules for Title

1.2.2.1   *Brief Rules for Title*

Recording at least one title, identifying phrase, or name for the work of art or architecture is required. If multiple Titles are recorded, one must be flagged as the preferred Title.

Preferred Title

For the preferred Title, use a concise descriptive title in the language of the catalog record (English in the United States). It should be a recent title provided by the owning institution, a concise inscribed title, or a title provided by the artist, if known and if it is sufficiently descriptive.

Examples

> **Title**: *Bust of Napoleon Bonaparte*
>
> **Title**: *Eight Scenes of the Xiao-Xiang Rivers*
>
> **Title**: *Gamble House*

If no appropriate authoritative descriptive title is known, the cataloger must create one.

Capitalization and Abbreviation

For titles derived from authoritative sources, follow the capitalization and punctuation of the source. For constructed titles in English, capitalize the first word and all nouns, pronouns, verbs, adverbs, adjectives, and subordinate conjunctions; use lowercase for articles, coordinate conjunctions, and prepositions, unless they are the first word of the Title.[1]

Examples

> **Title**: *View of a Walled City in a Landscape*
>
> **Title**: *Salomé with the Head of John the Baptist*

Title: *Two Griffins Attacking a Fallen Doe*

Title: *Tripod Table*

Title: *Facet-Cut Beaker*

Title: *Sears Tower*

Always capitalize proper names.

Example

Title: *Marguerite-Louise Lemonnier at Montparnasse, Paris*

For Titles in other languages, follow capitalization rules of that language.

Example

Title: *La vierge à l'hostie*

For the preferred title, avoid abbreviations. Include common abbreviations in alternate titles to provide access.

Example

Titles: *Saint Patrick's Cathedral* (preferred title) • *St. Patrick's Cathedral* (alternate title)

Initial Articles

Avoid initial articles. Exceptions include titles for which the initial article is critical to understanding the meaning (for example, removing the "La" from *La Vierge* would change the meaning of the phrase) or when the article is otherwise generally included in authoritative sources (for example, *The Nightwatch* by Rembrandt). In some cases the inclusion of an article will vary according to the language (for example, the title is generally *Mona Lisa* in English, but *La Gioconda* in Italian for the same painting).

Language of the Title

For the preferred Title, use a concise title in the language of the catalog record (English in the United States). Translate inscribed and other titles into English as necessary. Transcribe an inscribed title in the original foreign language as an alternate title.

Examples

Title: *The Bride Stripped Bare by Her Bachelors, Even* (preferred)

Title: *Roman Portrait Bust* (preferred)

Title: *View of Rome, Italy from the Northwest* (preferred)

Title: *Plan and Elevation of the Houses of Parliament* (preferred)

Title: *Design for a Table Sculpture Made from Sugar* (preferred)

Alternate titles in various languages may be included to provide better access. Use diacritics as required.

Example

Titles: *Madonna and Child with John the Baptist* (preferred) • *La Virgen y el Niño con el pequeño San Juan Bautista*

If the work is commonly known by a name or title in a language other than the language of the catalog record, however, use the commonly known title as the preferred title.

Examples

Title: *Notre Dame, Paris* (preferred)

Title: *Noli me tangere* (preferred)

Titles: *Mona Lisa* (preferred) • *Monna Lisa* • *La Gioconda* • *La Joconde* • *Portrait of the Wife of Francesco del Giocondo* (descriptive)

1.2.2.2 *Additional Recommendations for Title*

1.2.2.2.1 INDEX IMPORTANT INFORMATION

If there is important information in the title, index it in Work Type, Subject, Physical Characteristics, Location, or another appropriate element. Title is a free-text field, meaning that retrieval on it will not be optimal.

1.2.2.2.2 CONSTRUCTED TITLE

If no descriptive title is available in an authoritative source, construct a descriptive title. If an inscribed or repository title is overly long, in a foreign language, or does not describe the work, construct a concise descriptive title in the language of the catalog record. Constructed titles may refer to the subject, the materials, the form, or the function of the work.

1.2.2.2.3 VARIOUS TYPES OF WORKS

Titles, names, and other identifying phrases will differ depending on the type of work, the history and content of the work, and the available documentation.

Owner's Titles

Record the title or titles of the repository or owning institution; include the title preferred by the institution for use in publications and any additional repository titles: a brief title, a title for a special exhibition, or a title for use on a Web page. Visual resources collections should prefer the current owner's or repository's preferred title, if known.

Examples

[for a painting by Mary Cassatt in the Metropolitan Museum, New York]
> **Title**: *The Cup of Tea* (preferred)

[for a work in the National Gallery of Art, Washington]
> **Title**: *Chalice of the Abbot Suger of Saint-Denis* (preferred)

[for a building in Chicago]
> **Title**: *Wrigley Building* (preferred)

If the repository or owner's title is in a foreign language, translate it into the language of the catalog record (English, in the United States), if possible. Include the title in the original language as an alternate title.

[for a sculpture in the Louvre, Paris]

    Titles: *Winged Victory of Samothrace* (preferred) • *Victoire de Samothrace*

[for a painting by Rembrandt in the Rijksmuseum, Amsterdam]

    Titles: *The Nightwatch* (preferred) • *De Nachtwacht*

If the work is very well known by the repository or owner's title, however, make it the preferred title even if it is in a foreign language. See Language of the Title above.

Creator's Titles

Include the title preferred by the creator, if known. Museums and other repositories generally prefer the creator's title. If a cataloger for a visual resources collection discovers that the repository's title differs from the creator's title, he or she should flag the repository's title as preferred and include the creator's title as an alternate.

    Examples

    [for a painting by John Everett Millais]

        Title: *Ophelia* (preferred)

    [for a mobile by Alexander Calder]

        Title: *Hanging Spider* (preferred)

    [for a photograph by Alexander Gardner]

        Title: *Carnage at Antietam* (preferred)

    [for a performance piece by Harry Kipper]

        Title: *Psychic Attack* (preferred)

Inscribed Titles

If any work contains an inscription that was applied by the creator with the apparent purpose of giving it a title, record it as a title. For prints and books, record any title inscribed in the printing plate or on the title page. Punctuation and spelling should be preserved, if possible. The inscribed title may be repeated in fuller form in the Inscription element (see Chapter 3: Physical Characteristics). Inscriptions that are not titles should be recorded in the Inscription element. If the inscribed title does not describe the work concisely in the language of the catalog record, construct a descriptive title as indicated above.

    Examples

[for a famous painting by René Magritte]

    Titles: *Ceci n'est pas une pipe* (preferred, inscribed) • *This Is Not a Pipe* (alternate, translated)

[for a 19th-century print]

    Titles: *Hark! Charley* (preferred, inscribed) • *Young Mother and Infant* (alternate, descriptive)

The inscribed title need not be the preferred title. If the inscribed title is not well known and is in a foreign language, is too long, has abbreviations, or has obsolete or incorrect spelling, construct a preferred descriptive title.

Examples

[for a 19th-century American print]

Titles: *View of the Poor House, Hospital, and Lunatic Hospital of Northampton County, Pennsylvania* (preferred) • *Poor House, Hospital & Lunatick-Hospital of Northampton County, Pa.* (inscribed)

Titles: *Tarot or Trump Card Showing a Horse-Drawn Decorated Wagon in a Bavarian "Peasant Wedding" Procession* (preferred) • *Bey solchen Wierth: und Würthinen ist leicht in Schmaus und Hochzeit gehn* (inscribed)

Descriptive Titles

It is required to include a descriptive title, which is a concise title in the language of the catalog record (that is, in English) that indicates what the work is or what is depicted in it. If the repository title or another title is descriptive, the cataloger need not construct one. Descriptive titles should be flagged so they may be used in online results displays, wall labels, and so forth.

If an inscribed or repository title is in a foreign language, is too long for convenient display, or does not refer to the content of the work, construct a concise descriptive title that refers to the iconographic content of the work (that is, the figures, stories, or scenes portrayed in it). The subject matter should be more fully recorded and indexed in the Subject element (see Chapter 6). Descriptive titles may also refer to the Work Type or Physical Characteristics of the work; if so, the Work Type should be repeated in the Work Type element.

REFERRING TO HISTORICAL OR RELIGIOUS SUBJECTS

Where appropriate, list named historical, religious, mythological, literary, or allegorical themes or subjects.

Examples

[for an Indian sculpture]

Title: *Seated Buddha Preaching the First Sermon* (preferred)

[for a painting by Simone Martini]

Title: *The Annunciation* (preferred)

[for a Roman wall painting]

Title: *Odysseus in the Underworld* (preferred)

[for a painting by the Native American, Kicking Bear]

Title: *Battle of Little Big Horn* (preferred)

[for a drawing by François Boucher]

Title: *Allegory of Music* (preferred)

REFERRING TO FIGURES, WORKS, OR PLACES

Where appropriate, refer to named or anonymous figures, other works, or places depicted in the work. Include proper names, if they are known.

Examples

[for a sculpted head]

Title: *Portrait Head of Andrew Jackson* (preferred)

[for an architectural drawing]

Title: *Plan and Elevation of the Houses of Parliament, London* (preferred)

[for a Japanese screen]

Title: *Screen with Night Rain on Lake Biwa* (preferred)

[for a Tiffany vase decorated with flowers]

Title: *The Magnolia Vase* (preferred)

[for a pastel sketch]

Title: *Studies of a Female Nude* (preferred)

REFERRING TO THE WORK TYPE

For decorative works, non-Western art, archaeological works, architecture, or groups of works that do not have a title per se, include a descriptive phrase or name based on Work Types or a brief physical description of the work.

Examples

[for an ancient Greek vessel]

Title: *Red-Figure Amphora* (preferred)

[for an 18th-century French chandelier]

Title: *Chandelier* (preferred)

[for a 17th-century American vessel]

Title: *Silver Chocolate Pot* (preferred)

[for an African mask]

Title: *Helmet Mask* (preferred)

[for a group of drawings]

Title: *Portfolio of Sketches of Various Subjects* (preferred)

[for a Mesopotamian tablet]

Title: *Administrative Tablet with Cylinder Seal Impression of a Male Figure* (preferred)

Titles Referring to the Owner, Location, or History of the Work

Where appropriate, record a Title that includes the names of current or former owners, a current or former location, or other historical references.

Examples

[for a sculpture, the second title refers to a former owner]

Titles: *Statue of Hercules* (preferred) • *Lansdowne Herakles*

[for a textile, title refers to the place where it was first displayed]

Title: *Bayeux Tapestry* (preferred)

[for a set of china, title refers to the patron]

Title: *Franklin D. Roosevelt Service* (preferred)

Names of Buildings

For architecture, record a descriptive name, a name that refers to the owner, a dedication (for example, for a church), or a street address, as appropriate. Many buildings do not have names, in which case the title may refer to the Work Type (for example, *Amphitheater*) or it may be a longer descriptive phrase.

Examples

[for a ruin at Pompeii, Italy, title refers to the Work Type]

Title: *Amphitheater* (preferred)

[for an Italian church, title refers to location and dedication]

Titles: *Siena Cathedral* (preferred) • *Il Duomo di Siena* • *Santa Maria Assunta*

[for a Chinese temple, title refers to the denomination and style]

Title: *Taoist Temple* (preferred)

[for a skyscraper, title refers to the owner and address]

Titles: *Trump International Hotel and Tower* (preferred) • *One Central Park West*

[for an apartment building by Antoni Gaudí, the titles refer to the owner and the form of the building (pedrera means stone quarry)]

Titles: *Milá House* (preferred) • *Casa Milá* • *La Pedrera*

Numbered Titles

For manuscripts or other works, if appropriate, record an appellation based on a particular numbering system, such as a shelfmark.

Example

[for a Late Antique manuscript]

Titles: *Harley Golden Gospels* (preferred) • *British Museum Harley 2788*

1.2.2.2.4 MULTIPLE TITLES

Record multiple titles when a work is known by multiple titles or when a concise descriptive or other title must be constructed by the cataloger; use Title Type to flag one title as preferred.

Examples

[for a house by Frank Lloyd Wright]

Titles: *Edgar J. Kaufman House* (preferred) • *Fallingwater*

[for a painting by Bronzino]

Titles: *Allegory with Venus and Cupid* (preferred, repository title) • *Venus, Cupid, Time, and Folly* • *Allegory of Lust and Love*

[for a mosque]

Titles: *Selimiye Cami* (preferred) • *Mosque of Selim II*

Put each Title in a separate occurrence of the Title field. However, if a repository or creator's title includes multiple titles in the same field, enclose the second title in parentheses for display.

Example

[for a painting by Edward Steichen]

Title: *Le Tournesol (The Sunflower)* (preferred, repository title)

Translations and Former Titles

Include translations and former titles.

Examples

[for a painting by Pontormo, former title is included]

Titles: *Portrait of a Halberdier (Francesco Guardi?)* (preferred, repository title) • *Portrait of Cosimo I de' Medici* (former title)

[for a print, translated title]

Titles: *The Farewell of Telemachus and Eucharis* (preferred) • *Les Adieux de Télémaque et Eucharis*

Uncertainty in Descriptive Titles

Constructed titles may express uncertainty, if necessary.

Example

[for a leaf from an unknown manuscript]

Title: *Workers in a Field, Probably from a French Book of Hours*

1.2.2.2.5 UNKNOWN TITLES AND UNTITLED WORKS

For works for which a Title must be constructed, but where the Work Type and purpose are unknown, construct a descriptive Title using any generic information available.

Examples

[for a Paleolithic stone work of unknown Work Type, a constructed descriptive Title]

Title: *Stone Ritual Object* (preferred)

[for a Peruvian fabric of unknown purpose, a constructed descriptive Title]

Title: *Peruvian Textile* (preferred)

[for a contemporary painting with no iconographical subject, a constructed descriptive Title]

Title: *Abstract Composition* (preferred)

[for a building with no known name or unknown street address, a constructed descriptive Title]

Title: *House* (preferred)

Do not use the term *untitled* unless the creator has deliberately named the work *Untitled*.

Example

[for a contemporary print, titled by the creator]

Titles: *Untitled - 15* (preferred) • *Abstract Composition* (descriptive)

Although it is discouraged, the phrase *title unknown* may be used as a Title of last resort in the rare case when no title is known and none can be constructed. Record the phrase in all lowercase to distinguish it from a genuine title.

Example

[for an object of unknown origin, function, and work type]

Title: *title unknown*

1.2.2.2.6 TITLES FOR WHOLES AND PARTS

When a work is part of a larger whole, record the Title and other information about the whole using one of the methods discussed below. Subjects referred to in the title of either the part or the whole should be indexed in the appropriate record (see Chapter 6: Subject; see also Part 1: Related Works).

When Part and Whole Are Being Cataloged

If possible, catalog both the part and the whole separately; a link between the two Related Records would allow for a display of both Titles in the record for the part.

Examples

[for a panel in a polyptych by Matthias Grünewald]

Title: *Panel of Saint Sebastian* (preferred)
[link to the record for the entire altarpiece]
Related Work:
  Relationship Type: part of
  Related Work Title: *Isenheim Altarpiece* (preferred)

[for a part of an architectural complex]

Titles: *Pei's Pyramid* (preferred) • *Pyramide du Louvre* • *Pyramid Add-On*
[link to the record for the full complex]
Related Work:
  Relationship Type: part of
  Related Work Title: *The Louvre* (preferred)

[for a manuscript folio, the folio number may be included in the title]

Title: *Edmund Pierced by an Arrow, folio 14 recto* (preferred)
[link to the record for the manuscript]
Related Work:
  Relationship Type: part of
  Related Work Title: *Morgan Library MS M.736* (preferred)

In the record for the part, the related work may be displayed with information in addition to the title. See also Part 1: Related Works. In the example below, a label for the related work was created by concatenating the title and the free-text creator display from the record for the whole series (see Chapter 2: Creator Information).

Example

[for a print by Jacques Callot]

Title: *Attack on the Highway* (preferred)
[link to the record for the series]
Related Work:
  Relationship Type: part of
  Related Work *[concatenated label]*:
  Small Miseries of War Series; designed and etched by Jacques Callot, 1632-1633 in Nancy (France), first published posthumously in 1635 in Paris

When the Whole Is Not Cataloged

If the whole work is not cataloged, record the title for the whole in the record for the part (for example, when a repository holds a part of a work or series, but the whole work or series is not in the repository's collection, the repository may not wish to make a separate work record for the whole work or series; see Part 1: Related Works). There are two methods for making reference to the title of the whole in the record for the part.

THE WHOLE AND THE PART IN THE SAME TITLE

Refer to the title of the whole in the title of the part, if possible.

Examples

[for a historic room reassembled in the Metropolitan Museum]

Title: *Studiolo from the Ducal Palace in Gubbio* (preferred)

[for a leaf from a disassembled manuscript]

Title: *Feast of Sada, 22 verso, from the Shahnama (Book of Kings)* (preferred)

[for a panel of medieval stained glass]

Title: *Theodosius Arrives at Ephesus (Scene from the Legend of the Seven Sleepers of Ephesus)* (preferred)

COLLECTIVE TITLE

Alternatively, record a collective title, which is the title of the broader context of the work. When the title of the whole is recorded as a separate title in the record for the part, the title of the whole is known as the collective title. Use Title Type to indicate the type of title (for example, *collective title, series title,* and so forth).

Examples

[for a John James Audubon print from a disassembled volume]

Titles: *Carolina Parrot* (preferred) • *The Birds of America* (collective title)

[for a Gobelins tapestry from a series]

Titles: *Le Cheval Rayé* (preferred) • *Les Anciennes Indes* (series title)

[for an ancient Egyptian low-relief sculpture that is a fragment of a larger work]

Titles: *The Deceased in the Hall of Judgment* (preferred) • *Book of the Dead* (collective title)

[for a section of an Indian architectural work in a museum]

Titles: *Pillared Hall from a Temple* (preferred) • *Mandapa Temple* (collective title)

Two Parts Described in Same Title

If the parts of a work are not cataloged separately, include the titles of the two or more parts in the same title field.

Examples

[for a diptych depicting two separate scenes]

Title: *Stigmatization of St. Francis and An Angel Crowning Saints Cecilia and Valerian* (preferred)

[for a matched pair of works]

Title: *Pair of Globes: Celestial Globe and Terrestrial Globe* (preferred)

[for drawings on the recto and verso of a single sheet]

Title: *Two Standing Male Figures (recto); A Reclining Figure, Two Partial Figures (verso)* (preferred)

1.2.2.3 *Rules for Title Type*

Use Title Type to flag various types of Titles for displays or other purposes. Record a term that best describes the type of title. Titles may have more than one Title Type (for example, a single Title could be both the *inscribed title* and the *repository title*).

Preferred and Alternate Titles

Flag the preferred title to distinguish it from other types of titles.

> *Examples*
>
> [for a painting by Henri Matisse]
>> **Titles:**
>> *The Red Room* | **Title Type:** preferred
>> *Harmony in Red* | **Title Type:** alternate
>
> [for a building]
>> **Titles:**
>> *Centre George Pompidou* | **Title Type:** preferred
>> *Centre National d'Art et de Culture Georges Pompidou* | **Title Type:** alternate

Other Title Types

Use controlled vocabulary to record other Title Types, as warranted. Title Types could include the following terms: *owner's title, repository title, inscribed title, creator's title, descriptive title, constructed title, translated title, published title, former title, collective title, series title.*

> *Example*
>
> [for a photograph by Julia Margaret Cameron]
>> **Titles:**
>> *Mountain Nymph, Sweet Liberty* | **Title Type:** preferred • repository
>> *Portrait of a Young Woman* | **Title Type:** alternate • descriptive • constructed

1.2.2.4 *Rules for Language and Source*

Some institutions may wish to record additional information for titles, including the language and source of the title. Use controlled vocabulary for language. Record citations consistently, using the rules in CDWA, AACR, and the *Chicago Manual of Style.*

> *Example*
>
> [for a painting by Frida Kahlo]
>> **Title:** *The Two Fridas* (preferred title)
>>> **Language:** English
>>> **Source:** Ankori, Gannit. *Imaging Her Selves: Frida Kahlo's Poetics of Identity and Fragmentation.* Westport, Connecticut: Greenwood Press, 2002, figure 42.
>>
>> **Title:** *Las dos Fridas* (alternate title)
>>> **Language:** Spanish
>>> **Source:** *Frida Kahlo, 1907-1954: Salas Pablo Ruiz Picasso, Madrid, 30 de abril-15 de junio de 1985.* Madrid: Ministerio de Cultura, Dirección General de Bellas Artes y Archivos, 1992; **Page:** 159.

1.3   PRESENTATION OF THE DATA

1.3.1   Display and Indexing

1.3.1.1   *Free-Text vs. Controlled Fields*

For a discussion of when and why separate free-text and controlled fields are recommended, see Part 1: Database Design and Relationships: Display and Indexing.

1.3.1.2   *Fields in Authority File and Work Record*

Controlled Fields for Work Type

A repeatable controlled field should be used for Work Type. A free-text field for Work Type may be included, but it is generally not required. When a display is desired for multiple Work Types, it can be constructed by concatenating data from the repeatable controlled field.

> *Example*
>
> **Work Type displays** *[concatenated]*: panel painting; altarpiece
> **Controlled field**:
> **Work Types**: panel painting • altarpiece

Controlled Fields for Title

A repeatable free-text field should be used for Title. Given that retrieval on the free-text field will be inefficient, any important information in the title should be indexed in appropriate controlled fields (for example, Subject, Work Type, and Materials).

> *Example*
>
> [for an altarpiece by Hans Holbein the Elder]
>> **Work Types**: panel painting • altarpiece
>> **Titles**: *Adoration of the Magi* • *Die heiligen drei Könige* • *Hommages à la sainte famille*

Controlled Fields for Title Type

The preferred title must be flagged, using Title Type or another method. A repeatable controlled field should be used for Title Type. When a display is desired for multiple Title Types, it can be constructed by concatenating data from the repeatable controlled field.

Controlled Fields for Title Language and Source

Some institutions will wish to index the language and source of the title. Language should be a repeatable controlled field. Source should be linked to a bibliographic authority file. A brief title may be included for displays (see example below).

> *Example*
>
> **Work Type:** figurine
> **Title:** *Mezzetino: Character from the Commedia dell'arte*
> > **Title Type:** preferred
> > **Language:** English
> > **Source:** Bayerisches Nationalmuseum. *Bayerisches Nationalmuseum: Guide to the Collections*, 3rd ed. Munich: Bayerisches Nationalmuseum, 1971.
>
> **Title:** *Mezzetino: Figur der Commedia dell'arte*
> > **Title Type:** alternate
> > **Language:** German
> > **Source:** Bayerisches Nationalmuseum. *Bayerisches Nationalmuseum: Guide to the Collections*, 3rd ed. Munich: Bayerisches Nationalmuseum, 1971.

1.3.2 Examples

Examples of Work Records are included below. For additional examples, see the end of Part 1, the end of each chapter, and the CCO Web site. In the examples, *controlled* refers to values controlled by an authority file, controlled list, or other rules (for example, with dates). *Link* refers to a relationship between a Work Record and an Authority Record or between two Work Records. All links are controlled fields. In the examples that follow, Related Work Records are abbreviated for the sake of brevity. All Work Records should be as complete as possible. See the various chapters for discussions of individual metadata elements, whether they should be controlled, and the respective advantages of an authority file or a controlled list. In all examples in this manual, both within and at the end of each chapter, data values for repeatable fields are separated by bullet characters.

Required and recommended elements are marked with an asterisk.

Work Record

- **Class** *[controlled]*: ceramics • Greek and Roman art
- ***Work Type** *[link]*: Panathenaic amphora
- ***Title**: Panathenaic Prize Amphora and Lid I **Title Type**: preferred
- ***Creator display**: attributed to the Painter of the Wedding Procession as painter (Greek, 4th century BCE); signed by Nikodemos as potter (Greek, active 4th century BCE in Athens)
  - **Qualifier** *[controlled]*: attributed to I ***Role** *[link]*: painter I *[link]*: Painter of the Wedding Procession I ***Role** *[link]*: potter I *[link]*: Nikodemos
- ***Creation Date**: 363-362 BCE I *[controlled]*: **Earliest**: -0363; **Latest**: -0362
- **Extent**: general; ***Subject** *[links to authorities]*: religion and mythology • object (utilitarian) • ceremonial object I **Extent**: side A; ***Subject** *[links to authorities]*: Athena Promachos (Greek iconography) • human female I **Extent**: side B; ***Subject** *[links to authorities]*: Nike • Victor • competition • human females
- **Styles** *[link]*: Black-figure • Attic
- **Culture** *[link]*: Greek
- ***Current Location** *[link]*: J. Paul Getty Museum, Villa Collection (Malibu, California, United States) I **ID**: 93.AE.55
- ***Measurements**: height with lid, 89.5 cm (35 1/4 inches); circumference at shoulder, 115 cm (15 1/16 inches)
  - *[controlled]*: **Value**: 89.5; **Unit**: cm; **Type**: height I **Value**: 115; **Unit**: cm; **Type**: circumference
- ***Materials and Techniques**: wheel-turned terracotta, sintering
  - **Material** *[link]*: terracotta I **Technique** *[link]*: turning • sintering • vase painting
- **Inscriptions**: signed by Nikodemos
- **Description**: Side A: Athena Promachos; Side B: Nike Crowning the Victor, with the Judge on the Right and the Defeated Opponent on the Left. The figure of Athena is portrayed in an Archaistic style. The particular use of Nike figures atop the akanthos columns flanking Athena allow scholars to date this vase to precisely 363/362 BCE.
- **Description Source** *[link]*: J. Paul Getty Museum online. http://www.getty.edu (accessed February 10, 2004).

Concept Authority Record

- ***Terms**:
  - Panathenaic amphora (preferred, singular)
  - Panathenaic amphorae (preferred, plural)
  - Panathenaic amphoras
  - amphora, type c neck
  - amphora, type IIc
- ***Hierarchical position** *[links]*:
  - Objects Facet
  - .... Furnishings and Equipment
  - .... Containers
  - .... <storage vessels>
  - .... amphorae
  - .... neck amphorae
  - .... Panathenaic amphorae

- ***Note**: Refers to amphorae that were filled with olive oil from the sacred trees of Athena, given as prizes in the Panathenaic Games. They were neck amphorae with a large, broad body sharply tapering downward and a relatively thin neck. The standard decoration included images of Athena on one side and the contest at which the prize was won on the other, usually in the Black-figure technique.

- ***Source** *[link]*: *Art & Architecture Thesaurus* (1988-).

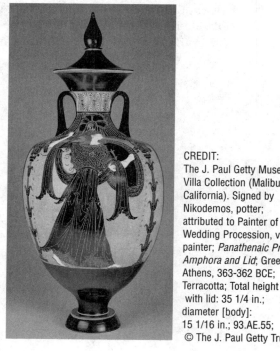

CREDIT:
The J. Paul Getty Museum, Villa Collection (Malibu, California). Signed by Nikodemos, potter; attributed to Painter of the Wedding Procession, vase-painter; *Panathenaic Prize Amphora and Lid*; Greek, Athens, 363-362 BCE; Terracotta; Total height with lid: 35 1/4 in.; diameter [body]: 15 1/16 in.; 93.AE.55; © The J. Paul Getty Trust.

Figure 11
Work Record Linked to an Authority Record for Work Type: Native American Fiddle[3]
Required and recommended elements are marked with an asterisk.

Work Record

- **Class** *[controlled]*: decorative arts • musical instruments • Native American art
- ***Work Type** *[link]*: <u>kízh kízh díhí</u>
- ***Title**: Tzii'edo' a 'tl (Apache Fiddle) | **Title Type**: repository
    Title: Kízh kízh díhí | **Title Type**: alternate
- ***Creator display**: unknown Athabascan family, Apache tribe
    *Role *[controlled]*: artist | *[link]*: unknown Athabascan
- ***Creation Date**: 19th century
    [controlled]: **Earliest**: 1800; **Latest**: 1899
- ***Subject** *[links to authorities]*: object (utilitarian) • music • entertainment
- **Culture** *[link]*: Athabascan (Apache)
- ***Current Location** *[link]*: Metropolitan Museum (New York, New York, United States) | **ID**: 89.4.2631 a,b
- **Creation Location** *[link]*: White Mountain Reservation (Southwest Culture Area, Arizona, United States)
- ***Measurements**: 44.5 cm (length) x 9 cm (diameter) (17 1/2 x 3 1/2 inches); bow length: 40.7 cm (16 inches)
    [controlled]: **Extent**: zither; **Value**: 44.5; **Unit**: cm; **Type**: length | **Value**: 9; **Unit**: cm; **Type**: diameter | **Extent**: bow; **Value**: 40.7; **Unit**: cm; **Type**: length
- ***Materials and Techniques**: agave flower stalk, wood, paint, horsehair
    Material *[link]*: agave • stalk • wood • paint • horsehair
- **Description Note**: Possibly created in the White Mountain Reservation. This two-stringed bowed zither was used for personal enjoyment or to entertain at home with songs and dances. The hollowed agave stalk body is decorated with traditional designs, and the strings attached to the ends of the tube are of horsehair.
- **Description Source** *[link]*: Metropolitan Museum of Art online. http://www.metmuseum.org (accessed February 1, 2004).

Concept Authority Record

- ***Terms**:
    kízh kízh díhí (preferred, singular)
    kízh kízh díhís (preferred, plural)
    tzii'edo' a 'tl
    Apache fiddle
    Navajo violin
- ***Hierarchical position** *[links]*:
    Objects Facet
    .... Furnishings and Equipment
    .... Sound Devices
    .... chordophones
    .... kízh kízh díhís

- ***Note**: Zitherlike instruments of the White Mountain and San Carlos Apache of Arizona and the Diegueño of California, consisting of a hollowed out mescal or other stalk either split lengthwise or whole, with one or two horsehair strings stretched over small rectangular bridges, one at each end. They are held horizontally with one end resting on the chest or abdomen, and played with a horsehair bow.

- ***Source** *[link]*: *Art & Architecture Thesaurus* (1988-).

CREDIT: *Tzii'edo' a 'tl* (Apache Fiddle), 19th century; Made by Athabascan Family, Apache Tribe; possibly White Mountain Reservation, Southwest Culture Area, Arizona, United States of America; Agave flower stalk, wood, paint, horse hair; length 17 1/2 in. (44.5 cm); diameter 3 1/2 in. (9 cm); bowl L. 16 in. (40.7 cm). The Metropolitan Museum of Art, The Crosby Brown Collection of Musical Instruments, 1989 (89.4.2631 a, b). Photograph © 1990 The Metropolitan Museum of Art.

Work Record

■ **Class** *[controlled]*: photographs • European art

■ ***Work Type** [link]*: albumen prints ◀————————

■ ***Title**: Views of Paris and Environs and the Exposition Universelle | **Title Type**: preferred

■ ***Creator display**: Neurdein Frères (French, active late 19th-early 20th centuries)
  ***Role** [link]*: photographers *[link]*: Neurdein Frères

■ ***Creation Date**: ca. 1889 | *[controlled]*: **Earliest**: 1885; **Latest**: 1894

■ ***Subject** [links to authorities]*: architecture • views • Paris (France) • International Exposition of 1889 (Paris, France) • Versailles Palace (Versailles, France) • Parc de Saint-Cloud (Paris, France) • Parc du Champ de Mars (Paris, France) • travel

■ ***Current Location** [link]*: Getty Research Institute, Research Library, Special Collections (Los Angeles, California, United States) | **ID**: 93-F101

■ ***Materials and Techniques**: albumen prints
  Technique *[link]*: albumen prints

■ ***Measurements**: 37 photographic prints; images 13 x 19 cm (5 1/8 x 7 1/2 inches), on sheets 19 x 25 cm (7 1/2 x 9 7/8 inches)
  [controlled]: **Extent**: items; **Value**: 37; **Type**: count || **Extent**: image; **Value**: 13; **Unit**: cm; **Type**: height | **Value**: 19; **Unit**: cm; **Type**: width || **Extent**: sheet; **Value**: 19; **Unit**: cm; **Type**: height | **Value**: 25; **Unit**: cm; **Type**: width

■ **Inscriptions**: captions in French, printed on mount above and below image.

■ **Description Note**: Mounted souvenir views of Paris and environs issued by Neurdein Frères for visitors to the 1889 Exposition universelle. Collection includes panoramas of Paris and views of its main avenues and monuments as well as views of Versailles and the Parc de Saint-Cloud. These images were probably printed from existing ones in the Neurdein Frères inventory. Six views of the Exposition universelle include a panoramic view taken from the Trocadero, a view of the Parc du Champ de Mars, and an exterior view of the Algerian pavilion.

Concept Authority Record

■ ***Terms**:
  albumen prints (preferred, plural)
  albumen print (preferred, singular)
  albumen photoprints
  albumen silver prints
  silver albumen prints

■ ***Hierarchical position** [link]*:
  Objects Facet
  .... Visual and Verbal Communication
  .... Visual Works
  .... <visual works by medium or technique>
  .... photographs
  .... positives
  .... photographic prints
  .... albumen prints

■ ***Note**: Refers to photographic prints having albumen as the binder; always black-and-white, though they may be toned to a monochrome hue.

■ ***Source** [link]*: *Art & Architecture Thesaurus* (1988-).

Figure 13
Work Record Linked to Another Work Record: Medieval Cathedral and Its Portal

Required and recommended elements are marked with an asterisk. Figure shows a hierarchical link between a building and a component of that building.

Work Record

- **Class** *[controlled]*: architecture
- ***Work Type** *[link to Concept Authority]*: basilica
- ***Title**: Chartres Cathedral | **Title Type**: preferred
  Title: Cathedral of Notre-Dame | **Title Type**: alternate
  Title: Notre-Dame d'Chartres | **Title Type**: alternate
- ***Creator display**: unknown French
  *Role *[controlled]*: architects | *[link to Personal and Corporate Name Authority]*: unknown French
- ***Creation Date**: construction was begun in 1194, consecrated in 1260; parts of earlier Romanesque building remain | *[controlled]*: **Earliest**: 1194; **Latest**: 1260
- ***Subject** *[link to authorities]*: Virgin Mary • worship • cathedral
- ***Current Location** *[link]*: Chartres (Eure-et-Loir, Centre region, France)
- ***Measurements**: height: 34 m (112 feet); length: 130 m (427 feet)
  [controlled]: **Value**: 34; **Unit**: m; **Type**: height | **Value**: 130; **Unit**: m; **Type**: length
- ***Materials and Techniques**: bearing masonry construction, limestone
  Material *[link]*: masonry • limestone | **Technique** *[link]*: load-bearing walls
- **Styles** *[link]*: Gothic
- **Description**: Noted for innovations in architectural construction and large number of sculptures and stained glass windows. The present cathedral was constructed on the foundations of the earlier church; the oldest parts of the cathedral are the crypt and Royal Portal (West Portal), remnants of a Romanesque church destroyed by fire in 1194.

Work Record

- **Class** *[controlled]*: architecture
- ***Work Type** *[link to Concept Authority]*: portal
- ***Title**: Portal (South Transept) | **Title Type**: preferred
- ***Creator display**: unknown French
  *Role *[controlled]*: architects | *[link]*: unknown French
- ***Creation Date** ca. 1205-ca. 1240
  [controlled]: **Earliest**: 1200; **Latest**: 1245
- ***Subject** *[link to authorities]*: portal • Last Judgment • Jesus Christ • martyrs • confessors • Saint Martin • Saint Nicholas
- ***Current Location** *[link]*: South Transept, Chartres Cathedral, Chartres (Eure-et-Loir, Centre region, France)
- ***Materials and Techniques**: limestone
  Material *[link]*: limestone
- **Styles** *[link]*: Gothic
- **Description**: The central portal depicts the Last Judgment; left portal portrays the Martyrs, tympanum portrays the martyrdom of St. Stephen; right portal portrays the Confessors, tympanum portrays good deeds of St. Martin and St. Nicholas.
- **Related Work**:
  Relationship Type *[controlled]*: part of
  [link to Work Record]: *Chartres Cathedral*; cathedral; unknown French; begun 1194, consecrated 1260; Chartres (Eure-et-Loir, Centre region, France)

Notes

1. For museums and other repositories of objects, common practice in English is to use title case, as advised here, for titles of works rather than sentence case, which is advised in AACR for book titles. Using title case helps ensure that the title of the work will be recognized among other descriptive text in wall labels and other displays.

2. This example is intended to illustrate metadata elements discussed in this manual. Field names and data values in the example do not necessarily represent the record for this work in the Getty Museum's database.

3. This example is intended to illustrate metadata elements discussed in this manual. Field names and data values in the example do not necessarily represent the record for this work in the Metropolitan Museum's database.

4. This example is intended to illustrate metadata elements discussed in this manual. Field names and data values in the example do not necessarily represent the record for this work in the database for the Getty Research Institute, Research Library.

Chapter *2*

Creator Information

Creator/Creator Role

2.1 ABOUT CREATOR INFORMATION

2.1.1 Discussion

The Creator of the work and the Role of the creator are critical elements in cataloging. The creator of a work may be one person, whether known by name or anonymous (that is, an artist whose name is not known, but who is known by some kind of appellation, such as *Achilles Painter*). Multiple creators may be responsible for designing and making a work. A creator may also be a corporate body—that is an organized group of individuals who work together to create art, such as an architectural firm or printmaking atelier. The creator may be unknown, and the responsibility therefore be assigned to a cultural group (that is, the hand or oeuvre is not known, and there thus is no associated appellation; see Various Types of Attributions below for a discussion of anonymous and unknown creators).

Creator

The Creator element identifies the individual, group of individuals, corporate body, cultural group, or other entity that contributed to creating, designing, producing, manufacturing, or altering the work.

Creator Role

The Creator Role element records the role or activity performed by the creator in the conception, design, or production of the work being cataloged.

Attribution Qualifier and Creator Extent

In addition to Creator and Role, other elements could include a qualification of the attribution (for example, *attributed to Raphael*) or an indication about which part (extent) of the work was completed by a particular creator when there are multiple creators (for example, *figures painted by Peter Paul Rubens, with landscape by Jan Breughel the Elder*) or multiple components (for example, *sculpted by Gian Lorenzo Bernini, with base by Vincenzo Pacetti and eagle by Lorenzo Cardelli*), or both.

Unknown Creators

Many works have creators whose names have been lost to history. When the creator is unknown, it is common in certain disciplines to use, in place of the name, a designation of the culture or geographic place that produced the work (for example, *Thai* or *unknown Thai*). The examples in CCO follow the unknown-plus-culture model. Given that creator is such an important field in retrieval, it is recommended to always record a value for creator in the work record, even if the creator is unknown. However, institutional practice may require that some institutions leave the field blank in the local database. In that case, another method should be devised in displays for users at the time of publication, such as filling in the creator area with *unknown* or with the name of the culture that created the work. For further discussion of issues surrounding unknown creators, see Part 3: Personal and Corporate Name Authority.

Ambiguity and Uncertainty

If scholarly opinion is divided regarding attribution, or if attribution is otherwise uncertain or ambiguous, this should be indicated in the free-text Creator display element. Such uncertainty may require that the multiple possibilities be indexed in controlled fields. For example, if it is uncertain which of two creators created a work, both should be indexed as such.

Organization of the Data

Creator and Creator Role are primary access points and therefore required. Both elements should be repeatable.

Museums and other collecting institutions may require more specialized access points for creator information than visual resources collections will need. Retrieval of works based on alternate creator names and basic biographical information, however, is likely to be important for all institutions.

Certain parts of creator information are best recorded in a free-text field for display in combination with controlled fields for access. Controlled fields should be linked to an authority file. If this is not possible, a controlled list of creators and their biographical information should be used to ensure consistency. Given that multiple creators may be responsible for a single work, the link to the authority records or controlled fields should be repeatable. In addition, one creator may fill multiple roles in creating a single work. The Creator Role field should therefore be repeatable for each creator.

The creator name and enough biographical information to identify the creator unambiguously should appear in a Work Record. When referring to the creator in the Work Record, the preferred name of the creator and a biography comprising the nationality and life dates should be displayed. This is most efficiently handled by a link to the Personal and Corporate Name Authority, in which a complete record of information about the creator can be stored, including variant names and biographical information. Creators in this authority file may include both individuals and corporate bodies, which may consist of any group of individuals who work together to create art, such as manufactories or architectural firms. See the discussion in Part 3: Personal and Corporate Name Authority. Additional discussion of creator information and attributions can be found in *Categories for the Description of Works of Art: Creation-Creator and Creator Identification.*

Recommended Elements

A list of the elements discussed in this chapter follows. Required elements are noted. (Creator display may be a free-text field or concatenated from controlled fields.)

> Creator display (required)
> Controlled creator field (link to authority file)
>> Role (required)
>> Creator extent
>> Attribution qualifier

About the Examples

The examples throughout this chapter are for illustration only. Local practice may vary. The examples tend to show the fullest possible use of display and indexing fields, which may not be necessary for visual resources collections and some other institutions.

2.1.2 Terminology

2.1.2.1 *Sources for Terminology*

2.1.2.1.1 CREATOR NAMES

Creator names should be controlled by using an authority record or controlled lists. Published sources of creator information include the following:

> Getty Vocabulary Program. *Union List of Artist Names* (ULAN). Los Angeles: J. Paul Getty Trust, 1988-. http://www.getty.edu/research/ conducting_research/vocabularies/ulan/.

> *Library of Congress Authorities.* Washington, DC: Library of Congress, 2002. http://authorities.loc.gov/.

> *Grove Dictionary of Art Online.* New York: Grove's Dictionaries, 2003. http://www.groveart.com/.

> Thieme, Ulrich, and Felix Becker, eds. *Allgemeines Lexikon der bildenden Künstler von der Antike bis zur Gegenwart.* 37 vols. 1907. Reprint, Leipzig: Veb E.A. Seemann Verlag, 1980-1986.

> Meissner, Günter, ed. *Allgemeines Künstlerlexikon: die bildenden Künstler aller Zeiten und Völker.* Munich: Saur, 1992-.

Bénézit, Emmanuel, ed. *Dictionnaire critique et documentaire des peintres, sculpteurs, dessinateurs et graveurs.* 1911-1923. Reprint, Paris: Librairie Gründ, 1976.

Macmillan Encyclopedia of Architects. Edited by Adolf K. Placzek. New York: Free Press; London: Collier Macmillan, 1982.

Additional general encyclopedias and dictionaries of creators exist. In addition, standard textbooks for art history and Web sites for art museums can serve as sources for names and biographical information about creators. You may also find more specialized sources of creator names, including national sources such as Bolaffi's *Dizionario dei pittori italiani* (1972-1976) for Italian artists, or Snodgrass's *American Indian Painters* for Native American artists.[1]

2.1.2.1.2 ROLES

Roles should be controlled by using a controlled list or authority file. Published sources of terminology for roles include the following:

Getty Vocabulary Program. *Art & Architecture Thesaurus* (AAT). Los Angeles: J. Paul Getty Trust, 1988-. http://www.getty.edu/research/ conducting_research/vocabularies/aat/. (Especially the Agents facet).

2.1.2.2 *Choice of Terminology*

2.1.2.2.1 CONSISTENCY

Using consistent terminology is especially important for controlled fields that are intended to provide access. Consistency is less important, but still desirable, in a free-text note than in a controlled field. Although uncontrolled terminology should be accommodated, terminology that is consistent with the terms in controlled fields is nonetheless recommended for the sake of clarity. Consistent style, grammar, and syntax are always recommended.

2.1.2.2.2 USING AN AUTHORITY RECORD

If possible, names and biographical information should be stored in an authority record linked to the Work Record. See Part 3: Personal and Corporate Name Authority.

To populate the authority records, use standard sources for creator names and biographical information. If information about a particular creator cannot be found in any of the standard published sources, use whatever scholarly sources are available and make a new authority record, citing the source from which the information was taken.

2.2 CATALOGING RULES

2.2.1 Rules for Creator

2.2.1.1 *Brief Rules for Creator*

Recording a creator is required. This can be the preferred name of the individual, a group of individuals, a corporate body, a cultural group, or any other entity that contributed to creating, designing, producing, manufacturing, or altering the work.

Use the most commonly used name, which is not necessarily the fullest name. In some cases, a pseudonym or nickname may be the preferred name. Take the name from an authoritative source. If sources disagree on the preferred form of the name, go down the list of preferred sources in the terminology section and use the name found in the source highest in the list of preferred sources.

A cursory discussion of issues regarding creators' names as they should appear in the Work Record follows. For a fuller discussion of how to choose preferred names, variant names, and other creator information, see Part 3: Personal and Corporate Name Authority.

Capitalization and Abbreviations

Capitalize surnames, initials, forenames, and honorifics. If a name includes an article or preposition (for example *de, des, la, l', della, von, von der*), use lowercase, except for relatively modern names, when the prefix is considered part of the last name and is capitalized. Determine capitalization by consulting an authoritative source. Avoid abbreviations, except for initials when they are part of the preferred name.

> *Examples*
>
> **Creator display**: James Ensor (Belgian, 1860-1949)
>
> **Creator display**: Giovanni della Chiesa (Italian, active 1494-1512)
>
> **Creator display**: Dante Della Manna (Brazilian, contemporary)
>
> **Creator display**: Abraham Louis van Loo (French, 1656-1712)
>
> **Creator display**: Nizami (Azerbaijan, probably 1141-1217)
>
> **Creator display**: Rebekah S. Munro (American, 1780-1803)

Language of the Names

Choose the name most commonly used in the language of the catalog record (English, in the United States). If there is no English version of the name, use the preferred name in the vernacular language. Note that most non-English names do not have English equivalents; thus English speakers use the name in the vernacular language of the creator. Determine which name is most commonly used by consulting an authoritative source. Use diacritics as appropriate.

> *Examples*
>
> **Creator display**: Raphael (Italian, 1483-1520)
>
> **Creator display**: Peter Le Lièvre (French, 1671-1745)

For constructed names (that is, for anonymous creators), use the language of the catalog record (for example, *Master of the Dominican Effigies* rather than *Maestro delle Effigi Domenicane*).

Natural Order and Inverted Names

In the Creator display, list the name in natural order, even if the source lists the name in inverted form.

> *Example*
>
>> **Creator display**: Vincent van Gogh (Dutch, 1853-1890)
>> **Controlled fields**:
>>> **Role**: painter
>>> *[link to Personal and Corporate Name Authority]*:
>>> Gogh, Vincent van

Constructing a Name

If the creator's name is not listed in standard sources and common usage therefore is not known, create a name using a standard such as *Anglo-American Cataloguing Rules* (AACR), informed by the usage of the name in publications (for example, journal articles). If no published source is available, refer to the signature on the work, if possible.

2.2.1.2 Additional Recommendations for Creator

2.2.1.2.1 SYNTAX

For the Creator display, list information in the following order: role or a reference to the process (optional, as necessary for clarity; for example, *painter* or *painted by*), the preferred name in natural order, nationality, and birth and death dates (or dates of activity).

> *Examples*
>
>> **Creator display**: Narciso Abeyta (Native American, 1918-1998)
>> **Controlled fields**:
>>> **Role**: painter
>>> *[link to Personal and Corporate Name Authority]*:
>>> Abeyta, Narciso
>>
>> **Creator display**: sculpted by Umberto Boccioni (Italian, 1882-1916)
>> **Controlled fields**:
>>> **Role**: sculptor
>>> *[link to Personal and Corporate Name Authority]*:
>>> Boccioni, Umberto
>>
>> **Creator display**: illuminated by the Limbourg Brothers (Flemish, active 1400-1416)
>> **Controlled fields**:
>>> **Role**: illuminators
>>> *[link to Personal and Corporate Name Authority]*:
>>> Limbourg Brothers

2.2.1.2.2 CONTEXT SENSITIVITY FOR NAMES

If an artist's or corporate body's names have been changed over time, record the name that was in use when the work was created, if known (for example, the work of Morris, Marshall, Faulkner and Company should be distinguished from the work of the later incarnation of the firm, Morris & Co.).

2.2.1.2.3 LISTING BIOGRAPHICAL INFORMATION

In an efficient system, biographical information in the Creator display in the Work Record should be automatically established through a link from the Personal and Corporate Name Authority. If, instead, the cataloger must enter the information by hand, use the rules below; see the further discussion of the creator's biographical information in Part 3: Personal and Corporate Name Authority.

What to Include in Biographical Information

Include nationality (or culture) and birth and death dates.

> *Examples*
>
>> William Morris (British, 1834-1896)
>>
>> Kicking Bear (Sioux, 1846-1904)
>>
>> Ishiguro Masayoshi (Japanese, 1772-after 1851)

Avoiding Confusion

Avoid phrasing the information in a way that could be confusing or ambiguous.

Uncertain Nationality

Indicate any uncertainty regarding nationality.

> *Example*
>
>> **Creator display**: draftsman: Jacques Daliwes (French or Flemish, 15th century)
>>
>> **Controlled fields**:
>>> **Role**: draftsman
>>>
>>> *[link to Personal and Corporate Name Authority]*:
>>> Daliwes, Jacques

Uncertain Dates

Indicate uncertain or ambiguous dates by using qualifiers such as *ca.* (which means circa), *after*, *before*, or by referring to spans of decades or centuries rather than to specific years (for example, *15th century*).

> *Examples*
>
>> **Creator display**: sculpted by Michel Erhart (German, ca. 1440-after 1522)
>>
>> **Controlled fields**:
>>> **Role**: sculptor
>>>
>>> *[link to Personal and Corporate Name Authority]*:
>>> Erhart, Michel

> **Creator display**: painted by Marten Heemskerck van der Heck (Dutch, active 1640s-1650s)
> **Controlled fields**:
> > **Role**: painter
> > *[link to Personal and Corporate Name Authority]*:
> > Heck, Marten Heemskerck van der

If *ca.* applies to both the birth and death date, repeat it for both (for example, *Chinese, ca. 1410-ca. 1465*). Do not use an apostrophe in date expressions such as *1650s* and *1900s*.

Active Dates

If life dates are unknown, list estimated life dates or dates of activity.

> *Example*
>
> > **Creator display**: painted by Ali Asghar (Persian painter, active from ca. 1525)
> > **Controlled fields**:
> > > **Role**: painter
> > > *[link to Personal and Corporate Name Authority]*:
> > > Ali Asghar

Locus of Activity

Include the place of activity (for example, *active in Italy*) if nationality is unknown or when the locus of activity is different from the artist's nationality or otherwise pertinent.

> *Example*
>
> > **Creator display**: sculpted by Josse de Corte (Flemish, 1627-1678, active in Italy)
> > **Controlled fields**:
> > > **Role**: sculptor
> > > *[link to Personal and Corporate Name Authority]*:
> > > Corte, Josse de

Biography for Anonymous Creators

For an anonymous creator or other creator with incomplete biographical information, include the deduced nationality (or locus of activity) and approximate dates of life or activity.

> *Example*
>
> > **Creator display**: engraved by Monogrammist B. G. (British, active late 19th century)
> > **Controlled fields**:
> > > **Role**: engraver
> > > *[link to Personal and Corporate Name Authority]*:
> > > Monogrammist B. G.

2.2.1.2.4 VARIOUS TYPES OF ATTRIBUTIONS

Record creator information appropriate to the work being cataloged. Various types of works require different creator information. Some works require only the simplest Creator display, but others require more complex explanations.

Simple Attributions

For works created by a single, known creator, make a straightforward reference to the creator.

> *Example*
>
> **[for a marble portrait bust]**
>> **Creator display**: Rombout Verhulst (Dutch, 1624-1698)
>> **Controlled fields**:
>>> **Role**: sculptor
>>> *[link to Personal and Corporate Name Authority]* :
>>> Verhulst, Rombout

Clarify the role of the creator if it will not be immediately apparent to the end user (for example, in the example below, *designed by* is included to clarify that this artist designed, but did not necessarily weave, the carpet).

> *Example*
>
> **[for a carpet]**
>> **Creator display**: designed by Maqsud of Kashan (Persian, active in 16th century)
>> **Controlled fields**:
>>> **Role**: designer
>>> *[link to Personal and Corporate Name Authority]* :
>>> Maqsud of Kashan

Multiple Creators

If multiple entities were involved in creating the work, record all of them. If there are too many to do so, record the most important or most prominent. If the role of the creator could be unclear or ambiguous to the end user—as when the creators contributed differently to the creation of the work—clearly explain roles and extent (see rules for Creator Role and Extent below; some institutions may not index Extent).

> *Examples*
>
> **[for an ancient Greek vessel]**
>> **Creator display**: potter was Euphronios (Greek, active ca. 520-ca. 470 BCE), painting attributed to Onesimos (Greek, active ca. 500-ca. 475 BCE)
>> **Controlled fields**:
>>> **Role**: potter
>>> *[link to Personal and Corporate Name Authority]* :
>>> Euphronios
>>>
>>> **Role**: painter
>>> **Qualifier**: attributed to
>>> *[link to Personal and Corporate Name Authority]* :
>>> Onesimos

[for a painting]

> **Creator display**: Marco Ricci (Italian, 1676-1730), figures by Sebastiano Ricci (Italian, 1659-1734)
> **Controlled fields**:
>> **Role**: painter
>> **Extents**: landscape • architecture
>> *[link to Personal and Corporate Name Authority]*:
>> Ricci, Marco
>>
>> **Role**: painter
>> **Extent**: figures
>> *[link to Personal and Corporate Name Authority]*:
>> Ricci, Sebastiano

[for a print]

> **Creator display**: designed by D. A. Alexander (British, 19th century), engraved and published by William Daniell (British, 1769-1837)
> **Controlled fields**:
>> **Role**: designer
>> *[link to Personal and Corporate Name Authority]*:
>> Alexander, D. A.
>>
>> **Roles**: engraver • publisher
>> *[link to Personal and Corporate Name Authority]*:
>> Daniell, William

[for a dome]

> **Creator display**: designed by Michelangelo Buonarroti (Italian, 1475-1564), design revised by Giacomo della Porta (Italian, born 1532 or 1533; died 1602)
> **Controlled fields**:
>> **Role**: designing architect
>> *[link to Personal and Corporate Name Authority]*:
>> Buonarotti, Michelangelo
>>
>> **Role**: design revisions by
>> *[link to Personal and Corporate Name Authority]*:
>> Porta, Giacomo della

[for an architectural drawing]

> **Creator display**: Henry Cobb (American, born 1926) for I. M. Pei and Partners (American, established 1955)
> **Controlled fields**:
>> **Role**: draftsman
>> *[link to Personal and Corporate Name Authority]*:
>> Cobb, Henry
>>
>> **Role**: architect
>> *[link to Personal and Corporate Name Authority]*:
>> I. M. Pei & Partners

Corporate Bodies as Creator

Record a studio, firm, or other group of persons that created the work, if appropriate.

FIRMS, MANUFACTORIES, AND STUDIOS

For decorative arts, photographs, and other works created in a studio, firm, or manufactory, record the studio, firm, or manufactory, with recognition given to any identified person responsible for decoration or other aspects of the work.

> *Examples*
>
> > **Creator display**: Manufacture royale de porcelaine de Sèvres (French, established 16th century); painted by Pierre-Antoine Méraud père (French, born 1735)
> > **Controlled fields**:
> > > **Role**: manufactory
> > > *[link to Personal and Corporate Name Authority]*:
> > > Sèvres Porcelain Manufactory
> > >
> > > **Role**: painter
> > > *[link to Personal and Corporate Name Authority]*:
> > > Méraud, Pierre-Antoine, père
> >
> > **Creator display**: Milton Kahl (American, 1909-1987), for the Walt Disney Company (American, founded 1923)
> > **Controlled fields**:
> > > **Role**: animator
> > > *[link to Personal and Corporate Name Authority]*:
> > > Kahl, Milton
> > >
> > > **Role***:* studio
> > > *[link to Personal and Corporate Name Authority]*:
> > > Walt Disney Company

FIRMS: ARCHITECTURAL DRAWINGS

For architectural drawings, record the name of the designer or draftsman, along with the name of the architectural firm.

> *Example*
>
> > **Creator display**: draftsman: Steven Forman (American, born 1954), for Richard Meier and Partners (American, founded 1970s)
> > **Controlled fields**:
> > > **Role**: draftsman
> > > *[link to Personal and Corporate Name Authority]*:
> > > Forman, Steven
> > >
> > > **Role**: architectural firm
> > > *[link to Personal and Corporate Name Authority]*:
> > > Richard Meier & Partners

FIRMS: BUILT WORKS

For structures, record the name of the main architect or the firm, or both.

Examples

> **Creator display**: John Russell Pope (American, 1874-1937)
> **Controlled fields**:
> > **Role**: architect
> > *[link to Personal and Corporate Name Authority]*:
> > Pope, John Russell

> **Creator display**: I. M. Pei and Partners (American, established 1955)
> **Controlled fields**:
> > **Role**: architectural firm
> > *[link to Personal and Corporate Name Authority]*:
> > I. M. Pei & Partners

CULTURAL GROUPS

If the artist is unknown and it is appropriate for the given discipline (for example, ancient art or African art), assign creation responsibility to a cultural group. See also Unknown Creators below and Part 3: Personal and Corporate Name Authority. Some institutions may choose to link to the Concept Authority, where culture terms are recorded.

Example

> **Creator display**: Mandinka People (West Africa, 19th century)
> **Controlled fields**:
> > **Role**: sculptor
> > *[link to Personal and Corporate Name Authority]*:
> > Mandinka People

Non-Artists

If appropriate, record individuals and corporate bodies even if they are not artists per se. These include all persons or groups of persons who contributed to the production, manufacture, or alteration of the work. For example, the patron of ancient architecture should often be included because it is likely that he contributed directly or indirectly to the design of a work he commissioned.[2] Important publishers of European prints, calligraphers of Chinese paintings, and others directly involved in the work should be included.

Examples

[for a patron]

> **Creator display**: unknown Roman architect, for the Emperor Hadrian (Roman, 76-138 CE, ruled 117-138)
> **Controlled fields**:
> > **Role**: architect
> > *[link to Personal and Corporate Name Authority]*:
> > unknown Roman

Role: patron
[link to Personal and Corporate Name Authority]:
Hadrian

[for inscribers]

Creator display: primary painter and calligrapher was Dai Xi (Chinese scholar, painter, 1801-1860), with additional inscriptions and colophons added by Luchuang Juren and Wen Jie
Controlled fields:
Roles: painter • calligrapher
[link to Personal and Corporate Name Authority]:
Dai Xi

Role*:* inscriber
[link to Personal and Corporate Name Authority]:
Luchuang Juren

Role*:* inscriber
[link to Personal and Corporate Name Authority]:
Wen Jie

[for a publisher]

Creator display: engraved by unknown French artist, published by Jean-Charles Pellerin (French, 1756-1836)
Controlled fields:
Role: engraver
[link to Personal and Corporate Name Authority]:
unknown French

Role*:* publisher
[link to Personal and Corporate Name Authority]:
Pellerin, Jean-Charles

[for a distributor of daguerreotypes]

Creator display: distributed by Atelier Héliographique (French, flourished 1840s)
Controlled fields:
Role: distributor
[link to Personal and Corporate Name Authority] :
Atelier Héliographique

[for an author and copyist]

Creator display: illuminations by unknown Syrian; author: Abu'l Izz Isma'il al-Jazari (Persian, 12th century); copyist: Farkh ibn 'Abd al-Latif (Persian, 14th century)
Controlled fields:
Role: illuminator
[link to Personal and Corporate Name Authority]:
unknown Syrian

Role: author
[link to Personal and Corporate Name Authority]:
Abu'l Izz Isma'il al-Jazari

Role: copyist
[link to Personal and Corporate Name Authority]:
Farkh ibn 'Abd al-Latif

For Groups of Works

For groups of works, include all the creators, if possible. If there are a large number, list the most important or most prominent in the Creator display; in the controlled indexing fields, however, index all the creators to enhance end-user access.

Examples

[for a box of photographs]

Creator display: photographers: Josiah Johnson Hawes (American, 1808-1901), Albert Sands Southworth (American, 1811-1894), and Joseph Pennell (American, 1866-1922)
Controlled fields:
Role: photographer
[link to Personal and Corporate Name Authority]:
Hawes, Josiah Johnson

Role: photographer
[link to Personal and Corporate Name Authority]:
Southworth, Albert Sands

Role: photographer
[link to Personal and Corporate Name Authority]:
Pennell, Joseph

[for a folder of drawings]

Creator display: architect: Frank Lloyd Wright (American, 1867-1959); draftsmen: Frank Lloyd Wright, John Howe (American, active 1940-1958)
Controlled fields:
Roles: architect • draftsman
[link to Personal and Corporate Name Authority]:
Wright, Frank Lloyd

Role: draftsman
[link to Personal and Corporate Name Authority]:
Howe, John

Uncertain Attributions

Indicate when the identity of the creator is uncertain or his or her role needs to be qualified. See also Attribution Qualifier below.

Examples

Creator display: attributed to Théophile-Alexandre Steinlen (Swiss, 1859-1923)
Controlled fields:
Role: painter
Qualifier: attributed to
[link to Personal and Corporate Name Authority]:
Steinlen, Théophile-Alexandre

Creator display: probably engraved by Pierre Le Pautre (French, 1660-1744)
Controlled fields:
>   **Role**: engraver
>   **Qualifier**: probably by
>   *[link to Personal and Corporate Name Authority]*:
>   Le Pautre, Pierre

Creator display: painted by Andrea di Bartolo (Sienese, active by 1389, died 1428); alternatively attributed to Bartolo di Fredi (Sienese, active by 1353, died 1410)
Controlled fields:
>   **Role**: painter
>   *[link to Personal and Corporate Name Authority]*:
>   Andrea di Bartolo
>
>   **Role**: painter
>   **Qualifier**: alternatively attributed to
>   *[link to Personal and Corporate Name Authority]*:
>   Bartolo di Fredi

Former Attributions

Include former attributions.

>   *Example*

>   **Creator display**: painting attributed to Qu Ding (Chinese, active ca. 1023-ca. 1056), formerly attributed to Yan Wengui (Chinese, active ca. 970-1030)
>   **Controlled fields**:
>>   **Role**: painter
>>   **Qualifier**: attributed to
>>   *[link to Personal and Corporate Name Authority]*:
>>   Qu Ding
>>
>>   **Role**: painter
>>   **Qualifier**: formerly attributed to
>>   *[link to Personal and Corporate Name Authority]*:
>>   Yan Wengui

Anonymous Creators

In the context of this manual, an *anonymous creator* is defined as one whose hand is identified and whose oeuvre is established, but whose name is not known (for example, *Master of the Dido Panels*). This type of creator is distinguished from *unknown creators*, discussed below.

For anonymous creators, record an appellation and biography that have been established by scholarly research. For further discussion, see Part 3: Personal and Corporate Name Authority.

Examples

> **Creator display**: painted by Master of the Dido Panels (Italian, active in 1440s)
> **Controlled fields**:
> > **Role**: painter
> > *[link to Personal and Corporate Name Authority]*:
> > Master of the Dido Panels

> **Creator display**: Achilles Painter (Greek, active ca. 450-ca. 420 BCE)
> **Controlled fields**:
> > **Role**: vase painter
> > *[link to Personal and Corporate Name Authority]*:
> > Achilles Painter

> **Creator display**: Borden Limner (American, active 1820s-1830s)
> **Controlled fields**:
> > **Role**: painter
> > *[link to Personal and Corporate Name Authority]*:
> > Borden Limner

Unknown Creators

If the identity of a hand and its oeuvre are not established, devise a generic identification to refer to the unknown creator. Unknown creators are common, especially in certain disciplines, including ancient art, Asian art, African art, aboriginal art, folk art, decorative arts, and Western art dating from the 16th century and earlier. Institutional practice varies in the way unknown creators are recorded and stored in authority files; whichever practice is followed, be consistent.

Although it is not recommended to leave the Creator element blank, because it is critical for retrieval, some institutions do leave the element blank when the creators are unknown, and then construct headings for display at the time of publication using the Culture element, with or without the word *unknown* (for example, *Italian*, or *unknown Italian*, or *unknown*). See the culture element in Chapter 4: Stylistic, Cultural, and Chronological Information and an illustration in Part 3: Personal and Corporate Name Authority.

If the creator is unknown and the identity of his or her hand is not established, devise a generic identification with which all unattributed works by unknown creators with similar attributes may be associated. Do not leave the element blank. Applying any one of the following methods is acceptable, provided it is done consistently and given the information at hand: Include the word *unknown* and the culture or nationality (for example, *unknown Korean*); list the culture alone (for example, *Korean*); list the word *unknown* alone, without reference to culture; include broad dates (for example, *unknown Korean 16th century* or *Korean 16th century*). The generic value for the unknown creator should be authority-controlled for consistency. For further discussion and examples of unknown creators, see Part 3: Personal and Corporate Name Authority. In the examples below, the unknown-plus-culture method, with a link to an Authority Record, is illustrated.

Examples

Creator display: unknown Maya
Controlled fields:
    Role: ceramicist
    [link to Personal and Corporate Name Authority]:
    unknown Maya

Creator display: unknown Indian, probably from Andhra Pradesh
Controlled fields:
    Role: sculptor
    [link to Personal and Corporate Name Authority]:
    unknown Indian

Creator display: Peter King (British, 18th century), with additions attributed to unknown draftsman in the Office of Nicholas Hawksmoor
Controlled fields:
    Role: architect
    [link to Personal and Corporate Name Authority]:
    King, Peter

    Role: draftsman
    Qualifier: attributed to
    Extent: additions
    [link to Personal and Corporate Name Authority]:
    unknown (Office of Nicholas Hawksmoor)

Creator display: Jean Fouquet (French painter, illuminator, ca.1420-ca.1480), formerly attributed to unknown 15th-century Italian
Controlled fields:
    Role: painter
    [link to Personal and Corporate Name Authority]:
    Fouquet, Jean

    Role*: painter
    Qualifier: formerly attributed to
    [link to Personal and Corporate Name Authority]:
    unknown Italian, 15th century

2.2.1.2.5 SUGGESTED TERMINOLOGY FOR QUALIFIER AND EXTENT

Use the following conventions and terminology.

For Creator Extent

Record the part of a work contributed by a particular creator, if necessary for clarity. Some examples of terminology follow:

execution	with additions
design	figures
predella	embroidery
cast	printed

Examples

[for a painting]

Creator display: figures by Peter Paul Rubens (Flemish, 1577-1640), landscape and still-life objects by Jan Brueghel the Elder (Flemish, 1568-1625)
Controlled fields:
Role: painter
Extent: figures
[link to Personal and Corporate Name Authority]:
Rubens, Peter Paul

Role: painter
Extents: landscape • still life
[link to Personal and Corporate Name Authority]:
Brueghel, Jan, the Elder

[for a globe]

Creator display: designed and assembled by Abbé Jean-Antoine Nollet (French, 1700-1770), decoration attributed to Martin brothers (French, active ca. 1725-1780)
Controlled fields:
Roles: designer • assembler
[link to Personal and Corporate Name Authority]:
Nollet, Jean-Antoine, Abbé

Role: painters
Extent: decoration
Qualifier: attributed to
[link to Personal and Corporate Name Authority]:
Martin brothers

For Attribution Qualifier

When the attribution is uncertain, is in dispute, or when there is a former attribution, clarify the attribution with a qualifier using the terminology below. Additional controlled vocabulary for qualifiers may be added as necessary.

ATTRIBUTIONS TO A KNOWN CREATOR

Use one of the following qualifiers to express uncertainty when the attribution of a work to a known creator or architect is in question or to note a former attribution (for example, *attributed to Frans Hals*):

attributed to	formerly attributed to
probably by	possibly by

UNKNOWN CREATORS LINKED TO KNOWN CREATOR

If the identity of a creator is unknown but he or she is known to have worked closely with a known creator, use an attribution qualifier to associate the work with the name of a known creator whose oeuvre is stylistically similar or otherwise related to the work at hand. In such cases, link to the known creator in the

Authority Record, and—in the Work Record—qualify the known creator's name with one of the qualifiers as described below:

Working Directly with Known Creator—Use one of the following qualifiers to indicate authorship by an unknown individual working directly for the named master, probably under his supervision (for example, *studio of Rembrandt, office of Christopher Wren,* or *workshop of Gislebertus*):

studio of	workshop of
office of	atelier of
assistant to	pupil of
associate of	manufactory of

The distinction between studio, workshop, office, and atelier typically depends on the historical period in question and the type of work being produced. Note that the Qualifier field should not be used to record the contribution of a corporate creator whose name happens to include such phrases as *office of* (for example, *Office of Public Buildings and Grounds*).

Not Working Directly with Known Creator—Use one of the following qualifiers to refer to an unknown artist in direct contact with the works of the named creator, and living at the same time or shortly after him or her, though not actually working in his or her studio (for example, *follower of Hokusai*):

follower of	circle of
school of	

Influenced by Known Creator—Use one of the following qualifiers to indicate an influence of (or an outright copy of) the style of the named master, but with the connotation that the named creator had little or nothing to do with the actual work at hand. The unknown creator need not necessarily be a contemporary of the named master (for example, *style of Raphael* or *copyist of Rodin*):

style of	after
copyist of	manner of

Examples

Creator display: possibly by Tuthmosis (Egyptian, 14th century BCE)
Controlled fields:
Role: master sculptor
Qualifier: possibly by
[link to Personal and Corporate Name Authority]:
Tuthmosis

Creator display: school of Rembrandt van Rijn (Dutch, 1606-1669)
Controlled fields:
Role: printmaker
Qualifier: school of
[link to Personal and Corporate Name Authority]:
Rembrandt van Rijn

For detailed definitions of qualifiers, see the *Categories for the Description of Works of Art: Creation-Creator-Qualifier.*

2.2.2 Rules for Creator Role

2.2.2.1 *Brief Rules for Creator Role*

Record a term or terms referring to the role or activity performed by the creator in the conception, design, production, or alteration of the work. Examples of roles include *artist, architect, painter, illustrator, sculptor, designer,* and *engraver.* This element is distinguished from life roles in the Personal and Corporate Name Authority; life roles include all of the different roles that a creator may have performed over a lifetime (see Part 3: Personal and Corporate Name Authority).

Record the most specific role of the creator, if known. The level of specificity may vary depending upon the type of work. For example, the role of the artist who designed and executed a sculpture may be simply *sculptor,* but a print may have been created by multiple individuals whose specific roles are listed, including a designer, engraver, and publisher.

Examples

> **Creator display**: sculpted by Edgar Degas (French, 1834-1917)
> **Controlled fields**:
> > **Role**: sculptor
> > *[link to Personal and Corporate Name Authority]:*
> > Degas, Edgar

> **Creator display**: engraved by Jacques Callot (French, 1592-1635), published by Israël Henriet (French, 1590-1661)
> **Controlled fields**:
> > **Role**: engraver
> > *[link to Personal and Corporate Name Authority]:*
> > Callot, Jacques

> > **Role**: publisher
> > *[link to Personal and Corporate Name Authority]:*
> > Henriet, Israël

If a specific role is not known for a given work, use a more general one. For example, if you do not know that an artist performed the specific role of *menuisier* (a type of joiner), list a more general role, such as *furniture worker.* If even the more general role is not known, use the most general, such as *artist.*

Example

> **Creator display**: François-Toussaint Foliot (French, 1748-ca. 1839)
> **Controlled fields**:
> > **Role**: furniture worker
> > *[link to Personal and Corporate Name Authority]:*
> > Foliot, François-Toussaint

2.2.2.2 *Additional Recommendations for Creator Role*

2.2.2.2.1 IN CREATOR DISPLAY AND INDEXED

In general, record the role in the free-text Creator display, using either an adjective (such as *designed by*) or a noun (such as *designer*). It should also be indexed for retrieval in a controlled field, using a noun (for example, *designer*) drawn from a controlled vocabulary.

> *Example*
>
> [for a painting]
>> **Creator display**: designed by Callot Soeurs (French, active 1895-1937)
>> **Controlled fields**:
>>> **Role**: designer
>>> *[link to Personal and Corporate Name Authority]*:
>>> Callot Soeurs

One exception applies when the role is obvious: If the creator's role is apparent to the end user within the context of the display, the role may be omitted from the Creator display. In all cases, however, the role should be indexed for retrieval.

> *Example*
>
> [for a painting]
>> **Creator display**: Edward Hopper (American, 1882-1967)
>> **Controlled fields**:
>>> **Role**: painter
>>> *[link to Personal and Corporate Name Authority]*:
>>> Hopper, Edward

2.2.2.2.2 CLARIFYING THE ROLE

If the role or attribution requires explanation, describe it in the Creator display and index it as appropriate. Examples include when there is uncertainty regarding the role, when one creator had multiple roles, or when multiple creators had different roles on the same work. See Various Types of Attributions above.

2.3   PRESENTATION OF THE DATA

2.3.1   Display and Indexing

2.3.1.1   *Free-Text vs. Controlled Fields*

For a discussion of when and why separate free-text and controlled fields are recommended, see Part 1: Database Design and Relationships: Display and Indexing.

2.3.1.1.1 HOW CREATOR DISPLAY IS INDEXED

The Creator display field presents a clear and comprehensible summary of the name and biographical information and is used to express nuance and uncertainty regarding the creator and role. Ideally, the Creator and the Creator Role should be recorded in both the free-text Creator display and in controlled fields that will be used for search and retrieval.

2.3.1.1.2 CONCATENATING CREATOR DISPLAY

If including a free-text field is not possible, a rudimentary display for the creator and the creator role can be constructed at the time of publication by concatenating data from controlled fields that are in the Work Record and the Authority Record.

Example

[display with role from the Work Record and Creator Name and Display Biography from the Personal and Corporate Name Authority]

Concatenated display:

designer	Soeurs, Callot	(French, active 1895-1937)
role	*artist preferred name*	*display biography*

Note that such concatenated displays work well for simple attributions, but they do not allow for the expression of nuance and uncertainty regarding more complex attributions. More complex attributions are better explained in a free-text Creator display.

2.3.1.2   *Fields in Authority File and Work Record*

2.3.1.2.1 MINIMUM CONTROLLED FIELDS

For Creator

Given that the creator will have variant names and biographical information critical to retrieval, the most efficient way to control this information is to link the Work Record to the Personal and Corporate Name Authority.

Example

[for a tapestry]

Creator display: Gobelins Tapestry Manufactory (French, established in 1662), based on designs by Albert Eckhout (Dutch, ca. 1610-1665)

Controlled fields:
   Role: manufacturer
   [link to Personal and Corporate Name Authority]:
   Gobelins Tapestry Manufactory

   Role: designer
   [link to Personal and Corporate Name Authority]:
   Eckhout, Albert

In the example above, the artists' preferred natural-order names are combined with biographical information for display to the end user. One way to generate this display is to link or pass the name and other information from the Authority Record, but then to allow the cataloger to edit the display in the Work Record as necessary.

Part TWO: Elements

For Role

For indexing, the Creator Role element should be linked to an authority or a controlled list of roles. It can be inserted into the Creator display manually or by a computer algorithm.

For Extent and Qualifier

Extent and Qualifier should be explained in the Creator display. Some owning institutions will wish to index these elements. If so, the values should be controlled by an authority or controlled list.

> *Example*
>
> **Creator display**: illuminations attributed to Simon Marmion (French, ca. 1425-1489); text inscribed by David Aubert (French, born 1435, active until at least 1479)
> **Controlled fields**:
>   **Role**: painter
>   **Extent**: illuminations
>   **Qualifier**: attributed to
>   *[link to Personal and Corporate Name Authority]*:
>   Marmion, Simon
>
>   **Role**: *scribe*
>   **Extent**: text
>   *[link to Personal and Corporate Name Authority]*:
>   Aubert, David

2.3.1.2.2 ELEMENTS TO INCLUDE IN AN AUTHORITY

The creator's preferred name, nationality, and life dates should be recorded in the Creator display in the Work Record, but ideally, these names and biographical information should be indexed for retrieval in a Personal and Corporate Name Authority record that is linked to the Work Record. In addition to the preferred name, life dates, and nationality, other fields in the authority file should include variant names, life roles, relationships to other artists, and further biographical information. See Part 3: Personal and Corporate Name Authority for further discussion.

2.3.2 Examples

Examples of Work Records are included below. For additional examples, see the end of Part 1, the end of each chapter, and the CCO Web site. In the examples, *controlled* refers to values controlled by an authority file, controlled list, or other rules (for example, with dates). *Link* refers to a relationship between a Work Record and an Authority Record or between two Work Records. All links are controlled fields. In the examples that follow, Related Work Records are abbreviated for the sake of brevity. All Work Records should be as complete as possible. See the various chapters for discussions of individual metadata elements, whether they should be controlled, and the respective advantages of an authority file or a controlled list. In all examples in this manual, both within and at the end of each chapter, data values for repeatable fields are separated by bullet characters.

Figure 14
Work Record Linked to a Personal and Corporate Name Authority Record: Oil Painting[3]

Required and recommended elements are marked with an asterisk.

Work Record

- **Class** *[controlled]*: paintings • European art
- ***Work Type** *[link]*: painting
- ***Title**: Landscape with Classical Ruins and Figures | **Title Type**: preferred
- ***Creator display**: Marco Ricci (Italian, 1676-1730), figures by Sebastiano Ricci (Italian, 1659-1734)
    - ***Role** *[link]*: painter | **Extent** *[controlled]*: landscape architecture | *[link]*: Ricci, Marco
    - ***Role** *[link]*: painter | **Extent** *[controlled]*: figures | *[link]*: Ricci, Sebastiano
- ***Creation Date**: ca. 1725/1730
    - *[controlled]*: **Earliest**: 1720; **Latest**: 1735
- ***Subject** *[links to authorities]*: landscape ruins • human figures • Dionysos (Greek deity) • Classical architecture
- **Culture** *[link]*: Italian
- ***Current Location** *[link]*: J. Paul Getty Museum (Los Angeles, California, United States) | **ID**:70.PA.33
- ***Measurements**: 123 x 161 cm (48 3/8 x 63 3/8 inches)
    - *[controlled]*: **Value**: 123; **Unit**: cm; **Type**: height | **Value**: 161; **Unit**: cm; **Type**: width
- ***Materials and Techniques**: oil on canvas
    - **Material** *[link]*: oil paint • canvas
- **Description**: In this fantastic vista, Marco Ricci combined ancient Roman monuments, such as an obelisk, sections of temples, and statues, to create a scene both picturesque and evocative of the power of the ancient world.
- **Description Source** *[link]*: J. Paul Getty Museum online. http:// www.getty.edu (accessed February 10, 2005).

Personal and Corporate Name Authority Record

- ***Names**:
    - Ricci, Marco (preferred, inverted)
    - Marco Ricci (preferred, natural order)
    - Richi, Marco
    - Ricci, Marchetto
    - Rizzi, Marco
    - Rizi, Marco
- ***Display Biography**: Italian painter, 1676-1730
- ***Nationalities** *[controlled]*: Italian • Venetian
- ***Birth Date** *[controlled]*: 1676; **Death Date**: 1730
- ***Life Roles** *[controlled]*: painter • draftsman
- **Place of Birth** *[link]*: Belluno (Veneto, Italy)
- **Place of Death** *[link]*: Venice (Veneto, Italy)
- **Places of Activity** *[link]*: Veneto (Italy), England
- **Related People**:
    - **Relationship Type** *[controlled]*: brother of *[link to related person]*: Sebastiano Ricci (Italian, 1659-1734)
- ***Sources** *[links]*:
    - *Union List of Artist Names* (1988-).
    - Thieme-Becker, *Allgemeines Lexikon der Künstler* (1980-1986).
    - Bolaffi, *Dizionario dei pittori italiani* (1972-1976).

CREDIT: The J. Paul Getty Museum (Los Angeles, California). Marco Ricci (Italian, 1676-1730) and Sebastiano Ricci (Italian, 1659-1734); Landscape with Classical Ruins and Figures, ca. 1725-1730; oil on canvas, 123 x 161 cm; 70.PA.33. © The J. Paul Getty Trust.

Figure 15

Work Record Linked to a Personal and Corporate Name Authority Record: Islamic Manuscript[4]

Required and recommended elements are marked with an asterisk.

Work Record

- ■ **Class** *[controlled]*: manuscripts • Islamic art
- ■ ***Work Type** *[link]*: illumination
- ■ ***Title**: Two Lovers | **Title Type**: preferred
- ■ ***Creator display**: Riza (Persian, ca. 1565-1635)
    ***Role** *[link]*: illuminator | *[link]*: Riza
- ■ ***Creation Date**: 1039 anno Hegirae (1629-1630 CE)
    [controlled]: **Earliest**: 1629; **Latest**: 1630
- ■ ***Subject** *[links to authorities]*: human figures • lovers • embracing
- ■ ***Current Location** *[link]*: Metropolitan Museum of Art (New York, New York, United States) | **ID**: 50.164
- ■ ***Measurements**: 18.1 x 11.9 cm (7 1/8 x 4 11/16 inches)
    [controlled]: **Value**: 18.1; **Unit**: cm; **Type**: height | **Value**: 11.9; **Unit**: cm; **Type**: width
- ■ ***Material and Technique**: tempera and gold on paper
    Material *[link]*: tempera • paper • gold
- ■ **Inscriptions**: signed: Riza-yi 'Abbasi; dated: A.H. 1039
- ■ **Description**: The artist was working at the court of Shah 'Abbas the Great (reigned 1588-1629); this work shows his renowned inventive palette and calligraphic line. The lovers are drawn as inextricably bound together, merged volumes confined within one outline.
- ■ **Description Source** *[link]*: Metropolitan Museum of Art online. http://www.metmuseum.org (accessed February 10, 2005).

Personal and Corporate Name Authority Record

- ■ ***Names**:
    Riza (preferred)
    Reza
    Riza 'Abbasi
    Riza-yi 'Abbasi
    Aqa Riza Kashani
- ■ ***Display Biography**: Persian ca. 1565-1635
- ■ ***Nationalities** *[controlled]*: Persian
- ■ ***Birth Date** *[controlled]*: 1560; **Death Date**: 1635
- ■ ***Life Roles** *[controlled]*: painter • court artist
- ■ **Place of Birth** *[link]*: Kashan (Esfahan Province, Iran)
- ■ **Place of Death** *[link]*: Esfahan (Esfahan Province, Iran)
- ■ **Place of Activity** *[link]*: Mashhad (Khorasan, Iran)
- ■ **Related People**:
    Relationship Type *[controlled]*: parent of
    [link to related person]: Muhammad Shafi' (Persian painter, active ca. 1628-1674)
- ■ **Note**: Riza, son of 'Ali Asghar, was a leading artist under the Safavid shah Abbas I (reigned 1588-1629). He is noted primarily for portraits and genre scenes. The various names for this artist and the attributions of paintings in his oeuvre are somewhat uncertain, since his signatures and contemporary documentary references to him are ambiguous.
- ■ ***Source** *[link]*: *Union List of Artist Names* (1988-).

CREDIT: *Two Lovers*, 1629-1630/ A.H. 1039; Safavid period (1501-1722); Riza 'Abbasi; Iran; Tempera and gold on paper; H. 7 1/8 in. x W. 4 11/16 in. (18.1 x 11.9 cm); The Metropolitan Museum of Art, Purchase, Francis M. Weld Gift, 1950 (50.164); Photograph © 1978 The Metropolitan Museum of Art.

Figure 16
Work Record Linked to Records for a Person and a Corporate Body: Modern Architecture
Required and recommended elements are marked with an asterisk.

Work Record

■ **Class** *[controlled]*: architecture • Modern art
■ ***Work Type** *[link]*: church
■ ***Title**: North Christian Church | **Title Type**: preferred
■ ***Creator display**: designed by Eero Saarinen (American, 1910-1961); posthumously, construction was supervised by firm of Eero Saarinen & Associates (American architectural firm, 1950-1961)
　***Role** *[link]*: architect | *[link]*: Saarinen, Eero
　***Role** *[link]*: architectural firm | *[link]*: Eero Saarinen & Associates
　***Role** *[link]*: general contractor | *[link]*: Repp and Mundt, Inc.
■ ***Creation Date**: designed 1961, completed 1964 *[controlled]*: **Earliest**: 1961; **Latest**: 1964
■ ***Subject** *[links to authorities]*: architecture • religion and mythology • church • Disciples of Christ (Protestant Christianity) • worship
■ ***Current Location** *[link]*: Columbus (Indiana, United States)
■ ***Measurements**: spire rises 58.5 m (192 feet) *[controlled]*: **Value**: 58.5; **Unit**: m; **Type**: height
■ ***Materials and Techniques**: hexagonal plan, concrete base, leaded copper spire, slate roof; welded steel buttresses support the roof and spire at the 6 axial corners
　Material *[link]*: steel • concrete • slate | **Technique** *[link]*: hexagonal plan • buttresses
■ **Description**: The architect was working on this building when he died unexpectedly. Building has a hexagonal plan elongated along the east-west axis; it is a one-story building with the lower level nested in a moat within an earthen berm. The massive roof and spire rest over a concrete base. The sanctuary is located at center of interior space, direct light from oculus high in the ceiling and ring of clerestory windows. Six rolled steel arch legs are supported on steel arch bases set on the concrete foundation. The roof slopes on all sides; the central spire is terminated with a cross.
■ **Sources** *[link to Source Records]*:
　Columbus Indiana: A Look At Architecture (1980); **Page**: 18.
　"Saarinen's Church." *Architectural Record*. vol. 136. September 1964; **Page**: 185-190.

Personal and Corporate Name Authority Record

■ ***Names**:
　Saarinen, Eero (preferred, inverted)
　Eero Saarinen (preferred, natural order)
■ *Display Biography: American architect, designer, 1910-1961
■ ***Nationalities** *[controlled]*: American • Finnish
■ ***Birth Date** *[controlled]*: 1910; **Death Date**: 1961
■ ***Life Roles** *[controlled]*: architect • furniture designer
　Related People and Corporate Bodies:
　Relationship Type *[controlled]*: son of
　[link to related person]: Eliel Saarinen (Finnish architect, 1873-1950, active in the United States)
　Relationship Type *[controlled]*: founder *[link to Related Corporate Body]*: Eero Saarinen & Associates (American architectural firm, 1950-1961)
■ ***Source** *[link to Source Record]*: Union List of Artist Names (1988-).

Personal and Corporate Name Authority Record

■ ***Names**:
　Saarinen & Associates, Eero (preferred, inverted)
　Eero Saarinen & Associates (preferred, natural order)
■ ***Display Biography**: American architectural firm, 1950-1961
■ ***Nationalities** *[controlled]*: American
■ ***Birth Date** *[controlled]*: 1950; **Death Date**: 1961
■ ***Life Roles** *[controlled]*: architectural firm
■ **Place/Locations** *[links]*: Birmingham (Michigan, United States) • Camden (Connecticut, United States)
■ **Related People**:
　Relationship Type *[controlled]*: founder
　[link to related person]: Eero Saarinen (American architect, 1910-1961)
■ ***Source** *[link to Source Record]*: Union List of Artist Names (1988-).

Notes

1. *Dizionario enciclopedico Bolaffi dei pittori e degli incisori italiani dall'XI al XX secolo.* Turin: Giulio Bolaffi, 1972-1976. Snodgrass, Jeanne O. *American Indian painters; a biographical directory.* New York: Museum of the American Indian, Heye Foundation, 1968.

2. For additional fields to record information about commissions and commissioners, see *Categories for the Description of Works of Art: Creation-Commission.*

3. This example is intended to illustrate metadata elements discussed in this manual. The field names and data values in the example do not necessarily represent the fields and values in the record for this object in the Getty Museum's collection management system.

4. This example is intended to illustrate metadata elements discussed in this manual. The field names and data values in the example do not necessarily represent the fields and values in the record for this object in the Metropolitan Museum's collection management system.

Chapter *3*

Physical Characteristics

Measurements / Materials and Techniques / State and Edition / Additional Physical Characteristics

3.1   ABOUT PHYSICAL CHARACTERISTICS

3.1.1   Discussion

Physical characteristics describe a work's appearance and the characteristics of its physical form. Metadata elements addressed here include Measurements, Materials and Techniques, and State and Edition. Additional elements are discussed as Additional Physical Characteristics and may be required by museums and collecting institutions, but typically will not be needed by visual resources collections. This chapter does not deal with the physical characteristics of the surrogate visual image. Visual resources collections, however, will typically require fields to document such information for surrogates as administrative metadata rather than descriptive metadata.

Measurements

The Measurements element contains information about the dimensions, size, or scale of the work. Measurements may be recorded according to different criteria, depending upon the type of work being measured. A two-dimensional painting will be measured differently than a three-dimensional statue. Measurements may vary depending on whether the work is framed, mounted, or installed. Measurements for architecture, clothing, and time-based media such as film and video each require different criteria. The recommendations given here are for recording a work's basic measurements (for example, the height and width of a canvas). Published sources listed in the bibliography, such as *Categories for the Description of Works of Art*, *Documenting Your Collections*, and *Info-Muse Network Documentation Guide*, provide more detailed information on how to document and measure original works. Whichever sources you use, it is important to maintain clear and consistent measuring and recording techniques within your institution.

Materials and Techniques

The Materials and Techniques element includes the substances or materials used in the creation of a work, as well as any production or manufacturing techniques, processes, or methods incorporated in its fabrication. This information includes a description of the technique, media, and support used in the creation of the work. It clarifies the relationship between the materials of which the work is made and the techniques used to apply them. Materials are the substances of which the work is composed. In many forms of art, a distinction is made between materials used as the media (such as *oil paint* or *chalk*) and materials used as the support (such as *canvas* or *paper*). Technique encompasses the instruments, processes, and methods used in the application of materials, such as *painting*, *etching*, *pen*, *burin*. In the example below, *pen* is the instrument, *ink and black chalk* are the media, and *paper* is the support.

> *Example*
>
> pen and ink and black chalk on paper

Materials and techniques may be recorded together or in separate fields, depending upon the needs of the cataloging institution. Furthermore, materials may be subdivided into media and support, if required by the institution. However, combining them all for display and access is recommended.

State and Edition

The State and Edition elements refer primarily to works produced in multiples. State describes the relationship of a work to other stages of the same work (for example, the third state of five total states, *3rd of 5 states*). State is most often used with prints, which may be pulled from a plate that has been altered repeatedly. State may sometimes refer to the creation of works other than prints, including any sequence of related stages that together build toward the creation of a work of art or architecture. Each variation in the plate or stage of production is identified as a particular state. The Edition element may identify a specific print or other work in the context of a limited number of identical or very similar works made or issued at the same time and from the same matrix. For prints, the number of the impression at hand is often juxtaposed with the number of prints in a run (for example, *2/32*). In addition to the numbered edition, a few other impressions may be printed (for example, artist's proofs, printer's proofs, hors de commerce). Edition may also be used in another sense, to describe an issuance of a work in relation to previous and subsequent editions; this use of edition often refers to books (*2nd edition*, for example). A new edition of a book usually involves substantive revisions to the intellectual content of the work, including alterations of the text or illustrations.

Additional Physical Characteristics

Museums and other collecting institutions may require additional elements, supplementing those listed in other sections of this chapter. These elements could include Inscriptions and Facture, among others.

Specificity

To guarantee accuracy, information regarding physical characteristics ideally should be determined, when possible, through direct physical examination, laboratory analysis, and research. Catalogers in museums and other collecting institutions would generally use documentation based on such examinations. Visual resources collections will necessarily obtain the information second- or third-hand from various sources rather than by direct physical examination.

Specificity refers to the degree of precision in the terminology used, ranging from broad, general terms to narrow, specific terms. For example, for the Materials and Techniques elements, should the cataloger use the more general term *wood*, or the specific term *poplar*? The cataloging institution should establish rules to ensure consistent levels of specificity across all records and guidelines for handling instances when information about a work is limited or unavailable. Criteria for establishing rules for specificity should include the size, focus, and requirements of the collection, and the expertise of the catalogers and the end users. The accuracy of the measurements of works may vary depending upon the needs of the institution. Records for visual resources collections generally do not require the level of specificity required by museums.

Exhaustivity

The level of completeness or exhaustivity in assigning terminology for physical attributes will depend on the requirements of the cataloging institution. How many aspects of the work will be cataloged? For example, for a print, will you record the sizes of the plate mark and the secondary support in addition to the size of the primary support? How many terms will be assigned to each work? For example, for a work constructed by various processes, will you list every process, only the primary process, or a phrase such as *various processes*? Criteria for making such decisions will depend on time limitations, available human resources, and the focus of the collection. Works may be cataloged in groups or only minimally in order to gain initial control of a collection; more thorough application of physical attributes terminology can be done later, in phases.

Approximations and Uncertainty

If analysis or documentation is inconclusive or impossible, or there is uncertainty about the physical attributes of a work, this should be indicated in a free-text display field (for example, *approximately 100 x 150 cm*, or *oil or oil and tempera on panel*). Such uncertainty may require that the multiple possibilities be indexed in the controlled fields. For example, if it is uncertain which of two materials was used, they should both be indexed in the controlled fields for retrieval.

Organization of Data

It is strongly advised to record measurements and materials and techniques if that information is available. Museums and other owning institutions generally require them. Edition information is required for books. State and edition information is recommended for prints, if known. For other types of works, state and edition information is generally not required, but should be recorded when the information is available.

Certain information about physical characteristics is best recorded in a free-text field for display in combination with controlled fields for access. Controlled fields should be repeatable. It is recommended to use controlled vocabularies, authorities, and consistent formatting of certain information to ensure efficient end-user retrieval. See the discussion in Part 1: Database Design and Relationships: Display and Indexing.

Recommended Elements

A list of the elements discussed in this chapter appears below. Required elements are noted. (Display may be a free-text field or concatenated from controlled fields.)

Measurements display (required)
- Value
- Unit
- Type
- Extent
- Qualifier
- Shape
- Format
- Scale

Material and Techniques display (required)
- Material
- Material Type
- Technique
- Color
- Mark
- Extent
- Qualifier

Edition display
- Impression Number
- Edition Size
- Edition Number

State display
- State Identification
- Known States
- Source of State

Inscriptions
- Inscription Type
- Inscription Location
- Inscription Author

Facture

Physical Description

Condition and Examination History

Conservation and Treatment History

About the Examples

The examples throughout this chapter are for illustration only. Local practice may vary. The examples tend to show the fullest possible use of display and indexing fields, which may not be necessary for visual resources collections and some other institutions.

3.1.2   Terminology

3.1.2.1   *Sources for Terminology*

3.1.2.1.1   MEASUREMENTS

Units of measurements should be controlled by using an authority file or controlled lists. Numeric values should be controlled. Published sources include the following:

National Institute of Standards and Technology General Table of Units and Measures. http://ts.nist.gov/ts/htdocs/230/235/appxc/appxc.htm

3.1.2.1.2 MATERIALS AND TECHNIQUES

Terms for materials and techniques should be controlled by using an authority file or controlled lists. Published sources include the following:

Getty Vocabulary Program. *Art & Architecture Thesaurus* (AAT). Los Angeles: J. Paul Getty Trust, 1988-. http://www.getty.edu/research/conducting_research/vocabularies/aat/.

Genre Terms: A Thesaurus for Use in Rare Book and Special Collections Cataloging. 2nd ed. Prepared by the Bibliographic Standards Committee of the Rare Books and Manuscripts Section (ACRL/ALA). Chicago: Association of College and Research Libraries, 1991.

Library of Congress. Prints and Photographs Division. *Thesaurus for Graphic Materials.* Washington, DC: Library of Congress, Cataloging Distribution Service, 1995. http://lcweb.loc.gov/rr/print/tgm2/.

3.1.2.1.3 STATE AND EDITION

Terminology should be controlled by using an authority file or controlled lists. Published sources include the following:

Getty Vocabulary Program. *Art & Architecture Thesaurus* (AAT). Los Angeles: J. Paul Getty Trust, 1988-. http://www.getty.edu/research/conducting_research/vocabularies/aat/. (Especially the Visual Works hierarchy).

Library of Congress. Prints and Photographs Division. *Thesaurus for Graphic Materials.* Washington, DC: Library of Congress, Cataloging Distribution Service, 1995. http://lcweb.loc.gov/rr/print/tgm2/.

3.1.2.2 *Choice of Terminology*

3.1.2.2.1 CONSISTENCY

Using consistent terminology is especially important for controlled fields that are intended to provide access. Consistency is less important, but still desirable, in a free-text note than in a controlled field. Although uncontrolled terminology should be accommodated, using terminology that is consistent with the terms in controlled fields is nonetheless recommended for the sake of clarity. Consistent style, grammar, and syntax are recommended.

3.1.2.2.2 USE OF AN AUTHORITY RECORD

If possible, terms should be stored in an Authority Record or controlled list, which is linked to the Work Record. To populate the authority file or list, use standard sources, combined with terminology developed for local usage as necessary.

3.2 CATALOGING RULES

3.2.1 Rules for Measurements

3.2.1.1 *Brief Rules for Measurements*

Recording measurements is required. Specify the dimensions or other measurements for the work, being sure to include the numerical value, the unit of measurement, and the type of measurement for each dimension.

Unit of Measurement

Display dimensions in both metric units and U.S. customary units (that is, feet and inches, also known as Imperial units), if possible. If using only one type of unit of measurement, use metric units because they are more universally understood. If your audience is solely American, use feet and inches.

> *Example*
>
> [for a ceramic tile]
>> **Measurements display**: 13.3 x 20.6 cm (5 1/4 x 8 1/8 inches)
>> **Controlled fields**:
>>> **Value**: 13.3; **Unit**: cm; **Type**: height
>>> **Value**: 20.6; **Unit**: cm; **Type**: width

Capitalization and Abbreviations

Write dimension type, extent, and unit in lowercase. Exceptions include proper names and certain types of symbols or abbreviations, such as those for some electronic file sizes (for example, *JPEG*). Avoid abbreviating the unit of measurement for U.S. customary units. Express metric units by the appropriate symbol (for example, cm; see Suggested Terminology below); do not use punctuation following the symbol. Put a space between the numeric value and the unit.

> *Example*
>
> [for a photograph]
>> **Measurements display**: 23.5 x 16 cm (9 1/4 x 6 3/8 inches)
>> **Controlled fields**:
>>> **Value**: 23.5; **Unit**: cm; **Type**: height
>>> **Value**: 16; **Unit**: cm; **Type**: width

In display, it is not necessary to repeat the unit for each value in the dimension, except when necessary to avoid confusion (as with feet and inches in the example below).

> *Example*
>
> [for an outdoor sculpture]
>> **Measurements display**: 436.9 x 718 x 777 cm (14 feet 4 inches x 23 feet 6 1/2 inches x 25 feet 6 inches)
>> **Controlled fields**:
>>> **Value**: 436.9; **Unit**: cm; **Type**: height
>>> **Value**: 718; **Unit**: cm; **Type**: width
>>> **Value**: 777; **Unit**: cm; **Type**: depth

3.2.1.2 *Additional Recommendations for Measurements*

3.2.1.2.1 SYNTAX

For display, express dimensions as height by width by depth (where pertinent); the orientation of the work (horizontal, vertical, and so on) is thus implied in the description of the dimensions. Place the second set of measurements (for example, U.S. customary units) in parentheses for clarity.

> *Example*
>
> [for a freestanding arch]
>> **Measurements display**: 198 x 233 x 82 cm (78 x 91 3/4 x 32 1/4 inches)
>> **Controlled fields**:
>>> **Value**: 198; **Unit**: cm; **Type**: height
>>> **Value**: 233; **Unit**: cm; **Type**: width
>>> **Value**: 82; **Unit**: cm; **Type**: depth

3.2.1.2.2 SUGGESTED TERMINOLOGY

Use the following conventions and terminology.

Numerical Value

For metric measurements, use whole numbers or decimal fractions (for example, *60, 238, 91.6, 17.25*). Inches may be expressed as whole numbers or fractions (for example, *17 1/4*). If feet are recorded, record feet and inches, rather than decimal fractions of feet.

Unit of Measurement

Examples of units of measurement include *millimeters, centimeters, meters, inches, feet, liters, kilograms, ounces, pounds, cubic centimeters, square feet, minutes, carats,* and *pixels.*

Abbreviate metric units according to ISO 31-0:1992, *Quantities and units* or the U.S. Metric Association's recommendations for metric symbols:

meter = m	kilogram = kg
centimeter = cm	kilobyte = kb
millimeter = mm	megabyte = Mb
gram = g	gigabyte = Gb

Type of Measurement

Examples of types of measurement include *height, width, depth, length, circumference, diameter, volume, weight, area,* and *running time.*

Additional Elements

Certain additional characteristics of measurements may be included as necessary.

EXTENT

Extent refers to the part of the work being measured. Examples of terminology include *overall, diameter, platemark, sheet, secondary support, mat, mount, frame, pattern repeat, lid, base, footprint, tessera, laid lines,* and *with base.*

MEASUREMENTS QUALIFIER

Qualifier refers to a word or phrase that elaborates on the nature of the dimensions of the work. Examples of terminology include *approximate, sight, maximum, assembled, before restoration, largest, variable, at corners, rounded,* and *framed.*

3.2.1.2.3 VARIOUS TYPES OF WORKS

Use descriptions of measurements appropriate to the particular work. Types of descriptions for measurements include *height* and *width, depth, diameter* and *circumference, shape, weight, volume* and *area, size, format, time, scale,* and *structural dimensions.*

Height and Width

Express measurements for a primarily two-dimensional work, such as a drawing or painting, as height by width.

> *Example*
>
> [for a panel painting]
>
> **Measurements display**: 46.1 x 60.9 cm (18 1/8 x 24 inches)
> **Controlled fields**:
>> **Value**: 46.1; **Unit**: cm; **Type**: height
>> **Value**: 60.9; **Unit**: cm; **Type**: width

Depth

Express measurements for a three-dimensional work, such as a sculpture or piece of furniture, as height by width by depth.

> *Example*
>
> [for a stained-glass panel]
>
> **Measurements display**: 33.5 x 25.4 x 7.78 cm (13 3/16 x 10 x 3 1/16 inches)
> **Controlled fields**:
>> **Value**: 33.5; **Unit**: cm; **Type**: height
>> **Value**: 25.4; **Unit**: cm; **Type**: width
>> **Value**: 7.78; **Unit**: cm; **Type**: depth

For basically rectangular works, generally measure the left side and bottom for height and width; generally measure depth at the lower left. For irregularly shaped works, measure the greatest dimensions.

Diameter and Circumference

Where appropriate, as for a round panel painting or a globe, record diameter, circumference, or another pertinent measurement. For a vessel or other pottery, record the circumference or diameter of the base or the mouth, if known.

Examples

[for a round painting]

Measurements display: 89 cm (35 inches) (diameter)
Controlled fields:
Value: 89; **Unit**: cm; **Type**: diameter

[for a ceramic vase]

Measurements display: 127 cm (50 inches) (circumference at the base); 139 cm (54 3/4 inches) (greatest circumference of the body)
Controlled fields:
Extent: base
Value: 127; **Unit**: cm; **Type**: circumference

Extent: body
Qualifier: largest dimensions
Value: 139; **Unit**: cm; **Type**: circumference

Shape

If it is an unusual or distinguishing characteristic, record an indication of the outline, form, or characteristic configuration of a work or part of a work, including its contours (for example, given that most paintings on canvas are rectangular, note when a painting on canvas is oval). Examples of terminology include *oval*, *cube*, *sphere*, rectangle, *circle*, and *irregular*.

Examples

[for an oval drawing]

Measurements display: 29.8 x 20.3 cm (11 3/4 x 8 inches) (oval)
Controlled fields:
Shape: oval
Value: 29.8; **Unit**: cm; **Type**: height
Value: 20.3; **Unit**: cm; **Type**: width

[for a globe]

Measurements display: 161.5 cm (63 5/8 inches) (circumference, sphere)
Controlled fields:
Shape: sphere
Value: 161.5; **Unit**: cm; **Type**: circumference

[for a wooden box]

Measurements display: 48.2 x 48.2 x 48.2 cm (16.5 x 16.5 x 16.5 inches) (cube)
Controlled fields:
Shape: cube
Value: 48.2; **Unit**: cm; **Type**: height
Value: 48.2; **Unit**: cm; **Type**: width
Value: 48.2; **Unit**: cm; **Type**: depth

Measurements for works of irregular shape should be expressed by their greatest height, width and depth (where appropriate).

Example

Measurements display: 19.1 x 23.5 x 13.9 cm (7 1/2 x 9 1/4 x 5 1/2 inches) (irregular, largest dimensions)
Controlled fields:
Shape: irregular
Qualifier: largest dimensions
Value: 19.1; **Unit**: cm; **Type**: height
Value: 23.5; **Unit**: cm; **Type**: width
Value: 13.9; **Unit**: cm; **Type**: depth

Weight

Include the weight of the work when it is significant (for example, for a coin or a megalithic stone).

Example

[for a carved gem]

Measurements display: 31 mm (1 1/8 inch) (diameter), 7.32 g (.2354 troy ounce)
Controlled fields:
Value: 31; **Unit**: mm; **Type**: diameter
Value: 7.32; **Unit**: gram; **Type**: weight

Volume and Area

Include volume or area where appropriate (for example, for a pool or garden).

Example

[for a garden]

Measurements display: approximately 5.18 square km (2 square miles) (area)
Controlled fields:
Qualifier: approximately
Value: 5.18; **Unit**: square km; **Type**: area

Size

Include size where appropriate (for example, for clothing).

Example

[for a jacket]

Measurements display: U.S. women's size 8; 50 inches (127 cm) (length at center back)
Controlled fields:
Extent: center back
Value: 127; **Unit**: cm; **Type**: length
Value: 8; **Unit**: U.S. women's; **Type**: size

Express measurements for digital images in pixels. Express measurements for computer art in file size, generally in kilobytes.

Examples

[for a digital work]

Measurements display: 2100 x 1557 pixels
Controlled fields:
    Value: 2100; **Unit**: pixels; **Type**: height
    Value: 1557; **Unit**: pixels; **Type**: width

[for computer art in a file]

Measurements display: 9585 kb (file size)
Controlled fields:
    Value: 9585; **Unit**: kb; **Type**: file size

Format of the Work

Describe the configuration of a work, including technical formats, when it is an important distinguishing characteristic. Measurements for graphic designs or photographs may include the format (for example, standard formats characterized by size, such as *cabinet photograph* or *vignette*). Examples of terminology include *cabinet photograph*, *vignette*, *VHS*, *IMAX*, and *DOS*. In some cases, the format of a work will be the same as its Work Type.

Examples

[for a Chinese scroll]

Measurements display: 32 x 254.5 cm (12 5/8 x 100 1/4 inches) (scroll)
Controlled fields:
    Format: scroll
    Value: 32; **Unit**: cm; **Type**: height
    Value: 254.5; **Unit**: cm; **Type**: width

[for a carte-de-visite]

Measurements display: approximately 8.25 x 5.72 cm (3 1/4 x 2 1/4 inches) (image, carte-de-visite format); 10.16 x 6.35 cm (4 x 2 1/2 inches) (sheet)
Controlled fields:
    Format: carte-de-visite

    Extent: image
    Qualifier: approximately
    Value: 8.25; **Unit**: cm; **Type**: height
    Value: 5.72; **Unit**: cm; **Type**: width

    Extent: sheet
    Qualifier: approximately
    Value: 10.16; **Unit**: cm; **Type**: height
    Value: 6.35; **Unit**: cm; **Type**: width

[for a digital file]

Measurements display: 17488 kb (JPEG)
Controlled fields:
    Format: JPEG
    Value: 17488; **Unit**: kb; **Type**: file size

[for a videotape]

Measurements display: 2 hours 32 minutes 40 seconds (VHS)
Controlled fields:
    Format: VHS
    Value: 2; **Unit**: hours | **Value**: 32; **Unit**: minutes
    Value: 40; **Unit**: seconds | **Type**: running time

[for an installation using DVD]

Measurements display: 4 channel DVD, 100 minutes, installed in a 418 square meter area
Controlled fields:
    Format: DVD
    Value: 100; **Unit**: minutes; **Type**: running time
    Extent: channels; **Value**: 4; **Unit**: N/A; **Type**: count
    Extent: installation; **Value**: 418; **Unit**: square m; **Type**: area

Time

Include running time and technical formats for a video or motion picture (see Formats above). Record time in minutes or in hours, minutes, and seconds. Include frames per second, if known.

Examples

[for a film]

Measurements display: 239 feet, 35 mm; 153 minutes, 24 frames per second (running time)
Controlled fields:
    Format: 35 mm
    Value: 239; **Unit**: feet; **Type**: length
    Value: 153; **Unit**: minutes; **Type**: running time
    Value: 24; **Unit**: frames per second; **Type**: running time

[for a DVD]

Measurements display: approximately 122 minutes (DVD)
Controlled fields:
    Format: DVD
    Qualifier: approximately
    Value: 122; **Unit**: minutes; **Type**: running time

Scale

For architectural drawings or other works where it is appropriate, include scale, which is an expression of the ratio between the size of the representation of something and that thing (for example, the size of the drawn structure and the actual built work). Examples of terminology include *1:10, 1/4 inch = 1 foot, 1-to-1, full-size, life-size,* and *monumental.* Record the scale as represented on the object. If it is in inches or feet, record it as such. For numeric scales (for example, *1:10*), for measurement type use *base* for the left side of the equation, and *target* for the right side of the equation.

Example

[for an architectural drawing]

Measurements display: 61.6 x 97.2 cm (24 1/4 x 38 1/4 inches); scale: 1 inch = 10 feet
Controlled fields:
    Value: 61.6; **Unit**: cm; **Type**: height
    Value: 97.2; **Unit**: cm; **Type**: width

    Scale: numeric
    Value: 1; **Unit**: inches; **Type**: base
    Value: 10; **Unit**: feet; **Type**: target

Structural Dimensions

Record structural dimensions, such as warp and weft, textile or wallpaper pattern repeats, and the spacing of chain and laid lines on a piece of paper, if pertinent.

Example

[for a 17th-century print]

Measurements display: 13.3 x 20.6 cm (5 1/4 x 8 1/8 inches)(sheet); 25 mm apart (15/16 inch) (chain lines); 14 per 20 mm (7/8 inch) (laid lines)
Controlled fields:
    Extent: sheet
    Value: 13.3; **Unit**: cm; **Type**: height
    Value: 20.6; **Unit**: cm; **Type**: width

    Extent: chain lines
    Value: 25; **Unit**: mm; **Type**: distance between

    Extent: laid lines per 20 mm
    Value: 14; **Unit**: N/A; **Type**: count

3.2.1.2.4 MEASURING PARTS

Clarify when only one dimension is known, when only a part or parts of the work have been measured, or when the extent of the measurement could otherwise be ambiguous.

Examples

[for a chapel]

Measurements display: 24 m (78 feet 9 inches) (height)
Controlled fields:
    Value: 24; **Unit**: m; **Type**: height

[for a table]

Measurements display: 56.8 cm (22 3/8 inches) (diameter)
Controlled fields:
    Value: 56.8; **Unit**: cm; **Type**: diameter

[for a polyptych]

> **Measurements display**: 183 x 187 cm (72 x 73 5/8 inches) (overall); 105 cm (41 3/8 inches) (width of central panel); 39 cm (15 3/8 inches) (width of each side panel)
> **Controlled fields**:
>> **Extent**: overall
>> **Value**: 183 **Unit**: cm **Type**: height
>> **Value**: 187 **Unit**: cm **Type**: width
>>
>> **Extent**: central panel
>> **Value**: 105 **Unit**: cm **Type**: width
>>
>> **Extent**: each side panel
>> **Value**: 39 **Unit**: cm **Type**: width

Image and Support

For two-dimensional works in which the image has dimensions that are significantly different from the support, include measurements for both, if known (for example, for an engraving, the dimensions of both the printing plate impression and the sheet may be included).

Example

[for an etching]

> **Measurements display**: 17.6 x 26.4 cm (6 15/16 x 10 3/8 inches) (plate mark); 24.5 x 30.7 cm (9 5/8 x 12 inches) (sheet)
> **Controlled fields**:
>> **Extent**: plate mark
>> **Value**: 17.6; **Unit**: cm; **Type**: height
>> **Value**: 26.4; **Unit**: cm; **Type**: width
>>
>> **Extent**: sheet
>> **Value**: 24.5; **Unit**: cm; **Type**: height
>> **Value**: 30.7; **Unit**: cm; **Type**: width

Measuring Components

For multiple-part works, record the dimensions of the components. Include a count of the components.

Examples

[for a screen]

> **Measurements display**: composed of 4 panels, 23 x 45 cm each (9 x 17 3/4 inches)
> **Controlled fields**:
>> **Extent**: panels
>> **Value**: 4; **Unit**: N/A; **Type**: count
>> **Value**: 23; **Unit**: cm; **Type**: height
>> **Value**: 45; **Unit**: cm; **Type**: width

[for a desk set]

> **Measurements display**: 5 components; candlesticks measure 29.97 x 9.53 cm (11 7/8 x 3 3/4 inches)
> **Controlled fields**:
>> **Extent**: components
>> **Value**: 5; **Unit**: N/A; **Type**: count
>>
>> **Extent**: candlesticks
>> **Value**: 29.97; **Unit**: cm; **Type**: height
>> **Value**: 9.53; **Unit**: cm; **Type**: width

Books and Manuscripts

For manuscripts and books, record the number of volumes (if more than one), a count of the leaves (foliation) or pages (pagination) as appropriate, the dimensions of the text block, then the number of columns and lines, if known. (For part-whole relationships, see the discussion in Part 1: Related Works; also see *Categories for the Description of Works of Art*, which records manuscript pagination and foliation counts and other component information in a separate subcategory, Object Work/ Component.)

> *Examples*

[for a manuscript]

> **Measurements display**: 468 leaves; text block: 17.78 x 23.18 cm (7 x 9 1/8 inches); 2 columns, 56 lines
> **Controlled fields**:
>> **Extent**: text block
>> **Value**: 17.78; **Unit**: cm; **Type**: height
>> **Value**: 23.18; **Unit**: cm; **Type**: width
>>
>> **Extent**: leaves
>> **Value**: 468; **Unit**: N/A; **Type**: count
>>
>> **Extent**: columns per page
>> **Value**: 2; **Unit**: N/A; **Type**: count
>>
>> **Extent**: lines per page
>> **Value**: 56; **Unit**: N/A; **Type**: count

[for a rare book]

> **Measurements display**: 3 volumes, 274 pages; text block: 47 x 32.2 cm (18 1/2 x 12 11/16 inches)
> **Controlled fields**:
>> **Extent**: text block
>> **Value**: 47; **Unit**: cm; **Type**: height
>> **Value**: 274; **Unit**: cm; **Type**: width
>>
>> **Extent**: pages
>> **Value**: 274; **Unit**: N/A; **Type**: count

Measuring Groups

For groups of items, record the range of measurements, if known. Record the number of items in the group, if known.

Examples

[for a group of design drawings]

Measurements display: 21 items; sheets range in size from 28.3 x 41.2 cm to 35.9 x 66.4 cm (11 1/8 x 16 1/4 inches to 14 1/8 x 26 1/8 inches)
Controlled fields:
Extent: items
Value: 21; **Unit**: N/A; **Type**: count

Qualifier: smallest
Value: 28.3; **Unit**: cm; **Type**: height
Value: 41.2; **Unit**: cm; **Type**: width

Qualifier: largest
Value: 35.9; **Unit**: cm; **Type**: height
Value: 66.4; **Unit**: cm; **Type**: width

[for a group of arrowheads]

Measurements display: 56 items; lengths range 36 mm to 64 mm (1 3/8 to 2 1/2 inches)
Controlled fields:
Extent: items
Value: 56; **Unit**: N/A; **Type**: count

Qualifier: smallest
Value: 36; **Unit**: mm; **Type**: length

Qualifier: largest
Value: 64; **Unit**: mm; **Type**: length

[for a group of drawings, models, and other items from an architect's office; items are very diverse and measurements are not available]

Measurements display: 152 items; various dimensions
Controlled fields:
Extent: items
Value: 152; **Unit**: N/A; **Type**: count

Measuring Architecture

Record measurements for an architectural work, if known. Generally, only incomplete measurements will be available. Record height or interior area, if known. If only the dimensions of a part are known (for example, the diameter of a dome), explain what the measurements represent.

Examples

[for a temple]

Measurements display: 43.59 m (143 feet) (diameter of dome); 43.59 m (143 feet) (interior height of dome from floor)
Controlled fields:
Extent: dome
Value: 43.59; **Unit**: m; **Type**: diameter

Extent: dome
Qualifier: interior
Value: 43.59; **Unit**: m; **Type**: height

[for an office building]

> **Measurements display**: 418 square m (4500 square feet) (interior area)
> **Controlled fields**:
>> **Extent**: interior
>> **Value**: 418; **Unit**: square m; **Type**: area

3.2.1.2.5 APPROXIMATE MEASUREMENTS

If accurate measurements cannot be made, record sight measurements (estimated measurements judged by eye, also called visible image measurements; for example, with a fragile framed pastel or an inaccessible ceiling fresco).

> *Example*

[for a watercolor]

> **Measurements display**: 86 x 93.35 cm (34 1/4 x 36 3/4 inches) (sight measurements, window of mat)
> **Controlled fields**:
>> **Extent**: window of mat
>> **Qualifier**: sight
>> **Value**: 86; **Unit**: cm; **Type**: height
>> **Value**: 93.35; **Unit**: cm; **Type**: width

Visual resources catalogers and others who are not measuring the original should not estimate approximate measurements, but instead should use approximate measurements that the repository of the object or another authoritative source supply.

3.2.1.2.6 ROUNDING

When measuring an object, generally include two decimal places for metric measurements, rounding to the next larger digit. For inches, round up to the nearest eighth of an inch. Small objects should be measured more precisely (for example, in millimeters for metric, or up to the nearest 1/16 of an inch). Very large works may be rounded more grossly (for example, in meters for metric measurements, or in feet rather than inches). The accuracy of measuring the works may vary depending on the needs and resources of the cataloging institution; it is important for an institution to have and follow consistent rules regarding rounding off measurements.

Visual resources catalogers and others who are not measuring the original object should not round off dimensions; instead, they should accurately record measurements as found in an authoritative source.

3.2.1.2.7 CONVERTING MEASUREMENTS

Measure the object using metric units, if possible, and convert to inches and feet. Measurements in metric units tend to be more precise than inches and feet. Thus, if measurements are made in inches and feet and then converted to metric units, it will give the impression that the measurements are more accurate than they actually are.

3.2.2 Rules for Materials and Techniques

3.2.2.1 *Brief Rules for Materials and Techniques*

Recording Materials and Techniques is required. Specify the matter, materials, or substances used to create a work, and the processes, techniques, and implements used to apply or form the materials, as appropriate.

Singular vs. Plural

In most cases, express terms for materials and techniques in the singular form.

> *Examples*
>
> > **Material**: ink
> >
> > **Material**: oil paint
> >
> > **Material**: charcoal
> >
> > **Material**: vernis Martin
> >
> > **Material**: laid paper
> >
> > **Material**: canvas
> >
> > **Material**: mother of pearl
> >
> > **Technique**: engraving
> >
> > **Technique**: gilding

Where appropriate, use the plural form of the term instead of the singular; that is, use terminology that reflects the characteristics of the work being cataloged, if possible. For example, if several feathers have been applied as a material, the plural term *feathers* should be used, particularly in the display field (for example, *beaded leather band with three eagle feathers*).

Capitalization and Abbreviations

For the sake of clarity and comprehensibility for end users, do not use abbreviations. Use lowercase except when a material is distinguished by a proper noun, such as *Carrara marble*, or is known by its brand name, such as *Formica*™. Do not use brand names unless the material is known exclusively or primarily by that term.

> *Examples*
>
> > **Material**: oak
> >
> > **Material**: India ink
> >
> > **Material**: Cor-Ten steel™
> >
> > **Material**: papyrus
> >
> > **Material**: polymer-impregnated cement

Language of the Terms

Use terminology in the language of the catalog record (English in the United States). Use non-English terms only when there is no English-language counterpart or when the English term is not customarily used in the context of fine arts or material culture. Include the appropriate diacritical marks.

Examples

Material: ivory

Material: cardboard

Material: stained glass

Material: papier-mâché

Material: pisé

Material: arriccio

3.2.2.2 *Additional Recommendations for Materials and Techniques*

3.2.2.2.1 SYNTAX

For display, use natural word order. List medium or media first, followed by the support (if pertinent). If there is no support, as with sculpture, list only the medium. Index materials and techniques as needed to facilitate search and retrieval. (In the examples below, technique is included among the indexing terms, although some institutions may wish to omit it or index it in the same repeating field as material; see also Display and Indexing below.)

Examples

[for an abstract painting]

Materials and Techniques display: oil on canvas
Controlled fields:
    Materials: oil paint • canvas
    Technique: painting

[for a sculpture]

Materials and Techniques display: marble
Controlled fields:
    Material: marble
    Technique: sculpting

Order among Multiple Media

If more than one technique or medium was used to create a work, list them in a logical order.

BY SEQUENCE OF APPLICATION

If the sequence in which materials or media were applied is known through analysis, examination, or documentation, list materials and techniques in the order of application. In the example below, graphite was applied first and the wash was applied last.

Example

[for a sketch]

> **Materials and Techniques display**: graphite, pen and black ink, with gray wash on white laid paper
> **Controlled fields**:
>> **Materials**: graphite • ink • wash • laid paper
>> **Techniques**: drawing • wash technique

BY IMPORTANCE

If importance or prominence of materials or techniques is obvious, list them in that order. In the example below, the squaring is considered less important than the materials used to create the image.

Example

[for a preparatory drawing]

> **Materials and Techniques display**: chalk and wash, squared in chalk, on prepared paper
> **Controlled fields**:
>> **Materials**: chalk • wash • prepared paper
>> **Techniques**: drawing • squared

3.2.2.2.2 SUGGESTED TERMINOLOGY

Use the following conventions and terminology.

Materials

For materials, record the matter, materials, or substances used to create a work. Examples of terminology include *canvas, glass, bronze, marble, wood, poplar, charcoal, vernis Martin, laid paper, paint, egg tempera, ink, iron gall ink, sound,* and *monitor.*

Techniques

For techniques, record processes, techniques, and implements used to apply or form materials in creating art or architecture. Examples of terminology include *drawing, painting, sculpting, casting, lost wax, stumping, pricking, engraving, etching, gilding, weaving, half-timber construction, wattle and daub, chisel, brush, palette knife, computer animation,* and *video installation.* Some institutions do not require technique as an indexing field.

Additional Elements

Some institutions may wish to display and index additional information regarding materials and techniques based on local needs. Add information if necessary, as defined below.

EXTENT

Extent refers to the specific part of a work composed of a certain material or created using a particular technique. Examples of terminology include *overall, surface, base, backing board, lower panel, jacket,* and *skirt.*

MATERIAL TYPE

For materials, some institutions may require separate retrieval on the media and the support to which they are applied. This distinction, known as *medium and support,* is typically important for two-dimensional works, including paintings, drawings, and prints.

Medium—Medium is the material applied to the support. Examples of terminology include *ink, paint, pastels, watercolor, charcoal, vernis Martin, mother of pearl, egg tempera, oil paint, gold leaf, iron gall ink, bronze, gouache, Conté crayon, deer bone, cinnabar, amethyst,* and *graphite.*

Support—Support is the surface upon which media have been applied. Examples of terminology include *canvas, oak panel, laid paper, wove paper, wood, copper, glass, marble, poplar, linen, burlap sacking, Foam-Cor™, Formica™,* and *fiberglass.*

DIVISIONS OF TECHNIQUES

For techniques, some institutions may require separate retrieval on processes-techniques and implements. For further discussion of this issue, see *Categories for the Description of Works of Art: Materials and Technique.*

Process—Process refers to the means, method, process, or technique by which a material was used in the creation of a work. Examples of terminology include *drawing, painting, fresco, sculpting, lost wax, stumping, pricking, intaglio, engraving, gilding, weaving, chasing, overpainting, montage, inlaid, collage, Red figure,* and *half-timber construction.*

Implement—Implement refers to any implement or tool used to create the work. Examples of terminology include *brush, pen, pencil, roulette, compass, chisel, eraser, chain saw, palette knife, felt tip pen, jacquard loom, burin, sable brush, scorper,* and *fingers.*

3.2.2.2.3 VARIOUS TYPES OF WORKS

Use descriptions of materials and techniques appropriate for the particular work at hand, in accordance with the recommendations below:

Paintings

For paintings, include media and support. In some cases, as with wall paintings, the term used to indicate the material or materials of which a work is made may be the same as the Work Type (for example, *fresco*).

Examples

[for a banner]

Materials and Techniques display: oil paint on linen canvas
Controlled fields:
Materials: oil paint • linen canvas
Technique: painting

[for an altarpiece]

Materials and Techniques display: egg-tempera paint with tooled gold-leaf halos on panel
Controlled fields:
Materials: egg tempera • gold leaf • wood panel
Techniques: painting • gold tooling

[for a mural]

Materials and Techniques display: fresco
Controlled fields:
Material: fresco
Technique: fresco painting

Drawings and Watercolors

For drawings and watercolors, include media and support. Techniques, processes, and implements (for example, *pen*) may be included, as appropriate. For drawings, include color if it is unusual or significant (see Color, below), but generally do not include color for watercolors.

Examples

[for a drawing]

Materials and Techniques display: pen and brown ink on ivory-colored paper
Controlled fields:
Materials: ink • paper
Techniques: pen • drawing

[for a drawing]

Materials and Techniques display: silverpoint, with white chalk heightening, on silver-gray prepared paper
Controlled fields:
Materials: chalk • prepared paper
Techniques: silverpoint • heightening • drawing

[for a watercolor]

Materials and Techniques display: watercolor on Arches™ paper
Controlled fields:
Materials: watercolor • Arches™ paper
Technique: painting

Prints

For prints, the display may refer to the technique alone, if appropriate (for example, *engraving*). If there are multiple techniques or the support is unusual, include this information to avoid ambiguity. The terms may repeat a term that is also used to denote the Work Type (for example, *lithograph*).

Examples

[for a modern print]

> **Materials and Techniques display**: lithograph
> **Controlled fields**:
>> **Materials**: ink • paper
>> **Technique**: lithograph

[for a manuscript illumination]

> **Materials and Techniques display**: etching, burin and drypoint on vellum
> **Controlled fields**:
>> **Materials**: ink • vellum
>> **Techniques**: etching • drypoint • burin

[for a photograph]

> **Materials and Techniques display**: albumen print
> **Controlled fields**:
>> **Material**: albumen paper
>> **Technique**: photography

[for a photograph]

> **Materials and Techniques display**: glycerine-developed platinum print
> **Controlled fields**:
>> **Material**: platinum paper
>> **Techniques**: glycerine process • photography

Sculpture and Other Three-Dimensional Works

For sculptures, record the primary material (for example, *bronze* or *marble*); include the technique if it is unusual or to avoid ambiguity. For sculptures, masks, and other three-dimensional works composed of multiple materials, if there are too many materials to list, include the most prominent or most important materials.

Examples

[for a modern sculpture]

> **Materials and Techniques display**: bronze
> **Controlled fields**:
>> **Material**: bronze
>> **Technique**: lost-wax process

[for a 19th-century sculpture]

Materials and Techniques display: white Carrara marble on gray granite base
Controlled fields:
    Extent: statue
    Material: Carrara marble
    Technique: carving

    Extent: base
    Material: granite
    Technique: carving

[for an African mask]

Materials and Techniques display: painted wood, with raffia, metal, and kaolin
Controlled fields:
    Materials: wood • raffia • metal • kaolin • paint
    Techniques: carving • sewing • gluing • painting

[for an automobile model]

Materials and Techniques display: fused deposition modeling
Controlled fields:
    Material: polycarbonate
    Technique: fused deposition modeling

Books and Manuscripts

For rare books, manuscripts, and modern artist's books, record the materials of the folios or the contents. Include the media of the art works depicted in the book, if known (for example, illuminations in a manuscript). Include information about the binding method or materials and the way in which text was produced, if known and if it is significant.

Examples

[for a pamphlet]

Materials and Techniques display: letterpress on pale yellow paper
Controlled fields:
    Material: paper
    Technique: letterpress printing

[for a rare book]

Materials and Techniques display: etchings on paper, casebound
Controlled fields:
    Materials: ink • paper
    Techniques: etching • case binding

[for a manuscript]

> **Materials and Techniques display**: ink and tempera on vellum (illuminations), leather and silver (binding)
> **Controlled fields**:
>> **Extent**: folios and illuminations
>> **Materials**: ink • tempera • vellum
>> **Techniques**: calligraphy • painting
>>
>> **Extent**: binding
>> **Materials**: leather • silver

Furniture and Architectural Details

For furniture, architectural components, windows, screens, and other such works, include the primary materials, which will vary according to the complexity of the work. Include the technique if it is unusual or significant.

Examples

[for a chest]

> **Materials and Techniques display**: maple
> **Controlled fields**:
>> **Material**: maple

[for a sofa]

> **Materials and Techniques display**: oak, veneered with rosewood, bronze mounts; horsehair upholstery
> **Controlled fields**:
>> **Materials**: oak • rosewood • bronze • horsehair
>> **Technique**: veneering

[for a stained-glass screen]

> **Materials and Techniques display**: stained glass in fruitwood frame
> **Controlled fields**:
>> **Materials**: stained glass • lead • fruitwood

Ceramics and Glass Works

For vessels and other types of ceramics and glass works, record the media and techniques as appropriate for the composition of the work. List style terms, such as *Black-figure*, when they refer to a technique. If style is recorded here, it should be repeated in the style element.

Examples

[for a bowl]

> **Materials and Techniques display**: terracotta
> **Controlled fields**:
>> **Material**: terracotta
>> **Technique**: coiling

[for a vase]

Materials and Techniques display: free-blown glass
Controlled fields:
  Material: free-blown glass

[for a pedestal plate]

Materials and Techniques display: painted and glazed earthenware
Controlled fields:
  Materials: earthenware • paint • glaze
  Technique: throwing

Jewelry and Utilitarian Works

Include the primary materials and techniques for jewelry, costume accessories, works for serving or consuming food, liturgical works, and other precious or utilitarian works. Explain the use of materials where necessary to avoid ambiguity.

Examples

[for a necklace]

Materials and Techniques display: gold repoussé work
Controlled fields:
  Material: gold
  Technique: repoussé

[for a snuff box]

Materials and Techniques display: laminated copper and gold with inlays of shell and mother of pearl
Controlled fields:
  Materials: copper • gold • shell • mother of pearl
  Techniques: laminating • inlay • soldering

[for a chalice]

Materials and Techniques display: silver plate over copper, with semiprecious stones
Controlled fields:
  Materials: copper • silver • semi-precious stones
  Techniques: casting • French plating

Architecture

For architecture, include the primary exterior and interior materials. Include references to the methods of construction or the form of the building, including the frame or the plan, if known.

Examples

[for an office buliding]

Materials and Techniques display: steel frame with glass panels
Controlled fields:
  Materials: steel • glass
  Techniques: steel frame • glass curtain wall

[for a house]

Materials and Techniques display: wood frame and adobe, with red tile roof
Controlled fields:
    Extent: frame
    Material: wood

    Extent: walls
    Material: adobe

    Extent: roof
    Material: tile
    Technique: wood frame

[for a church]

Materials and Techniques display: Greek cross plan, limestone and sandstone, bearing masonry
Controlled fields:
    Materials: limestone • sandstone
    Techniques: Greek cross plan • load-bearing walls • vaulting • buttressing

Textiles and Clothing

For textiles, include the composition of the fibers. Include techniques, such as a reference to the finish of the fabric (for example, *satin*), if known.

Examples

[for an apron]

Materials and Techniques display: linen
Controlled fields:
    Material: linen
    Technique: weaving

[for a mola]

Materials and Techniques display: cotton appliqué
Controlled fields:
    Material: cotton
    Technique: appliqué

[for a vestment]

Materials and Techniques display: silk satin with stencil-dyed pattern, embroidered in gold thread
Controlled fields:
    Materials: silk • dye • gold thread
    Techniques: satin weaving • stencil-dyed • embroidery

Performance Art and Installations

For performance art and other ephemeral works, include a simple generic description; alternatively, a more complex description may be included, if known. Include works or other objects that are used as materials (for example, *metal chair* in the example below).

Examples

[for an installation]

Materials and Techniques display: multimedia installation
Controlled fields:
    Material: multimedia
    Technique: installation

[for performance art]

Materials and Techniques display: wooden stage, phonograph, one living human actor, metal chair
Controlled fields:
    Materials: wooden stage • phonograph • actor • metal chair
    Techniques: installation • performance

[for an installation]

Materials and Techniques display: four-channel video projection with sound
Controlled fields:
    Materials: video • sound • audiovisual equipment
    Techniques: installation • projection

Film and Video

For a video or motion picture, record the specific media and audio and video techniques, if known. The material may be the same as the Work Type. The format of these media is also important; see Measurements above.

Examples

[for a videotape]

Materials and Techniques display: black-and-white videotape with sound
Controlled fields:
    Materials: videotape • sound
    Colors: black-and-white

[for an animation cel]

Materials and Techniques display: nitrate (cels), courvoisier on wood veneer background
Controlled fields:
    Materials: nitrate film • wood veneer
    Technique: courvoisier

Electronic and Digital Media

Include terms appropriate for electronic works. For computer graphics, techniques may combine concepts from various media. The material may be the same as the Work Type. For a discussion of format, see Measurements above.

Examples

[for a digital image]

Materials and Techniques display: digital image
Controlled fields:
    Material: digital image

[for a Web site]

Materials and Techniques display: interactive networked code, Java applet with server database and servlets
Controlled fields:
    Materials: computer code • digital images • audio
    Techniques: HTML • FLASH • networked • interactive

3.2.2.2.4 MATERIALS AND TECHNIQUES FOR PARTS

If various parts of a work are constructed of different materials, clearly explain this in the display.

Examples

[for a ring]

Materials and Techniques display: garnet in a gold setting
Controlled fields:
    Materials: garnet • gold
    Technique: casting

[for a lamp]

Materials and Techniques display: bronze base, leaded glass shade
Controlled fields:
    Extent: base
    Material: bronze

    Extent: shade
    Material: lead glass

[for a carpet]

Materials and Techniques display: wool and silk (pile), cotton (warp and weft), with symmetrical knots
Controlled fields:
    Extent: pile
    Materials: wool • silk

    Extent: warp and weft
    Material: cotton

    Extent: overall
    Techniques: weaving • symmetrical knots

3.2.2.2.5 GROUPS

For a group of works, describe all the materials and techniques used to create items in the group. If there are too many to describe, list the most important or most typical materials and techniques evident in the group.

Example

[for a group of drawings]

> **Materials and Techniques display**: pen and ink on paper, chalk on paper, tempera on academy board
> **Controlled fields**:
> > **Materials**: ink • paper
> > **Techniques**: pen • drawing
>
> > **Materials**: chalk • paper
> > **Technique**: drawing
>
> > **Materials**: tempera • academy board
> > **Technique**: painting

3.2.2.2.6 UNCERTAIN AND ALTERED MEDIA

Clearly indicate if uncertainty exists regarding the materials of which a work is made. Note when a support or other characteristic regarding the work has been lost, destroyed, or altered (for example, *transferred to canvas*). If a specific medium is unknown, list a more general one. For example, use *color photograph* if it is uncertain if the technique or process is *dye transfer, Kodachrome, Kodacolor,* and so on. When there are multiple possibilities, index each of them.

Examples

[for a portrait painting, tempera is indexed as a material and the uncertainty is explained in the display]

> **Materials and Techniques display**: oil or oil and tempera on panel transferred to canvas
> **Controlled fields**:
> > **Materials**: oil paint • tempera • panel • canvas
> > **Technique**: painting

[for a tray]

> **Materials and Techniques display**: probably soft paste porcelain
> **Controlled fields**:
> > **Material**: soft paste porcelain

3.2.2.2.7 COLOR

If color is an unusual or important characteristic of the work, note the color, tint, or hue of the material of which a work is composed. When extremely accurate records of the color are required, a color chart should be maintained for comparison. If the color has iconographic or symbolic meaning, record it also in the Subject element.

Examples

[for a statue]

Materials and Techniques display: gray granite
Controlled fields:
    Material: granite | **Color**: gray
    Technique: carving

[for a drawing]

Materials and Techniques display: pen and black ink and brown chalk on ivory-colored laid paper
Controlled fields:
    Material: ink | **Color**: black
    Material: chalk | **Color**: brown
    Material: laid paper | **Color**: ivory
    Techniques: pen • drawing

[for a garment]

Materials and Techniques display: blue Chinese silk with red samite appliqués
Controlled fields:
    Extent: overall
    Material: Chinese silk | **Color**: blue
    Technique: weaving

    Extent: appliqués
    Material: samite | **Color**: red

3.2.2.2.8 MARKS

For works on paper and as appropriate for other works, include a description and identification of watermarks, stationers' stamps, and other marks inherent in or applied to the material before it was fashioned into the work of art, if known. Marks are a characteristic of the material, generally a paper support; they are typically not a part of the artistic creation. The location of the mark on the work may be noted.

Examples

[for a print]

Materials and Techniques display: engraving on laid paper, watermark lower left: foolscap
Controlled fields:
    Material: laid paper
    Mark: foolscap

    Material: ink
    Technique: engraving

[for a drawing]

    Materials and Techniques display: pen and sepia ink on laid paper, watermark: star in circle with cross (like *Briquet 6088*)

    Controlled fields:

        Material: laid paper

        Mark: Briquet 6088: star in circle with cross

        Source: Briquet, C.-M. *Les filigranes: dictionnaire historique des marques du papier dès leur apparition vers 1282 jusqu'en 1600.* A facsimile of the 1907 edition with supplementary material contributed by a number of scholars. Edited by Allan Stevenson. Amsterdam: Paper Publications Society, 1968.

        Material: sepia

        Technique: drawing

If the mark is published in an authority, make a reference to the authority (for example, *Briquet* above). The full citation for the source should be available, ideally in a bibliographic authority file.

3.2.3   Rules for State and Edition

3.2.3.1 *Brief Rules for State*

For prints and as appropriate for other works produced in multiples, record an indication of the relationship of the work to other stages of the same work, if known. Any stage in the development of a printing plate at which impressions are taken is a state; a new state occurs when the matrix (plate) is altered (for example, lines are added or erased).

Capitalization and Abbreviations

Avoid abbreviations, except for abbreviations for numbers (for example, use *2nd* rather than *second*). Use lowercase.

    Examples

        State display: 3rd state

        State display: 2nd of 8 states

        State display: artist's proof

Language of the Terms

Use ordinal numerals (for example, *4th*) and Arabic cardinal numbers (for example, *5*), as appropriate. Record other terminology in the language of the catalog record (English in the United States). If no English term exists and non-English terms must be used, include the appropriate diacritical marks.

    Examples

        State display: 4th of 5 states

        State display: printer's proof

        State display: bon à tirer

        State display: hors de commerce

3.2.3.2 *Additional Recommendations for State*

3.2.3.2.1 SYNTAX

For display, use natural word order. List the ratio of the state of the work to the total number of known states (for example, *3rd of 5 states*). If the number of states is unknown, list the numeric indication of the state (for example, *3rd state*). For unnumbered states, record the appropriate term.

> *Examples*
>
> **State display**: 3rd of 5 states
> **Controlled fields**:
> > **State identification**: 3
> > **Known states**: 5
>
> **State display**: artist's proof
> **Controlled fields**:
> > **State identification**: artist's proof
> > **Known states**: N/A

3.2.3.2.2 SUGGESTED TERMINOLOGY

Use the following conventions and terminology.

Numerical Indicators

For most indications of state, record numerical references, as described in Syntax above.

Names for States

For named states, use the following terminology.

ARTIST'S PROOF

Use *artist's proof*, also known as *epreuve d'artiste*, for impressions printed especially for the artist and excluded from the numbering of an edition. On the print, you may find it abbreviated as *AP* or *EA*, and numbered with an edition number according to the number of artist's proofs pulled (for example, *AP 2/12*).

BON À TIRER

Use *bon à tirer*, occasionally known as *right to print*, for the proof approved by the artist to establish the standard for all of the other prints in the edition.

PRINTER'S PROOF

Use *printer's proof* for impressions printed as tests for the printer and excluded from the numbering of an edition. You may find it abbreviated *PP* on the print.

HORS DE COMMERCE

Use *hors de commerce*, meaning *outside the commercial edition*, for proofs that were excluded from the numbering of an edition, were not originally intended for sale, are not artist's proofs, printer's proofs, or bon à tirer. You may find it abbreviated *HC* on the print.

ADDITIONAL TERMS

In addition, the AAT, the CDWA standard textbooks, and Web sites related to printmaking can serve as sources for additional terminology about states (for example, the National Gallery of Art's Gemini G.E.L. Online Catalogue Raisonné at http://www.nga.gov/gemini/glossary.htm). If no published source is available, refer to the inscription on the work, if possible.

3.2.3.2.3 AMBIGUITY AND UNCERTAINTY

If scholars disagree or are uncertain about the state, clearly indicate this in the display.

> *Example*
>
> > **State display**: possibly 3rd of 4 states
> > **Controlled fields**:
> > > **State identification**: 3
> > > **Known states**: 4

If you do not know the total number of states, include the known state and omit the total number of states.

> *Examples*
>
> > **State display**: 2nd state
> > **Controlled fields**:
> > > **State identification**: 2
> > > **Known states**: unknown
>
> > **State display**: final state
> > **Controlled fields**:
> > > **State identification**: final
> > > **Known states**: unknown

3.2.3.2.4 SOURCES OF STATES

If scholars disagree about the order or number of states, or when a single scholarly study provides the indication of state, include a brief reference to the catalogue raisonné or other source that you used to identify the state, for example, *Robison (1986)*. The full citation should be available, ideally in a bibliographic authority file.

> *Example*
>
> > **State display**: 1st of 3 states (Robison (1986))
> > **Controlled fields**:
> > > **State identification**: 1
> > > **Known states**: 3
> > **Source**: Robison, Andrew. *Early Architectural Fantasies: A Catalogue Raisonné of the Piranesi Etchings.* Washington, DC: National Gallery of Art, 1986.

3.2.3.3   Brief Rules for Edition

For prints and other works produced in multiples, if known, record the edition, which is a notation that identifies a specific print or other work in the context of a limited number of identical or very similar works made or issued at the same time and from the same matrix (for example, *2/50*).

For books, if known, record an indication of the position of the issuance of the work in relation to previous and subsequent editions (for example, *2nd edition*). A new edition of a book should involve substantive revisions to the intellectual content of the work, including alterations of the text or illustrations.

Capitalization and Abbreviations

Avoid abbreviations, except for ordinal numerals (for example, use *3rd* rather than *third*). Use lowercase except when a term includes a proper name.

> *Examples*
>
> > **Edition display**: 46/500
> >
> > **Edition display**: 3rd edition
> >
> > **Edition display**: Victoria edition

Language of the Terms

Use Arabic cardinal numbers (for example, *5*) and ordinal numbers (for example, *4th*), as appropriate. Record terminology in the language of the catalog record (English in the United States). Include the appropriate diacritical marks. If there is an edition statement on the work, accurately transcribe it in the original language (transliterated into the Roman alphabet when necessary).

> *Examples*
>
> > **Edition display**: 4/50
> >
> > **Edition display**: Édition Müller

3.2.3.4   Additional Recommendations for Edition

3.2.3.4.1   SYNTAX

For Prints

For prints or other works issued in multiples at the same time, record a fractional number. Record the impression number, forward slash, and the edition size (for example, *51/250*).

> *Example*
>
> [for a print]
>
> > **Edition display**: 3/20
> > **Controlled fields**:
> > > **Impression number**: 3
> > > **Edition size**: 20

For Books

For books and other works produced in the context of prior or later issuances, record the number or name of the edition followed by the word *edition* (for example, *5th edition*).

> *Examples*
>
> [for a book]
>
> > **Edition display**: 2nd edition
> > **Controlled fields**:
> > > **Edition number-name**: 2
>
> [for a book]
>
> > **Edition display**: Kennedy edition
> > **Controlled fields**:
> > > **Edition number-name**: Kennedy

Editions Both Numbered and Named

If an edition is both numbered and named, record the name followed by the impression number and edition size.

> *Example*
>
> [for a print]
>
> > **Edition display**: Sagot and Le Garrec edition, 98/150
> > **Controlled fields**:
> > > **Impression number**: 98
> > > **Edition size**: 150
> > > **Edition number-name**: Sagot and Le Garrec

3.2.3.4.2 SUGGESTED TERMINOLOGY

Use the following conventions and terminology.

Impression Number

For impression number, record the number assigned to a particular item within a specific edition or production run, such as *1, 30, 241*.

Edition Size

For edition size, record the total number of works created in a particular production run, such as *50, 250, 500*.

Edition Number or Name

For edition number or name, record the term for the specific edition to which a work belongs. Terminology can include proper names (such as *Kennedy edition*) or terms (such as *3rd edition, subscriber's edition*, or *revised edition*).

3.2.3.4.3 AMBIGUITY AND UNCERTAINTY

If the impression number or edition size is uncertain, clearly indicate this in the display.

Example

[for a print]

Edition display: probably 34/50
Controlled fields:
    Impression number: 34
    Edition size: 50

If the edition size is known but the impression number is unknown, record the edition size.

Example

[for a cast sculpture]

Edition display: edition of 20
Controlled fields:
    Impression number: unknown
    Edition size: 20

3.2.3.5 *Versions*

Record different versions as separate, related works (see Part 1: Related Works for a discussion of related works). Note that different versions of a work, such as copies after a work, re-creations, replicas, or reproductions of it, are not considered states or editions. Versions include the following examples: *1/4-scale version, small version, version A*. The distinction is that states and editions refer to multiples of the same physical or intellectual work, and versions are not considered to be multiples.

3.2.4 Rules for Additional Physical Characteristics

3.2.4.1 *Brief Rules for Inscriptions*

Describe or transcribe any distinguishing or identifying physical lettering, annotations, texts, markings, or labels that are affixed, applied, stamped, written, inscribed, or attached to the work, excluding any mark or text inherent in the materials of which the work is made. (For marks applied to the materials, see Materials and Techniques above.)

Among the various types of inscriptions, it is a priority to record signatures, dates, and inscribed titles. Inscribed titles should be recorded in the Title element (see Chapter 1), but they may be repeated or recorded in fuller form in the Inscription element.

Capitalization and Abbreviations

Record the transcription so that it accurately reflects case and abbreviations of the inscription on the work. Fill in abbreviated text if necessary for clarity, but place your editorial additions in brackets to distinguish them from the actual transcription (for example, the "ou" in *Petersbourg* below). For other descriptive text in the field, such as *signed* and *dated*, avoid abbreviations and use lowercase.

Examples

[for a print]

> **Inscription display**: signed and dated in the plate, lower right: Benedicti / Castilionis / 1647

[for an album]

> **Inscription display**: lower center: PROJETS / POUR LA VILLE / DE / ST. PETERSB[ou]RG

Language of Terms in Inscription

Record the transcription so that it accurately reflects the language, spelling, case, and diacritics of the original text, noting line breaks and illegible sections as necessary. Record descriptive editorial text, such as an indication of the location on the work (for example, *lower center*), in the language of the catalog record (English in the United States).

Examples

[for an oil painting]

> **Inscription display**: signed, lower right: Vincent

[for a ceramic box]

> **Inscription display**: inscribed on back under foot: 1508 adi 12 de setéb / facta fu í Castel durát / Zouá maria vró

3.2.4.2 *Additional Recommendations for Inscriptions*

3.2.4.2.1 SYNTAX

Record an indication of the nature and position of the inscription (for example, *lower center*, *recto*, or *verso*), followed by a colon, and then the accurate transcription of the text. To indicate line breaks in the original text, use a forward slash. Use brackets for any editorial comment that appears after the colon in the body of the transcription. Use a semicolon to separate descriptions of multiple inscriptions.

Examples

[for a drawing]

> **Inscription display**: signed in lower left: GBPiazzetta; inscribed and dated verso, in a later hand: S. Maria dei Servi / 1735

[for a print]

> **Inscription display**: signed in the plate, lower center: Iullius Parigu Inv. Iacobus Callot F.

[for a painting]

> **Inscription display**: inscribed lower center: COSMO MEDICI / DVCII / FLORENTINOR.ET.SENESNS. / URBIS ROMAE / AEDIFICIORVM ILLVSTRIVMQVAE / SVPERSVNT RELIQVIAE SVMMA [...]

[for a chair]

> **Inscription display**: stamped under the back seat rail: IAVISSE [for Jean Avisse]

3.2.4.2.2 INDEX IMPORTANT INFORMATION

Record important information contained in the inscription, such as the name of the artist, date of execution, subject matter, or title, in the appropriate elements elsewhere in the Work Record.

3.2.4.2.3 SUGGESTED TERMINOLOGY

Terminology for the editorial comments in the Inscription element include *type of inscription, location on work,* and *typeface and letterform.*

Type of Inscription

Examples of terminology include *signed, dated, titled, maker's mark, colophon, collector's mark, impressed, graffito,* and *not inscribed.*

Location on Work

Examples of terminology include *lower right, upper center verso, below the left handle,* and *within printing plate.*

Typeface and Letterform

Examples of terminology include *Helvetica 9 pt bold, open letters, Carolingian minuscule, rustic capitals,* and *dotted delta.*

3.2.4.2.4 EXHAUSTIVITY

If the inscription is too long to transcribe, describe it instead of transcribing. Alternatively, transcribe part of it and indicate missing text with an ellipsis.

Examples

[for an illustration, the inscription is described]

Inscription display: rotunda Gothic script, beginning of the last canto of Dante's Inferno, in Italian with the first line of the new section in Latin

[for a poster, the long inscription is truncated]

Inscription display: text of Shakespeare's Twelfth Night, Act 1: Scene 1: IF MUSIC be the Food / of Love, / play on; Give me / excess of it, that, surfeiting, / The appetite / may sicken, and so die [...]

3.2.4.2.5 TRANSLATIONS

If the cataloger or a source has translated the text from the original language (for example, if the original text is in a non-Roman alphabet), clearly indicate the translation by placing it in brackets.

Example

[for a painting]

Inscription display: inscribed in Slavonic in upper right on scroll held by angel: [The souls of the righteous are now in the hands of the Lord. The heavenly powers open the gates to receive the soul of the great Tsar Alexander]

3.2.4.2.6 AMBIGUITY AND UNCERTAINTY

Clearly indicate any uncertainty. Use words such as *probably* when scholarly opinion varies or is uncertain. Within the transcription, place editorial commentary in square brackets as necessary to distinguish it from the accurately inscribed text. For example, in the example below, *[—?]* indicates an illegible word and *179[4?]* an illegible numeral.

Examples

[for a drawing]

> **Inscription display**: inscribed in pen and gray ink over graphite, upper right: hic.corona.exit. [—?] / .ob.diminuitionem. / colonna[rum] / 179[4?]

[for a book]

> **Inscription display**: medicinal recipes in Arabic, owner's inscription at lower left and marginalia are probably by the same hand

3.2.4.3 *Recommendations for Other Physical Characteristics*

3.2.4.3.1 RECORDING FACTURE

Record a detailed description of the way in which the work was made, including an assessment of its workmanship or characteristics of execution, the construction methods used, or the specific applications of techniques. This element can be used to record how to put together an installation or carry out performance art. For further discussion, see *Categories for the Description of Works of Art*. Index important elements as necessary, for example, in Materials and Techniques.

Examples

[for a print]

> **Facture display**: Multiple plate intaglio print was made using three separate aquatint plates inked in dark brown, blue, and pale green.

[for a pyramid]

> **Facture display**: In its earliest form, the pyramid was a seven-stepped structure finished with a casing of dressed limestone. Later, it was enlarged into an eight-stepped pyramid by extending all seven original steps, and adding a new platform on top. In a final building campaign, it was changed into a smooth-sided pyramid by filling in the steps with casing blocks.

[for an installation]

> **Facture display**: Work comprised of four channels of video and four channels of audio; displayed using four DVD players, four projectors, speakers, and a synchronizer in a spacious gallery.

3.2.4.3.2 RECORDING PHYSICAL DESCRIPTION

Record a description of the appearance of a work expressed in generic terms, without reference to the subject depicted. This includes the names of any recognizable patterns, motifs, or textures used in the decoration of the work. Index important characteristics in Materials and Techniques, Subject, or another appropriate element. Many institutions may include this information as a descriptive note; specialized collections may require a separate field for physical description.

Examples

[for a carpet]

Physical Description display: Carpet is kilim type, with smooth, flat surface. Field is decorated with 15 medallions which are connected by stylized scrolling vine motif; medallions contain various flowers and fruit trees with small birds; borders are decorated with alternating geometric designs and arabesques.

[for a jar]

Physical Description display: Jar has a high waist, short collar-like neck, plain rim, plain base, and lug handles.

[for a desk]

Physical Description display: The interior behind the roll top has numerous drawers which spring open at the pressure of concealed buttons and levers. In the superstructure is a folding reading stand and compartments with an inkwell and sand pot. At the back of the desk is a removable panel for access to the movement.

Examples of terminology for motifs and patterns include *guilloche, egg and dart moldings, Greek key pattern, pomegranate pattern, coat of arms, griffins, false drawer, rigaree,* and *cut-cardwork.*

3.2.4.3.3 RECORDING CONDITION AND EXAMINATION HISTORY

Record a description assessing the overall physical condition, characteristics, and completeness of a work of art or architecture at a particular time. This includes examinations of the work under special conditions, such as ultraviolet light.

Example

[for a carpet]

Condition History display: Oxidized metallic areas, oxidized browns, applied fringe one end, missing minor guards both ends, minor areas of restoration. Warp: Cotton Z4-6S, alternate warp strongly depressed, natural white; Weft: Cotton, 2Z, (sometimes 3Z), then 2 strands of unplied silk (light to dark shades of beige and red). The silk alternating between 2 rows of 2Z cotton, 3 shoots; Pile: Silk, with metallic-wrapped silk threads, asymmetrical knot open to the left; Density: 15-17 horizontal, 13-15 vertical.

For further discussion and a list of fields, see *Categories for the Description of Works of Art.*

3.2.4.3.4 RECORDING CONSERVATION AND TREATMENT HISTORY

Record the procedures or actions that a work has undergone to repair, conserve, or stabilize it.

Example

[for a low relief sculpture]

> **Conservation and Treatment History display**: Removed hardened surface salt with chelating agent; removed excess salts from within body by electrophoresis; rinsed with passified deionized water until conductivity measurements indicated that no more salts could be removed; slow dried; consolidated sections with Rohm & Haas AC33 aq. Dispersion of ethyl acrylate/methyl methacrylate copolymer (Feller Class I stability).

For further discussion and a list of fields, see *Categories for the Description of Works of Art.*

3.3   PRESENTATION OF THE DATA

3.3.1   Display and Indexing

3.3.1.1   *Free-Text vs. Controlled Fields*

For a discussion of when and why separate free-text and controlled fields are recommended, see Part 1: Database Design and Relationships: Display and Indexing.

Ideally, Measurements, Materials and Techniques, State and Edition, and any Additional Physical Characteristics should be recorded in free-text fields for display, in combination with controlled fields that will be used for indexing and retrieval. If including a free-text field for an element is not possible, a rudimentary display for each can be constructed by concatenating data from controlled fields.

Controlled fields should contain all information pertinent to retrieval of information for the physical characteristics. Requirements will vary from institution to institution. Rules should be established to meet local requirements.

Controlled fields do not necessarily need to include all the information in the free-text display field (for example, color), if these characteristics are not required for retrieval. Conversely, in some cases controlled fields may contain more information than is explicitly stated in the free-text field (for example, *ink*, which may be implied but not stated in a free-text field).

Some institutions may not need to retrieve information for the physical characteristics, though they may wish to display the information (for example, visual resources collections may not need to retrieve on measurements; some institutions may not need to retrieve on state and edition or inscriptions). In such cases, a free-text field alone may be used for any of those elements, without controlled fields.

3.3.1.2   *Fields in Authority File and Work Record*

3.3.1.2.1   MINIMUM CONTROLLED FIELDS

For Measurements

The minimum recommended controlled fields for measurements are numerical value, unit of measurement, and type of measurement.

> **Measurements display**: 13.3 x 20.6 cm (5 1/4 x 8 1/8 inches)
> **Controlled fields**:
>> **Value**: 13.3; **Unit**: cm; **Type**: height
>> **Value**: 20.6; **Unit**: cm; **Type**: width

If inches rather than metric units are stored in the controlled fields, typically decimal fractions should be used to better facilitate calculations (for example, *17 1/4 inches* would be stored as *17.25*). Ideally, both inches and metric units would be stored for each work (or the system could calculate the translation from one to the other), to allow retrieval by either measurement system.

Additional controlled fields could include extent, qualifier, shape, format, and scale.

Examples

> **Measurements display**: approximately 3 1/4 x 2 1/4 inches (image, carte-de-visite format); 4 x 2 1/2 inches (sheet)
> **Controlled fields**:
>> **Format**: carte-de-visite
>>
>> **Extent**: image
>> **Qualifier**: approximately
>> **Value**: 3.25; **Unit**: inches; **Type**: height
>> **Value**: 2.25; **Unit**: inches; **Type**: width
>>
>> **Extent**: sheet
>> **Qualifier**: approximately
>> **Value**: 4; **Unit**: inches; **Type**: height
>> **Value**: 2.5; **Unit**: inches; **Type**: width

> **Measurements display**: 24 1/4 x 38 1/4 inches; scale: 1 inch = 10 feet
> **Controlled fields**:
>> **Value**: 24.25; **Unit**: inches; **Type**: height
>> **Value**: 38.25; **Unit**: inches; **Type**: width
>> **Scale**: numeric; **Value**: 1; **Unit**: inches; **Equals Value**: 10; **Unit**: feet

> **Measurements display**: 29.8 x 20.3 cm (11 3/4 x 8 inches) (oval)
> **Controlled fields**:
>> **Shape**: oval
>> **Value**: 29.8; **Unit**: cm; **Type**: height
>> **Value**: 20.3; **Unit**: cm; **Type**: width

For Materials and Techniques

At minimum, one repeatable controlled field is recommended. In the example below, materials and techniques are both indexed in the same repeatable field.

Example

> **Materials and Techniques display**: etching and drypoint on laid paper
> **Controlled field**:
>> **Materials and Techniques**: ink • etching • drypoint • laid paper

Depending upon local requirements, materials and techniques may be indexed separately in the information system, but they should be available together for display.

Example

> **Materials and Techniques display**: engraving with watercolor on white laid paper
> **Controlled fields**:
>> **Materials**: ink • watercolor • laid paper
>> **Techniques**: engraving • painting

Additional controlled fields could include extent, qualifier, color, a subdivision of materials into medium and support, and a subdivision of techniques into process and implement.

Examples

> **Materials and Techniques display**: ink and tempera on vellum (illuminations), leather and silver (binding)
> **Controlled fields**:
>> **Extent**: folios and illuminations
>> **Materials**: ink • tempera • vellum
>> **Techniques**: calligraphy • painting
>>
>> **Extent**: binding
>> **Materials**: leather • silver

> **Materials and Techniques display**: pen and black ink and brown chalk on ivory-colored laid paper
> **Controlled fields**:
>> **Material**: ink | **Color**: black
>> **Material**: chalk | **Color**: brown
>> **Material**: laid paper | **Color**: ivory
>> **Techniques**: pen • drawing

For State and Edition

Most institutions will require only a free-text field for State and Edition because they do not need to retrieve that information. If controlled fields are required, they should contain all information pertinent to retrieval. Numbers and terms in controlled fields should be strictly controlled.

STATE

Suggested controlled fields for state are State Identification and Known States. Source should also be controlled.

Example

> **State display**: Bartsch 133, state 1 of 3
> **Controlled fields**:
> > **State identification**: 1
> > **Known states**: 3
> > **Source**: *The Illustrated Bartsch*. New York: Abaris Books, 1980, 39/1:269.

EDITION

Suggested controlled fields for edition are Impression Number, Edition Size, and Edition Number-name.

Examples

> **Edition display**: 5/125
> **Controlled fields**:
> > **Impression number**: 5
> > **Edition size**: 125

> **Edition display**: Millennium edition
> **Controlled fields**:
> > **Edition number-name**: Millennium edition

> **Edition display**: 10th edition
> **Controlled fields**:
> > **Edition number-name**: 10th edition

For Inscriptions

If retrieval on inscriptions is required, controlled fields could include the type of inscription, location on the work, and the typeface or letterform. The author, date, and language of the inscription could also be recorded in controlled fields. Important information contained in the inscription, such as the name of the artist, date of execution, subject matter, or title, should be indexed in the appropriate elements elsewhere in the Work Record.

Example

> **Inscription display**: signed and dated upper right: Rembrandt f. / 1635
> **Controlled fields**:
> > **Inscription types**: signed • dated
> > **Inscription location**: upper right
> > **Inscription author**: Rembrandt van Rijn (Dutch, 1606-1669)

For Facture

Facture may be described in a free-text field. Most institutions will not need controlled fields for information on the facture of works. Pertinent information, such as materials and techniques, should be indexed in appropriate elements elsewhere in the Work Record.

For Physical Description

Indexing of the physical description display may be important when cataloging decorative arts, including carpets, other textiles, wallpaper, ceramics, furniture, and architectural elements. If retrieval on specific categories of information is required, controlled fields should be used to index characteristics that are not indexed elsewhere, for example, the major motifs or patterns.

For Condition and Examination History

Museums and other repositories will typically require both free-text and controlled fields for condition and examination history. This information is generally not included in displays available to the public. See the discussion in the *Categories for Description of Works of Art.*

For Conservation and Treatment History

Most museums and other repositories need to maintain detailed records on conservation history, including free-text and controlled fields that document the dates, the names of conservators, and types of conservation applied. This information is generally not included in displays available to the public. See the discussion in the *Categories for Description of Works of Art.*

3.3.1.2.2 AUTHORITY FILE ELEMENTS

Ideally, terminology in the controlled fields should be stored in separate authority records. See further discussion in Part 1: Authority Files and Controlled Vocabularies and Part 3: Concept Authority. If linking to an authority file is not possible, terminology for indexing should be linked to a controlled list.

In the controlled indexing fields, a computer system that allows catalogers to use any term, either preferred or variant, in the authority file is the most effective. If working without such a system, catalogers should be consistent in using the preferred form of term or name used for indexing the physical description. See Part 3: Concept Authority for further discussion.

3.3.2 Examples

Examples of Work Records are included below. For additional examples, see the end of Part 1, the end of each chapter, and the CCO Web site. In the examples, *controlled* refers to values controlled by an authority file, controlled list, or other rules (for example, rules for recording dates). *Link* refers to a relationship between a Work Record and an Authority Record or between two Work Records. All links are controlled fields. In the examples that follow, Related Work Records are abbreviated for the sake of brevity. All Work Records should be as complete as possible. See the various chapters for discussions of individual metadata elements, whether they should be controlled, and the respective advantages of an authority file or a controlled list. In all examples in this manual, both within and at the end of each chapter, data values for repeatable fields are separated by bullet characters.

Figure 17

Work Record Linked to a Concept Authority Record: Engraving[1]

Required and recommended elements are marked with an asterisk.

Work Record

- **Class** *[controlled]*: prints and drawings • European art
- ***Work Type** *[link]*: engraving
- ***Title**: Apollo, Pan, and a Putto Blowing a Horn | **Title Type**: preferred
- ***Creator display**: Giorgio Ghisi (Italian, ca. 1520-1582), after a painting by Primaticcio
    *Role *[link]*: printmaker | *[link]*: Ghisi, Giorgio
- ***Creation Date**: 1560s | *[controlled]*: **Earliest**: 1560; **Latest**: 1569
- ***Subject** *[links to authorities]*: religion and mythology • landscape • Apollo • Pan • putto • competition • human figures • male • music • horn • Ovid (Roman, 43 BCE-17 CE) • *Metamorphoses*
- ***Current Location** *[link]*: Research Library, Getty Research Institute (Los Angeles, California, United States) | **ID** #2000.PR.2
- ***Measurements**: plate mark: 29.6 x 17 cm, folio: 30.7 x 18.3 cm
    [controlled]: **Extent**: plate mark; **Value**: 29.6; **Unit**: cm; **Type**: height | **Value**: 17; **Unit**: cm; **Type**: width | **Extent**: folio; **Value**: 30.7; **Unit**: cm; **Type**: height | **Value**: 18.3; **Unit**: cm; **Type**: width
- ***Materials and Techniques**: copper engraving on laid paper
    Material *[links]*: laid paper • black ink | **Technique** *[link]*: copper engraving
- **State**: 5th of 5
- **Description**: The subject of this print comes from Ovid's *Metamorphoses*, the musical competition between Pan and Apollo. The engraving is after a lost painting by Primaticcio in the vault of the fourth bay of the Galerie d'Ulysse at Fontainebleau. It is one of four prints based on compositions surrounding a central image of Venus and the three Fates.
- **Related Work**:
    Relationship Type *[controlled]*: after
    [link to Related Work]: Apollo, Pan, and Putto; painting; Francesco Primaticcio (Italian, 1504-1570); 1559-1560; lost, formerly in Galerie d'Ulysse, Fontainebleau (Ile-de-France, France)

Concept Authority Record

- ***Terms**:
    copper engraving (preferred)
    chalcography
    copper plate engraving
    copperplate engraving
- ***Note**: Process of engraving for printing using copper plates; replaced in the early 19th century by the use of more durable plates, either of steel or steel-faced copper.
- ***Hierarchical position** *[link]*:
    Activities Facet
    .... Processes and Techniques
    .... <printing processes>
    .... <intaglio printing processes>
    .... engraving (printing process)
    .... copper engraving (printing process)
- ***Source** *[link]*: *Art & Architecture Thesaurus* (1988-).

CREDIT: Giorgio Ghisi; *Apollo, Pan, and a Putto Blowing a Horn*. 1560s; copper engraving on laid paper. Research Library. The Getty Research Institute (Los Angeles, California), Special Collections, ID#2000.PR.2. © The J. Paul Getty Trust.

Figure 18
Work Record Linked to a Concept Authority Record: Japanese Screen[2]

Required and recommended elements are marked with an asterisk.

Work Record

- **Class** *[controlled]*: paintings • Asian art
- ***Work Type** *[link]*: screen
- ***Title**: Eight-Planked Bridge (Yatsuhashi) | **Title Type**: preferred
- ***Creator display**: Ogata Korin (Japanese, 1658-1716)
    *Role *[link]*: painter | *[link]*: Ogata Korin
- ***Creation Date**: probably done sometime between 1711 and 1716
    [controlled]: **Earliest**: 1711; **Latest**: 1716
- ***Subject** *[links to authorities]*: landscape • bridge • irises • love
  • longing • journeying • Ise Monogatari (Japanese literature, poems)
- ***Current Location** *[link]*: Metropolitan Museum of Art (New York,
  New York, United States) | **ID**: 53.7.1-2
- ***Measurements**: pair of six-panel folding screens; each 179.1 x
  371.5 cm (5 feet 10 1/2 inches x 12 feet 2 1/4 inches)
    [controlled]: **Extent**: parts; **Value**: 2; **Type**: count | **Extent**: each
    part; **Value**: 179.1; **Unit**: cm; **Type**: height | **Value**: 371.5; **Unit**:
    cm; **Type**: width | **Extent**: components; **Value**: 2; **Type**: count
- ***Materials and Techniques**: ink, color, and gold-leaf on paper, using
  tarashikomi (color blending technique)
    Material *[link]*: ink • paint • gold leaf • paper | **Technique** *[link]*:
    tarashikomi
- **Inscriptions**: right hand screen: Korin's signature with honorary title
  hokkyo; round seals read Masatoki
- **Style** *[link]*: Edo (Japanese)
- **Description**: Represents a popular episode in the 10th-century
  Ise Monogatari (The Tales of Ise) series of poems on love and
  journeying; in this episode, a young aristocrat comes to a place
  called Eight Bridges (Yatsuhashi) where a river branched into eight
  channels, each spanned by a bridge. He writes a poem of five lines
  about irises growing there. The poem expresses his longing for his
  wife left behind in the capital city.
- **Description Source** *[link]*: Metropolitan Museum of Art online.
  http://www.metmuseum.org (accessed February 1, 2005).

Concept Authority Record

- ***Term**:
    tarashikomi (preferred)
- ***Note**: A technique involving the
  pooling of pigments to create
  distinctive blurred effects. Color is
  applied with a wet brush and a second
  color is then applied before the first
  has dried. It was most often seen in
  Japanese Rimpa-style painting.
- ***Hierarchical position** *[link]*:
    Activities Facet
    .... Processes and Techniques
    .... painting techniques
    .... tarashikomi
- ***Source** *[link]*: *Art & Architecture
  Thesaurus* (1988-).

CREDIT: *Eight-Planked Bridge (Yatsuhashi).* Edo period (1615-1868), 18th century; Korin (Japanese,
1658-1716); Japan; Pair of six-panel folding screens; ink, color, and gold-leaf on paper; Each 70 1/2 x
12 ft. 2 1/4 in. (179.1 x 371.5 cm) The Metropolitan Museum of Art, Purchase, Louisa Eldridge
McBurney Gift, 1953; (53.7.1-2); Photograph © 1993 The Metropolitan Museum of Art.

Work Record

- **Class** *[controlled]*: architecture • European art
- ***Work Type** *[link]*: observation tower
- ***Title**: Eiffel Tower | **Title Type**: preferred
  Title: Tour Eiffel | **Title Type**: alternate
  Title: Three-Hundred-Metre Tower | **Title Type**: former
- ***Creator display**: architect: Gustave Eiffel (French, 1832-1923)
  *Role *[link]*: architect | *[link]*: Eiffel, Gustave
- ***Creation Date**: 1887-1889 | *[controlled]*: **Earliest**: 1887; **Latest**: 1889
- ***Subject** *[links to authorities]*: architecture • industrial exposition • International Exposition of 1889 (Paris, France)
- **Style** *[link]*: Belle Époque
- ***Current Location** *[link]*: Paris (France)
- ***Measurements**: 300 m (height) (984 feet)
  [controlled]: **Value**: 300; **Unit**: m; **Type**: height
- ***Materials and Techniques**: wrought iron, exposed iron construction
  Material *[link]*: wrought iron • structural iron | **Technique** *[link]*: exposed construction
- **Description**: Commission was awarded by competition; the competition sought a plan for a monument for the International Exposition of 1889, celebrating the centenary of the French Revolution. The tower is built almost entirely of open-lattice wrought iron. It was the entrance gateway to the exposition.

Concept Authority Record

- ***Terms**:
  wrought iron (preferred)
  wrought-iron
- ***Note**: Iron alloy of fibrous nature made by melting white cast iron, passing an oxidizing flame over it, and rolling it into a mass; valued for its corrosion resistance and ductility.
- ***Hierarchical position** *[controlled]*:
  Materials Facet
  .... Materials
  .... inorganic material
  .... metal
  .... iron alloy
  .... wrought iron
- ***Source** *[link]*: *Art & Architecture Thesaurus* (1988-).

CREDIT: Eiffel Tower, Paris, France © 2005 Patricia Harpring. All rights reserved.

Work Record

- **Class** *[controlled]*: decorative arts • costume jewelry • Egyptian art
- ***Work Type** *[link]*: pectoral
- ***Title**: Pectoral with the Name of Senwosret II I **Title Type**: preferred
- ***Creator display**: unknown ancient Egyptian, Twelfth Dynasty
  - ***Role** *[link]*: artist *[link]*: unknown ancient Egyptian
- ***Creation Date**: reigns of Senwosret II-Amenemhat III, ca. 1897-ca. 1878 BCE
  - *[controlled]*: **Earliest**: -1907; **Latest**: -1868
- ***Subject** *[links to authorities]*: religion and mythology • human figures • apparel • adornment • Senwosret II (Egyptian king) • Sit-hathor-yunet (Egyptian princess) • falcons • water • ankh • life • cobras • Nekhbet (Egyptian deity) • Udjo (Egyptian deity) • Heh (Egyptian deity)
- ***Current Location** *[link]*: Metropolitan Museum (New York, New York, United States) I **ID**: 16.1.3
- **Discovery Location** *[link]*: Al Lahun (Upper Egypt region, Egypt)
- ***Measurements**: length of pectoral, excluding necklace: 8.3 cm (3 1/4 inches)
  - **Extent** *[controlled]*: pectoral; **Value**: 8.3; **Unit**: cm; **Type**: length
- ***Materials and Techniques**: gold, carnelian, feldspar, garnet, and turquoise; cloisonné
  - **Material** *[link]*: carnelian • gold • feldspar • garnet • turquoise I **Technique** *[link]*: cloisonné
- **Inscriptions**: hieroglyphic of the design reads: the god of the rising sun grants life and dominion over all that the sun encircles for one million one hundred thousand years [that is, eternity] to King Khakheperre [Senwosret II].
- **Style** *[link]*: Egyptian • Middle Kingdom
- **Culture** *[link]*: Egyptian
- **Description**: The cloisonné pectoral is inlaid with 372 carefully cut pieces of semiprecious stones. The focus of the pectoral is the throne name of King Senwosret II. It was found among the jewelry of Princess Sit-hathor-yunet in her underground tomb beside the pyramid of Senwosret II. Jewelry worn by royal women during the Middle Kingdom was symbolic of concepts and myths surrounding Egyptian royalty. Jewelry imbued a royal woman with superhuman powers and thus enabled her to support the king in his role as guarantor of divine order on earth.
- **Description Source** *[link to Source Record]*: Metropolitan Museum of Art online. http://www.metmuseum.org (accessed February 1, 2005).

Concept Authority Record

- ***Terms**:
  - carnelian (preferred)
  - cornelian
- ***Note**: A translucent red or orange variety of chalcedony, containing iron impurities. It is often used for seals and signet rings.
- ***Hierarchical position** *[link]*:
  - Materials Facet
  - .... Materials
  - .... inorganic material
  - .... mineral
  - .... quartz
  - .... chalcedony
  - .... carnelian
- ***Source** *[link]*: *Art & Architecture Thesaurus* (1988-).

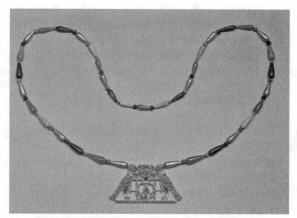

CREDIT: *Pectoral with the Name of Senwosret II*, ca. 1897-1878 B.C.E.; Dynasty 12, reigns of Senwosret II-Amenemhat III; Middle Kingdom; Egyptian; Lahun; Gold, carnelian, feldspar, garnet, turquoise; L. of pectoral 3 1/4 in. (8.3 cm); The Metropolitan Museum of Art, Rogers Fund and Henry Walters Gift, 1916 (16.1.3). Photograph © 1983 The Metropolitan Museum of Art.

Figure 21
Work Record Linked to a Concept Authority Record: Byzantine Architecture
Required and recommended elements are marked with an asterisk.

Work Record

- **Class** *[controlled]*: architecture
- ***Work Type** *[link]*: basilica • cathedral
- ***Title**: Saint Mark's Basilica | **Title Type**: preferred
  Title: Basilica di San Marco | **Title Type**: alternate
  Title: San Marco | **Title Type**: alternate
  Title: St. Mark's | **Title Type**: alternate
- ***Creator display**: probably designed by Italian and Byzantine architects
  *Role *[controlled]*: architect | *[link]*: unknown Italian
  *Role *[controlled]*: architect | *[link]*: unknown Byzantine
- ***Creation Date**: current structure completed in 1071
  [controlled]: **Earliest**: 1042; **Latest**: 1071
- ***Subject** *[link to authorities]*: Saint Mark • pilgrimage • worship • cathedral
- ***Current Location** *[link]*: Venice (Italy)
- ***Measurements**: diameter of central dome: 13.8 m (42 feet)
  [controlled]: **Extent**: central dome; **Value**: 13.8; **Unit**: m; **Type**: diameter
- ***Materials and Techniques**: Greek cross plan surmounted by five domes; bearing masonry construction and timber frame domes; richly decorated interior and exterior with sculpture, mosaics and ceremonial objects
  Material *[link]*: masonry | **Technique** *[link]*: load-bearing walls • Greek cross plan
- **Style** *[link]*: Byzantine
- **Culture**: Italian • Byzantine
- **Description**: Original church was begun in 829 (consecrated in 832) to house the remains of St. Mark, which had been brought from Alexandria. St. Mark thus replaced St. Theodore as the patron saint of Venice. The first basilica burned in 976 during an uprising against doge Pietro Candiano IV. Present basilica built by his successor, Doge Domenico Contarini and completed in 1071. It is believed that both Byzantine and Italian architects and craftsmen were responsible for the construction and decoration. The basilica stands beside the Doges' Palace and served as the doge's chapel. It did not become the cathedral church of Venice until 1807.
- **Description Source** *[link]*: Gloag, *Western Architecture* (1958); **Page**: 101 ff.

Concept Authority Record

- ***Terms**:
  Greek cross plan (preferred)
  Greek-cross plan
- ***Note**: Refers to buildings in which the plan is shaped like a Greek cross, with a square central mass and four arms of equal length. The Greek-cross plan was widely used in Byzantine architecture and in Western churches inspired by Byzantine examples.
- ***Hierarchical position** *[controlled]*:
  Physical Attributes Facet
  .... Attributes and Properties
  .... <building plan attributes>
  .... Greek cross plan
- ***Source** *[controlled]*: *Art & Architecture Thesaurus* (1988-).

CREDIT: St. Mark's Basilica, Venice, Italy © Patricia Harpring 2005. All rights reserved.

Notes

1. This example is intended to illustrate metadata elements discussed in this manual. Field names and data values in the example do not necessarily represent the record for this object in the Getty Research Institute Research Library's information system.

2. This example is intended to illustrate metadata elements discussed in this manual. Field names and data values in the example do not necessarily represent the record for this object in the Metropolitan Museum's information system.

3. This example is intended to illustrate metadata elements discussed in this manual. Field names and data values in the example do not necessarily represent the record for this object in the Metropolitan Museum's information system.

Chapter *4*

Stylistic, Cultural, and Chronological Information

Style / Culture / Date

4.1   ABOUT STYLISTIC, CULTURAL, AND CHRONOLOGICAL INFORMATION

4.1.1   Discussion

This chapter introduces the Style, Culture, and Date elements that refer to a work's stylistic characteristics, cultural origins, and date of design or creation.

Style

The Style element identifies the named, defined style, historical or artistic period, movement, group, or school whose characteristics are represented in the work being cataloged. Designations of style, period, group, or movement are derived from scholarly tradition within given fields of expertise. The terminology places the work in the context of other works created in the same or a similar style.

Often styles or periods take their names from a technique used in a particular place at a certain time. Terms such as *Red-figure*, *Black-figure*, and *Pointillist* are examples of styles based on technique. Some terms, such as *Surrealist*, may refer to a style or artistic movement not necessarily tied to a particular period or a single technique. Stylistic similarities may be the basis for the concept of school, which can refer to movements such as the American *Ashcan School* or to artistic families or groups such as the Japanese *Kano School*.

Terms referring to style or period may be based on historical eras and thus have a chronological reference; for example, periods may be delimited by dates associated with certain rulers or governments. The names of dynasties, such as *Ming*, are used for artistic periods in China, Japan, and Egypt. Ruling families provide names for periods and styles such as *Tudor* or *Stuart*. A style term may refer to the reign of a specific monarch, such as *Louis XIV, Napoleonic, Victorian,* or *Ptolemaic.* Certain broad terms, such as *Ancient Greek, Medieval,* or *Renaissance,* have generally accepted chronological boundaries; they may be subdivided into well-known secondary eras, for example, *Archaic, Classical, Hellenistic.*

For further discussion of style, see *Categories for the Description of Works of Art: Styles/Periods/Groups/Movements.*

Culture

The Culture element contains the name of the culture, people, or nationality from which the work originated. This element is useful to institutions that wish to note the culture associated with the work in order to place the work in the context of other works created in the same culture.

Nationality and culture are also included in elements of creator information, detailed in Chapter 2: Creator Information and in Part 3: Personal and Corporate Name Authority. If you wish to avoid the redundancy of recording culture-nationality with both the creator and the work, record the nationality or culture with the creator information (instead of in the Culture element discussed in this chapter), even when the creator is unknown. Unknown creators are discussed in Chapter 2: Creator Information.

Given that the culture that produced the work is nearly always the same as the creator's culture, the Culture element in this chapter may seem redundant; however, it may be a necessary element for some institutions. It is recognized that, for unknown creators, some institutions may choose to leave the creator fields blank and construct headings for display, for example, *unknown Italian* or *Italian.* Where such local practice exists, this Culture element becomes critical for works with unknown creators. It is generally not necessary to enter a value in the Culture element when the work has a known creator, such as Matisse, who was French (because the nationality/culture of Matisse would be recorded in the authority).

Date

The Date element records the date or range of dates associated with the creation, design, production, presentation, performance, construction, or alteration of the work or its components. This chapter does not deal with the date of the surrogate visual image, although it is recognized that visual resources collections will typically require fields to document dates for images. See also Part 1: Works and Images and Chapter 9: View Information: View Date.

The Creation Date for a work of art may simply be a single year. In other cases, a work of art or architecture may have more complex dates. It may have been created over a span of time or may have multiple dates associated with phases or activities surrounding its creation. For example, a manuscript may have been illuminated in one century and bound in another. Architectural structures may have been created over a period of years, decades, or centuries, often completed in multiple building campaigns during different periods of time. Other types of works may have been completed in several separate and discrete stages. For example, the dates of a photographic negative and the prints made from it can differ widely (for example, negatives, such as those of Ansel Adams, are often reprinted). Some types of works, such as ephemeral street art or installations, may have a finite range of dates associated with their existence. Performance art or happenings may require a date more specific than the year; they may have taken place on a specific day and time of day.

Uncertainty will often be a factor in recording a date. Approximate dates may represent a range of a few years or a broad range of a century or more. Dates may be qualified with terms such as *circa* (*ca.*), *about*, *before*, or *after* (for example, *after 1611* or *ca. 830 BCE*). Dates may also be recorded by century (for example, *12th century*).

Specificity

Style and culture should be recorded at the most specific level appropriate, keeping in mind the scope of the collection, available information, and the expertise of the cataloger and intended users; a hierarchical authority file should be used to provide access through broader concepts. For example, if a narrow, specific term such as *Hadrianic* or *Norse* is used for style/period, the concept authority would provide access to the broader terms such as *Roman* or *Scandinavian* to facilitate retrieval and understanding of context.

In the free-text date field, the date of the work should be recorded with the greatest level of specificity known, but expressed in a way that conveys the correct level of uncertainty or ambiguity to the end user (for example, *ca. 1820*). The indexing fields, earliest and latest dates, should indicate the broadest span relevant for the free-text date (for example, *Earliest: 1815* and *Latest: 1825*). The Earliest and Latest Dates should not be visible to the end user, but should be used only in record retrieval.

Organization of the Data

Style and culture should be recorded in repeatable controlled fields. Terminology for both should be controlled by an authority file or controlled list. See Part 3: Concept Authority, which could be used to control the terms for style and culture. Style is not a required element. Culture is not required, except in the situation discussed above, where an institution does not record creator information for unknown creators, but instead wishes to construct displays for unknown creators by using culture and other elements.

Date of Creation is a required element. It is recommended that both display and indexing fields be included. Dates can be recorded in a free-text field, which should then be indexed using two numbers to delimit the beginning and end of the implied date span.

Example

Display Date: late 14th century
Earliest: 1375; **Latest**: 1399

Sets of dates should be repeatable (for example, some institutions will differentiate dates of design, construction, and so forth in separate sets).

Recommended Elements

A list of the elements discussed in this chapter appears below. Required elements are noted. Display may be a free-text field or concatenated from controlled fields.

Style
    Style Qualifier
Culture
Display Date (required)
    Earliest Date
    Latest Date
    Date Qualifier

About the Examples

The examples throughout this chapter are for illustration only. Local practice may vary. The examples tend to show the fullest possible use of display and indexing fields, which may not be necessary for visual resources collections and some other institutions.

4.1.2   Terminology

4.1.2.1   *Sources for Terminology*

4.1.2.1.1 STYLE AND CULTURE

Style and culture terminology should be controlled by using an authority file or controlled lists. The terms used for each may often be derived from the same sources, and may thus overlap. Sources of terminology may include the following

Getty Vocabulary Program. *Art & Architecture Thesaurus* (AAT). Los Angeles: J. Paul Getty Trust, 1988-. http://www.getty.edu/research/ conducting_research/vocabularies/aat/. (Especially the Styles and Periods hierarchy).

Library of Congress Authorities. *Library of Congress Subject Headings.* Washington, DC: Library of Congress, 2005. http://authorities .loc.gov/.

Grove Dictionary of Art Online. New York: Grove's Dictionaries, 2003. http://www.groveart.com/.

Levinson, David, ed. *Encyclopedia of World Cultures.* Boston: G. K. Hall, 1991-1996.

4.1.2.1.2 DATE

Date information must be formatted consistently to allow retrieval. Local rules should be in place. Suggested formats are available in the ISO standard and *W3C XML Schema Part 2.*[1]

ISO 8601:2004 Numeric representation of Dates and Time. *Data elements and interchange formats. Information interchange. Representation of dates and times.* Geneva, Switzerland: International Organization for Standardization, 2004.

XML Schema Part 2: Datatypes, 2001. http://www.w3.org/TR/ xmlschema-2/.

4.1.2.2 *Choice of Terminology*

4.1.2.2.1 CONSISTENCY

Consistent terminology for style and culture elements is essential to efficient retrieval. Consistency in data format within the Date elements used for retrieval is especially critical. Consistency is less important, but still desirable, in a free-text note than in a controlled field. Although uncontrolled terminology should be accommodated, terminology that is consistent with the terms in controlled fields is nonetheless recommended for the sake of clarity. Consistent style, grammar, and syntax are recommended.

4.1.2.2.2 USE OF AN AUTHORITY RECORD

If possible, style and culture terminology and definitions (for example, scope notes) should be stored in a hierarchical authority file, which is linked to the Work Record. See Part 3: Concept Authority. If it is not possible to use an authority file, terms may be taken from controlled lists.

4.2 CATALOGING RULES

4.2.1 Rules for Style

4.2.1.1 *Brief Rules for Style*

Record one or more terms that denote the style, historical period, group, movement, or school whose characteristics are represented in the work being cataloged. If necessary, write a fuller description of the style of the work in the Description element (see Chapter 8).

Adjectival Forms

Generally use the adjectival form of terms for style and period.

> *Examples*
>
>> **Style**: Byzantine
>>
>> **Style**: Constantinopolitan
>>
>> **Style**: Medieval
>>
>> **Style**: Baroque
>>
>> **Style**: Impressionist
>>
>> **Style**: Neo-Pop

Record nouns or gerunds when they are used as adjectives, as appropriate.

> *Examples*
>
>> **Style**: Early Bronze Age
>>
>> **Style**: Black-figure
>>
>> **Style**: Orientalizing

Alternatively, the noun form of terms (for example, *Impressionism* rather than *Impressionist*) may be used to accommodate local practice. Be consistent.

Capitalization and Abbreviations

Capitalize terms for styles and periods. Some exceptions occur, for example, with very broad designations (such as *protohistoric*); use capitalization as indicated in your source (for example, the AAT). Avoid abbreviations.

> *Examples*
>
> **Style**: Old Kingdom (Egyptian)
>
> **Style**: Renaissance
>
> **Style**: Pre-Raphaelite
>
> **Style**: Postmodern
>
> **Style**: Cameroonian
>
> **Style**: Nayarit
>
> **Style**: Western Arctic Inuit
>
> **Style**: protohistoric

Language of the Terms

Use terminology in the language of the catalog record (English in the United States), except in cases where no exact English-language equivalent exists. Use diacritics as required.

> *Examples*
>
> **Style**: Abstract Expressionist
>
> **Style**: Louis XVI
>
> **Style**: Bäzäklik
>
> **Style**: Ch'ien-lung
>
> **Style**: Ya' Furid

4.2.1.2 Additional Recommendations for Style

4.2.1.2.1 VARIOUS TYPES OF STYLE TERMS

Terms for style, period, group, or movement vary depending on the discipline and the kind of work being cataloged. When the meaning of a style term overlaps with data designated in another element (for example, culture or date, as described below), record the pertinent information in that element as well.

Referring to Visual Appearance

Record a style term if the visual appearance, configuration of artistic elements, method of creation, geographic reference, and time frame of creation of the work correspond to the definition of a particular style. For definitions of the individual styles, see the AAT.

> *Examples*
>
> [for a drawing by Parmigianino]
>
> **Style**: Mannerist

[for a building by Charles Moore]
> **Style**: Postmodern

[for porcelain figures by the Doccia porcelain factory]
> **Style**: Rococo

[for a painting by Claude Monet]
> **Style**: Impressionist

[for a 19th-century house]
> **Style**: Gothic Revival

Referring to a Technique

If the style is defined by a medium or technique, repeat the information in Materials and Techniques (see Chapter 3).

Example

[for a Panathenaic amphora, *Black-figure* refers to technique]
> **Styles**: Black-figure • Attic

[for an 11th-century Chinese painting, style term refers to both medium and subject][2]
> **Style**: Ink-bamboo

Referring to Theme or Subject of the Work

If the style term refers explicitly or implicitly to the subject or other thematic or visual content of the work, repeat the information in the Subject element (see Chapter 6).

Examples

[for a Scythian ornament, reference to subject is explicit]
> **Style**: Animal Style

[for a painting by Caspar David Friedrich, reference to subject is implicit]
> **Style**: Romantic

Referring to a Place

If the style term refers to a geographic or geopolitical entity, repeat the information in the Location element (see Chapter 5). Such style terms may also overlap with culture (see Culture below).

Examples

[for a 12th-century tomb]
> **Style**: Catalan

[for an 18th-century painted chest]
> **Style**: French Colonial

Referring to a Period

If the style or period term refers to a chronological period, repeat the information in the Date element.

Examples

[for a Kouros statue]

Style: Archaic (Greek)

[for an ancient Egyptian crown]

Style: Middle Kingdom (Egyptian)

For the purposes of cataloging, a century is not a period per se; do not record centuries in the Style/Period element. Use the Date element for recording centuries (for example, *14th century*).

Referring to a Ruler

If the style or period term refers to the reign of a ruler or to a dynasty, you may repeat the information in fields for donor or patron, if your institution captures such information (see Chapter 2: Creator Information).

Examples

[for a 10th-century Indian statue of Shiva]

Style: Chola

[for 14th-century Japanese armor]

Style: Kamakura

[for a 16th-century carpet by Maqsud of Kashan]

Styles: Safavid • Persian

[for an ancient Roman building]

Style: Hadrianic

Referring to a Cultural Group

If the term for style or period refers to a culture or group, it will probably overlap with the Culture element, which is also discussed in this chapter. Institutions that require culture should repeat this information in the Culture element.

Examples

[for a Pre-Columbian vessel]

Style: Maya

[for an African mask from the Congo]

Style: Chokwe

4.2.1.2.2 GROUPS OF WORKS

For a group of items, include all the styles represented in the group. If there are too many to list them all, include the most important within the context of the group or the most typical styles evident in the group.

Example

[for a group of pastel drawings]

Styles: Impressionist • Post-Impressionist

4.2.1.2.3 UNCERTAINTY

When in doubt regarding the specific style, period, group, or movement to which a work belongs, choose a broader term about which you are certain. For example, use the broader term *Roman* if it is uncertain whether the period is *Monarchic* or *Early Imperial*.

4.2.1.2.4 QUALIFIERS OF STYLE/PERIOD

Some institutions may wish to distinguish if the term refers to the style, period, group, movement, or dynasty, thereby differentiating between each type. Qualifiers may be used for this purpose. Given the overlap between these concepts, assigning qualifiers is often difficult and unnecessary, unless retrieval is required based on these distinctions. The qualifier would best be recorded in the Concept Authority rather than in individual Work Records.

Example

[for a chair]

> **Style**: Arts and Crafts
> **Qualifier**: movement

4.2.2 Rules for Culture

4.2.2.1 *Brief Rules for Culture*

Record the culture or nationality from which the work originated. See Part 3: Personal and Corporate Name Authority: Nationality for further discussion on how to record culture and nationality.

Adjectival Forms

Generally use the adjectival form of a proper noun for a culture, region, nation, or continent.

Examples

> **Culture**: Celtic
> **Culture**: Italian
> **Culture**: Siberian
> **Culture**: African
> **Culture**: Pre-Columbian
> **Culture**: Middle Eastern

In rare cases, when there is no commonly used adjectival form for a term, use the noun form.

> *Example*
>
>> **Culture**: Asia Minor

Capitalization and Abbreviations

Capitalize terms for culture and nationality. Avoid abbreviations.

> *Examples*
>
>> **Culture**: Abbevillian
>>
>> **Culture**: French
>>
>> **Culture**: Sienese
>>
>> **Culture**: East Asian
>>
>> **Culture**: Native American

Language of the Terms

Use terms in the language of the catalog record (English in the United States), except in cases where no exact English-language equivalent exists. Use diacritics as required.

> *Examples*
>
>> **Culture**: Russian
>>
>> **Culture**: Il Chamus
>>
>> **Culture**: Canaliño

4.2.2.2 Additional Recommendations for Culture

4.2.2.2.1 VARIOUS TYPES OF TERMS FOR CULTURE

Terms for culture or nationality may be adjectival forms of a name for a tribe, band, ethnic group, linguistic group, cultural group, civilization, religious group, nation, country, city-state, continent, or general region. For further discussion of issues surrounding culture and nationality, see Part 3: Personal and Corporate Name Authority.

> *Examples*
>
> [terms refer to a culture]
>
>> **Culture**: Celtic
>>
>> **Culture**: Khoikhoi
>>
>> **Culture**: Sioux
>
> [terms refer to a nation, country, or city-state, present or historical]
>
>> **Culture**: Italian
>>
>> **Culture**: Burgundian
>>
>> **Culture**: Egyptian
>>
>> **Culture**: Sienese

[terms refer to a continent]

    Culture: African

    Culture: Asian

[terms refer to an ethnicity or racial group]

    Culture: Hispanic

    Culture: Polynesian

[terms refer to a religious group]

    Culture: Islamic

    Culture: Buddhist

4.2.2.2.2 GROUPS OF WORKS

For a group of items, include all the cultures represented in the group. If there are too many to list them all, include the most important or the most typical cultures evident in the group.

4.2.2.2.3 UNCERTAINTY

When in doubt about which specific culture or nationality produced a work, choose a broader concept about which you are certain. For example, use the more general *Western Sudanese* if it is uncertain whether the culture is *Dogon* or *Bamana*.

4.2.2.2.4 UNKNOWN CREATORS

Record unknown creators in the Creator elements (see Chapter 2: Creator Information). Alternatively, when local practice forbids this, if the creator of the work is unknown and the creator field is not filled in, the Culture element is required.

4.2.2.2.5 OVERLAP WITH STYLE

Because a culture may have a recognizable style, the terminology used to describe the culture may also be recorded in the Style element (see above).

4.2.3 Rules for Date

4.2.3.1 *Brief Rules for Date*

Recording the date of either design or creation is required. In the Display Date, record a year, a span of years, or a phrase that describes the specific or approximate date when the work was designed or created. In Earliest and Latest Dates, record years that delimit the span stated or implied in the Display Date. Earliest and Latest Date will be hidden from end users.

Example

    Display Date: ca. 1750

      Earliest: 1745; **Latest**: 1755

Use the proleptic Gregorian calendar, which is produced by extending the Gregorian calendar to dates preceding its official introduction. See also Gregorian and Other Calendars, below.

Format

In the Display Date, use natural word order. For Earliest and Latest Dates, record appropriate numbers following ISO 8061 or *W3C XML Schema Part 2*.

> *Example*
>
> > **Display Date**: completed between 1950 and 1952
> > **Earliest**: 1950; **Latest**: 1952

Capitalization and Abbreviation

Do not capitalize words other than proper nouns or period names. Avoid abbreviations, except with *ca.* (for circa), the numbers in century or dynasty designations (for example, *17th century*), and *BCE* and *CE*.

> *Examples*
>
> > **Display Date**: constructed ca. 1730-ca. 1750
> > **Earliest**: 1725; **Latest**: 1755
>
> > **Display Date**: 17th century
> > **Earliest**: 1600; **Latest**: 1699
>
> > **Display Date**: New Kingdom, 18th dynasty (1404-1365 BCE)
> > **Earliest**: -1404; **Latest**: -1365

Include all digits for both years in a span; for example, with four-digit years, do not abbreviate the second year (for example, record *1780-1795*, not *1780-95*).

Language

In the Display Date, use ordinal numbers (for example, *4th*) and Arabic numbers (for example, *1959*), as appropriate. Express words and phrases in the language of the catalog record (English in the United States), except in rare cases where no English-language equivalent exists or where the foreign term is most commonly used, such as with the name of a period. Use diacritics as required.

4.2.3.2 *Additional Recommendations for Date*

4.2.3.2.1 SYNTAX: DISPLAY DATES

If a specific date is known, record the year. If a span of dates is applicable (as when a work was completed over several years), record the year beginning the span, followed by a dash and the year ending the span.

> *Examples*
>
> > **Display Date**: 1944
> > **Earliest**: 1944; **Latest**: 1944
>
> > **Display Date**: 1821-1826
> > **Earliest**: 1821; **Latest**: 1826

To express uncertainty or otherwise clarify the dates, place editorial commentary before the years (for example, *ca.*, *designed*, and the like) when possible. Use natural word order.

Examples

> **Display Date**: ca. 1610
> > **Earliest**: 1605; **Latest**: 1615

> **Display Date**: designed 1911 or 1912
> > **Earliest**: 1911; **Latest**: 1912

> **Display Date**: probably late 12th century
> > **Earliest**: 1150; **Latest**: 1220

4.2.3.2.2 SYNTAX: EARLIEST AND LATEST DATES

Years

For Earliest and Latest Dates for retrieval, record years without commas or other punctuation, except for the dash, which is used to express negative numbers for dates BCE. Use four digits for most years. If possible, for years that require fewer than four digits, follow the standards, which suggest inserting leading zeroes (for example, *0009*). Dates BCE may require more than four digits (for example, *-10000*).

Examples

[for a four-digit year CE]

> **Display Date**: 1997
> > **Earliest**: 1997; **Latest**: 1997

[for a date BCE]

> **Display Date**: 12-9 BCE
> > **Earliest**: -0012; **Latest**: -0009

Day and Time

Generally, recording the year a work was created is specific enough for good retrieval; for ephemeral art or performances, however, record the precise day and time, if possible. Use the following syntax: *YYYY-MM-DD* (year, month, day, separated by dashes), if possible. Format time as *hh:mm:ss* (hours, minutes, seconds, separated by colons). The standards suggest alternate possibilities. You may use an alternative syntax if you are consistent and it is compliant with the standards.

Examples

[for an ephemeral installation]

> **Display Date**: 1 January through 25 May 2000
> > **Earliest**: 2000-01-01; **Latest**: 2000-05-25

[for performance art, includes time]

> **Display Date**: 5 November 1983, midnight-2:30 pm
> > **Earliest**: 1983-11-05 00:00:00; **Latest**: 1983-11-05 14:30:00

TIME ZONE

A date and time designation as written above is assumed to be in a local time zone. There is no international standard for abbreviations for civil time zones such as PDT (Pacific Daylight Time) or CET (Central European Time). If your institution wishes to record the time zone, be consistent. In order to indicate that a time is measured in Universal Time (UTC, which has replaced Greenwich Mean Time), the standards suggest appending a capital letter *Z* (for *zero meridian*) to a time, as in *14:30:00Z*. Local times are then recorded as plus or minus UTC (for example, U.S. and Canadian Eastern Standard Time is the UTC minus five hours). See the pertinent standards for further guidance.

4.2.3.2.3 DATES BCE AND CE

In the display date, use *BCE* (Before Common Era) to indicate dates before the year 1 in the proleptic Gregorian calendar.

> *Examples*
>
> [for a Greek amphora]
> > **Display Date**: 463 BCE
> > > **Earliest**: -0463; **Latest**: -0463
>
> [for a Chinese sculpture, where date is a span in BCE]
> > **Display Date**: 221-206 BCE
> > > **Earliest**: -0221; **Latest**: -0206

For dates after the year 1, do not include the designation *CE* (Current Era), except where confusion may occur because either the span of dates begins *BCE* and ends *CE* (for example, *75 BCE-10 CE*) or the date is within the first few centuries of the Current Era. Do not use *BC* (Before Christ) or *AD* (Anno Domini). Indicate dates *BCE* with negative numbers in earliest and latest dates.

> *Examples*
>
> [for an Indian bracelet, where date is a span in BCE and CE]
> > **Display Date**: 15 BCE-20 CE
> > > **Earliest**: -0015; **Latest**: 0020
>
> [for a Roman monumental arch]
> > **Display Date**: 312-315 CE
> > > **Earliest**: 0312; **Latest**: 0315

Dates "Years Ago" or "Before Present"

For very ancient works, artifacts, and in certain other disciplines (for example, in pre-Columbian studies), *BCE* is often not appropriate. Use the phrases *years ago* or *before present* if your source indicates age relative to the present rather than an absolute date. Do not abbreviate designations (do not, for example, use *y.a.* or *B.P.*).

> *Example*
>
> [for rock carvings in Jinmium, Australia]
> > **Display Date**: created about 75,000 years ago
> > > **Earliest**: -76000; **Latest**: -70000

For Earliest and Latest Dates, translate the dates into the proleptic Gregorian calendar. Use an appropriate calibration table, if possible. Alternatively, if your computer system can accept multiple dating systems, record the dates as given in the source and flag them as *years ago* or *before present*.[3]

4.2.3.2.4 GREGORIAN AND OTHER CALENDARS

In general, record dates in the Display Date according to the proleptic Gregorian calendar. If your source provides a date in another calendar (for example, Julian, Napoleonic, or Islamic calendars), record it in the Display Date element, clearly designating the alternate calendar. Also include the year in the proleptic Gregorian calendar to avoid confusion. Index the dates in the Earliest and Latest Dates elements using the proleptic Gregorian calendar.

Examples

[for a Persian carpet, expressed according to the Islamic lunar calendar]

Display Date: 946 anno Hegirae (1540 CE)
Earliest: 1540; **Latest**: 1540

[for a French print, in the French revolutionary calendar]

Display Date: année II de la Rèpublique (1794 CE)
Earliest: 1794; **Latest**: 1794

4.2.3.2.5 SPECIFICITY: YEAR OF COMPLETION

Record the year of completion, if known. If the Display Date is a single year, put that year in both Earliest and Latest Dates. Do not leave a field blank.

Examples

[for a painting]

Display Date: 1862
Earliest: 1862; **Latest**: 1862

[for a skyscraper]

Display Date: 1976
Earliest: 1976; **Latest**: 1976

If the single year does not refer to the year of completion, explain the significance of the year in the Display Date. In Earliest and Latest Dates, record the estimated span of time during which the creation of the work took place.

Examples

[for a Korean temple]

Display Date: construction began in 689
Earliest: 0689; **Latest**: 0720

[for a church completed in the 17th century]

Display Date: dedicated in 1643
Earliest: 1550; **Latest**: 1643

4.2.3.2.6 SPECIFICITY: SPANS OF YEARS

For architecture and other works that were constructed over a period of time, express the dates as a span of years, if known. Explain the significance of the span in the Display Date.

> *Example*
>
> [for a fortified complex]
>
> > **Display Date**: constructed 1378-1485
> > **Earliest**: 1378; **Latest**: 1485

Also record a span of dates when the date of design and production are separated by a period of time.

> *Example*
>
> [for a sculpture]
>
> > **Display Date**: designed in 1462, cast in 1469
> > **Earliest**: 1462; **Latest**: 1469

For ongoing works, such as an interactive Web site, record the date when the work was begun. For the latest date, estimate the end of a broad span during which the work could continue.

> *Example*
>
> [for a Web site]
>
> > **Display Date**: begun in 2004
> > **Earliest**: 2004; **Latest**: 2054

4.2.3.2.7 SPECIFICITY: UNCERTAIN AND APPROXIMATE DATES

If the specific year or years is not known, record dates with the greatest accuracy known. In the guidelines below, the conventions are arranged from greatest level of accuracy to the least; use the greatest possible level of accuracy, based on the information at hand.

Probably

If there is doubt among scholars regarding the date of a work, indicate this in the Display Date by using the word *probably* or a question mark. Index such dates with Earliest and Latest Dates representing an appropriate span based on available information. In the example below, for example, a span of one year on either side of 1937 was allowed.

> *Example*
>
> [for a Mexican costume]
>
> > **Display Date**: probably 1937
> > **Earliest**: 1936; **Latest**: 1938

Or

If the date of a work is known to be one particular year or another, indicate this in the Display Date by using the word *or.*

Example

[for an engraving]

Display Date: 1568 or 1569
Earliest: 1568; **Latest**: 1569

Circa

If the precise date is unknown, preface the year with *ca.* (for *circa*) or *about*. Estimate Earliest and Latest Dates based on available information about the work and conventions surrounding various historical periods.

Examples

[for a photograph]

Display Date: ca. 1935
Earliest: 1930; **Latest**: 1940

[for an ancient palace]

Display Date: ca. 500 BCE
Earliest: -0550; **Latest**: -0450

For works produced within the last few centuries, use a ten-year span for approximated (*ca.*) Earliest and Latest Dates. For example, subtract five years from earliest and add five years to latest to create a ten-year span. Thus *ca. 1860* could be indexed as *Earliest: 1855; Latest: 1865*. For ancient works, use a 100-year span. For example, *ca. 1200 BCE* could be indexed as *Earliest: -1250; Latest: -1150*. Alter these recommendations to allow an appropriately greater or lesser span if warranted by available information.

If *ca.* is used with a span of dates, repeat it as necessary to indicate whether it applies to the beginning year, the ending year, or both. Estimate Earliest and Latest Dates as appropriate.

Examples

[for a large carved altar, completed over several years, but both the beginning and the end of the span are uncertain]

Display Date: ca. 1505-ca.1510
Earliest: 1500; **Latest**: 1515

[for a house, where only the beginning year of construction is uncertain]

Display Date: constructed ca. 1750-1756
Earliest: 1745; **Latest**: 1756

[for a shrine, where only the ending year of construction is uncertain]

Display Date: constructed 1834-ca. 1850
Earliest: 1834; **Latest**: 1855

Preface centuries or other broad dates with *ca.* as needed. Estimate Earliest and Latest Dates appropriately, based on available information.

Example

[for an African mask]

> **Display Date**: ca. 19th century
> **Earliest**: 1775; **Latest**: 1925

For very ancient works, use the word *about* rather than *ca.* (for example, *about <x> years ago* or *about <x> years before present*).

Example

[for a tool kit from Dyuktai Cave, Siberia]

> **Display Date**: about 18,000 years ago
> **Earliest**: -19000; **Latest**: -13000

Before and After

When an exact date is unknown, express dates relative to a *terminus ante quem* or a *terminus post quem* (meaning *date before which* and *date after which*), if appropriate. In the display date, use the words *before* or *after*. Estimate earliest and latest dates based on available information; allow a ten-year span if nothing else is known.

Examples

[for an architectural garden pavilion]

> **Display Date**: before 1758
> **Earliest**: 1748; **Latest**: 1758

[for a wall mosaic]

> **Display Date**: after 547
> **Earliest**: 0547; **Latest**: 0557

Spans Indicating Uncertainty

When an exact date is unknown, record the span of years during which the creation took place, if appropriate. Distinguish between the span indicating that a precise date is unknown, but the work was created at some point during the span, and the span that is known, during which the creation process took place over a number of years (for example, for architecture, which is discussed in Specificity: Spans of Years, above). When necessary to avoid ambiguity, clearly describe the meaning of the date in the Display Date.

Examples

[for a drawing]

> **Display Date**: created between 1859 and 1862
> **Earliest**: 1859; **Latest**: 1862

[for a textile, the free-text date implies a broad span]

> **Display Date**: 3rd or 2nd century BCE
> **Earliest**: -0299; **Latest**: -0100

A dash or forward slash may be used in certain ways, provided it will be clear to the user what is meant. Use the dash to indicate a span during which a work was made, as when a building was constructed over several years. For example, *ca. 1435-ca. 1560* means that construction took many years, from ca. 1435 to ca. 1560. Use the forward slash when a specific date is not known, to indicate a span that contains some year or years when the work was made. For example, for a bowl, *1735/1745* means that the date is uncertain but that creation occurred sometime between 1735 and 1745.

Example

[for a building, the start and end date of the span in the Display Date field are themselves a span]

Display Date: constructed 118/119-125/128 CE
Earliest: 118; **Latest**: 128

Decades and Centuries

When the exact date is unknown, indicate the date to the nearest decade or century, when appropriate. Do not use an apostrophe with decades (for example, *1890s*, not *1890's*).

Examples

[for an American poster]

Display Date: 1890s
Earliest: 1890; **Latest**: 1899

[for a Peruvian textile]

Display Date: 16th century
Earliest: 1500; **Latest**: 1599

[for a Tibetan building]

Display Date: 2nd century BCE
Earliest: -0199; **Latest**: -0100

Qualify decades or centuries with *early*, *mid-*, and *late*, as warranted. Assign appropriate Earliest and Latest Dates by dividing the decade or century into thirds (for example, *late 18th century* may be indexed as *Earliest: 1770, Latest: 1799*), unless this formula is contradicted by available information.

Examples

[for a German chair]

Display Date: late 18th century
Earliest: 1770; **Latest**: 1799

[for an American silver tray]

Display Date: 1720s or 1730s
Earliest: 1720; **Latest**: 1739

[for a Chinese ceremonial vessel]

Display Date: late 12th or early 11th century BCE
Earliest: -1130; **Latest**: -1070

Dates by Period or Era

If there is no more precise date known than the broad period or the reign of a ruler, express dates according to a named period, dynasty, or ruler's reign, as appropriate. The periods may be divided into *early*, *middle*, or *late*. Earliest and Latest Dates for retrieval should be based on dates applicable for that period, if no more specific date for the work is known. In some cases, the period named in the Date element may be the same as the period recorded in the Style or Culture element.

Examples

[for a North American Woodland Indian bannerstone; earliest and latest dates refer to the period]

Display Date: Late Archaic Period
Earliest: -2000; **Latest**: -1000

[for a Spanish crucifix; earliest and latest dates refer broadly to the period]

Display Date: Medieval
Earliest: 1100; **Latest**: 1499

[for a Precolumbian Chilean ceramic vessel; ca. 2300 BCE refers to the vessel at hand, which is within the range and culture of Diaguita Phase II; Diaguita could be repeated in the style or culture elements as well]

Display Date: ca. 2300 BCE (Diaguita Phase II)
Earliest: -2500; **Latest**: -2100

[for a Mughal textile; the parenthetical date span refers to the reign of the Shah, not specifically to the particular textile at hand, because no more accurate date for the textile is known]

Display Date: reign of Shah Jahan (1628-1657)
Earliest: 1628; **Latest**: 1657

No Date

Do not use *n.d.* to indicate *no date*. Do not leave the date fields blank. If a date is uncertain, determine a possible date range based on available information, including the dates of other art works, associated historical events, or the birth and death dates of the artist. For example, unless the work was completed after his or her death, the death date of the artist would be the *terminus ante quem* for the work he or she created.

4.2.3.2.8 GROUPS OF WORKS

Groups of works commonly contain items created over a period of time. For the group, record either the *inclusive* or the *bulk dates*. Inclusive dates, also called *span dates*, are the years of the earliest and latest dated works in the group (for example, *1911-1951*). Bulk dates are the years representing the earliest and latest dates for the most important or principal body of items in the group. There may be multiple sets of bulk dates for any group (for example, *1914-1918 and 1939-1945*). Indicate in the Display Date if the dates are inclusive dates or bulk dates (for example, use parentheses as in the examples below).

Examples

[for a box of photographs]

Display Date: 1887-1894 (bulk dates)
Earliest: 1887; **Latest**: 1894

[for a group of Japanese musical instruments]

Display Date: ca. 1673-ca. 1695 (inclusive dates)
Earliest: 1668; **Latest**: 1700

The type of dates used for groups may be indexed with the Qualifier element. See Date Qualifiers below.

Example

[for a group of architectural drawings]

Display Date: 1968-1978 (inclusive dates)
Qualifier: inclusive
Earliest: 1968; **Latest**: 1978

4.2.3.2.9 CREATIVE ACTIVITIES ON DIFFERENT DATES

When it is known that different activities in the creative process took place at different times, indicate this in the free-text date field.

Example

[for a sculpture]

Display Date: 1372, reworked 1377-1379
Earliest: 1372; **Latest**: 1379

Date Qualifiers

Some institutions may wish to use date qualifiers. If your institution follows this practice, when the span of time between different creative activities is significant, use repeating sets of earliest and latest dates to index the various activities separately, if possible. Use qualifiers to label the various sets of dates. Examples of terminology for qualifiers include *creation*, *design*, *execution*, *alteration*, *restoration*, and *addition*. See also Groups of Works above.

Examples

[for a monumental sculpture]

Display Date: designed 1482, executed 1532-1534
Qualifier: design
Earliest: 1482; **Latest**: 1482

Qualifier: execution
Earliest: 1532; **Latest**: 1534

[for a sofa by Duncan Phyfe]

Display Date: ca. 1815, reupholstered in 1895
Qualifier: execution
Earliest: 1810; **Latest**: 1820

Qualifier: restoration
Earliest: 1895; **Latest**: 1895

[for Beauvais Cathedral]

Display Date: plans drawn in the 1230s, construction began in 1247, vaults collapsed in 1284, construction ended ca. 1500
Qualifier: design
Earliest: 1230; **Latest**: 1239

Qualifier: execution
Earliest: 1247; **Latest**: 1510

4.3   PRESENTATION OF THE DATA

4.3.1   Display and Indexing

4.3.1.1   *Free-Text vs. Controlled Fields*

For a discussion of when and why separate free-text and controlled fields are recommended, see Part 1: Database Design and Relationships: Display and Indexing.

4.3.1.2   *Fields in Authority File and Work Record*

Controlled Fields for Style

For the Style element, a repeatable controlled field should be used for indexing the style, period, group, or movement in which the work being cataloged was created. A free-text display field is not required, but may be used whenever it is necessary to express uncertainty or ambiguity. Where multiple styles or periods are assigned, if a display is desired, it can be constructed by concatenating data from the repeatable controlled field.

Example

Style displays *[concatenated]*: Gothic; Rayonnant

Styles: Gothic • Rayonnant

Controlled Fields for Culture

For the Culture element, a repeatable controlled field should be used for indexing culture or nationality. A free-text display field is not required, but may be used whenever it is necessary to express uncertainty or ambiguity. Where multiple cultures or nationalities are assigned, if a display is desired, it can be constructed by concatenating data from the repeatable controlled field.

Controlled Fields for Date

The Date element should ideally consist of a set of three fields: a free-text field to express nuances of the date to the user, and two indexing fields representing the earliest and latest dates implied in the Display Date. Earliest and Latest Dates are controlled fields intended to provide consistently formatted data that will be used in retrieval but not visible to the end user.

Example

Display Date: constructed 1378-1485
Earliest: 1378; **Latest**: 1485

The Earliest and Latest Dates should be controlled by rules in ISO or W3C standards (see Terminology section). It is recognized that practical considerations, such as the limitations of the institution's computer system, may require departure from the standards (for example, some systems do not allow storage of leading zeroes with numbers).

Controlled Field for Date Qualifier

Some institutions require qualifiers for dates. The values should be controlled by a controlled list.

4.3.2   Examples

Examples of Work Records are included below. For additional examples, see the end of Part 1, the end of each chapter, and the CCO Web site. In the examples, *controlled* refers to values controlled by an authority file, controlled list, or other rules (for example, rules for recording dates). *Link* refers to a relationship between a Work Record and an Authority Record or between two Work Records. All links are controlled fields. In the examples that follow, Related Work Records are abbreviated for the sake of brevity. All Work Records should be as complete as possible. See the various chapters for discussions of individual metadata elements, whether they should be controlled, and the respective advantages of an authority file or a controlled list. In all examples in this manual, both within and at the end of each chapter, data values for repeatable fields are separated by bullet characters.

Figure 22
Work Record Linked to an Authority Record for Culture: Ottonian Manuscript[4]
Required and recommended elements are marked with an asterisk.

Work Record

- **Class** *[controlled]*: manuscripts • European art
- ***Work Type** *[link]*: sacramentary • illuminated manuscript
- ***Title**: Sacramentary I **Title Type**: preferred
- ***Creator display**: illuminated by unknown German active in Mainz or Fulda, binding by unknown Mosan artist
    *Role *[link]*: illuminator I **Extent** *[controlled]*: illuminations I *[link]*: unknown German
    *Role *[link]*: artist I **Extent** *[controlled]*: binding I *[link]*: unknown Mosan
- ***Creation Date**: illuminated in 2nd quarter of 11th century, binding from 12th century, with later additions
    [controlled]: **Qualifier**: illuminations; **Earliest**: 1025; **Latest**: 1060 I **Qualifier**: binding; **Earliest**: 1100; **Latest**: 1199
- ***Subject** *[links to authorities]*: **Extent**: overall; **Terms**: service book • sacramentary • prayers • Mass I **Extent**: cover; **Terms**: Christ in Majesty • Ascension
- **Culture** *[link]*: Ottonian
- ***Current Location** *[link]*: J. Paul Getty Museum (Los Angeles, California, United States) I **IDs**: MS. LUDWIG V 2; 83.MF.77
- **Creation Location display**: binding: Mainz or Fulda (in modern Germany); illuminations: Mosan region (in modern Belgium)
- **Creation Locations** *[links]*: Fulda (Hessen, Germany) • Mainz (Rheinland-Pfalz, Germany) • Mosan (Europe) • Liège Province (Belgium)
- ***Measurements**: 179 leaves; text block: 26.6 x 19.1 cm (10 1/2 x 7 1/2 inches); text area: 17 x 13 cm (6 3/4 x 5 1/8 inches); oak covers: 27.3 x 19.8 cm (10 3/4 x 7 7/8 inches)
    [controlled]: **Extent**: leaf; **Value**: 26.6; **Unit**: cm; **Type**: height I **Value**: 19.1; **Unit**: cm; **Type**: width II
    Extent: text area; **Value**: 17; **Unit**: cm; **Type**: height I **Value**: 13; **Unit**: cm; **Type**: width II
    Extent: cover; **Value**: 27.3; **Unit**: cm; **Type**: height I **Value**: 19.8; **Unit**: cm; **Type**: width
- ***Materials and Techniques**: tempera colors, gold, silver, and ink on parchment, with hammered and engraved binding of copper gilt, silver, brass, and niello
    Extent: illuminations; **Material** *[link]*: tempera • ink • parchment I **Extent**: binding; **Material** *[link]*: gilt silver • brass • oak I **Technique** *[link]*: niello
- **Description**: Although the Ottonian book was written and illuminated in Germany, the binding was produced in Mosan, a region in present-day Belgium noted for medieval metalwork and enamel traditions.
- **Description Source** *[link]*:
    J. Paul Getty Museum online. http://www.getty.edu (accessed February 10, 2004).

Concept Authority Record

- ***Term**:
    Ottonian (preferred)
- ***Note**: Refers to the period, style, and culture associated with the rule of the Ottonian emperors (919-1024) and Salian rulers Conrad II and Henry III, through most of the 11th century. The style is an amalgam of elements including the ideals of the Carolingian art, a renewed interest in Early Christian art, and the influence of contemporary Byzantine art.
- ***Hierarchical position** *[link]*:
    Styles and Periods Facet
    .... Styles and Periods
    .... European
    .... Medieval
    .... Ottonian
- ***Source** *[link]*: *Art & Architecture Thesaurus* (1988-).

CREDIT: The J. Paul Getty Museum (Los Angeles, California). Illuminated by unknown German active in Mainz or Fulda, binding by unknown Mosan artist; *Christ in Majesty* (cover), and *The Ascension* (illumination), from *Sacramentary*; illuminated 2nd quarter of 11th century, binding from 12th century, with later additions; oak boards covered in red silk fitted with hammered and engraved silver and copper (cover); tempera colors and gold on parchment (illumination), 26.6 x 19.1 cm, text area 17 x 13 cm, oak covers 27.3 x 19.8 cm; Ms. Ludwig V2, 83.MF.77.20, (illumination), fol. 23 recto and 83.MF.77. cover. © The J. Paul Getty Trust.

Figure 23
Work Record Linked to an Authority Record: Corinthian Temple

Required and recommended elements are marked with an asterisk.

Work Record

- **Class** *[controlled]*: architecture
- ***Work Type** *[link]*: temple • town hall • dwelling • stable • church • museum
- ***Title**: Maison Carée | **Title Type**: preferred
  Title: Nîmes Temple | **Title Type**: alternate
- ***Creator display**: unknown Roman
  *Role *[controlled]*: architect | *[link]*: unknown Roman
- ***Creation Date**: 16 CE
  [controlled]: **Earliest**: -0016; **Latest**: -0016
- ***Subject** *[link to authorities]*: Roman temple • Gaius Caesar • Lucius Caesar
- ***Current Location** *[link]*: Nîmes (Languedoc-Roussillon, France)
- ***Measurements**: length: 25 m (82 feet); width: 12 m (40 feet)
  [controlled]: **Value**: 25; **Unit**: m; **Type**: length | **Value**: 12; **Unit**: m; **Type**: width
- ***Materials and Techniques**: cut stone, bearing masonry construction
  Material *[link]*: masonry | **Technique** *[link]*: dimension stone • load-bearing walls
- **Style** *[link]*: Corinthian
- **Culture** *[link]*: Ancient Roman • Gallo-Roman
- **Description**: Temple was dedicated to Gaius and Lucius Caesar, adopted sons of the first Roman emperor Augustus. Noted as best-preserved Roman building remaining in Gaul.

Concept Authority Record

- ***Term**:
  Corinthian (preferred)
- ***Note**: Refers to the third of both the three Greek architectural orders and the later five traditional classical orders of architecture that, with Doric, Ionic, Tuscan, and Composite, was used by the Romans and through the Renaissance and beyond. It seems to have been influenced by Egyptian architecture, though it probably developed in Greece in interior architecture, and was used in exterior architecture by the 3rd century BCE. In Greek architecture it is characterized by a form that is lighter and more ornate than Doric or Ionic, a bell-shaped capital with acanthus stalks emerging to support graceful volutes, and a column that is seated on a base and usually fluted. It was the most common of Greek styles in Roman architecture, and in Roman and later architecture the style was often modified. It is distinct from "Corinthian order," since an architectural order refers strictly to the specific system or assemblage of parts that is subject to uniform established rules and proportions, regulated by the role that each part has to perform.
- ***Hierarchical position** *[link]*:
  Styles and Periods Facet
  .... Mediterranean
  .... Aegean
  .... <Aegean styles>
  .... Corinthian
- ***Source** *[link]*: *Art & Architecture Thesaurus* (1988-).

Work Record

■ **Class** *[controlled]*: architecture • American art
■ ***Work Type** *[link]*: mansion • president's dwelling
■ ***Title**: White House I **Title Type**: preferred
　　Title: Executive Mansion I **Title Type**: former
　　Title: President's Palace I **Title Type**: former
　　Title: President's House I **Title Type**: former
■ ***Creator display**: James Hoban (American, 1762-1831)
　　*Role *[link]*: architect I *[link]*: Hoban, James
■ ***Creation Date**: 1793 to 1801, burned 1814, porticos
　1824 to 1829
　　[controlled]: **Earliest**: 1793; **Latest**: 1829
■ ***Subject** *[links to authorities]*: architecture • presidency
　• power
■ **Style** *[link]*: Georgian • Neoclassical • Palladian
■ ***Current Location** *[link]*: Washington (DC, United States)
■ ***Measurements**: 3 stories, over 100 rooms, White
　House and the grounds occupy 7.2 hectares (18 acres)
　　[controlled]: **Extent**: rooms; **Value**: 104; **Type**: count
　I **Extent**: stories; **Value**: 3; **Type**: count I **Extent**:
　grounds; **Value**: 7.2; **Unit**: hectares; **Type**: area
■ ***Materials and Techniques**: cut-stone bearing masonry
　construction
　　Material *[link]*: masonry I **Technique** *[link]*:
　dimension stone • load-bearing walls
■ **Description**: Design was the result of a public
　competition in 1792. Among the entrants was Thomas
　Jefferson, later president of the United States. James
　Hoban won the commission with a plan for a Georgian
　mansion in the Palladian style.

Concept Authority Record

▨ ***Terms**:
　　Neoclassical (preferred)
　　Neo-Classical
　　Neoclassicism
▨ ***Note**: Refers to the style of European and American
　architecture and fine and decorative arts between the
　mid-18th century and the mid-19th century inspired
　by archaeological discoveries in the Mediterranean
　and Near East and characterized by the imitation of
　Greek and Roman forms and motifs. Also considered
　a reaction to Rococo opulence, Neoclassical works
　are often linear, symmetrical, and even severe.
▨ ***Hierarchical position** *[link]*:
　　Styles and Periods Facet
　　.... Styles and Periods
　　.......... European
　　.................. <modern European styles>
　　............................ Neoclassical
▨ ***Source** *[link]*: *Art & Architecture Thesaurus* (1988-).

Concept Authority Record

▨ ***Term**:
　　Georgian (preferred)
▨ ***Note**: Refers to the style in architecture, interior
　design, and decorative arts in Britain and Ireland and
　spread to the United States during the reigns of
　George I to George IV, between 1714 and 1830. Some
　authors omit the reign of George IV and refer to the
　period ca.1790 to 1830 as Regency. Though Classical
　forms and motifs dominate, the style encompasses
　Renaissance and Rococo forms as well as a range of
　Neoclassical styles such as Pompeiian Revival and
　Etruscan style.
▨ ***Hierarchical position** *[link]*:
　　Styles and Periods Facet
　　.... Styles and Periods
　　.......... European
　　.................. <Renaissance-Baroque styles>
　　............................ Georgian
▨ ***Source** *[link]*: *Art & Architecture Thesaurus* (1988-).

Notes

1. The ISO standard recognizes year zero. Humanities projects, however, will generally omit it in calculations of earliest and latest dates.

2. *Ink-bamboo* painting was a style of Chinese painting that emphasized a distinctive relationship between ink as a medium and bamboo as a subject.

3. Years in ages estimated by radiocarbon dating, potassium/argon dating, and other such relative dating methods do not necessarily correspond to years recorded in a calendar; therefore, calibration tables are designed for the particular circumstances surrounding the specific relative dating process. Calibration tables are often unavailable; however, dates should still be estimated, because the fields must not be left blank and slight inaccuracies in earliest and latest dates will not affect overall retrieval.

4. This example is intended to illustrate metadata elements discussed in this manual. Field names and data values in the example do not necessarily represent the record for this object in the Getty Museum's information system.

Chapter 5

Location and Geography

Current Location / Creation Location / Discovery Location / Former Location

5.1   ABOUT LOCATION AND GEOGRAPHY

5.1.1 Discussion

This chapter deals with elements that record geographic or other location information. Location information will be pertinent for Current Location, Creation Location, Discovery Location, and other types of former locations.

Most cultural works have a variety of geographic associations. Examples include the nation where a pot was made, the city of the museum that currently houses a painting, or the village where an architectural work is located. Another aspect of location information is more specific, for example, the building inside which the work is located (for example, a fresco in a church), or the museum or other institution that owns or has control of the work. Works that can be moved (*movable*, for example, a sculpture or drawing in a museum or other institution) may have changing relationships to repositories and geography over time, whereas those that are monumental, architectural, or otherwise stationary (for example, a fresco attached to the wall of a church) may not, because they have remained in the same place since they created. At least four questions about location are generally of interest when describing a cultural object or work:

- Where is it now?
- Where was it before?
- Where was it made?
- Where was it discovered?

Geographic Places and Repositories

Data values for Location elements can comprise two types of data: a geographic place (for example, *Florence (Italy)*) and a named repository or building (for example, *Gallerie degli Uffizi*). Geographic places may be administrative entities, such as a city or nation (for example, *Tokyo (Japan)*) or physical features (for example, *Lascaux Cave (Dordogne, Aquitaine, France)*). Deserted settlements (for example, *Machu Picchu (Peru)*) and former nations or empires (for example, *Flanders*) may be included. Repositories for museum objects are generally recorded by the name of the institution or organization that owns or has control of the object (for example, *National Gallery of Art (London, England, United Kingdom)*). For works not housed in a museum or other collecting institution, locations may also include the name of the building in which the work is located (for example, the church of *Santa Croce (Florence, Italy)*), which is not necessarily the same as the name of the institution that has control of the work (for example, for works in Santa Croce, *Soprintendenza ai Beni artistici e storici per le province di Firenze, Prato e Pistoia*). The issues are further complicated by the fact that buildings may also be cataloged as art works in their own right. For works owned by individuals, location may include the city or address of the home of the owner. For further discussion, see Part 3: Geographic Place, Personal and Corporate Name, and Subject Authorities.

Current Location

The Current Location element includes the geographic location of the work of art or architecture and the building or repository that currently houses the work, where applicable. The current location is important to researchers and most other users of art information. If catalog records are being created within a single owning institution, it may seem unnecessary to explicitly record repository and geographic place for every Work Record. However, this information should be included when data is exchanged between institutions or when data is available online in a larger context, such as a union catalog or federated database. If the current location is unknown, that fact should be indicated and the last known location should be included. The repository number is also typically a component of Current Location information, particularly for works in museums; this number or alphanumeric code uniquely identifies the work in the holding institution, and is critical for researchers wishing to find a particular work. For additional discussion, see *Categories for the Description of Works of Art: Current Location*.

Creation Location

Creation Location is where the work or its components was or were created, designed, or produced; it may also be the presumed original location of the work. It is usually a geographic place, but it may include the name of a corporate body or building. Creation Location is critical for retrieval, but is often not known. Therefore, geographic place information related to the creator (recorded in the Personal and Corporate Name Authority) is often substituted in queries. Location information about the creator includes the geographic place implicit in nationality or culture, and geographic places recorded as the creator's loci of activity, birth place, and death place. See Part 3: Personal and Corporate Name Authority for further discussion.

Discovery Location

Discovery Location is the geographic place where a work was excavated or discovered. This can be a general or a specific place, including the excavation site and the plot or section within the site. The Discovery Location becomes especially important when little else is known about a work or its creation; an example is the disposition of artifacts in the Sutton Hoo ship-burial hoard. For further discussion, see *Categories for the Description of Works of Art: Context-Archaeological: Excavation Place*.

Former Locations

Additional types of former location may be important for the Work Record, including locations related to the ownership or collecting history of the work. Places related to the exhibition, loan history, conservation, and historical context of the work may be included. A specific architectural work, building, or site within which the work of art or architecture was incorporated or displayed may be included. For elements related to these other types of former locations, see *Categories for the Description of Works of Art*.

Location as Subject

The subject depicted in or on a work of art may be a geographic place (see Chapter 6: Subject).

Specificity

The level of specificity applied in recording location information will depend upon the requirements of the cataloging institution and the available information. Location may be recorded at the most general level, such as the continent (for example, *Europe*), or at the most specific level, such as a street address (for example, *13 Coventry Street (London, England, United Kingdom)*). The most common location designation will include city, administrative subdivision (if applicable), and nation (for example, *London (England, United Kingdom)*), preceded by the name of the repository, when applicable.

Ambiguity and Uncertainty

The data structure and cataloging rules should allow for uncertainty and ambiguity inherent in certain works to be noted in the record; for example, a work may have been discovered *near Peking, China*, or was *probably originally located in the Collegiata (San Gimignano, Italy)*. This is most easily achieved by combining a free-text field with controlled fields. In some cases (for example, *created at La Cruz, Costa Rica or Peñas Blancas, Nicaragua*), it may be necessary to index multiple possibilities in repeatable fields controlled by a list or authority file.

Organization of the Data

Cataloging institutions must make decisions regarding the level of complexity and granularity necessary for recording and controlling location information. Location information should be controlled, ideally in authorities.

One important issue involves how location information is categorized and controlled. If a simple approach is adequate, all location terminology may be stored together in a controlled list or a single authority file. Some institutions will require more granular data. They may need to make distinctions between buildings and administrative repositories because their users need to know the physical location of the work in the present or past and what entity has or has had control of the work. If such distinctions are necessary to facilitate research or retrieval, the data model must be able to separate different types of entities into different authorities, because the characteristics and therefore the fields of these authorities will differ. Some institutions will also need to record repository buildings as architectural works in their own right. If so, records for these buildings as architectural works should be recorded separately with other Work Records. For further discussion of these issues, see Part 3: Geographic Place Authority and Personal and Corporate Name Authority.

Another important issue concerns how many fields are considered necessary for location information in a Work Record. Several areas of a museum Work Record will have a geographic component. Visual resource collections may require fewer location fields than museums or research databases. In *VRA Core Categories*, each location term is qualified with a type attribute that specifies what kind of location is being recorded. The *VRA Core 4.0 XML* schema's controlled list of data values for this type of attribute currently include creation, site (used for current locations for architecture and archaeology), formerSite, discovery, repository, former-Repository, owner, formerOwner, installation, exhibition, performance, context (used for related works cited as a location), publication, and other. Individual cataloging agencies may choose to record fewer or more location types, but it is recommended that any additional terms be derived from a controlled list. *Categories for the Description of Works of Art* is tailored more to museums and researchers. It lays out a thorough set of categories, with separate location fields clustered with related fields. For example, former ownership locations are clustered with the personal names, dates, method of acquisition, and other information related to the provenance for the work.

Authorities

Names used to describe locations should be drawn from one or more authority files, depending on the needs of the cataloging institution. The pertinent authorities are the Geographic Place Authority (for names of cities, nations, and physical features), the Personal and Corporate Name Authority (for names of repositories, libraries, other institutions or agencies, or private collectors), and the Subject Authority (for buildings). Names should be taken from standard controlled vocabularies. Ideally, the authority files should be based on hierarchical structures that include narrower and broader terms.

Location information may require fields that are indexed and controlled as well as fields that permit a free-text description that will be more meaningful for display and will allow the expression of ambiguity, nuance, and context. Multiple location terms may apply to each work or image, so the authority-controlled location fields should be repeatable.

See further discussion of authorities and vocabularies in Part 3: Geographic Place, Personal and Corporate Name, and Subject Authorities and in *Categories for the Description of Works of Art*.

Recommended Elements

A list of elements in this chapter appears below. Required elements are noted. Display may be a free-text field or concatenated from controlled fields.

> Current Location display (required)
>> Controlled location (link to corporate body or geographic authority)
>
> Creation Location display
>> Controlled location (link to corporate body or geographic authority)
>
> Discovery Location display
>> Controlled location (link to corporate body or geographic authority)
>
> Former Location display
>> Controlled location (link to corporate body or geographic authority)

Other Location Information

A repository or owner may assign a unique identifier to a work; this information may be recorded as a separate element within the location area of the record. Some institutions may require location associated with elements other than those discussed in this chapter. For further discussion, see the place-location fields in *Categories for the Description of Works of Art: Ownership/Collecting History, Copyright/Restrictions, Exhibition/Loan History, Condition/Examination History, Conservation/Treatment History, Context: Historical,* and *Context: Architectural.*

About the Examples

The examples throughout this chapter are for illustration only. Local practice may vary. The examples tend to show the fullest possible use of display and indexing fields, which may not be necessary for visual resource collections and some other institutions.

5.1.2 Terminology

5.1.2.1 *Sources for Terminology*

Location names should be controlled by means of a link to an authority file or controlled lists. Published sources of names address both geographic place names and buildings and repositories:

Geographic Place Names

> Getty Vocabulary Program. *Getty Thesaurus of Geographic Names* (TGN). Los Angeles: J. Paul Getty Trust, 1988-. http://www.getty.edu/ research/conducting_research/vocabularies/tgn/.
>
> United States Geological Survey (USGS). *Geographic Names Information System* (GNIS). http://geonames.usgs.gov/ [domestic names].
>
> National Geospatial Intelligence Agency (NGA); formerly United States National Imagery and Mapping Agency (NIMA). (Advised by the US

Board on Geographic Names. USBGN). GEOnet Names Server (GNS). http://earth-info.nga.mil/gns/html/ [foreign names].

Library of Congress Authorities. *Library of Congress Subject Headings.* Washington, DC: Library of Congress, http://authorities.loc.gov/.

Lavall, Cherry. *British Archaeological Thesaurus.* London: Council for British Archaeology, 1989.

Columbia Lippincott Gazetteer of the World. Edited by Leon E. Seltzer. Morningside Heights, NY: Columbia University Press, 1961.

Princeton Encyclopedia of Classical Sites. 2nd ed. Princeton, NJ: Princeton University Press, 1979.

Barraclough, Geoffrey, ed. *Times Atlas of World History.* 4th ed. Edited by Geoffrey Parker. Maplewood, NJ: Hammond, 1994.

Times Atlas of the World. 10th comprehensive ed. New York: Times Books, 1999.

Webster's New Geographical Dictionary. Springfield, MA: Merriam-Webster, 1984.

Rand McNally. *New International Atlas.* Chicago: Rand McNally, 1995.

Names of Repositories and Buildings

Library of Congress Authorities. *Library of Congress Name Authorities.* Washington, DC: Library of Congress, 2005. http://authorities .loc.gov/.

International Directory of the Arts. Berlin: Deutsche Zentraldruckerei, 1953-.

International Directory of Arts & Museums of the World. Munich: K. G. Saur, 1998-.

Official Museum Directory. Washington, DC: American Association of Museums, 1971-.

Avery Architecture & Fine Arts Library. *Avery Index to Architectural Periodicals at Columbia University.* Los Angeles: J. Paul Getty Trust, 1994-. Online by subscription at http://www.getty.edu/research/ conducting_research/avery_index/.

Macmillan Encyclopedia of Architects. Edited by Adolf K. Placzek. New York: Free Press; London: Collier Macmillan, 1982.

America Preserved: A Checklist of Historic Buildings, Structures, and Sites. 60th ed. Washington, DC: Library of Congress, Cataloging Distribution Service, 1995.

Fletcher, Sir Banister. *History of Architecture.* 20th ed. Oxford; Boston: Architectural Press, 1996.

Grove Dictionary of Art Online. New York: Grove's Dictionaries, 2003. http://www.groveart.com/.

Additional sources of geographic names may be used, including atlases, maps, and gazetteers.

5.1.2.2 *Choice of Terminology*

5.1.2.2.1 CONSISTENCY

Use controlled fields for location information. Some institutions may also require free-text fields to allow for the expression of ambiguous and uncertain location information. Consistency is less important, but still desirable, in a free-text note than in a controlled field. Although uncontrolled terminology should be accommodated, terminology that is consistent with the terms in controlled fields is nonetheless recommended for the sake of clarity. Consistent style, grammar, and syntax are recommended.

5.1.2.2.2 USE OF AN AUTHORITY FILE

Geographic place and repository names should be controlled by one or more authorities. If multiple authorities are used, they will be the Geographic Place Authority for cities, nations, archaeological sites, and physical features, the Personal and Corporate Name Authority for museums and other administrative repositories, and the Subject Authority for buildings.

Authorities should be populated with values from published controlled vocabularies wherever possible. New terms should be created as necessary. See the rules and discussion regarding the creation of new names in Part 3: Geographic Place, Personal and Corporate Name, and Subject Authorities.

5.2 CATALOGING RULES

5.2.1 Rules for Location

5.2.1.1 *Brief Rules for Location*

5.2.1.1.1 TYPES OF LOCATION

Record the types of locations indicated below.

Current Location

Recording the current location of the work is required. Specify the geographic place, building, or repository (for example, a museum) where the work is currently located. If the work is no longer extant or the location is unknown, information to that effect must be indicated.

Creation Location

If it is known, you need to record the place where the creation, design, or production of the work or its components took place. Alternatively, record the original location of the work, if that is known.

Discovery Location

For works found in an archaeological site or other works with unknown creation locations, record the place where the work was excavated or discovered, if this information is known.

Other Types of Former Location

If required by the cataloging institution, record locations related to the historical context, ownership, collecting history, exhibition, loan history, or conservation of the work.

5.2.1.1.2 RECORDING THE LOCATION

For all the types of locations described, record the preferred name for the geographic place, building, or repository where the work is or was located. Record the most commonly used name, which is not necessarily the fullest or official name. Take the name from an authoritative source. A brief discussion is given below. See Part 3: Geographic Place, Personal and Corporate Name, and Subject Authorities for more information on how to formulate names.

Capitalization

Capitalize all proper names, including the names of buildings, repositories, villages, towns, cities, provinces, states, nations, empires, kingdoms, and physical features. If a name includes an article or preposition (for example *de, des, la, l'*), generally use lowercase except when it is the first word in the name.

> *Examples*
>
> [geographic places]
>
> > **Current Location**: Agroha (Haryana state, India)
> >
> > **Current Location**: East Hinson Indian Mounds (Collier County, Florida, United States)
> >
> > **Creation Location**: Lombardy (Carolingian Empire)
> >
> > **Current Location**: Aire-sur-la-Lys (Nord-Pas-de-Calais, France)
> >
> > **Current Location**: La Chapelle (Louisiana, United States)
>
> [a building as location]
>
> > **Current Location**: Notre Dame (Paris, France)
>
> [a repository as location]
>
> > **Current Location**: Museo Nacional (Guatemala City, Guatemala)

Capitalization of names in languages other than English may vary. For guidance in capitalizing institution names, refer to official publications or the institution's official Web site and the sources listed in Sources for Terminology. For geographic names, use the listed sources.

Abbreviations

Avoid abbreviations. For the preferred name, spell out the name of the repository; do not use abbreviations or initials (for example, not *MoMA* or *NGA*).

Examples

[geographic places]

> **Current Location**: Santa Maria (Azores, Portugal)
>
> **Current Location**: Falaba (Northern Province, Sierra Leone)
>
> **Current Location**: Antietam National Battlefield Site (Sharpsburg, Maryland, United States)

[a repository]

> **Current Location**: Museum of Modern Art (New York, New York, United States)

If abbreviations—such as standard ISO codes for country names or U.S. Postal Code abbreviations for state names in the United States—are used in local applications, convert the abbreviations into the full name for display.

Language of the Names

For the preferred name, use a name commonly used in sources in the language of the catalog record. In the United States, for example, use *Florence (Italy)* rather than *Firenze (Italia)*. Rely on authoritative sources to determine the preferred name.

> *Example*
>
> **Current Location**: Florence (Tuscany, Italy)

Do not use obsolete English names or other names that are not commonly used. For example, do not use *Leghorn (Italy)*, because modern English sources prefer the Italian name, *Livorno (Italy)*.

FOR GEOGRAPHIC PLACE NAMES

If there is no commonly used English name for a geographic place, use the preferred vernacular name (that is, the name in the local language). The names of most nations have English counterparts (for example, *Germany* rather than *Deutschland*). The largest inhabited places will often have English names; however, for most other inhabited places in non-English-speaking nations, there is no English name. Use diacritics as appropriate.

> *Examples*
>
> **Current Location**: Rio de Janeiro (Sudeste region, Brazil)
>
> **Current Location**: Altomünster (Bavaria, Germany)
>
> **Current Location**: Cap-Haïtien (Haiti)

Use the repository or building name most commonly found in authoritative English-language sources; some names will be in English, and others will be in the vernacular. Use diacritics as appropriate.

Examples

> **Current Location**: Opéra (Paris, France)
>
> **Current Location**: Museum of Islamic Art (Cairo, Egypt)
>
> **Current Location**: Archaeological Museum (Delphi, Greece)
>
> **Current Location**: State Hermitage Museum (Saint Petersburg, Russia)
>
> **Current Location**: Temple of Heaven (near Beijing, China)

For French, Spanish, Italian, and German, English-language sources generally (but not always) use the vernacular, for example, *Santa Croce (Florence, Italy)* rather than *Holy Cross (Florence, Italy)*. For names in other languages, sources generally, but not always, translate the name into English, for example, *National Museum (Prague, Czech Republic)* rather than *Národní Muzeum (Prague, Czech Republic)*. For further discussion, see Part 3: Personal and Corporate Name Authority and Subject Authority.

Examples

[two institutions in Italy, one name is generally in Italian in English sources, and the other generally in English in English sources]

> **Current Location**: Pinacoteca Nazionale (Siena, Italy)
>
> **Current Location**: Vatican Library (Holy See, Rome, Italy)

Constructing a Name

If the geographic place, repository, or building name is not listed in an authoritative source and common usage is therefore not known, create a name using a standard such as *Anglo-American Cataloguing Rules* (AACR). See Part 3: Personal and Corporate Name, Geographic Place, and Subject Authorities for further discussion.

5.2.1.2 *Additional Recommendations for Location*

5.2.1.2.1 CONVEYING NUANCE AND AMBIGUITY

Some of the recommendations and examples given imply a free-text field dedicated to location. If such a free-text field is not available, record the nuance in the Description element (see Chapter 8, see also Display and Indexing below).

5.2.1.2.2 SYNTAX

In an efficient system, location names in the Work Record should be automatically constructed by links from the Geographic Place or Personal and Corporate Name Authorities. If, instead, the cataloger must enter the information by hand, use the rules for syntax below.

For Geographic Places

To refer to a geographic place, list the preferred name followed by enough broader contexts to unambiguously refer to the place in the following order: inhabited place (city), province or other subdivision, nation. Include the continent if necessary. Place the broader contexts in parentheses or otherwise distinguish them for clarity.[1]

Examples

[for the Medina Azahara palace]

Current Location display: Córdoba (Andalusia, Spain)

[for the outdoor sculpture Large Arch by Henry Moore]

Current Location display: Columbus (Indiana, United States)

[for a sculpture]

Creation Location display: Rufisque (Dakar Region, Senegal)

[for a textile]

Creation Location display: Alamo Navajo Indian Reservation (Socorro County, New Mexico, United States)

For Repositories and Buildings

For a building or repository, list the preferred name of the building or repository followed by the geographic location in the following order: inhabited place (city), province or other subdivision (as needed), nation. Place the geographic place names in parentheses or otherwise distinguish them for clarity.

Examples

[for a drawing in a repository]

Current Location display: Graphische Sammlung Albertina (Vienna, Austria)

[for a painting]

Current Location display: Yamatane Museum of Art (Tokyo, Japan)

[for a fresco in a ruined building in a deserted city]

Current Location display: Villa of the Mysteries (Pompeii, Campania, Italy)

[for an altarpiece in a church]

Current Location display: Santa Maria Tonantzintla (Puebla, Mexico)

5.2.1.2.3 VARIOUS TYPES OF WORKS

Movable Works

If the work is movable, that is, is not attached to architecture and is small enough to have changed locations over time (for example, a panel painting or sculpture), record the Current Location. Record the Creation Location, the Discovery Location, or any other significant Former Location, if any of these are known.

Examples

[for an amphora]

Current Location display: J. Paul Getty Museum (Los Angeles, California, United States)
Creation Location display: Athens (Greece)

[for a ceramic plate]

Current Location display: Freer Gallery of Art (Washington, DC, United States)
Discovery Location display: near Delhi (India)

[for a panel painting]

Current Location display: Pinacoteca Nazionale (Siena,Tuscany, Italy)
Former Location display: Duomo (Siena, Tuscany, Italy)

Stationary Works

For architecture, works that are large or monumental, or works that are attached to architecture (for example, a fresco), record the Current Location.

Examples

[for a jamb statue]

Current Location display: Notre Dame Cathedral (Reims, Marne, Champagne-Ardenne, France)

[for a burial mound]

Current Location display: Adams County (Ohio, United States)

[for a cave temple]

Current Location display: Dunhuang (Gansu Province, China)

Creation Location, Discovery Location, and Former Location will generally not be pertinent for stationary works. However, exceptions are possible, because seemingly large and stationary works can in fact be and have been moved.

Examples

[for an obelisk]

Current Location display: Piazza di Montecitorio (Rome, Lazio, Italy)
Creation Location display: Heliopolis (Egypt)

[for a house]

Current Location display: Old Sturbridge Village (Massachusetts, United States)
Creation Location display: Charlton (Massachusetts, United States)

Lost Works

For works that are lost or destroyed, include either the Creation Location or the last known location, or both. For Current Location, record appropriate terminology, such as *unknown* or *not applicable*.

Examples

[for a mural painting]

Current Location display: not applicable
Creation Location display: Rockefeller Center (New York, New York, United States)

[for a stained glass window]

Current Location display: not applicable
Creation Location display: Gedächtniskirche (Berlin, Germany)

[for an oil painting]

Current Location display: unknown
Former Location display: Van Gogh Museum (Amsterdam, The Netherlands)

Performance Art

For performance art or environmental art, record the location where the work was performed or created.

Example

[for a piece of performance art]

Current Location display: not applicable
Creation Location display: Times Square (New York, New York, United States)

5.2.1.2.4 SPECIFICITY OF LOCATION

Record the most specific level of location known or applicable, using the guidelines below.

Repository

If the work is or was in a repository or building, record the name of the repository or building, as well as its geographic location.

Examples

[for a Native American woven basket]

Current Location display: Heard Museum (Phoenix, Arizona, United States)

[for a painting by Piet Mondrian]

Current Location display: San Francisco Museum of Modern Art (San Francisco, California, United States)

If the repository has multiple sites, include the specific location for the work, if known. For large or complex institutions, include the division or department that controls the work.

Examples

[for an altarpiece by Bartolo di Fredi]

Current Location display: The Cloisters, Metropolitan Museum of Art (New York, New York, United States)

[for a drawing by Rembrandt van Rijn]

> **Current Location display**: Department of Prints, Drawings, and Photographs, National Gallery of Art (Washington, DC, United States)

Private Collection

If the work is in a private collection, record the name of the collection, if it is known. If the name of the collection is unknown or if the owner wishes to remain anonymous, record the phrase *private collection* (lowercase); include the geographic location, if it is known.

> *Example*
>
> [for an oil painting]
>
> > **Current Location display**: Luciano Conti Collection (Beverly Hills, California, United States)
>
> [for pastel sketch]
>
> > **Current Location display**: private collection (Montreal, Canada)

Building

If the work is or was in a church or other building, include the name of the building.

> *Example*
>
> [for a pietra dura frieze]
>
> > **Current Location display**: Golden Temple (Amritsar, Punjab, India)

Record the part of the building, if known.

> *Example*
>
> [for a fresco by Masaccio]
>
> > **Current Location display**: Brancacci Chapel, Santa Maria del Carmine (Florence, Italy)

City

For Current Location for architecture and other works not in a repository or building, record the name of the city and its broader contexts. For Creation Location for other works, record the city and its broader contexts.

> *Example*
>
> [for the building Hagia Sophia]
>
> > **Current Location display**: Istanbul (Marmara region, Turkey)
>
> [for a walking stick]
>
> > **Creation Location display**: Am Loubia (Batha Prefecture, Chad)

When the City Is Not Known

If the city is not known or appropriate, record the nation. If the nation is not known, record the region or continent.

Example

[for a mask, the region is recorded]

Creation Location display: North Africa

Neighborhoods and Addresses

Neighborhoods and street addresses may be included where pertinent.

Examples

[for a house in a neighborhood]

Current Location display: Georgetown (Washington, DC, United States)

[street address for a church]

Current Location display: 17, Rue St.-Antoine (Le Marais, Paris, France)

Archaeological Sites

For archaeological sites, include the plot number, trench number, or other specific designation, if known and where appropriate.

Example

[for a ruined structure]

Discovery Location display: plot #125, hill 78-098 (Great Zimbabwe Ruins National Park, Victoria, Zimbabwe)

Physical Features

For works that are or were not in an inhabited place, but are or were located on or in a named physical feature, name the physical feature.

Example

[for a leather boot]

Discovery Location display: Ötztaler Alps (Europe)

Unnamed Location

If a location is unnamed, record the nearest named town, city, or physical feature. Qualify it with the phrase *near* in the Location display. Optionally, if the site is named but not well known, include the name of a better known nearby location in the Location display, if possible.

Examples

[for a Megalithic tomb]

Current Location display: near Valencia de Alcántara (Spain)
[link to Geographic Place Authority]: Valencia de Alcántara (Spain)

[for a bas-relief sculpture]

Discovery Location display: Tomb 7, Monte Albán, near Oaxaca City (Mexico)
[link to Geographic Place Authority]: Tomb 7 (Monte Albán, Mexico)

[for a figurine]

> **Discovery Location display**: unnamed camp site, along the Danube River in Niederösterreich, northeastern Austria
>> *[links to Geographic Place Authority]*: Danube River (Europe) • Niederösterreich (Austria)

For an unnamed site that is not near a well-known place, record the name of the smallest administrative entity that contains the site (for example, a *county*).

> *Example*

> [for an arrowhead]

>> **Discovery Location display**: excavated in Franklin County, Indiana, United States
>>> *[link to Geographic Place Authority]*: Franklin County (Indiana, United States)

Little-Known Places

If the place name is not well known and the place type is not evident from the name, include a term describing the type of place for clarity, if possible (for example, *deserted settlement, quarry, cliff face*).

> *Examples*

> [for a stupa]

>> **Discovery Location display**: deserted settlement Mohenjo-daro, Sind Province, Pakistan
>>> *[link to Geographic Place Authority]*: Mohenjo-daro (Sind Province, Pakistan)

> [for a stone tool]

>> **Discovery Location display**: Buxton Limeworks quarry, near Taung, Bophuthatswana, South Africa
>>> *[link to Geographic Place Authority]*: Buxton Limeworks (Bophuthatswana, South Africa)

> [for a rock painting]

>> **Current Location display**: cliff face, near Huashan, Shaanxi Province, China
>>> *[link to Geographic Place Authority]*: Huashan (Shaanxi Province, China)

Uncertain Location

If the location is uncertain, indicate this in the display; index the probable place or places.

> *Examples*

> [for a ceremonial mace]

>> **Former Location display**: probably from the burial mound at Bush Barrow, Wiltshire, southern England
>>> *[link to Geographic Place Authority]*: Bush Barrow (Wiltshire, England, United Kingdom)

[for a textile]

    Creation Location display: probably from Batticaloa or Trincomalee, Eastern Province, Sri Lanka

        [links to Geographic Place Authority]: Trincomalee (Eastern Province, Sri Lanka)

        • Batticaloa (Eastern Province, Sri Lanka)

Historical Places

For current locations, use the current name of the location. For Creation Location and other pertinent former locations, avoid anachronistic displays in the Work Record, when possible. Ideally, if a historical name is pertinent to the work, the historical name for the place or repository should be used (for example, for a late-15th-century Flemish altarpiece, the Creation Location should be noted as *Antwerp (Flanders)* rather than *Antwerp (Belgium)* because the nation of Belgium did not exist until 1831). Anachronisms are most likely to occur for Creation Location, Discovery Location, and other types of former locations.

For historical places that are likely to be unfamiliar to end users, include the modern counterpart in the display field.

    Example

    [for a sculpture]

        Creation Location display: Rhakotis, now called Alexandria, Egypt

        [link to Geographic Place Authority]: Alexandria (Egypt)

Locations of Parts and the Whole

For works that were formerly part of other works, such as spolia and disassembled manuscript folios or altarpiece panels, include the location of original, intact work, if known. Architectural works may or may not be stored in the Geographic Place Authority.

    Example

    [for a carved capital]

        Former Location display: spolia, originally from the Baths of Caracalla, Rome, Italy

        [link to Subject Authority]: Baths of Caracalla (Rome, Lazio, Italy)

        Current Location display: Santa Maria in Trastevere (Rome, Italy)

        [link to Subject Authority]: Santa Maria in Trastevere (Rome, Lazio, Italy)

If possible, also use related works to link the original intact work and the current part; see Part 1: Related Works.

Intended and Former Locations

Include intended or former locations, if possible.

> *Examples*
>
> [for a sculpture]
>
>> **Discovery Location display**: found near the ruins of the villa of the Roman emperor Hadrian at Tivoli
>>> *[link to Subject Authority]*: Hadrian's Villa (Tivoli, Lazio, Italy)
>>
>> **Current Location display**: J. Paul Getty Museum (Los Angeles, California, United States)
>>> *[link to Personal and Corporate Name Authority]*: J. Paul Getty Museum (Los Angeles, California, United States)
>
> [for a sculpture]
>
>> **Former Locations display**: originally designed for a high location on a buttress of the Cathedral of Florence, but never displayed there; first displayed in front of the Palazzo Vecchio, Piazza della Signoria; later moved to the Accademia to protect the work
>>> *[links to Subject Authority]*: Cathedral of Santa Maria del Fiore (Florence, Tuscany, Italy) • Palazzo Vecchio, Piazza della Signoria (Florence, Tuscany, Italy)
>>
>> **Current Location display**: Galleria dell'Accademia (Florence, Italy)
>>> *[link to Personal and Corporate Name Authority]*: Galleria dell'Accademia (Florence, Tuscany, Italy)

5.2.1.2.5 OWNERSHIP HISTORY

If your institution is recording provenance (that is, a full history of ownership), record the ownership history of the work as a continuous chronological sequence.

> *Example*
>
> [for an altarpiece]
>
>> **Former Locations display**: before 1835, Abbazia di Sant'Antimo near Montalcino; 1835-1846, Cardinal Fesch Collection, Rome; 1846-1863, Campana Collection, Rome; since 1863, Musée du Louvre, Paris.
>>> *[link to Subject Authority]*: Abbazia di Sant'Antimo (Siena province, Tuscany, Italy)
>>>
>>> *[links to Personal and Corporate Name Authority]*: Cardinal Joseph Fesch Collection (Rome, Italy) • Marquis Giampietro Campana Collection (Rome, Italy) • Musée du Louvre (Paris, France)

Note that museums and other holding institutions will probably require a thorough treatment of ownership history, including various controlled fields for dates of ownership and methods of acquisition. For further discussion, see *Categories for the Description of Works of Art: Ownership/Collecting History*.

5.2.1.2.6 LOANS

Note when a work is housed in one location on long-term loan and is owned by another repository or agency.

> *Example*
>
> [for an oil painting]
>
>> **Current Location display**: Hart Senate Office Building (Washington, DC); on loan from the National Portrait Gallery (Washington, DC)
>>
>>> *[link to Personal and Corporate Name Authority]*: National Portrait Gallery (Washington, DC, United States)
>>>
>>> *[link to Subject Authority]*: Hart Senate Office Building (Washington, DC, United States)

Museums and other owning institutions will probably need several controlled fields to track loans. See *Categories for the Description of Works of Art: Exhibition/Loan History* for further discussion.

5.2.1.2.7 GEOSPATIAL DATA

Some institutions may require detailed geospatial data such as latitude and longitude. Ideally, this information should be in the Authority Record to which the Work Record is linked. For a discussion of geographic coordinates, see Part 3: Geographic Place Authority.

> *Example*
>
> [for a ruined farmhouse]
>
>> **Current Location display**: located outside Barcelona, Spain
>>
>>> *[link to Geographic Place Authority]*: Barcelona (Catalonia, Spain)
>>> **Coordinates**:
>>> **Lat**: 41 23 N; **Long**: 002 11 E

5.3 PRESENTATION OF THE DATA

5.3.1 Display and Indexing

5.3.1.1 *Free-Text vs. Controlled Fields*

For a discussion of when and why separate free-text and controlled fields are recommended, see Part 1: Database Design and Relationships: Display and Indexing.

Controlled fields for location information are essential. It is equally essential to be able to indicate in a free-text display field any uncertainty, ambiguity, approximations, and other information that might require explanation. This may be achieved with display fields dedicated to location information. Alternatively, the Description field may be used instead (see Chapter 8: Description), and displays for location information can be constructed by concatenating information from the appropriate authorities.

Example

[Option 1: with required current location and discovery location discussed in description]

> **Current Location display** *[concatenated from Personal and Corporate Name Authority]*: Kunsthistorisches Museum (Vienna, Austria)
>
> **Description element**: Was discovered along the Danube River in Niederösterreich, northeastern Austria.

[Option 2: with Current Location display and Discovery Location display, both indexed]

> **Current Location display**: Kunsthistorisches Museum (Vienna, Austria)
> > *[link to Personal and Corporate Name Authority]*: Kunsthistorisches Museum (Vienna, Austria)
>
> **Discovery Location display**: unnamed camp site, along the Danube River in Niederösterreich, northeastern Austria
> > *[link to Geographic Place Authority]*: Danube River (Niederösterreich, Austria)

5.3.1.2 *Fields in the Authorities and Work Record*

Location information may be linked to one of three authorities, depending on the type of location. Geographic places should be linked to the Geographic Place Authority. Buildings may be linked to the Subject Authority (or the Geographic Place Authority if that is the local practice); they may also be recorded as works in their own right. Repositories should be linked to the Personal and Corporate Name Authority, given that the owner of the work is a corporate body, not a building, even if the building happens to have the same name, such as the *National Gallery of Art*.

These authorities should include preferred and variant names for the geographic place or location, hierarchical links to broader contexts, and other information. See Part 3: Geographic Place Authority and Personal and Corporate Name Authority.

In the controlled fields used for indexing, a computer system or program that allows catalogers to use any term (preferred or variant) in the authority is ideal. If such a system is not an option, catalogers should be consistent in using the preferred form of the term or name when indexing the location.

5.3.2 Examples

Examples of Work Records are included below. For additional examples, see the end of Part 1, the end of each chapter, and the CCO Web site. In the examples, *controlled* refers to values controlled by an authority file, controlled list, or other rules (for example, with dates). *Link* refers to a relationship between a Work Record and an Authority Record or between two Work Records. All links are controlled fields. In the examples that follow, Related Work Records are abbreviated for the sake of brevity. All Work Records should be as complete as possible. See the various chapters for discussions of individual metadata elements, whether they should be controlled, and the respective advantages of an authority file or a controlled list. In all examples in this manual, both within and at the end of each chapter, data values for repeatable fields are separated by bullet characters.

Work Record

- ■ **Class** *[controlled]*: paintings • European art
- ■ ***Work Type** [link]*: painting
- ■ ***Title**: Wheatstacks, Snow Effect, Morning | **Title Type**: preferred
- ■ ***Creator display**: Claude Monet (French, 1840-1926)
    ***Role** [link]*: painter | *[link]*: Monet, Claude
- ■ ***Creation Date**: 1891
    [controlled]: **Earliest**: 1891; **Latest**: 1891
- ■ ***Subject** [links to authorities]*: landscape • Giverny (Haute-Normandie, France) • wheatstacks • field • snow • light
- ■ **Style** *[link]*: Impressionist
- ■ ***Current Location** [link]*: J. Paul Getty Museum (Los Angeles, California, United States) | **ID**:95.PA.63
- ■ **Creation Location** *[link]*: Giverny (Haute-Normandie, France)
- ■ ***Measurements**: 65 x 100 cm (25 1/2 x 39 1/4 inches)
    [controlled]: **Value**: 65; **Unit**: cm; **Type**: height | **Value**: 100; **Unit**: cm; **Type**: width
- ■ ***Materials and Techniques**: oil on canvas
    Material *[link]*: oil paint • canvas
- ■ **Description**: In May 1891, Monet began his first series, using wheatstacks just outside his garden at Giverny, producing 30 canvases depicting wheatstacks in various conditions of light and weather.

Personal and Corporate Name Authority Record

- ▨ ***Name**:
    J. Paul Getty Museum (preferred)
- ▨ ***Display Biography**: American museum, established 1953
- ▨ ***Nationality** [controlled]*: American
    ***[controlled]*: **Start**: 1953; **End**: 9999
- ▨ ***Role** [controlled]*: museum
- ▨ ***Location** [link to authority]*: Los Angeles (California, United States)

CREDIT: The J. Paul Getty Museum (Los Angeles, California), *Wheatstacks, Snow Effect, Morning,* (*Meules, Effet de Neige, Le Matin*) 1891; Claude Monet (French, 1840-1926); oil on canvas, 65 x 100 cm (25 1/2 x 39 1/4 inches); 95.PA.63. © The J. Paul Getty Trust.

Geographic Place Authority Record

- ▨ ***Names**:
    Giverny (preferred)
    Warnacum (historical)
- ▨ ***Hierarchical position** [link]*:
    .... Europe (continent)
    .... France (nation)
    .... Haute-Normandie (region)
    .... Eure (department)
    .... Giverny (inhabited place)
- ▨ ***Place Type** [controlled]*: inhabited place
- ▨ **Coordinates** *[controlled]*:
    Lat: 49 04 00 N degrees minutes
    Long: 001 32 00 E degrees minutes
    (**Lat**: 49.0667 decimal degrees)
    (**Long**: 1.5333 decimal degrees)
- ▨ **Note**: Located on the right bank of the River Seine, at its confluence with one of the two branches of the River Epte. Settlement was ancient, artifacts discovered here include a neolithic monument and Gallo-Roman graves ...
- ▨ ***Source** [link]*: Getty Thesaurus of Geographic Names (1988-).

Geographic Place Authority Record

- ▨ ***Names**:
    Los Angeles (preferred)
    L.A.
    Pueblo de Nuestra Señora la Reina de los Angeles de Porciuncula (historical)
- ▨ ***Hierarchical position** [link]*:
    North and Central America (continent)
    .... United States (nation)
    .... California (state)
    .... Los Angeles County (county)
    .... Los Angeles (inhabited place)
- ▨ ***Place Type** [controlled]*: inhabited place
- ▨ **Dates**: settled by Spanish expedition headed by Gaspar de Portolá in search of mission sites, on August 2, 1769; founded in 1781
    [controlled]: **Start**: 1769; **End**: 9999
- ▨ **Coordinates** *[controlled]*:
    Lat: 34 03 00 N degrees minutes
    Long: 118 14 00 W degrees minutes
    (**Lat**: 34.0500 decimal degrees)
    (**Long**: -118.2333 decimal degrees)
- ▨ **Note**: State's largest city; expanded rapidly in late 19th and early 20th centuries due to cattle ranching, railroads, and motion-picture industry ...
- ▨ ***Source** [link]*: Getty Thesaurus of Geographic Names (1988-).

Work Record

- **Class** *[controlled]*: sculpture • Asian art
- ***Work Type** *[link]*: statue
- ***Title**: Standing Parvati | **Title Type**: preferred
- ***Creator display**: unknown Indian (Tamil Nadu)
- ***Role** *[link]*: sculptor | *[link]*: unknown Indian
- ***Creation Date**: ca. first quarter of the 10th century
  [controlled]: **Earliest**: 0890; **Latest**: 0935
- ***Subject** *[links to authorities]*: religion and mythology • human figure
  • female • Parvati (Hindu deity) • sensuality • tribhanga • dance
- **Style** *[link]*: Chola period
- **Culture** *[link]*: Indian
- ***Current Location** *[link]*: Metropolitan Museum (New York, New York,
  United States) | **ID**:57.51.3
- **Creation Location** *[link]*: Tamil Nadu state (India)
- ***Measurements**: 69.5 cm (height) (27 3/8 inches)
  [controlled]: **Value**: 69.5; **Unit**: cm; **Type**: height
- ***Materials and Techniques**: copper alloy, lost-wax process
  Material *[link]*: copper alloy | **Technique** *[link]*: lost-wax process
- **Description Note**: As was typical of this period, this sculpture was
  created using the lost-wax technique, meaning each sculpture requires a
  separate wax model and thus is unique. Iconographic conventions for this
  figure include the conical crown with mountain-like (karandamukuta)
  tiers, swaying hips in a triple-bend (tribhanga) pose, and the one hand is
  posed as if holding a flower. Parvati in this pose is often placed beside
  Shiva in his role as Lord of the Dance (Nataraja).
- **Description Source** *[link]*: Metropolitan Museum of Art online.
  http://www.metmuseum.org (accessed February 1, 2005).

CREDIT: *Standing Parvati*, Chola period (880-1279), ca. first quarter of the 10th century; India (Tamil Nadu); Copper alloy; height: 27 3/8 in. (69.5 cm); view #1; The Metropolitan Museum of Art. Bequest of Cora Timken Burnett, 1956 (57.51.3). Photograph © 1994 The Metropolitan Museum of Art.

Geographic Place Authority Record

- ***Names**:
  Tamil Nadu (preferred)
  Madras (historical)
- ***Hierarchical position** *[link]*:
  Asia (continent)
  .... India (nation)
  .... Tamil Nadu (state)
- ***Place Type** *[controlled]*: state
- **Coordinates** *[controlled]*:
  Lat: 11 00 00 N degrees minutes
  Long: 078 00 00 E degrees minutes
  (**Lat**: 11.0000 decimal degrees)
  (**Long**: 78.0000 decimal degrees)
- **Note**: Cultural center of Dravidians during ancient times; was the base of
  Chola Empire 10th-13th century, and of Vijayanagara Kingdom 1335-
  1565. European colonization took place in the 1500s; area was under the
  control of Great Britain by the early 19th century; became an autonomous
  province in 1937; reorganized in 1956.
- ***Source** *[link]*: *Getty Thesaurus of Geographic Names* (1988-).

Figure 27

Work Record Linked to Authority Record: 19th-Century Building

Required and recommended elements are marked with an asterisk.

Work Record

- **Class** *[controlled]*: architecture • American art
- ***Work Type** *[link]*: courthouse
- ***Title**: Columbus Courthouse | **Title Type**: preferred
- ***Creator display**: Isaac Hodgson (American, born 1826 in Ireland)
     *Role *[link]*: architect | *[link]*: Hodgson, Isaac
- ***Creation Date**: ground broken in 1871, completed in 1874
     [controlled]: **Earliest**: 1871; **Latest**: 1874
- ***Subject** *[links to authorities]*: architecture • courthouse • government
- **Style** *[link]*: Second Empire
- ***Current Location** *[link]*: Columbus (Indiana, United States)
- ***Measurements**: 2 story
     [controlled]: **Extent**: stories; **Value**: 2; **Type**: count
- ***Materials and Techniques**: limestone foundation, limestone and facing brick, iron roof truss
     Material *[link]*: limestone • face brick | **Technique** *[link]*: iron trusses
- **Description**: Replaced an earlier courthouse located in the middle of Central Square. This new structure was noted for being heated with steam, lighted with gas chandeliers, and being fireproof: fireproofing included the original slate roof (now copper) and a method of using dirt and sand to fill the joist space between floor and ceiling.
- **Description Sources** *[link]*:
     National Register of Historic Places online (accessed February 4, 2005).
     Columbus Indiana: A Look At Architecture (1980); **Page**: 18.

CREDIT: Columbus Courthouse, Columbus, Indiana

Geographic Place Authority Record

- ***Names**:
     Columbus (preferred)
     Tiptonia (historical)
- ***Hierarchical position** *[link]*:
     North and Central America (continent)
     .... United States (nation)
     .... Indiana (state)
     .... Bartholomew (county)
     .... Columbus (inhabited place)
- ***Place Type** *[controlled]*: inhabited place
- **Coordinates** *[controlled]*:
     Lat: 39 12 00 N degrees minutes
     Long: 085 55 00 W degrees minutes
     (**Lat**: 39.2000 decimal degrees)
     (**Long**: -85.9167 decimal degrees)
- **Note**: Located on East Fork of White River; is a diversified industrial community surrounded by fertile prairie land; noted for modern architecture designed by distinguished architects, including I. M. Pei, the Saarinens, Harry Weese, and Robert Trent Jones.
- ***Source** *[link]*: *Getty Thesaurus of Geographic Names* (1988-).

Notes

1. The broader contexts may be added through the link to the Geographic Place Authority by using a broader context display field in the authority (see the discussion in Geographic Place Authority). Alternatively, the broader contexts may be concatenated by algorithm from the hierarchical parents for the place in the authority. If the broader contexts are thus added by algorithm rather than constructed by hand, develop a formula to consistently include the English name (if any) for the first-level administrative level and nation to display as parents with the city name (for example, *Lazio (Italy)* to display with *Rome*). Suitable algorithms may also be developed to display broader contexts for physical features, regions, and other types of geographic entities.

2. This example is intended to illustrate metadata elements discussed in this manual. Field names and data values in the example do not necessarily represent the record for this object in the Getty Museum's information system.

3. This example is intended to illustrate metadata elements discussed in this manual. Field names and data values in the example do not necessarily represent the record for this object in the Metropolitan Museum's information system.

Chapter *6*

Subject

Subject

6.1   ABOUT SUBJECT

6.1.1   Discussion

The Subject element contains an identification, description, or interpretation of what is depicted in and by a work or image. Subjects include things, places, activities, abstract shapes, decorations, stories, and events from literature, mythology, religion, or history. Philosophical, theoretical, symbolic, and allegorical themes and concepts may be subjects. Subjects of representational (figurative) works may be narrative, meaning that they tell a story or represent an episode in a story. They may also be nonnarrative, representing persons, animals, plants, buildings, or objects depicted in portraits, still lifes, landscapes, genre scenes, architectural drawings, allegories, and so on. Nonrepresentational works also have subject matter, which may include a reference to abstract content, decoration, function, or implied themes or attributes. Subject should be recorded for all works and images, even those that have no narrative or figurative subject matter in the traditional sense. For abstract works, architecture, decorative arts, furniture, and other works with no narrative or figurative subject matter, their content may be the function of the works and important aspects of their form or composition.

Determining the Subject

When analyzing subject content, the cataloger should answer the question: what is the work of or about? Traditionally, what a work is about (often called *about-ness*) is defined as its iconographical, narrative, thematic, or symbolic meaning; what the work is of (often called *of-ness*) is what would be seen in the work by an objective, nonexpert viewer. A methodical approach to subject analysis is

207

recommended. Posing the questions who, what, when, and where is one method of analyzing subject. Another method is a top-down approach that examines various levels of specificity based loosely on theories of human perception and recognition of meaning in images described by the scholar Erwin Panofsky.[1] Panofsky identified three primary levels of meaning in art: pre-iconographical description, expressional analysis or identification, and iconographical interpretation. Using a simplified and more practical application of this traditional art-historical approach can be helpful in indexing subjects for purposes of retrieval. The first level—description—refers to the generic elements depicted in or by the work (for example, *man*). The second level—identification—refers to the specific subject, including named mythological, fictional, religious, or historical subjects (for example, *George Washington*). The third level—interpretation—refers to the meaning or themes represented by the subjects and includes a conceptual analysis of what the work is about (for example, *political power*). For a more detailed discussion of this method, see *Categories for the Description of Works of Art: Subject Matter.*

Specificity

Include a general subject designation (for example, *portrait* or *landscape*). For other terms, the level of specificity and inclusiveness applied to cataloging the subject content of a work of art or architecture will depend upon various factors, including the depth of the cataloger's expertise and the quality and extent of information available. Do not include information, such as interpretation, if you do not have scholarly opinion to support it; furthermore, if expert knowledge is unavailable, it is better to be broad and accurate rather than specific and incorrect. For example, index a creature broadly as *bird* rather than specifically as *goldfinch* if you are uncertain of the species.

Adapt your approach to the characteristics of the collection being cataloged, the available time, human resources, and technology, and the needs of users for retrieval. Remember to accommodate both expert and nonexpert users. Answer these questions in the context of the institution's requirements. Is it useful to index every item in the scene? If not, where do you draw the limit? Will your system link a specific term to its broader context and synonyms in an authority file? If not, you should include important broader contexts and synonyms in the work record. The greater the depth of subject analysis, the better the access will be. Not all institutions, however, can afford the time and provide the expertise required for detailed subject analysis.

Although it may appear that subject terms applied to some types of works, such as architecture and utilitarian objects, repeat or overlap with terms applied to other elements such as Title or Work Type, a thorough description and indexing of the subject content should be done separately in the Subject element. Noting the subject of a work in fields or metadata elements dedicated specifically to subject content ensures that the subject is consistently recorded and indexed in the same place, using the same conventions for all works in the database.

Exhaustivity

To ensure consistent indexing, cataloging guidelines should be established regarding the number of terms to be assigned and the method to be used for analyzing a work or image to determine its subject. Catalogers can go through the levels of description, identification, and interpretation. They might go through a mental checklist of objects, persons, events, activities, places, and periods corresponding to the who, what, when, and where questions. They might read a work from left to right, from top to bottom, from foreground to background, or from the most prominent to least prominent subjects in the work. Works with a primarily functional purpose, such as architecture and utilitarian objects, should also be analyzed for subject, possibly including the work's function or form, or both. Some institutions may have the resources to assign only a few terms to each work; others may require more extensive cataloging.

Examples

[with only a few subject terms]
> **Subject**: still life • flowers

[with more extensive indexing]
> **Subject**:
> still life • flowers • Austrian copper rose • Floribunda rose • Jadis rose • lilac • Ming vase • embroidered tablecloth • Monarch butterfly

Ambiguity and Uncertainty

If scholarly opinion is divided regarding subject content, or if subject information is otherwise uncertain or ambiguous, this should be indicated in a free-text field (for example, *probably represents Zeus and a female consort, but possibly Poseidon and Amphitrite*). Such uncertainty may require that multiple possibilities be indexed in the field controlled by a vocabulary or authority file. For example, if scholarly opinion is divided regarding whether a figure represents Zeus or Poseidon, the names of both gods should be indexed for retrieval.

Organization of the Data

Subject is an important access point and indexing this element is strongly recommended. Some institutions, however, may not be able to record subject terminology. The Subject element should be repeatable. To ensure that broader contexts are applied and synonyms are accessible, names and terms used to describe subject matter should be drawn from the subject authority and the other three authorities. For example, the *Three Kings*, *Three Wise Men*, and the *Three Magi* are synonyms for the same biblical characters and all can provide end-user access to works depicting that subject. Ideally, the subject authority should be arranged in hierarchical structures that include narrower and broader relationships. For example, the 18th-century *Battle of Concord* could be linked to the broader subject *U.S. Revolutionary War* to facilitate end-user access. If maintaining a subject authority and other appropriate authorities is not possible, a controlled list of subjects should be used to ensure consistency. Because of the all-encompassing nature of subject content, several sources of subject terminology will certainly be required; furthermore, the system should allow for adding local terminology as needed.

Subject should ideally be recorded in a free-text field for display in combination with controlled fields for access. This may be done in a free-text field dedicated to subject or by including a discussion of the subject in the Description element (see Chapter 8). In any case, controlled fields for indexing subject are strongly recommended. It is likely that multiple subject terms will apply to each work or image, so the authority-controlled fields should be repeatable. Even though the subject matter of a work may be referred to in the Title and Work Type elements, a thorough description and indexing of the subject content should be done in the Subject element.

This chapter discusses subject information that is recorded in the Work Record. Image collections will often have more than one view of a work, including interior and exterior views of an architectural work, an image of a detail of a painting or sculpture, and so on. Users of an image collection require access to particular views of a work, in addition to all views of the same work. For example, users must be able to retrieve particular images of *tierceron ribs* in the vaults of the larger contexts, *Lincoln Cathedral* and *King's College Chapel* in Cambridge. See Chapter 9: View Information: View Description and View Subject, and Part 3: Subject Authority for further information. Additional discussion of issues surrounding the recording of subjects can be found in *Categories for the Description of Works of Art: Subject Matter* and the subject identification authority. Issues related to subject matter and subject identification are discussed in some depth in *Introduction to Art Image Access.*[2]

Authorities for Subject

Local practice, resources, and database functionality will dictate which terms are stored in a dedicated subject authority file. However, subject terminology can and usually does cover a broad range of terminology. Ideally, the Subject Authority would comprise only terminology that falls outside the scope of the other authorities. It would likely contain proper names for iconography, such as the names of literary, mythological, or religious characters or themes, historical events and themes, and any other named iconographical subject. Given that subject matter may include types of terminology that are also applied to other parts of the Work Record, terms used in the Subject fields may be found in various authority files; given the overlap in terminology needed for various elements, it is typically more efficient to include any given term in a single authority file to avoid redundant entry of the same term in multiple authorities. For example, personal names for subjects (for example, *Galileo Galilei (Italian scientist, philosopher, 1564-1642)*) could be found in the Personal and Corporate Name Authority, in which records for artists and other persons related to the works are also contained; records for persons, whether artists, patrons, or subjects, have similar characteristics, require similar fields, and therefore can be stored in the same authority file (life roles can be used to separate artist names from other kinds of personal names in the authority file, when necessary). In addition, the same person can have multiple roles related to various works, such as *subject*, *patron*, or *artist*. Geographic names needed for subject (for example, *Tokyo (Japan)*) could be found in the Geographic Place Authority, because such names will also be used in other fields in the Work Record. Terminology (for example, *cathedral*, *marble*, *chisel*) needed for Work Type, physical characteristics, and other fields may also be required for Subject; this could be stored in the Concept Authority, along with the terms used to index the generic elements depicted in a work (for example, *woman*, *tree*, *horse*).

Architecture and other works may be the subjects of other works; named architectural and other works may be included in the subject authority or cataloged as works in their own right in Work Records. For further discussion, see Part 3: Subject Authority.

Recommended Elements

A list of the elements discussed in this chapter appears below. Required elements are noted. Display may be a free-text field or concatenated from controlled fields.

> Subject display or Description element (if you do not include a subject display, describe the subject in the description element as necessary)
>> Controlled Subject (required) (ideally links to several authorities: persons/corporate bodies, geographic places, concepts, or iconographical subject authority)
>> Extent
>> Subject Type

About the Examples

The examples throughout this chapter are for illustration only. Local practice may vary. The examples tend to show the fullest possible use of display and indexing fields, which may not be necessary for visual resources collections and some other institutions.

6.1.2   Terminology

6.1.2.1   *Sources for Terminology*

Subject terminology should be controlled by using authority files or controlled lists.

Note that subject terminology may be stored in the Geographic Place Authority, Personal and Corporate Name Authority, and the Concept Authority (for general concepts), as well as in a dedicated Subject Authority. See the discussion at the beginning of this chapter and in Part 3: Subject Authority.

Subject indexing generally requires the use of terms from many different vocabularies; note that local terminology will also probably be necessary. Published sources of terms that may be appropriate for subjects include the following.

Generic Concepts

> Getty Vocabulary Program. *Art & Architecture Thesaurus* (AAT). Los Angeles: J. Paul Getty Trust, 1988-. http://www.getty.edu/research/ conducting_research/vocabularies/aat/.

> Library of Congress Authorities. *Library of Congress Subject Headings*. Washington, DC: Library of Congress, 2005. http://authorities.loc .gov/.

> Fleming, John. *Penguin Dictionary of Architecture and Building Terms*. London: Penguin, 1999.

> Grech, Chris. *Multilingual Dictionary of Architecture and Building Terms*. New York: E. and F. N. Spon, 1998.

Iconographic Themes

ICONCLASS. http://www.iconclass.nl/. (Most useful for Western religious and mythological subjects).

Garnier, François. *Thesaurus iconographique: système descriptif des représentations.* Paris: Léopard d'or, 1984.

Roberts, Helene E., ed. *Encyclopedia of Comparative Iconography: Themes Depicted in Works of Art.* 2 vols. Chicago: Fitzroy Dearborn, 1998.

Stutley, Margaret. *Illustrated Dictionary of Hindu Iconography.* London: Routledge and Kegan Paul, 1985.

Narkiss, Bezalel, et al. *Index of Jewish Art: An Iconographical Index of Hebrew Illuminated Manuscripts.* Jerusalem: Israel Academy of Sciences and Humanities; Paris: Institut de recherche et d'histoire des textes, 1976-1988.

Fictional Characters

Seymour-Smith, Martin, and William Freeman. *Dictionary of Fictional Characters.* Rev. ed. Boston: The Writer, 1992

Persons or Groups of Persons

Library of Congress Authorities. *Library of Congress Name Authorities.* Washington, DC: Library of Congress. http://authorities.loc.gov/.

The International Who's Who. London: Europa Publications Ltd., 1935-.

Hunt, Kimberly N. *Encyclopedia of Associations: National Organizations.* 38th ed. 2 vols. Farmington Hills, MI: Gale Group, 2002.

Atterberry, Tara E. *Encyclopedia of Associations: International Organizations.* 37th ed. 2 vols. Detroit, MI: Gale Group, 2001.

Biography and Genealogy Master Index. Farmington Hills, MI: Thomson-Gale, 1998. Online by subscription at http://galenet.gale.com/a/acp/bgmi (accessed November 18, 2002).

Canadiana: The National Bibliography on CD-ROM. Ottawa: National Library of Canada, 2001-.

Getty Vocabulary Program. *Union List of Artist Names (ULAN).* Los Angeles: J. Paul Getty Trust, 2000. http://www.getty.edu/research/conducting_research/vocabularies/ulan/.

Names of Buildings

Avery Architectural & Fine Arts Library. *Avery Index to Architectural Periodicals at Columbia University.* Los Angeles: J. Paul Getty Trust, 1994-. Online by subscription at http://www.getty.edu/research/conducting_research/avery_index/.

Macmillan Encyclopedia of Architects. Edited by Adolf K. Placzek. New York: Free Press; London: Collier Macmillan, 1982.

America Preserved: Checklist of Historic Buildings, Structures, and Sites.
    60th ed. Washington, DC: Library of Congress, Cataloging
    Distribution Service, 1995.

Fletcher, Sir Banister. *History of Architecture.* 20th ed. Oxford; Boston:
    Architectural Press, 1996.

Grove Dictionary of Art Online. New York: Grove's Dictionaries, 2003.
    http://www.groveart.com/.

Library of Congress Authorities. *Library of Congress Subject Headings
    and Name Authorities.* Washington, DC: Library of Congress.
    http://authorities.loc.gov/.

Geographic Names

Getty Vocabulary Program. *Getty Thesaurus of Geographic Names* (TGN).
    Los Angeles: J. Paul Getty Trust, 1988-. http://www.getty.edu/
    research/conducting_research/vocabularies/tgn/.

United States Geological Survey (USGS). *Geographic Names Information
    System* (GNIS). http://geonames.usgs.gov/ [domestic names]

National Geospatial Intelligence Agency (NGA), formerly United States
    National Imagery and Mapping Agency (NIMA). (Advised by the U.S.
    Board on Geographic Names. USBGN). *GEOnet Names Server* (GNS).
    http://earth-info.nga.mil/gns/html/ [foreign names]

Library of Congress Authorities. *Library of Congress Subject Headings.*
    Washington, DC: Library of Congress. http://authorities.loc.gov/.

Seltzer, Leon E., ed. *Columbia Lippincott Gazetteer of the World.*
    Morningside Heights, NY: Columbia University Press, 1961.

Princeton Encyclopedia of Classical Sites. 2nd ed. Princeton, NJ:
    Princeton University Press, 1979.

Barraclough, Geoffrey, ed. *Times Atlas of World History.* 4th ed. edited by
    Geoffrey Parker. Maplewood, NJ: Hammond, 1994.

Times Atlas of the World. 10th comprehensive ed. New York: Times
    Books, 1999.

Webster's New Geographical Dictionary. Springfield, MA: Merriam-
    Webster, 1984.

Rand McNally. *New International Atlas.* Chicago: Rand McNally, 1995.

Archaeological Terms

Lavell, Cherry. *British Archaeological Thesaurus: For Use with British
    Archaeological Abstracts and Other Publications with British
    Archaeology.* London: Council for British Archaeology, 1989.

Museum Documentation Association. *MDA Archaeological Objects
    Thesaurus.* Cambridge: MDA, English Heritage & Royal Commission
    on the Historical Monuments of England, 1997. http://www.mda
    .org.uk/archobj/archint.htm#Foreword.

Getty Vocabulary Program. *Art & Architecture Thesaurus* (AAT). Los Angeles: J. Paul Getty Trust, 1988-. www.getty.edu/research/ conducting_research/vocabularies/aat/.

Animals

Animal Diversity Web. University of Michigan Museum of Zoology, 1995-2002. http://animaldiversity.ummz.umich.edu/index.html.

Grzimek, Bernhard, and George M. Narita, eds. *Grzimek's Animal Life Encyclopedia.* 13 vols. New York: Van Nostrand Reinhold, 1972-1975.

Plants

USDA, NRCS. 2001. *The PLANTS Database*, Version 3.1. National Plant Data Center, Baton Rouge, LA 70874-4490 USA. http://plants .usda.gov.

Events

Library of Congress Authorities. *Library of Congress Subject Headings.* Washington, DC: Library of Congress. http://authorities.loc.gov/.

Mellersh, H. E. L., and Neville Williams. *Chronology of World History.* 4 vols. Santa Barbara, CA: ABC-CLIO, 1999.

Grun, Bernard. *Timetables of History: A Horizontal Linkage of People and Events.* 3rd ed. New York: Simon and Schuster, 1991.

Thompson, Sue Ellen, and Helene Henderson, comp. *Holidays, Festivals, and Celebrations of the World Dictionary.* 2nd ed. Detroit: Omnigraphics, 1997.

Kohn, George Childs. *Dictionary of Wars.* Rev. ed. New York: Facts on File, 2000.

Human Anatomy and Medical Topics

Medical Subject Headings (MeSH). Bethesda, MD: National Library of Medicine, nd. http://www.nlm.nih.gov/mesh/MBrowser.html.

General Science, Astronomy, Aerospace Information

NASA Scientific and Technical Information Office. *NASA Thesaurus, 1998 Edition.* 2 vols. Plus Supplement. Washington, DC: National Aeronautics and Space Administration, 1998. http://www.sti.nasa .gov/thesfrm1.htm.

6.1.2.2   *Choice of Terminology*

6.1.2.2.1   CONSISTENCY

Using consistent terminology is especially important for controlled fields that are intended to provide access. Consistency is less important, but still desirable, in a free-text note than in a controlled field. Although uncontrolled terminology should be accommodated, terminology that is consistent with the terms in controlled fields is nonetheless recommended for the sake of clarity. Consistent style, grammar, and syntax are recommended.

6.1.2.2.2 USE OF AUTHORITY FILES

If possible, subject terms and related information should be stored in authorities linked to the work record.

To populate the authorities, use standard sources for subject terms and other appropriate terminology. If a particular subject cannot be found in any of the standard published sources, make a new authority record, citing the source from which the information was taken.

6.2 CATALOGING RULES

6.2.1 Rules for Subject

6.2.1.1 *Brief Rules for Subject*

Record one or more terms that characterize the persons and groups of persons, things, places, activities, abstract shapes, decorations, stories, events from literature, mythology, religion, or history, and philosophical, theoretical, symbolic, or allegorical themes depicted in the work.

Singular vs. Plural

Use the proper names of iconographical themes, mythological events, persons, places, and the like, as appropriate; issues of singular vs. plural generally do not apply to proper names. For generic terms, generally use the singular form of the term. When the singular is inappropriate, use the plural term, as warranted by the subject being cataloged. For example, if a single tree is depicted in a painting, use the singular *tree*; if two or more trees are depicted, use the plural *trees*.[3]

> *Examples*
>
> **Subject**: Annunciation (Life of the Virgin cycle)
>
> **Subject**: Buddha (Buddhist iconography)
>
> **Subject**: fruit
>
> **Subject**: tree
>
> **Subject**: horses

Capitalization and Abbreviations

Capitalize proper names; for other terms, use lowercase. Avoid abbreviations.

> *Examples*
>
> **Subject**: Abraham Lincoln (American president, 1809-1865, president 1861-1865)
>
> **Subject**: Coronation of Charlemagne (Life of Charlemagne)
>
> **Subject**: Cairo (Egypt)
>
> **Subject**: flowers
>
> **Subject**: landscape

Language of the Terms

Use terminology in the language of the catalog record (English in the United States), except for proper names and other cases where no English-language equivalent exists. Use diacritics as required for non-English terms.

Examples

Subject: bridge

Subject: lake

Subject: caritas romana

Subject: fin-de-siècle

Subject: André-Marie Ampère (French physicist, 1775-1836)

6.2.1.2 *Additional Recommendations for Subject*

6.2.1.2.1 CONVEYING NUANCE AND AMBIGUITY

The recommendations and examples below imply either a free-text field dedicated to subject or using the Description element to express the nuance regarding subject (see Chapter 8). See Display and Indexing below.

6.2.1.2.2 SYNTAX

Express the subject in natural word order. Place broader contexts, biographical information for persons, and the like in parentheses or with other punctuation for clarity.

6.2.1.2.3 CONTEXT SENSITIVITY

Use terminology that is context-sensitive to the work being cataloged, if possible. For example, if the work portrays the Greek goddess Aphrodite, use that name to describe her rather than the Roman name, Venus.

6.2.1.2.4 SPECIFICITY

Include both general and specific terms as described.

General Subject

In the indexing terms, include terms that describe the subject matter in a general way, as warranted. Note that the general subject will not necessarily be a broader context for the specific subject in an authority file. For example, *portrait* is a general type, *ruler* and *Shah Jahan* are more specific, but none of the three terms will have a genus-species relationship in the authority file.

Example

Subject display or Description element:
Shah Jahan on horseback, dressed for the hunt.

Controlled Subject fields (repeatable):
portrait • ruler • horse • hunt • Shah Jahan (Mughal emperor of India, 1592-1666, ruled 1628-1658)

In the list of general subject terms below, terms with the word "and" refer to the same subject, interpretation of which may differ depending on the user's point of view. Is a subject religious or mythological, history or legend? It is often a point of view and the terms are therefore combined with an "and" to avoid advocating one or the other view in subject indexing. The individual terms should map to the Concept Authority. When local systems or sources of vocabulary do not accommodate combined terms, catalogers might instead link to both terms in the authority.

advertising and commercial	allegory	animal
apparel	architecture	botanical
ceremonial object	cityscape	funerary art
genre	history and legend	human figure
interior architecture	landscape	literary theme
machine	military	mixed motif
object (utilitarian)	nonrepresentational art	portrait
didactic and propaganda	religion and mythology	seascape
still life		

Specific Subject

Include terms to describe the subject as specifically as possible, as warranted by the information available and the expertise of the catalogers. For example, if you know that a flower is a rose, use the specific term *rose* or use the species name, *Rosa soulieana*. If you do not know what kind of flower it is, use a more general term, such as *flower*.

6.2.1.2.5 VARIOUS TYPES OF SUBJECTS AND WORKS

Choose terms appropriate to the type of subject being cataloged.

Proper Names

Include proper nouns that identify persons, places, activities, and events, if known (for example, *Napoleon Bonaparte, Venus, Cusco (Peru), African diaspora, Mexican Independence Day*).

> *Example*
>
> **Subject display or Description element**:
> Battle of Little Big Horn from the Native American point of view.
>
> **Controlled Subject fields (repeatable)**:
> history and legend • Battle of Little Big Horn (Indian Wars) • war • death • Lakota • Cheyenne • horses • United States Army 7th Cavalry

Allegory and Themes

Include terms to describe thematic and allegorical concepts, as the cataloger's expertise or authoritative documentation permits, for example, *truth, war, democracy, materialism.*

Example

Subject display or Description element:
Ancient plum tree with two new shoots

Controlled Subject fields (repeatable):
allegory • Spring • botanical • birth • plum tree • renewal

Narrative Subjects

For subjects that tell a story, describe the narrative sequence or the episode from the story represented in or by the work. The examples below illustrate a brief and a fuller cataloging of narrative subjects (see Figure 28).

Examples

Subject display or Description element:
Saint Bruno sees a heavenly vision while meditating in the wilderness.

Controlled Subject fields (repeatable):
religion and mythology • Saint Bruno (French cleric, 11th century) • vision • heaven • angels • wilderness • Carthusian order (Christian monastic order) • meditation

Subject display or Description element:
In a continuous narrative designed for the side of a wedding chest, the scene depicts Paris, a shepherd who is the most handsome man in the world. Paris must judge a competition between three goddesses; he hands an apple inscribed "For the fairest" to Aphrodite without even looking at her rival goddesses, Hera and Athena. He thus chooses the love of Helen, the world's most beautiful woman, over greatness or warlike prowess. As a reward, he is granted the fair Helen, and takes her on his horse to the town in the distance.

Controlled Subject fields (repeatable):

religion and mythology	landscape
Greek mythology	human male
Aphrodite (Greek goddess)	human female
Athena (Greek goddess)	castle
Hera (Greek goddess)	fortified city
Paris (Greek legendary character)	horse
Helen (Greek legendary character)	beauty
Trojan War (Greek legends)	love
contest	marriage
victory of love over war	Judgment of Paris

Figure 28
Iconographical Subjects: Judgment of Paris

CREDIT: The J. Paul Getty Museum (Los Angeles, California). Francesco di Giorgio Martini (Italian 1439-1502). *Story of Paris* [center panel]; ca. 1460s; tempera on wood; 34.9 x 108.7 cm (13 3/4 x 42 7/8 inches); 70.PB.45. © The J. Paul Getty Trust.

Representational Subject, Nonnarrative

For nonnarrative subjects, include the primary persons, places, things, events, allegorical content, and other pertinent subject matter.

Examples

Subject display or Description element:
Forest with a winding road and bridge, with a castle in the distance.

Controlled Subject fields (repeatable): landscape • castle • road • forest • bridge

The following are full subject descriptions for Figures 29 and 30. For a more limited indexing of subject for the painting in Figure 29, see Part 1: Examples.

Examples

Subject display or Description element:
Still life of drooping flowers spilling onto a ledge, some decaying and being eaten by insects; represents the senses of sight and smell; the decay and broken stems symbolize the transient nature of life, youth, and beauty; the ledge pushed up to the picture plane resembles the ledge seen in posthumous portraits, thus symbolizing death. The crown of thorns flower at the top symbolizes the Passion of Christ.

Controlled Subject fields (repeatable):

still life	roses	eggs	crown of thorns plant
botanical	violet	transience	Passion of Christ
flowers	lilies	life	Pronkstilleven
tulips	primrose	Vanitas	caterpillar
narcissus	cyclamen	beauty	bird's nest
sweetpeas	peonies	smell	ledge
urn	hyacinth	senses	death

Figure 29
Still Life: Flowers

Figure 30
Albumen Print: Portraits, Civil War

Part TWO: Elements

Subject display or Description element:
President Abraham Lincoln on the Antietam battlefield, with Major Allan Pinkerton, chief of the Secret Service, and Major John McClernand.

Controlled Subject fields (repeatable):
portraits • Battle of Antietam (American Civil War) • United States Army • president • war • soldier • Allan Pinkerton (American Secret Service agent, detective, 1819-1884) • John McClernand (American Union General, 1812-1900) • history and legend • army camp • tent • campstool • stovepipe hat • officer • Abraham Lincoln (American president, 1809-1865) • Antietam Battlefield (Sharpsburg, Maryland)

Nonrepresentational Works

For works with no figurative or narrative content, such as nonrepresentational or abstract art, describe the visual elements of the composition (for example, *geometric patterns*, *friezes*, *spheres*) and thematic or symbolic meaning.

Example

Subject display or Description element:
The objects used by Man Ray to create this image are not apparent; the rapid alternation of light and dark on the page stimulates the eye; the stippled spots of black interact with the texture of the paper to activate the surface of the print and suggest positive and negative space.

Controlled Subject fields (repeatable):
nonrepresentational • light • light and dark • texture • spots • positive and negative space

Figure 31
Abstract, Rayograph

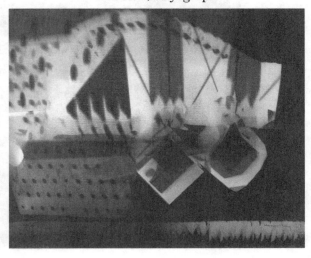

CREDIT: The J. Paul Getty Museum (Los Angeles, California). Man Ray (American, 1890-1976, died in France). *Untitled Rayograph (Light Patterns)*. 1927. Gelatin silver print rayograph. 9 15/16 x 11 7/8 inches (25.15 x 29.97 cm). 84.XM.1000.153. © Man Ray Trust ARS-ADAGP. © The J. Paul Getty Trust.

Decorative Arts

For decorative arts and material culture objects that are primarily functional, describe the object's function (for example, *watering cans*, *prayer rugs*, *divination objects*) and themes or allegorical meanings, if any.

Example

Subject display or Description element:
Strewn with flowers, vessels filled with fruit and flowers, and large acanthus leaf scrolls, the design of this large carpet centers on a prominent central sunflower, the symbol of the Sun King Louis XIV. Images of Chinese blue-and-white porcelain bowls decorate the border.

Controlled Subject fields (repeatable):
object (utilitaritian) • carpet • fruit • flowers • bowls • sunflower • acanthus leaf scrolls • Chinese porcelain • Sun King • Louis XIV (French king, 1638-1715, reigned 1643-1715)

Figure 32
French Carpet

CREDIT: The J. Paul Getty Museum (Los Angeles, California). Savonnerie Manufactory (*French carpet factory, active from 1627 to the present*), made in the Chaillot workshops of Philippe Lourdet. Carpet. ca. 1666. Wool and linen. L: 428.8 x W: 642.1 cm (L: 21 feet 4/5 inches x W: 14 feet 4/5 inches). 70.DC.63. Gift of J. Paul Getty. © The J. Paul Getty Trust.

Architecture

For works of architecture, architectural complexes, and sites, use terms that describe the work's purpose or primary function. This can include its function based on its ownership, activities associated with its use, or its purpose based on developmental design (for example, *corporate headquarters*, *church*, *religious building*, *tract houses*). The subject term may repeat the object type. For churches and other buildings with dedications, record the dedication as a subject.

> *Example*
>
> **Subject display or Description element**:
> Pantheon, formerly dedicated to Santa Maria ad Martyres.
>
> **Controlled Subject fields (repeatable)**:
> architecture • planetary gods • museum • Queen of Martyrs (Veneration of the Virgin Mary) • worship • church • temple

6.2.1.2.6 MULTIPLE SUBJECTS

When a work contains multiple subjects, include a clarification in the display field and index all subjects in the controlled fields.

> *Example*
>
> **Subject display or Description element**:
> Panathenaic amphora. Side A: Athena Promachos; Side B: Nike crowning the Victor, with the judge on the right and the defeated opponent on the left.
>
> **Controlled Subject fields (repeatable)**:
> religion and mythology • human males • human females • ceremonial object • competition • prize • Nike (Greek goddess) • object (utilitarian) • victor • Athena Promachos (Greek iconography)

Extent

In the indexing fields, some institutions may wish to designate the part of the work for which the subject terms are pertinent. Examples of Extent could include *side A*, *side B*, *recto*, *verso*, *main panel*, *predella*, and the like. Using Extent generally or for the overall subject is not necessary, except to distinguish it from the subject of the parts.

> *Example*
>
> [for a Panathenaic amphora, subject overall and for each side]
> **Extent**: overall
> **Controlled Subject fields**:
> religion and mythology • ceremonial object
>
> **Extent**: side A
> **Controlled Subject fields**:
> Athena Promachos (Greek iconography) • human female
>
> **Extent**: side B
> **Controlled Subject fields**:
> Nike (Greek goddess) • victor • human females • prize • competition

6.2.1.2.7 SUBJECT AS PART OF A LARGER SUBJECT

When the subject is part of a larger literary work or story, a larger subject that is typically portrayed in a series, a historical event that is part of a larger theme, and the like, provide access to the subject of the larger context as well as to the specific subject of the work being cataloged.

> *Example*
>
> **Subject display or Description element:**
> Krishna battles the armies of the demon Naraka, from the Bhagavata Purana (Ancient Stories of Lord Vishnu).
>
> **Controlled Subject fields (repeatable):**
> Krishna and Naraka (Bhagavata Purana, Hindu literature) • Krishna (incarnation of Vishnu, Hindu diety) • Naraka (Hindu demon) • warriors • religion and mythology • elephants • war • horses

Linking to a hierarchical authority is the most efficient way to link a subject to its broader contexts; see Part 3: Subject Authority. If this is not possible, include the subject of the larger context in the record for the work being cataloged.

Note that if the work itself is part of a series of works, this may be mentioned in the subject display, but the item should be linked to the series through Related Works, if possible. See Part 1: Related Works and Chapter 1: Object Naming.

> *Example*
>
> **Subject display or Description element:**
> The work is part of the Gobelins series *Les Anciennes Indes*, featuring exotic life of the Indies and South America. This tapestry depicts unusual plant and animal life of Brazil. Many of the plants, fish, birds, and other animals woven in this hanging were taken from life drawings made in South America; however, French artists at the Gobelins manufactory added other animals, such as the Indian rhinoceros and striped horse or zebra.
>
> **Controlled Subject fields (repeatable):**
> object (utilitarian) • landscape • hunt • travel • plants • fish • bow and arrow • spear • Brazil • Dutch expansion • animals • Indies • human figures • Amerindians • zebra • turtle • crane • parrot • rhinoceros • South America • Native Americans

6.2.1.2.8 WHEN SUBJECT IS ANOTHER WORK

If a work depicts another work, record the depicted work as a subject. Examples include architecture or other art works depicted in drawings, photographs, and paintings. In addition, if both works are being cataloged, link them as Related Works. See Part 1: Related Works. In the example, the cataloging institution has made a separate Work Record for the depicted work, linking the work at hand to the record for the depicted work; in other words, *Wells Cathedral* is both the Subject and a Related Work.

> *Example*
>
> **[for a 19th-century albumen print by Frederick Henry Evans]**
>
> **Subject display or Description element:**
> west end of the nave, Wells Cathedral (Somerset, England)

Controlled Subject fields (repeatable):

⟶ interior architecture • arches • <u>Wells Cathedral (Somerset, England)</u> • columns • nave
• light

[linked to another Work Record]

Related Work:
Relationship Type: depiction of
[concatenated label for the Related Work]:

⟶ <u>Wells Cathedral (Somerset, England, United Kingdom)</u>. Current structure begun
ca. 1180.

6.2.1.2.9 RECORDING SUBJECT AS DEPICTED IN WORK

Indicate when the subject as depicted in the work is a view, a detail, incorrect, or otherwise does not accurately represent the named subject.

Subject as Depicted vs. Reality

For designs for and depictions of architecture, cartographical and topographical materials, and technical and scientific renderings, describe the subject as depicted in the work.[4] In the example below, the design as depicted does not portray the design of the Lincoln Memorial as built. The drawing is linked to the authority record for the Lincoln Memorial, but important characteristics of the subject as depicted have also been included (for example, *pyramid, reflecting pool*).

Example

Subject display or Description element:
Presentation drawing. Pope's design for the Lincoln Memorial in the shape of a pyramid (1912 competition) included entrances with façades in the form of a Greek temple on all four sides; there was a reflecting pool on the east side.

Controlled Subject fields (repeatable):
architecture • Lincoln Memorial (Washington, DC) • presentation drawing • pyramid
• reflecting pool • Greek temple plan

Subject as Depicted in a Detail

If the work portrays a detail or a partial or particular view of a subject, record the important characteristics of the subject as depicted in the work.

Examples

Subject display or Description element:
Extreme close-up of the left eye and lips of Marilyn Monroe.

Controlled Subject fields (repeatable):
portrait • extreme close-up • Marilyn Monroe (American actress, 1926-1962) • eye
• nostril • lips

Subject display or Description element:
Section and elevation of the drum and dome of Saint Peter's, Rome.

Controlled Subject fields (repeatable):
architecture • dome • drum • lantern • buttresses • pilasters • Saint Peter's (Rome, Italy)
• section • elevation • cathedral • basilica • papal authority

Subject Characteristics Particular to Surrogate Images

For cataloging subjects of surrogate images, see the discussion in Chapter 9: View Information.

6.2.1.2.10 UNCERTAIN SUBJECTS

If the subject of the work is in dispute or otherwise uncertain among scholars, note this in the free-text field and index alternative subjects in the controlled fields.

Example

[for a painting by Dosso Dossi]

Subject display or Description element:
The painting's precise meaning is uncertain, though it seems to be an allegory with the message that prosperity in life is transitory and dependent on luck. The nude woman apparently represents Fortune, holding a cornucopia containing the bounty that she could bring; however, she sits on a bubble, which could burst at any moment. The man personifies chance; he holds up lottery tickets, which he is about to place inside a golden urn, a timely reference to the civic lotteries that had just become popular in Italy. The tickets may also refer to the painting's probable patron, Isabella d'Este, Marchioness of Mantua. One of her emblems was a bundle of lots, denoting her personal experience with fluctuating fortune.

Controlled Subject fields (repeatable):
allegory • bubble • cornucopia • fruit • lottery tickets • urn • wind • female nude • male nude • Fortune • Chance • good fortune • misfortune • luck • Isabella d'Este (Italian noblewoman, 1473-1539)

6.2.1.2.11 FORMER SUBJECTS

If opinions regarding the subject designation have changed over time, note this in the display field and index former subjects in the controlled fields.

Example

Subject display or Description element:
The portrait was formerly believed to represent Cosimo I de'Medici; it is now held that the sitter may be Francesco Guardi, a young nobleman. He holds a halberd, a military weapon used during the 15th and 16th centuries; a halberd was a combination spear and battle-ax, used in battle but also as a symbol indicating a member of the civic guard.

Controlled Subject fields (repeatable):
portrait • halberd • halberdier • soldier • spear • weapon • civic guard • human male • nobleman • sword • ax • battle-ax • Mannerist costume • Francesco Guardi (Italian nobleman, born 1514) • Cosimo I de' Medici (Italian nobleman, 1519-1574, Grand Duke of Tuscany 1569-1574)

6.2.1.2.12 GROUPS OF WORKS

For a group of works, include all of the subjects represented in the group, if possible. If there are too many subjects to include them all, include the most important or most prominent subjects.

Example

[for a group of works]

Subject display or Description element:
The group of drawings includes general views, bird's-eye views, cadastral maps, and other images of several cities in Italy, including Venice, Naples, Rome and Florence.

Controlled Subject fields (repeatable):
views • cadastral maps • cityscapes • Rome (Italy) • Naples (Italy) • Turin (Italy) • Lake Garda (Italy) • wind • bird's-eye views • topographical views • Venice (Italy) • Florence (Italy) • San Gimignano (Italy) • Siena (Italy) • landscapes • architecture

6.2.1.2.13 SUBJECT TYPE

Some institutions may want to designate the type of subject being described. The Subject Type element may be used to distinguish between subjects that reflect what the work is of (description and identification) from terms indicating what the work is about (interpretation).

Example

[for a Jasper Francis Cropsey landscape]

Subject display or Description element:
Monumental view of the Hudson River Valley with a high vantage point, looking southeast toward the distant Hudson River and the flank of Storm King Mountain.

Subject Type: description
Subject Terms: landscape • autumn • dawn • hunters • dogs

Subject Type: identification
Subject Terms: Hudson River (New York, United States) • Storm King Mountain (Orange County, New York, United States)

Subject Type: interpretation
Subject Terms: peace • man in harmony with nature

6.3 PRESENTATION OF THE DATA

6.3.1 Display and Indexing

6.3.1.1 *Free-Text vs. Controlled Fields*

For a discussion of when and why separate free-text and controlled fields are recommended, see Part 1: Database Design and Relationships: Display and Indexing.

Ideally, subject should be recorded in a free-text field for display and controlled fields that will be used for retrieval.[5] Either include a free-text field reserved for subject or include a description of the subject in the Description element.

Alternatively, a rudimentary display can be constructed by concatenating terms from controlled fields.

Example

Subject display or Description element:
Interior view of Saint Bavo, Haarlem. The artist departed from reality when, for a clear glass window with a door beneath, he substituted an altar and a stained glass window with a scene of the Immaculate Conception, calling to mind perhaps the state of the Catholic church before it was transformed into a whitewashed Dutch Protestant church.

Controlled Subject fields (repeatable):
architecture • interior • church • Saint Bavo (Haarlem, the Netherlands) • Gothic architecture • Immaculate Conception (Life of the Virgin cycle) • Protestant Reformation • Catholicism

6.3.1.2 *Fields in Authority Files and Work Record*

6.3.1.2.1 MINIMUM CONTROLLED FIELDS IN THE WORK RECORD

A repeatable field for controlled subject terminology is required in the Work Record. A free-text field, either one dedicated to subject or description, may be included in the Work Record.

6.3.1.2.2 AUTHORITY FILE ELEMENTS

Ideally, controlled subject terminology should be stored in separate Authority Records. In a cataloging system, there may be several authority files from which subject terminology may be drawn. See further discussion in Part 3: Subject Authority. If linking to an authority file is not possible, terminology for indexing should be linked to a controlled list.

For the Controlled Subject field, the terms in the examples are sometimes shown with a display biography (for persons) or broader contexts in parentheses, as if these values were concatenated from hierarchical authorities. See the sections on each authority file for recommendations for displaying terminology in the Work or Image Record, specifically, Part 3: Subject Authority, Personal and Corporate Name Authority, Geographic Place Authority, and Concept Authority.

In the controlled, indexing fields, it is most effective to use a computer system that efficiently allows catalogers to use any term or name form linked to a given subject in the authority file. Lacking such a system, catalogers should be consistent in using the preferred form of term or name used for indexing the subject. See Part 3 for further discussion.

6.3.2   Examples

Examples of Work Records are included below. For additional examples, see the end of Part 1, the end of each chapter, and the CCO Web site. In the examples, *controlled* refers to values controlled by an authority file, controlled list, or other rules (for example, rules for recording dates). *Link* refers to a relationship between a Work Record and an Authority Record or between two Work Records. All links are controlled fields. In the examples that follow, Related Work Records are abbreviated for the sake of brevity. All Work Records should be as complete as possible. See the various chapters for discussions of individual metadata elements, whether they should be controlled, and the respective advantages of an authority file or a controlled list. In all examples in this manual, both within and at the end of each chapter, data values for repeatable fields are separated by bullet characters.

Figure 33

Work Record Linked to a Subject Authority: Pre-Columbian Vessel[6]

Required and recommended elements are marked with an asterisk.

Work Record

▪ **Class** *[controlled]*: ceramics • Pre-Columbian art

▪ ***Work Type** [link]*: cup

▪ ***Title**: Vessel with Mythological Scene of the Maya Underworld | **Title Type**: preferred

▪ ***Creator display**: unknown Maya
   ***Role** [link]*: artist | *[link]*: unknown Maya

▪ ***Creation Date**: 8th century
   [controlled]: **Earliest**: 0700; **Latest**: 0799

▪ ***Subject** [links to authorities]*: religion and mythology • object (utilitarian) • Xibalbá (Maya iconography) • underworld
   • skeleton • death • ax • altar • celebration • sacrifice • Baby Jaguar • ceremonial object

▪ **Culture**: Maya

▪ ***Current Location** [link]*: Metropolitan Museum of Art (New York, New York, United States) | **ID**: 1978.412.206

▪ **Creation Location** *[link]*: Petén Department (Guatemala)

▪ ***Measurements**: 14 cm (height) (5 1/2 inches)
   [controlled]: **Value**: 14; **Unit**: cm; **Type**: height

▪ ***Materials and Techniques**: terracotta
   Material *[link]*: terracotta | **Technique** *[link]*: vase painting

▪ **Description**: Straight-sided ceramic vessels with painted decoration comprising complex scenes were common in 8th-century Maya art. The "codex-style" painting depicts a scene in the realm of the Lords of Death, where a dancing figure holds a long-handled axe and a handstone. On a monster-head altar lies Baby Jaguar, a deity figure, and beside the altar is a dancing, skeletal death figure. The meaning has been variously interpreted as depicting either sacrifice or celebration.

▪ **Description Source** *[link]*: Metropolitan Museum of Art online. http://www.metmuseum.org (accessed February 1, 2004).

CREDIT: *Vessel with Mythological Scene*, 8th century; Maya peoples; Guatemala, Petén Department; Ceramic; height 5 1/2 in. (14 cm). View #1. The Metropolitan Museum of Art, Michael C. Rockefeller Memorial Collection, Purchase, Nelson A. Rockefeller, Gift, 1968. (1978.412.206); Photograph © 1981 The Metropolitan Museum of Art.

Subject Authority Record

▪ ***Subject Names**:
   Xibalbá (preferred)
   Place of Fear
   Underworld

▪ ***Hierarchical position** [link]*:
   Maya iconography
   ...... legends from the Popol Vuh
   .... Xibalbá

▪ ***Indexing Terms** [controlled]*: underworld • demons
   • Hero Twins • Vucub-Camé (demon) • Hun-Camé (demon)

▪ **Note**: In the creation myth of the highland Quiché Maya, the underground realm called Xibalbá was ruled by the demon kings Hun-Camé and Vukub-Camé. It was a dangerous place accessed by a steep and difficult path. The Hero Twins, Hun-Hunapú and Vukub-Hunapú, were lured to Xibalbá by a ball game challenge, but were then tricked and slaughtered. However, the twins were avenged by Hun-Hunapú's sons, Hunapú and Xbalanqué.

▪ ***Source** [links]*: *Larousse World Mythology* (1981); **Page**: 473 ff.

Work Record

- **Class** *[controlled]*: sculpture • Greek and Roman art
- ***Work Type** [link]*: statue
- ***Title**: Lansdowne Herakles I **Title Type**: preferred
- ***Creator display**: unknown Roman
    - ***Role** [link]*: sculptor I *[link]*: unknown Roman
- ***Creation Date**: ca. 125 CE
    - *[controlled]*: **Earliest**: 0120; **Latest**: 0130
- ***Subject** [links to authorities]*: religion and mythology • <u>Hercules</u> (Greek/Roman hero) • human figure • male • nude • lion skin • Nemean Lion • club
- **Culture** *[link]*: Roman
- ***Current Location** [link]*: Paul Getty Museum, Villa Collection (Malibu, California, USA) I **ID**: 70.AA.109
- **Discovery Location** *[link]*: Hadrian's Villa (Tivoli, Lazio, Italy)
- ***Measurements**: 193.5 cm (height) (76 3/16 inches)
    - *[controlled]*: **Value**: 193.5; **Unit**: cm; **Type**: height
- ***Materials and Techniques**: Pentelic marble
    - **Material** *[link]*: Pentelic marble
- **Description**: Hercules standing in contrapposto, holding his attributes, the skin of the Nemean lion and a club. This statue was found in Tivoli ca. 1790, in the ruins of Hadrian's Villa; it was in the collection of the Marquess of Lansdowne until 1951. It is related in appearance to works attributed to 4th-century BCE Greek sculptors; however, the work has an eclectic style that is purely Roman.
- **Description Source** *[link]*: J. Paul Getty Museum. *Handbook of the Collections*. Los Angeles: J. Paul Getty Museum, 1991; **Page**: 6.

Subject Authority Record

- ***Subject Names**:
    - <u>Hercules</u> (preferred)
    - Herakles
    - Heracles
    - Ercole
    - Hercule
    - Hércules
- ***Hierarchical position** [links]*:
    - Classical Mythology
    - ...... Greek heroic legends
    - .... Story of Hercules
    - .... Hercules
- ***Indexing Terms** [controlled]*: Greek hero • king • strength • fortitude • perseverance • Argos • Thebes
- **Note**: Probably based on an actual historical figure, a king of ancient Argos. The legendary figure was the son of Zeus and Alcmene ...
- **Related Subjects** *[links]*:
    - Labors of Hercules
    - Zeus (Greek god)
    - Alcmene (Greek heroine)
    - Hera (Greek goddess)
- **Dates**: Story developed in Argos, but was taken over at early date by Thebes; literary sources are late, though earlier texts may be surmised.
    - *[controlled]*: **Earliest**: -1000; **Latest**: 9999
- ***Sources** [links]*:
    - ICONCLASS
    - http://www.iconclass.nl/.
    - Grant, Michael and John Hazel. *Gods and Mortals in Classical Mythology*. Springfield, MA: G & C Merriam, 1973; **Page**: 212 ff.

231

Figure 35

Work Record with Geographic Subject: Book of Maps[8]

Required and recommended elements are marked with an asterisk. In this example, the subject is discussed in the description rather than in a dedicated subject display.

Work Record

- ■ **Class** *[controlled]*: Special Collections • rare books
- ■ ***Work Type** [link]*: book • etchings • maps • plans • panoramas
- ■ ***Title**: Theatrum civitatum nec non admirandorum Neapolis et Siciliae regnorum | **Title Type**: preferred
- ■ ***Creator display**: Joan Blaeu (Dutch, 1596-1673), with Bastiaen Stopendaal (Dutch, 1637-before 1707)
  - * **Role** *[controlled]*: printmaker | *[link]*: Blaeu, Joan
  - * **Role** *[controlled]*: printmaker | *[link]*: Stopendaal, Bastiaen
- ■ ***Creation Date**: 1663
  - *[controlled]*: **Earliest**: 1663; **Latest**: 1663
- ■ ***Subject** [link to Geographic Place Authority]*: Sicily (Italy) • <u>Naples</u> (Campania, Italy)
- ■ ***Current Location** [link]*: Research Library, Getty Research Institute (Los Angeles, California, United States) | **ID**: 92-B27718
- ■ **Publication Location** *[link]*: Amsterdam (The Netherlands)
- ■ ***Measurements**: 78 pages, 2 folded leaves
  - *[controlled]*: **Extent**: pages; **Value**: 78; **Type**: count
- ■ ***Materials and Techniques**: handcolored etchings • printing | **Technique** *[link]*: etching • printing
- ■ **Description**: With the exception of 2 double folded leaves of plates, all etchings are on pages backed with text. There are 8 half-page, 1 single-, 22 double-page etchings, all colored.
- ■ **Description Source** *[link]*: Research Library, Getty Research Institute, Special Collections.

Geographic Place Authority Record

- ■ ***Names**:
  - <u>Naples</u> (preferred)
  - Napoli
  - Nápoles
  - Neapel
  - Neapolis
- ■ ***Hierarchical position** [link]*:
  - Europe (continent)
  - .... Italy (nation)
  - .... Campania (region)
  - .... Napoli (province)
  - .... Naples (inhabited place)
- ■ ***Place Type** [controlled]*: inhabited place
- ■ **Coordinates** *[controlled]*:
  - **Lat**: 40 50 00 N degrees minutes
  - **Long**: 014 15 00 E degrees minutes
  - (**Lat**: 40.8333 decimal degrees)
  - (**Long**: 14.2500 decimal degrees)
- ■ ***Source** [link]*: *Getty Thesaurus of Geographic Names* (1988-).

Work Record

- ■ **Class** *[controlled]*: prints and drawings • European art • rare books
- ■ ***Work Type** [link]*: etching
- ■ ***Title**: View of Naples | **Title Type**: preferred | **Title**: Napoli | **Title Type**: inscribed
- ■ ***Creator display**: Bastiaen Stopendaal (Dutch, 1637-before 1707)
  - * **Role** *[link]*: printmaker *[link]*: Stopendaal, Bastiaen
- ■ ***Creation Date**: 1663
  - *[controlled]*: **Earliest**: 1663; **Latest**: 1663
- ■ ***Subject** [links to authorities]*: cityscape • <u>Naples</u> (Campania, Italy) • panorama • harbor
- ■ ***Current Location** [link]*: Research Library, Getty Research Institute (Los Angeles, California, United States) | **ID**: 92-B27718 -plate 1
- ■ ***Measurements**: 52 cm (length) (20 1/2 inches)
  - *[controlled]*: **Value**: 52; **Unit**: cm; **Type**: length
- ■ ***Materials and Techniques**: hand-colored etching
  - **Material** *[link]*: paper | **Technique** *[link]*: etching • hand coloring
- ■ **Inscriptions**: titled: Napoli; signed in the plate
- ■ **Related Work**:
  - **Relationship Type** *[controlled]*: part of
  - *[link to Work Record]*: *Theatrum civitatum nec non admirandorum Neapolis et Siciliae regnorum*; book; Joan Blaeu (Dutch, 1596-1673); 1663; Amsterdam (The Netherlands)

CREDIT: View of Naples, from Joan Blaeu, *Theatrum civitatum nec non admirandorum Neapolis et Siciliae regnorum*, 1663; Research Library, The Getty Research Institute (Los Angeles, California), ID#92-B27718. © The J. Paul Getty Trust.

Figure 36
Work Record Linked to Other Authorities for Subject: Portrait[9]
Required and recommended elements are marked with an asterisk.

Work Record

- **Class** *[controlled]*: paintings • European art
- ***Work Type** *[link]*: painting
- ***Title**: Magdaleine Pinceloup de la Grange | **Title Type**: preferred
- ***Creator display**: Jean-Baptiste Perronneau (French, ca. 1715-1783)
    - ***Role** *[link]*: painter | *[link]*: Perronneau, Jean-Baptiste
- ***Creation Date**: 1747
    - *[controlled]*: **Earliest**: 1747; **Latest**: 1747
- ***Subjects** *[links]*: portrait • Pinceloup de la Grange, Magdaleine (French aristocrat, 18th century) • domestic cat
- ***Current Location** *[link]*: J. Paul Getty Museum (Los Angeles, California, United States) | **ID**: 84.PA.664
- **Style** *[link]*: Rococo | **Culture** *[link]*: French
- ***Measurements**: 65 x 54 cm (25 5/8 x 21 3/8 inches)
    - *[controlled]*: **Value**: 65; **Unit**: cm; **Type**: height | **Value**: 54; **Unit**: cm; **Type**: width
- ***Materials and Techniques**: oil on canvas
    - **Material** *[link]*: oil paint • canvas
- **Description**: The sitter was from the provincial French region of Orléans, but the artist imbued her with Parisian sophistication. The cat she holds is known as a "Chartreux cat," descriptions of which first appeared in 18th-century France. While some at this time valued this breed as a companion animal, it was primarily bred for its fur.
- **Description Source** *[link]*:
    - J. Paul Getty Museum online. http://www.getty.edu (accessed February 10, 2005).
- **Related Work**:
    - **Relationship Type** *[controlled]*: pendant of
    - *[link to Work Record]*: *Charles-François Pinceloup de la Grange*; painting; Jean-Baptiste Perronneau (French, ca. 1715-1783); 1747; J. Paul Getty Museum (Los Angeles, California, United States); 84.PA.664

Personal and Corporate Name Authority Record

- ***Names**:
    - Pinceloup de la Grange, Magdaleine (preferred, inverted)
    - Magdaleine Pinceloup de la Grange (preferred, natural order)
    - Parseval, Magdaleine
    - Pinceloup de la Grange, Madaleine
- ***Display Biography**: French aristocrat, 18th century
- ***Nationality** *[controlled]*: French
    - *[controlled]*: ***Birth Date**: 1700; ***Death Date**: 1799
- ***Life Roles** *[controlled]*: aristocrat
- **Place of Activity** *[link]*: Orléans (France)
- **Related People**:
    - **Relationship Type** *[controlled]*: spouse of
    - *[link to Personal and Corporate Name Authority]*: Charles-François Pinceloup de la Grange
- ***Sources** *[link]*: J. Paul Getty Museum (online).

Concept Authority Record

- ***Terms**:
    - Felis domesticus (preferred, species name)
    - domestic cat (preferred, common name)
    - Felis catus
    - house cat
- ***Hierarchical position** *[link]*:
    - Animal Kingdom
    - .... Vertebrates (subphylum)
    - .... Mammalia (class)
    - .... Carnivora (order)
    - .... Felidae (family)
    - .... Felis domesticus
- ***Note**: Domesticated member of the genus Felis, first domesticated in Egypt ca. 2000 BCE. Probably descended from Felis sylvestris; in some taxonomies, Felis domesticus and Felis sylvestris are the same species.
- **Related Concept**:
    - **Relationship Type** *[controlled]*: descended from
    - *[link to Concept Authority]*: Felis silvestris
- ***Sources** *[link to Source Records]*:
    - Animal Diversity Web. University of Michigan Museum of Zoology, 1995-2002. http://animal-diversity.ummz.umich.edu/ (accessed February 5, 2004).
    - "Cat, domestic." *Encyclopaedia Britannica* online (accessed February 4, 2004).

CREDIT:
The J. Paul Getty Museum (Los Angeles, California). Jean-Baptiste Perronneau, *Magdaleine Pinceloup de la Grange, née de Parseval*. French, 1747, Oil on canvas, 25 9/16 x 20 11/16 in.; 84.PA.665. © The J. Paul Getty Trust.

Notes

1. Panofsky, Erwin. *Studies in Iconology: Humanistic Themes in the Art of the Renaissance.* New York: Oxford University Press, 1939.

2. Murtha Baca, ed. *Introduction to Art Image Access: Issues, Tools, Standards, Strategies.* Los Angeles: Getty Research Institute, 2002.

3. Local practice may vary. Note that Library of Congress subject terms are plurals, thus users committed to using that authority will probably use plural terms in all cases.

4. For a discussion of architectural drawings and their relationship to the subject "as built," and how some institutions may require separate fields for method of representation and point of view for architectural drawings, see the *ADAG/FDA Guide to the Description of Architectural Drawings.*

5. Some institutions may wish to include flags or multiple controlled fields to distinguish between indexing terms indicating what the work is "of" from terms indicating what it is "about." For a discussion of this point of view, see Sara Shatford Layne, "Subject Access to Art Images," in *Introduction to Art Image Access: Issues, Tools, Standards, Strategies,* edited by Murtha Baca. Los Angeles: Getty Research Institute, 2002, 1 ff.

6. This example is intended to illustrate metadata elements discussed in this manual. Field names and data values in the example do not necessarily represent the record for this object in the Metropolitan Museum's database.

7. This example is intended to illustrate metadata elements discussed in this manual. Field names and data values in the example do not necessarily represent the record for this object in the Getty Museum's database.

8. This example is intended to illustrate metadata elements discussed in this manual. Field names and data values in the example do not necessarily represent the record for this work in the database for the Research Library, Getty Research Institute.

9. This example is intended to illustrate metadata elements discussed in this manual. Field names and data values in the example do not necessarily represent the record for this object in the Getty Museum's database.

Chapter 7

Class

Class

7.1   ABOUT CLASS

7.1.1   Discussion

The Class element is used to relate a specific work to others with similar characteristics, often based on the organizational scheme of a particular repository or
collection. The purpose is to place the work within a broader context, categorizing
it on the basis of similar characteristics, including materials, form, shape, function, region of origin, cultural context, or historical or stylistic period. Class terms
may represent a hierarchy, a typology, or some other grouping of items, implying
similarities among works within the logic of the classification.

Assigning a Class Designation

Using Class to place the work within a broader context and relate it to other
works in a collection helps end users browse groupings of works that are related
or share characteristics. The class scheme can be a useful starting point in the
discovery of works contained in the collection. It introduces the collection and
indicates both its organizational structure and its general focus.

Terms entered in this element should be assigned based on local guidelines pertinent for the individual collection. For example, in museum collections, the class of
an object may correspond to the collection of a particular curatorial department
(for example, *decorative arts, furniture, paintings, sculpture, prints and drawings*);
in visual resources collections, it may be based on art historical periods or styles,
such as *Prehistoric, Egyptian, Romanesque, Renaissance*. A work may belong
simultaneously to different classes in different schemes, depending on the scheme
used or the point of view.

The Class element may refer to a category within the collection arrangement of the owning institution as described, or it may refer to organizational schemes applied to visual resource collections, union catalogs, and shared cataloging initiatives. For example, when an image of a work of art from a museum is used in a visual resources collection, it may be classified differently from the museum's classification, depending on the scope and use requirements of the visual resources collection. In a shared cataloging initiative or union catalog, yet another classification may be required. In such situations, however, it is useful to end users to include the original class designation of the art work's repository as well.

Class carries no connotation of quality; it is not a categorization of objects according to grade or value. For a more complete discussion of class as a cataloging element, see *Categories for the Description of Works of Art: Classification*.

Specificity

The level of specificity to which a work is classified (for example, in the case of a Brewster chair, whether more broadly as *decorative arts*, or more specifically as *furniture* or *chairs*) will depend on the perspective of the cataloging institution and the requirements of end users. More general terms than those recorded in Work Type should be recorded in Class. For example, if a work is identified as a carpet in Work Type, it could be classified as *decorative arts* in Class. Ideally, Class does not duplicate information in the Work Type element, though such overlap may sometimes be necessary or even inevitable.

Organization of the Data

Class should be recorded in a repeatable controlled field. Terminology should be controlled by an authority file or controlled list. Terms may be taken from published or unpublished sources; they may derive from ordered systems of categories or from published, hierarchically structured thesauri. The scheme for Class should be documented with a statement describing the purpose, intended audience, and focus of the collection. Terms should be defined so that it is clear which kinds of works belong to a particular class.

Recommended Elements

This chapter discusses the display and indexing fields for Class. Display may be a free-text field or concatenated from controlled fields.

> Class display
>
> > Class

About the Examples

The examples throughout this chapter are for illustration only. Local practice may vary.

7.1.2   Terminology

7.1.2.1   *Sources for Terminology*

Terminology should be controlled by using an authority file or controlled lists. Although the scheme for Class is locally defined, terms to populate that scheme may be taken from ordered systems of categories or from a published or local hierarchically structured thesauri, or they may be based on common usage within a particular institution or discipline. Sources of terminology may include the following:

> Getty Vocabulary Program. *Art & Architecture Thesaurus* (AAT). Los Angeles: J. Paul Getty Trust, 1988-. http://www.getty.edu/research/conducting_research/vocabularies/aat/. (Especially the Objects facet).

> Library of Congress. Prints and Photographs Division. *Thesaurus for Graphic Materials: Genre and Physical Characteristics Terms.* Washington, DC: Library of Congress, Cataloging Distribution Service, 1995. http://lcweb.loc.gov/rr/print/tgm2.

> Library of Congress Authorities. *Library of Congress Subject Headings.* Washington, DC: Library of Congress, 2005. http://authorities.loc.gov/.

> Chenhall, Robert G. *Revised Nomenclature for Museum Cataloging: A Revised and Expanded Version of Robert G. Chenhall's System for Classifying Man-made Objects.* Edited by James R. Blackaby, Patricia Greeno, and The Nomenclature Committee. Nashville, TN: AASLH Press, 1988.

> *Genre Terms: A Thesaurus for Use in Rare Book and Special Collections Cataloging.* 2nd ed. Prepared by the Bibliographic Standards Committee of the Rare Books and Manuscripts Section (ACRL/ALA). Chicago: Association of College and Research Libraries, 1991.

> *Paper Terms: A Thesaurus for Use in Rare Book and Special Collections Cataloging.* Prepared by the Bibliographic Standards Committee of the Rare Book and Manuscripts Section (ACRL/ALA). Chicago: Association of College and Research Libraries, 1990.

> Lavell, Cherry. *British Archaeological Thesaurus: For Use with British Archaeological Abstracts and Other Publications with British Archaeology.* London: Council for British Archaeology, 1989.

> *Tozzer Library Index to Anthropological Subject Headings.* Harvard University. 2nd rev. ed. Boston: G. K. Hall, 1981.

7.1.2.2 *Choice of Terminology*

7.1.2.2.1 CONSISTENCY

Using consistent terminology in this element is strongly recommended.

7.1.2.2.2 USE OF AN AUTHORITY RECORD

If possible, Class element terminology and definitions (for example, scope notes) should be stored in an authority file linked to the Work Record. Define the purpose and intended audience of the Class scheme. Class terms may also be stored in the Concept Authority described in Part 3. On the other hand, given that there will be a limited number of Class terms, some institutions may instead choose to control Class with a simple controlled list.

7.2 CATALOGING RULES

7.2.1 Rules for Class

7.2.1.1 *Brief Rules for Class*

Record one or more terms that relate the work to other works with similar characteristics, including materials, form, shape, function, region of origin, cultural context, or historical or stylistic period, based on the organizational scheme of a particular repository or collection.

Singular vs. Plural

Generally use the plural form of nouns, because classifications represent groups of similar items, not an individual item.

> *Examples*
>
> > **Class**: paintings
> >
> > **Class**: prints and drawings
> >
> > **Class**: religious objects
> >
> > **Class**: manuscripts
> >
> > **Class**: graphic arts
> >
> > **Class**: decorative arts

When the term refers to a broad type and the plural form is not appropriate, use the singular.

> *Examples*
>
> > **Class**: sculpture
> >
> > **Class**: architecture
> >
> > **Class**: costume
> >
> > **Class**: furniture
> >
> > **Class**: performance art

Compound Concepts

Use compound concepts for the Class element when appropriate for a particular collection. Compound concepts are terms composed of multiple concepts such as *European paintings*. This is unlike the AAT or other standards-compliant thesauri, in which each record represents a single concept.

> *Examples*
>
> > **Class**: European paintings
> >
> > **Class**: Maya ceremonial objects

Capitalization and Abbreviations

Capitalize the proper names of culture, nationality, period, or style where appropriate. For other terms, use lowercase. Avoid abbreviations.

Examples

> **Class**: textiles
>
> **Class**: ceramics
>
> **Class**: Pre-Columbian textiles
>
> **Class**: American paintings
>
> **Class**: African art
>
> **Class**: Baroque paintings

If your institution uses a classification scheme made up of abbreviations or numeric or alphanumeric codes that might seem meaningless to an end user, map these to controlled terms that will be meaningful in a display. In an online database or kiosk system, for example, a local classification code such as *P20FR* should be translated to *20th-century French paintings*.

7.2.1.2 *Additional Recommendations for Class*

7.2.1.2.1 SPECIFICITY

If possible, do not duplicate any term used in the Work Type element. When the Class term is based on Work Type, select a term that categorizes the work more broadly than the term used in Work Type, if possible. In the examples below, the Work Type field is included to clarify the relationship between it and Class. See Chapter 1: Object Naming for a discussion of Work Type.

Examples

> **Controlled fields**:
> > **Work Type**: temple
> > **Class**: architecture
>
> **Controlled fields**:
> > **Work Type**: drum
> > **Class**: musical instruments
>
> **Controlled fields**:
> > **Work Type**: lithograph
> > **Class**: prints

In some cases, however, it is impossible to avoid duplicating the Work Type term.

Example

> **Controlled fields**:
> > **Work Type**: painting
> > **Class**: paintings

7.2.1.2.2 VARIOUS TYPES OF COLLECTIONS

Use terms and an overall scheme that will facilitate browsing or retrieval at a level of specificity consistent with the depth of the collection and the needs of the intended users. The example illustrates how the same work type, *cartonnier*, could be classified with class terms that are more or less specific, depending on the scope of the collection.

Examples

> **Work Type**: cartonnier
> **Class**: furniture

> **Work Type**: cartonnier
> **Class**: French decorative arts

> **Work Type**: cartonnier
> **Class**: decorative arts

7.2.1.2.3 MULTIPLE CLASS DESIGNATIONS

Assign multiple Class designations, if necessary.

Example

> **Work Type**: magic scroll
> **Class**: works on paper • medicinal objects • Ethiopian works

7.3 PRESENTATION OF THE DATA

7.3.1 Display and Indexing

For a discussion of when and why separate free-text and controlled fields are recommended, see Part 1: Database Design and Relationships: Display and Indexing.

A repeatable controlled field for Class should be used for indexing. A free-text display field for Class may be included, but is generally not required. Where multiple designations of Class occur, if a display is desired, it can be constructed by concatenating data from the repeatable controlled field. The example below illustrates a work with multiple Class designations.

Example

[for a painted Chinese screen]

> **Free-Text Class display field or Concatenated display of Class**:
> Asian art; furniture; paintings
> **Controlled field (repeatable)**:
> > **Class**: Asian art • furniture • paintings

7.3.2 Examples

Examples of Work Records are included below. For additional examples, see the end of Part 1, the end of each chapter, and the CCO Web site. In the examples, *controlled* refers to values controlled by an authority file, controlled list, or other rules (for example, rules for recording dates). *Link* refers to a relationship between a Work Record and an Authority Record or between two Work Records. All links are controlled fields. In the examples that follow, Related Work Records are abbreviated for the sake of brevity. All Work Records should be as complete as possible. See the various chapters for discussions of individual metadata elements, whether they should be controlled, and the respective advantages of an authority file or a controlled list. In all examples in this manual, both within and at the end of each chapter, data values for repeatable fields are separated by bullet characters.

Figure 37
Work Record Linked to an Authority Record for Class: Globe[1]
Required and recommended elements are marked with an asterisk.

Work Record

- **Class** *[link]*: <u>decorative arts</u> • furniture • scientific instruments • European art
- ***Work Type** *[link]*: globe
- ***Title**: Terrestrial Globe I **Title Type**: preferred
- ***Creator display**: globe made by Jean-Antoine Nollet (French, 1700-1770); map engraved by Louis Borde (French, active 1730s-1740s); wood stand painted with vernis Martin (possibly applied by the Martin brothers' studio)
    Extent *[controlled]*: globe I ***Role** *[link]*: creator I *[link]*: Nollet, Jean-Antoine
    Extent *[controlled]*: map I ***Role** *[link]*: engraver I *[link]*: Borde, Louis
    Extent *[controlled]*: stand I **Qualifier**: possibly by I ***Role** *[link]*: painters I *[link]*: Martin brothers
- ***Creation Date**: 1728
    [controlled]: **Earliest**: 1728; **Latest**: 1728
- ***Subjects** *[links to authorities]*: object (utilitarian) • Earth • geography • cartography
- ***Current Location** *[link]*: J. Paul Getty Museum (Los Angeles, California, United States) I **ID**: 86.DH.705.1
- ***Measurements**: 109.9 (height) x 44.5 (diameter of globe) x 31.8 cm (depth of the stand) (43 1/4 x 17 1/2 x 12 1/2 inches)
    [controlled]: **Value**: 109.9; **Unit**: cm; **Type**: height I **Value**: 31.8; **Unit**: cm; **Type**: diameter I **Value**: 31.8; **Unit**: cm; **Type**: depth
- ***Materials and Techniques**: papier mâché, printed paper, and gilt bronze on a wooden (poplar, spruce, and alder) stand painted with vernis Martin
    Material *[link]*: papier mâché • paper • bronze • poplar • spruce • alder
    Technique *[link]*: vernis Martin
- **Inscriptions**: dedication to duchesse du Maine, wife of Louis XIV's first illegitimate child
- **Description**: The globe and its pendant were designed by the popular scientist who taught physics to the royal children. Owning a globe was very fashionable in the 18th century, and considered essential for the libraries of the aristocracy.
- **Description Source** *[link]*: J. Paul Getty Museum online. http://www.getty.edu (accessed February 10, 2004).
- **Related Work**:
    Relationship type *[controlled]*: pendant of
    [link to Work Record]: *Celestial Globe*; globe; Nicolas Bailleul le jeune (French, active 1740-1750); 1730; J. Paul Getty Museum (Los Angeles, California, United States); 86.DH.705.2

Authority Record

- ***Term**:
    <u>decorative arts</u> (preferred)
- ***Note**: Designation for those arts involving the creation of works that serve utilitarian as well as aesthetic purposes, or involving the decoration and embellishment of utilitarian objects.
- ***Source** *[link]*: *Art & Architecture Thesaurus* (1988-).

CREDIT: The J. Paul Getty Museum (Los Angeles, California). Globe made and assembled by Jean-Antoine Nollet, scientist; Map by Louis Borde, engraver. *Terrestrial Globe.* 1728. Wood painted with vernis Martin; papier mâché; printed paper; bronze. 109.9 x 44.5 x 31.8 cm (43 1/4 x 17 1/2 x 12 1/2 inches). 86.DH.705.1. © The J. Paul Getty Trust.

Figure 38
Work Record Linked to an Authority Record for Class: Medieval Building

Required and recommended elements are marked with an asterisk.

Work Record

- **Class** *[link to authority]*: <u>architecture</u>
- ***Work Type** *[link]*: basilica
- ***Title**: Prato Cathedral | **Title Type**: preferred
    - **Title**: Duomo di Prato | **Title Type**: alternate
    - **Title**: Cattedrale di Santo Stefano | **Title Type**: alternate
    - **Title**: Santo Stefano di Borgo al Cornio | **Title Type**: former
- ***Creator display**: architect: Guidetto da Como (Italian, 13th century) from 1211, other unknown architects
    - ***Role** *[controlled]*: architect | *[link]*: Guidetto da Como
- ***Creation Date**: original church dates from 10th century, current church was begun in 12th century, façade and campanile date from 12th-15th century
    - *[controlled]*: **Earliest**: 1100; **Latest**: 1499
- ***Subjects**: *[link to authorities]*: architecture • Saint Stephen • cathedral • worship
- ***Current Location** *[link]*: Prato (Tuscany, Italy)
- ***Materials and Techniques**: bearing masonry construction, green and white striped marble façade
    - **Material** *[link]*: masonry | **Technique** *[link]*: bearing walls | **Extent** *[controlled]*: façade | **Material** *[link]*: marble • striped pattern
- **Style** *[link]*: Romanesque • Gothic
- **Description**: The current church is an enlargement of a 10th-century parish church. The cathedral was a pilgrimage site noted for the relic of the Virgin Mary's belt, the Sacro Cingolo, and important 15th-century frescoes.

Authority Record

- ***Term**:
    - architecture (preferred)
- ***Note**: Designation for the built environment, including structures, parts of structures, landscape architecture, and city planning.
- ***Source** *[link]*: *Art & Architecture Thesaurus* (1988-).

CREDIT:
Prato Cathedral, Prato, Italy
© 2005 Patricia Harpring.
All rights reserved.

Note

1. This example is intended to illustrate fields discussed in this manual. Field names and data values in the example do not necessarily represent the record for this object in the Getty Museum's collections information system.

Chapter 8

Description

*Description /
Other Descriptive Notes*

8.1   ABOUT DESCRIPTION AND OTHER NOTES

8.1.1   Discussion

The Description element and other types of notes may be associated with particular fields throughout the Work Record.

Description

The element consists of a descriptive note that is generally a relatively brief essay-like text, detailing the content and context of the work. It is a free-text field used to record comments and an interpretation that may supplement, qualify, or explain information indexed in various other elements.

The element should contain a single coherent statement covering some or all of the salient characteristics and historical significance of the work of art or architecture. Topics covered may include a discussion of the subject, function, or significance of the work. For a more exhaustive discussion of the element, see *Categories for the Description of Works of Art: Descriptive Note.*

Other Notes

Some institutions may require additional element-specific free-text notes to explain or qualify information in a number of particular elements throughout the Work Record—a Subject Note, Date Note, or Title Note, for example. These are useful because they can contain the nuances of language necessary to convey uncertainty and ambiguity that cannot otherwise easily be captured in controlled fields within any single element. Making such notes integral to a cataloging system ensures against the loss of those important details that are essential to study but cannot be fully understood without elaboration. Museums typically require notes, often combined with controlled fields, to record information about the physical description, condition, conservation, and collecting history of the work. A note may also be used to record administrative information or issues relevant to the record itself, such as a reference to the origin of the information as transcribed or exported from one system to another. If a cataloger needs to cite a particular publication as the source of information about the work, notes may be used for that purpose as well. This is especially useful if a system does not have a bibliographic authority file (see Part 1: Authority Files and Controlled Vocabularies: Source Authority).

Some notes may be published, and others may contain administrative information that will not be. For further discussion of these various types of notes, see *Categories for the Description of Works of Art*, where such notes, called *remarks* or *description*, are included for every category.

Specificity

As mentioned, and as a supplement to information recorded in controlled fields, free-text notes allow for the nuance and detail necessary to capture a precise description that cannot be fully addressed in other elements.

Organization of the Data

Description and other descriptive notes are free-text fields; thus, if a note contains any information that is significant for retrieval, that information should also be recorded in the appropriate metadata element for indexing. Any significant persons, corporate bodies, subjects, dates, media, and techniques in a note should be indexed.

Recommended Elements

A list of the elements discussed in this chapter appears below.

>   Description (descriptive note)
>   Sources
>   Other Descriptive Notes
>   Sources

The examples throughout this chapter are for illustration only. Local practice may vary.

8.1.2   Terminology

8.1.2.1   *Sources for Terminology*

Published sources of information may include general reference works, art encyclopedias and dictionaries, and standard textbooks for art history. A few sources for Western art follow:

>   Gardner, Helen. *Gardner's Art through the Ages*. 11th ed. Edited by Fred S. Kleiner, Christin J. Mamiya, and Richard G. Tansey. Fort Worth, TX: Harcourt Brace Publishers, 2001.

Grove Dictionary of Art Online. New York: Grove's Dictionaries, 2003. http://www.groveart.com/

Hartt, Frederick. *Art: History of Painting, Sculpture, and Architecture.* 2nd ed. New York: Harry N. Abrams, 1985.

Janson, H. W. *History of Art.* 7th ed. Upper Saddle River, NJ: Prentice Hall Art, 2006.

Catalogues raisonnés of specific artists, collection catalogs, monographs on specific built works, standard textbooks dealing with specific cultures and periods, and exhibition catalogs are also important sources for detailed information about specific works. Online resources are also useful; for example, some owning institutions have extensive information about their works available on their Web sites.

8.1.2.2 *Choice of Terminology*

Consistency is less important, but still desirable, in a free-text note than in a controlled field. Although uncontrolled terminology should be accommodated, terminology that is consistent with the terms in controlled fields is nonetheless recommended for the sake of clarity. Consistent style, grammar, and sentence structure are recommended.

8.2 CATALOGING RULES

8.2.1 Rules for Description

8.2.1.1 *Brief Rules for Description*

Record a descriptive note discussing some or all of the salient characteristics and historical significance of the work of art or architecture. Discuss the significance, function, or subject of the work (see also Chapter 6: Subject).

Brevity

Enter information clearly and concisely. Capture salient points not already fully described in other elements.

Examples

[for a building]

Description field:
The Pantheon was dedicated to the seven planetary gods in 128 CE. It was consecrated as a Christian church in the early 7th century. It is the major surviving example of Roman concrete-vaulted architecture.

[for a pastel portrait]

Description field:
Liotard exhibited remarkable skill in the difficult medium of pastels, which he preferred when creating portraits of children. Surfaces, textures, and volume are described with subtle gradations of color. At the time he was working on this picture, portraits of children were becoming very popular in Western Europe.

Syntax and Order of Topics

Use natural word order. Use complete sentences. List information in the order of importance, chronologically, or from general to specific, depending on which is appropriate for the particular work.

Example

[for a photograph by André Kertész]

Description field:
Characteristic of Kertész' work as a Naturalist-Surrealist, this work combines prosaic observations of life combined with surrealistic perspective.

If none of these ways of ordering applies to the work, list information in this order: what is the work (Work Type, Subject, Style), who is responsible for it, where was it made, when was it made. Omit any of these if they are not significant or are explained adequately in other elements.

Example

[for a sacramentary]

Description field:
This volume contains prayers that would be said by a priest at mass. It includes seven full-page Ottonian miniatures. Scenes are set against colored, ornamented bands. Because it includes prayers for saints venerated at Beauvais, the book may have been commissioned at the request of the bishop of Beauvais for presentation to Robert the Pious, king of France. The writing and illumination have been attributed to Nivardus of Milan, who worked at the Benedictine monastery of Saint-Benoît-sur-Loire, at Fleury, France in the early 11th century.

Capitalization and Abbreviations

Use sentence case and capitalize proper names. Avoid abbreviations.

Examples

[for a Persian carpet]

Description field:
This large carpet was made for the mosque of Safi-ud-din in Ardabil, which is the holiest of Persian religious shrines. Because the artist was from Kashan, the carpet was probably actually produced there, and not made in Ardabil, which produces a different style of carpet. In this carpet, the central medallion with radiating pendants was ultimately derived from contemporary and earlier bookbinding and manuscript illumination.

[for a Maya pot]

Description field:
This straight-sided ceramic vessel with painted decoration comprising complex scenes was a common type in 8th-century Maya art. The codex-style painting depicts a scene in the realm of the Lords of Death, where a dancing figure holds a long-handled axe and a handstone. On a monster-head altar lies Baby Jaguar, a deity figure, and beside the altar is a dancing skeletal death figure. The meaning has been variously interpreted as depicting either sacrifice or celebration.

Language

Write the note in the language of the catalog record (English in the United States). Names and other words in foreign languages may be used within the note when there is no commonly used English equivalent. Use diacritics as appropriate.

Examples

[for an Indian sculpture]

Description field:
Chola-period bronzes were created using the lost wax technique, meaning that each sculpture is unique. Parvati wears her signature conical crown with *karandamukuta* tiers, and she stands in the *tribhanga*, or triple-bend pose. Judging from her pose, this sculpture may have been placed to the left of an image of Shiva in his role as Nataraja, or Lord of the Dance.

[for a lidded bowl]

Description field:
Madame Louise of France, the eighth daughter of the French King Louis XV, probably drank from this bowl. Known as an *écuelle*, it would have held bouillon—a light, nourishing broth taken as a snack between meals. Madame Louise's monogram ML and the coat of arms of an unmarried royal princess are painted on the lid and dish. Lidded bowls with accompanying dishes were produced in large numbers at the Vincennes and Sèvres Porcelain Manufactory in a variety of shapes, sizes, and decorative schemes. This bowl is an example of the restrained transitional style characteristic of the 1760s, when the effusive Rococo style was being replaced by the tenets of the new Neoclassical style.

8.2.1.2 *Additional Recommendations for Description*

8.2.1.2.1 INDEX IMPORTANT INFORMATION

Repeat all information that is in the note and is required for retrieval as necessary in other display fields. Index it in appropriate controlled fields elsewhere in the Work Record.

Example

Free-Text Description field:
This is the largest of Turner's four extant watercolors of this medieval castle on the northern coast of Wales. Turner portrays the landscape and ocean in a dramatic fashion, using angry clouds, sunshine, and roiling waves to animate the scene and emphasize the struggle of the fishermen.

Creator display: Joseph Mallord William Turner (British, 1775-1851)
Controlled fields:
    Role*:* painter
    [link to Personal and Corporate Name Authority]:
    Turner, Joseph Mallord William Turner

Materials and Techniques: watercolor and gum arabic with graphite underdrawing
Controlled Material fields (repeatable):
    wood • gum arabic • graphite • underdrawing
Controlled Subject fields (repeatable):
    Conway Castle (Wales) • ocean • coast • fishermen • castle • seascape • rocks
    • struggle

8.2.1.2.2 TOPICS IN THE DESCRIPTION

Appropriate topics for the Description field include the subject of the work, its function, its relationship to other works, its style, and any aspects of it that might be either disputed or uncertain.

Subject and Method of Representation

Include a concise description and discussion of the subject content and the method of representation, if appropriate.

Examples

[for an architectural drawing]

Description field:
The drawing depicts a longitudinal section of the cathedral, showing that the main dome and minor ones are constructed differently.

[for the Lincoln Memorial, Washington, DC]

Description field:
The design was influenced by the Greek Parthenon. Built into the design are symbols of the Union; for example, the 36 exterior Doric columns represent the 36 states in the Union at the time of Lincoln's death.

Function, Manufacture, Condition

Include a concise description and discussion of the function or use of the work, and the circumstances surrounding its manufacture or condition, if significant.

Examples

[for a Mississippian culture bannerstone]

Description field:
This bannerstone is a double-crescent-shaped stone, typical of the *winged* type. Although the purpose of bannerstones is uncertain, it is assumed that they were status symbols in the form of adornments or insignia, perhaps carried on a wooden staff (with the holes arranged vertically); many scholars believe that bannerstones formed part of an atlatl (a stick used in pre-Columbian cultures to throw spears).

[for a work by contemporary artist, Robert Smithson]

Description field:

The *Spiral Jetty* was a counterclockwise coil of mud, salt crystals, rocks, which were hauled in by truck, but were indigenous elements of the landscape at Great Salt Lake. Although clockwise spirals were powerful positive forces, the artist equated this counterclockwise spiral with destruction and entropy, drawing on symbolism from many cultures.

Relationship to Other Works

Include a concise description and discussion of the significance of the work related to others from the same period, place, artistic school, and so on, if significant.

Example

[for a drawing of Apollo and the Muses on Parnassus]

Description field:

Poussin used this study in formulating a painting now in the Museo del Prado. This drawing is based on Raphael's famous fresco in the Stanza della Segnatura in the Vatican. The drawing is more animated than is typical for Poussin, but shows his characteristic tendency to abstract forms and to use wash quite broadly.

Stylistic, Technical Development

If significant, include a discussion of the artist's style, technical expertise, and how this work is representative of the artist's oeuvre.

Example

[for a sculpture]

Description field:

The virtuosity of the sculptor is apparent in the rendering of a variety of textures, including flesh, hair, lace, and satins. Verhulst has employed decorative foliage and curving volutes below the armor to mitigate the truncation of the figure at the shoulders and chest.

Disputed Issues

Include a clarification of disputed or uncertain issues concerning attribution, original location, identification of subjects, dating, or other relevant historical information, if appropriate.

Example

[for a medieval panel painting]

Description field:

The *Adoration of the Magi in Siena* was produced by Bartolo's workshop but probably executed primarily by Bartolo di Fredi himself. Although it is unknown where the altarpiece originally stood, the quality of the materials, large size, and the influence that the work had on other artists are all evidence of an expensive commission and prominent location, possibly in the cathedral of Siena. It illustrates the artist's late stylistic concerns and was extremely influential in Siena and elsewhere.

8.2.2   Rules for Other Descriptive Notes

If descriptive notes are attached to various fields in the database, rules for brevity, syntax, language, capitalization, and abbreviation in these other descriptive notes should be the same as the rules for the general Description element (above).

Depending on the needs of the cataloging institution, use notes specific to individual elements to clarify or supplement information recorded in that element. In the examples below, the name of each note indicates the specific area of the record to which it corresponds.

Subject Display (Note)

Example

[for a drawing]

Subject display (Note):
This drawing may have been a preparatory study for a religious composition, possibly for a *Marriage of the Virgin or Apostles with the Virgin Mary.*

Controlled Subject field:
Marriage of the Virgin • Spozalizio • male figures • Virgin Mary • Saint Joseph • female figure • apostles • drapery

Controlled Work Type field:
preparatory study

Physical Description Display (Note)

Example

[for a Koran]

Physical Description display (Note):
The *Ibn al-Bawwab Koran* is a small volume containing 286 brownish paper folios. Each text has fifteen lines of round script written with a straight-cut reed pen to produce letters of uniform thickness. The brown ink is enhanced with blue and gold.
Source: Bloom, Jonathan, and Sheila Blair. *Islamic Arts*. London: Phaidon Press, 1997; **Page**: 195.

Materials and Techniques display:
brown ink with blue tempera and gold leaf
Controlled Materials and Techniques field:
ink • tempera • gold leaf

Date Note

Example

[for St. Peter's, the Vatican]

Date Note:
Between 1452 and 1455, Bernardo Rossellino drafted a plan to extend the foundation of Old Saint Peter's. In 1506, Pope Julius commissioned Donato Bramante to continue plans to rebuild it, but by 1515, upon Bramante's death, only four large pilasters had been erected. In 1546, Michelangelo took over as lead architect. By 1564, upon Michelangelo's death, plans and construction for the dome were under way, but the

dome was not completed until 1593 under the architects Dominico Fontana and Giacomo della Porta. Between 1603 and 1614, Carlo Maderno directed the construction of the nave and portico, and Bernini laid out the Piazza San Pietro 1656-1667.

Creation Date display:
designs begun 1451, constructed 1506-1615, piazza finished 1667
Controlled Date fields:
Earliest: 1451; **Latest**: 1615

8.2.3 Rules for Sources for Notes

Cite the source or sources used to compose notes. This is particularly critical when a published text has been used extensively or copied verbatim. Sources may be recorded in a dedicated source field, which may be linked to a controlled bibliographic authority file.

Example

[for an ancient Egyptian bas relief]

Description field:
Mentuhotep II was the founder of the Middle Kingdom, reuniting Egypt after the chaotic First Intermediate Period. This relief comes from his mortuary temple at Deir el-Bahri in western Thebes. The high standards of the royal Theban workshops are evident in the delicately modeled low relief and the finely painted details.
Source: Hibbard, Howard. *Metropolitan Museum of Art*. New York: Harrison House, 1986; **Page**: 30.

If a quote is taken largely verbatim from a source, indicate the source in the note itself, if necessary for clarity. Ideally, all such sources should also be linked to an authority record for the citation.

Example

[for a portrait]

Description field:
Gertrude Stein said of Picasso's famous 1905-1906 portrait of her (now in the Metropolitan Museum, New York): "... for me, it is I, and it is the only reproduction of me which is always I, for me." (Stein, Gertrude. *Picasso*, 1948)
Source: Stein, Gertrude. *Picasso*. London: B. T. Batsford, Ltd., 1948; **Page**: 8.

8.3 PRESENTATION OF THE DATA

8.3.1 Display and Indexing

8.3.1.1 *Free-Text vs. Controlled Fields*

For a discussion of when and why separate free-text and controlled fields are recommended, see Part 1: Database Design and Relationships: Display and Indexing.

8.3.1.1.1 INDEXING NOTES

Description and other descriptive notes are free-text fields. Important information in the note must be indexed in appropriate controlled fields for optimal retrieval.

Some notes (for example, a note containing museum acquisition information) may be inappropriate for display to the public; institutions should decide which notes will be displayed to end users and which are not for publication.

8.3.1.1.2 INDEXING SOURCES

Ideally, a Source field will be associated with the note, and linked to a bibliographic authority file to control values. See the discussion in Part 1: Authority Files and Controlled Vocabularies: Source Authority.

Example

[for the Chrysler Building, New York]

Description field:
Van Alen's building was famous as Manhattan's tallest structure in the early 1930s. Its massing of forms, use of fenestration as a design element, and surface treatment are similar to examples of late 1920s commercial architecture. However, its ornamentation makes it an Art Deco classic; this is particularly evident in the seven floors that make up the elongated dome, comprising a series of tiered arched forms with a triangular dormer. In a striking feat of showmanship, Van Alen's 27-ton steel spire pushed the building's height to 1,046 feet, making it higher than the Eiffel Tower.
Source: Duncan, Alistair. *Art Deco*. London: Thames and Hudson, 1988; **Page**: 186.

Record citations consistently, using the rules in the *Chicago Manual of Style*.

8.3.2 Examples

Examples of Work Records are included below. For additional examples, see the end of Part 1, the end of each chapter, and the CCO Web site. In the examples, *controlled* refers to values controlled by an authority file, controlled list, or other rules (for example, rules for recording dates). *Link* refers to a relationship between a Work Record and an Authority Record or between two Work Records. All links are controlled fields. In the examples that follow, Related Work Records are abbreviated for the sake of brevity. All Work Records should be as complete as possible. See the various chapters for a discussion of the individual metadata elements, whether they should be controlled, and the respective advantages of an authority file or a controlled list. In all examples in this manual, both within and at the end of each chapter, data values for repeatable fields are separated by bullet characters.

Work Record

- **Class** *[controlled]*: paintings
- ***Work Type** *[link]*: painting
- ***Title**: Irises I **Title Type**: preferred
- ***Creator display**: Vincent van Gogh (Dutch, 1853-1890)
    ***Role** *[link]*: painter I *[link]*: Gogh, Vincent van
- ***Creation Date**: 1889
    [controlled]: **Earliest**: 1889; **Latest**: 1889
- ***Subjects** *[links to authorities]*: botanical • irises • regeneration • soil • nature
- ***Current Location** *[link]*: J. Paul Getty Museum (Los Angeles, California, United States) I **ID**:90.PA.20
- **Creation Location**: Saint-Rémy-de-Provence (Provence-Alpes-Côte d'Azur, France)
- ***Measurements**: 71 x 93 cm (28 x 36 5/8 inches)
    [controlled]: **Value**: 71; **Unit**: cm; **Type**: height I **Value**: 93; **Unit**: cm; **Type**: width
- ***Materials and Techniques**: oil on canvas, applied with brush and palette knife
    Material *[link]*: oil paint • canvas I **Technique/Implement** *[link]*: brush • palette knife
- **Inscriptions**: signed lower right: Vincent
- **Style** *[link]*: Impressionist • Post-Impressionist
- **Description**: This work was painted when the artist was recuperating from a severe attack of mental illness; it depicts the garden at the asylum at Saint-Rémy. The cropped composition, divided into broad areas of vivid color with monumental irises overflowing the borders of the picture, was probably influenced by the decorative patterning of Japanese woodblock prints. There are no known drawings for this painting; Van Gogh himself considered it a study. His brother Theo recognized its quality and submitted it to the Salon des Indépendants in September 1889, writing to Vincent of the exhibition: "[It] strikes the eye from afar. It is a beautiful study full of air and life."
- **Description Source** *[link]*: J. Paul Getty Museum. *Handbook of the Collections*. Los Angeles: J. Paul Getty Museum, 1991; **Page**: 129.

CREDIT: The J. Paul Getty Museum (Los Angeles, California), Vincent van Gogh (Dutch, 1853-1890); *Irises*, 1889; oil on canvas, 71 x 93 cm; (28 x 36 5/8 inches); 90.PA.20. © The J. Paul Getty Trust.

Figure 40
Work Record with a Description: Modern Painting[2]

Required and recommended elements are marked with an asterisk.

Work Record

- **Class** *[controlled]*: paintings • American art
- ***Work Type** *[link]*: painting
- ***Title**: The Figure 5 in Gold | **Title Type**: preferred
    Title: *Five in Gold* | **Title Type**: alternate
- ***Creator display**: Charles Demuth (American, 1883-1935)
    ***Role** *[link]*: painter | *[link]*: Demuth, Charles
- ***Creation Date**: 1928 | *[controlled]*: **Earliest**: 1928; **Latest**: 1928
- ***Subjects** *[links to authorities]*: portrait • William Carlos Williams (American poet, 1883-1963) • Williams, William Carlos • "The Great Figure" (poem) • industry • fire • fire engine
- ***Current Location** *[link]*: Metropolitan Museum of Art (New York; New York, United States) | **ID**:49.59.1
- ***Measurements**: 90.2 x 76.2 cm (35 1/2 x 30 inches)
    [controlled]: **Value**: 90.2; **Unit**: cm; **Type**: height | **Value**: 76.2; **Unit**: cm; **Type**: width
- ***Materials and Techniques**: oil on cardboard
    Material *[link]*: oil paint • cardboard
- **Style** *[link]*: Futurist • Cubist
- **Description**: In the 1920s Demuth produced a series of poster-portraits honoring his contemporaries, inspired by Gertrude Stein's word-portraits. This painting pays homage to a poem by William Carlos Williams, "The Great Figure." This portrait consists not of a physical likeness of the poet, but of images associated with him, the poet's initials, and the names "Bill" and "Carlos." Williams' poem describes the experience of seeing a red fire engine with the number 5 painted on it racing through the city streets.
- **Description Source** *[link]*:
    Metropolitan Museum of Art online. http://www.metmuseum.org (accessed February 1, 2005).

CREDIT: *The Figure 5 in Gold*, 1928; Charles Demuth (American, 1883-1935); Oil on cardboard; H. 35-1/2, W. 30 in. (90.2 x 76.2 cm); The Metropolitan Museum of Art, Alfred Stieglitz Collection, 1949 (49.59.1); Photograph © 1986 The Metropolitan Museum of Art.

Figure 41
Work Record with a Description: Romanesque Tower

Required and recommended elements are marked with an asterisk.

Work Record

- **Class** *[link]*: architecture • European art
- ***Work Type** *[link]*: campanile
- ***Title**: Leaning Tower of Pisa | **Title Type**: preferred
    Title: Campanile | **Title Type**: alternate
    Title: Torre Pendente | **Title Type**: alternate
- ***Creator display**: architect and engineer: begun by Bonanno Pisano (Italian, active late 12th century) or Gherardo di Gherardo (Italian, active late 12th century); continued by Giovanni Pisano (Italian, born ca. 1240, died before 1320) and Giovanni di Simone (Italian, active ca. 1260-ca. 1286); finished by Tommaso Pisano (Italian, died after 1372)
    *Role *[link]*: architect | *[link]*: Bonanno Pisano || ***Role** *[link]*: architect | *[link]*: Gherardo di Gherardo || ***Role** *[link]*: architect | *[link]*: Giovanni Pisano || ***Role** *[link]*: architect | *[link]*: Giovanni di Simone || ***Role** *[link]*: architect | *[link]*: Tommaso Pisano
- ***Creation Date**: tower was begun in 1173 and completed in the 14th century
    [controlled]: **Earliest**: 1173; **Latest**: 1399
- ***Subjects** *[links to authorities]*: architecture • religion and mythology • bell tower
- **Style** *[link]*: Romanesque
- ***Current Location** *[link]*: Pisa (Tuscany, Italy)
- ***Measurements**: 8 stories, 56 m (height) (185 feet), inclination is about 4.9 m (16 feet) off the perpendicular
    [controlled]: **Value**: 56; **Unit**: m; **Type**: height | **Extent**: stories; **Value**: 8; **Type**: count
- ***Materials and Techniques**: bearing masonry, cut stone construction, round plan, white marble inlaid on the exterior with colored marble
    Material *[link]*: marble | **Technique** *[link]*: bearing walls • dimension stone • round plan • inlaying
- **Description**: Vasari reports that the tower was begun by Bonanno Pisano, but modern research indicates the plan may have been by Gherardo di Gherardo. The uneven settling of the campanile's foundations during its construction caused the tower to lean. The work was continued by Giovanni Pisano and Giovanni di Simone in 1275, with the addition of another three floors in a direction that bent opposite to the inclination to compensate for the flaw; but the added weight caused the tower to lean even more. According to Vasari, Tommaso di Andrea Pisano completed the belfry between 1350 and 1372. Modern efforts are underway to prevent the further leaning and ultimate collapse of the tower.
- **Description Sources** *[link]*:
    Touring Club Italiano: Toscana (1984); **Page**: 117 ff.
    Soprintendenza ai Beni Ambientali Architettonici Artistici e Storici per le provincie di Pisa Livorno Lucca Massa Carrara online http://www.ambientepi.arti.beniculturali.it/ (accessed February 4, 2005).
- **Related Work**:
    Relationship Type *[controlled]*: part of
    [link to Related Work]: *Cathedral of Pisa*; cathedral; unknown Italian; 1063-1350; Piazza del Duomo (Siena, Italy)

CREDIT:
Leaning Tower of Pisa, Pisa,
Italy © 2005 Patricia Harpring.
All rights reserved.

Notes

1. This example is intended to illustrate metadata elements discussed in this manual. Field names and data values in the example do not necessarily represent the record for this object in the Getty Museum's collections information system.

2. This example is intended to illustrate metadata elements discussed in this manual. Field names and data values in the example do not necessarily represent the record for this object in the Metropolitan Museum's collections information system.

Chapter **9**

View Information

View Description / View Type /
View Subject / View Date

9.1   ABOUT VIEW INFORMATION

9.1.1   Discussion

The View Information elements include details about the view of the work as it appears in an image (surrogate) of the work. Elements addressed here include View Description, View Type, View Subject, and View Date, which are only a few of the fields needed to catalog images. For additional information regarding cataloging images, see Part 1: Works and Images and Database Design and Relationships. A more in-depth discussion is available in *Categories for the Description of Works of Art: Related Visual Documentation* and *VRA Core 4.0.*

It is important to record information about the view of an image regardless of its format (photograph, negative, slide, microfiche, videotape, streaming video, or digital image) or type of institution (visual resources collection, library, museum, or archival collection). Visual surrogates can provide access to works that would be otherwise unavailable due to their remote locations or other restrictions that would limit direct contact. When an image rather than the original work is the only visual access, a description of the view helps provide a more complete experience and understanding of the work as seen in the image; this is particularly true for three-dimensional works such as sculpture or architecture.

View Description

View Description is a free-text field that elaborates on the spatial, chronological, or contextual aspects of the work as captured in the image view (for example, *detail of the lower left-hand corner,* *view facing the northwest,* or *view of building at sunset*). Whereas the View Type element describes the vantage point using limited and controlled vocabulary, the View Description element places the vantage point within a fuller context and elaborates on the perspective by describing details, parts, cardinal directions, and so forth. Together with View Type, View Description helps the end user evaluate the nature of the information within the image and differentiate among multiple images of the same work.

View Type

View Type records the specific vantage point or perspective, such as profile view, close-up view, or interior view. It helps the user differentiate among multiple images of the same work.

View Subject

View Subject may include terms or phrases that characterize the subject matter of the work as it is depicted in a specific image. Recording the subject matter of the view helps differentiate among multiple images of the same work and enables end users to identify specific images that illustrate a particular concept or detail. It is especially useful for details, complex works, and built works that may include many different views and details. For example, given subject access to an image with a view of a room that includes the term *skylights*, users who need examples of skylights can quickly locate an image that contains that detail.

Not every image will require that the View Subject element be completed. For example, if the image depicts a two-dimensional painting in full, the subject of the image will be adequately covered by the subject of the work itself. View Subject is required when the subject matter depicted in the image is specific to the image and distinct from that of the work in general. For further discussion of View Subject and related topics, see Chapter 6: Subject.

View Date

The View Date element includes any date or range of dates associated with the creation or production of the image. Although not required, it should be recorded when it is known. An image of Villa Savoy taken in 1935 will provide information about the villa that will be different from the information gleaned from a photograph of it taken in 1999. The visual document may also be the only record of a damaged or lost work, and can be vital to the work's restoration or recovery. Knowing the date of the view can aid in restoration of a work. For example, a view of the Basilica of San Francesco in Assisi taken in 1996, just before the earthquake of 1997, would be a possibly significant visual record of the building's condition just before it was damaged.

It is important to distinguish between a view date and other collection administration dates. For example, consider an image showing the Taj Mahal taken in 1969 in a 35-mm slide format and copied to a digital format in 2003. The date of the digital image is 2003, but the date of the view is 1969. Such distinctions should be made clear in the Image Record. The Creation Date for the copy is generally recorded with other administrative data and should not be confused with the View Date.

Organization of Data

Ideally, both a View Description (display) and controlled fields for View Type, View Date, and View Subject will be used. View Type and View Subject should be repeatable fields. Using controlled vocabularies, authorities, and consistent formatting to ensure efficient end-user retrieval is recommended.

View Information fields are part of the Image Record, although they should be linked to the appropriate Work Record. How the Image Record and the Work Record are linked is a local database implementation issue. Note that an institution may require multiple Image Records to be linked to a single Work Record. For example, a painting (Work Record) may be linked to image records for slides of the full view of the painting and various details; a building (Work Record) might be linked to multiple records for digital images showing different views and details of the building. See Part 1: Works and Images. In database systems that link Work and Image Records, it should be possible to narrow searches to retrieve images of a particular detail or view of a given work, based on values in the View Type and View Subject elements.

Recommendations for recording certain information about the view, particularly for the View Date and the View Subject, may duplicate recommendations already stated elsewhere in this guide; where appropriate, the reader is directed to additional relevant sections in the guide.

Recommended Elements

A list of the elements discussed in this chapter appears below. Required elements are noted. Display may be a free-text field or concatenated from controlled fields.

> View Description (required)
> View Type (required)
> View Subject display
> View Subject controlled (required)
> View Display Date
> View Earliest Date
> View Latest Date

About the Examples

The examples throughout this chapter are for illustration only. Local practice may vary. The examples tend to show the fullest possible use of display and indexing fields, which may not be necessary for all institutions.

9.1.2   Terminology

9.1.2.1   *Sources of Terminology*

9.1.2.1.1   VIEW DESCRIPTION

View Description is a free-text field that describes the view in as much detail as necessary. Terminology should be as consistent as possible.

9.1.2.1.2 VIEW TYPE

Use of a controlled vocabulary linked to an authority file is recommended. Some examples include the following:

> Getty Vocabulary Program. *Art & Architecture Thesaurus* (AAT). Los Angeles: J. Paul Getty Trust, 1988-. http://www.getty.edu/research/conducting_research/vocabularies/aat/. (Especially Visual Works: Views).

> Library of Congress. *Thesaurus for Graphic Materials 2, Genre and Physical Characteristics.* Washington, DC: Library of Crongress. http://lcweb.loc.gov/rr/print/tgm2/.

9.1.2.1.3 VIEW SUBJECT

Subject terminology should be controlled by using an authority file or controlled list. See suggestions for terminology in Chapter 6: Subject.

9.1.2.1.4 VIEW DATE

Date information must be formatted consistently to enable effective searching and retrieval on dates. Local rules should be in place. Suggested formats are available in the ISO standard and *W3C XML Schema Part 2*.[1] See additional guidance regarding dates in Chapter 4.

> ISO 8601:2004 Numeric representation of Dates and Time. *Data elements and interchange formats. Information interchange. Representation of dates and times.* Geneva, Switzerland: International Organization for Standardization, 2004.

> *XML Schema Part 2: Datatypes, 2001.* http://www.w3.org.

9.1.2.2 *Choice of Terminology*

9.1.2.2.1 CONSISTENCY

Using consistent terminology is especially important for controlled fields that are intended to provide access. Consistency is less important, but still desirable, in a free-text note than in a controlled field. Although uncontrolled terminology should be accommodated, terminology that is consistent with the terms in controlled fields is nonetheless recommended for the sake of clarity. Consistent style, grammar, and syntax are recommended.

9.1.2.2.2 USE OF AN AUTHORITY FILE

If possible, terms should be stored in an authority or controlled list, which is linked to the Image Record. To populate the authority file or list, use standard sources combined with local terminology as necessary.

9.2 CATALOGING RULES

9.2.1 Rules for View Description and View Type

9.2.1.1 *Brief Rules for View Description*

Describe the spatial, chronological, or contextual aspects of the work as captured in the image view. The View Type and Subject may be mentioned.

Capitalization and Abbreviations

Capitalize proper names. For other words, use lowercase. Do not capitalize cardinal directions (east, west, north, and south). Avoid abbreviations.

> *Examples*
>
> > **View Description**: distant view from the east
> >
> > **View Description**: detail of the signature in the lower right corner
> >
> > **View Description**: detail of the face of the lamb and Jesus' hand

Syntax

Use natural word order.

Language

Write the description in the language of the catalog record (English in the United States).

9.2.1.2 *Brief Rules for View Type*

Choose terms to indicate the position, angle, range, orientation, extent, or portion of the work depicted in the image view.

Capitalization and Abbreviations

Use lowercase. Avoid abbreviations.

> *Examples*
>
> > **View Type**: close-up view
> >
> > **View Type**: exterior view

Language of the Terms

Use terms in the language of the catalog record (English in the United States).

> *Examples*
>
> > **View Type**: oblique view
> >
> > **View Type**: worm's-eye view

9.2.1.3 *Additional Recommendations for View Description and Type*

The descriptions and indexing of image views may vary depending on the view and content of the image, as outlined.

Portion or Extent

If a view includes a portion of the entire work, indicate this (for example, *partial view*). Describe the part that is captured in the view (see also Controlled Fields for View Subject below).

Examples

[for a detail of a painting]

View Description (display):
detail of the artist's initials in lower left-hand corner

View Type (controlled):
detail view

[for a detail of a Scythian pectoral]

View Description (display):
detail of the lion in the lower center of the pectoral

View Type (controlled):
detail view

[for a partial view of a rock-cut temple]

View Description (display):
partial exterior view showing column and lintel of eastern entrance

View Types (controlled):
exterior view • partial view

[for an interior view of an art center]

View Description (display):
interior view with atrium and staircase

View Types (controlled):
interior view • partial view

Range or Position

If a view is taken from a particular range or position, indicate this.

Examples

[for a distant view of the Parthenon]

View Description (display):
distant view facing west

View Type (controlled):
distant view

[for a close-up view of a wall mosaic]

View Description (display):
close-up view of Justinian's eyes

View Type (controlled):
close-up view

Angle or Perspective

If a view is taken from a particular angle or perspective, indicate this.

Examples

[for an oblique view of a Roman arch]

View Description (display):
oblique view facing north

View Type (controlled):
oblique view

[for a view inside the Guggenheim Museum]

View Description (display):
interior overhead view from the top level down to the main gallery, taken from the ceiling

View Types (controlled):
overhead view • interior view

Interior or Exterior

For architecture and other works that contain interior space, indicate the view relative to the work's interior or exterior space where relevant.

Examples

[for an exterior view of a Mexican pyramid]

View Description (display):
exterior view facing southwest

View Type (controlled):
exterior view

[for an interior view of a Black-figure kylix]

View Description (display):
interior, detail view of the Chimaera

View Types (controlled):
interior view • detail view

Three-Dimensional Works

For three-dimensional works, use controlled terms that indicate positional attributes relative to the whole.

Examples

[for an African ancestral figure sculpture]

View Description (display):
profile view of the face and shoulders from the left

View Type (controlled):
profile view

[for a Renaissance sculpture of a horse]

    View Description (display):
    view of the hindquarters

    View Type (controlled):
    back view

Multiple Objects in One View

For views that include multiple objects, locate them within the context of the particular vantage point.

Example

[for a medieval church complex]

    View Description (display):
    bell tower in foreground with baptistery to the left

    View Types (controlled):
    exterior view • partial view

Environment and Lighting

For views that include the work within an environmental setting or under noteworthy lighting conditions, indicate the conditions.

Examples

[for a modern museum building]

    View Description (display):
    exterior view of the courtyard facing east at sunset

    View Types (controlled):
    exterior view • partial view

[for a monumental abstract sculpture]

    View Description (display):
    partial view in the fog

    View Type (controlled):
    partial view

If retrieval on the lighting (for example, raking light) or environmental conditions is required, this information should be indexed in View Type and View Subject.

Example

[for a drawing in pastels]

    View Description (display):
    detail of the surface in raking light

    View Types (controlled):
    raking light view • extreme close-up view

Cardinal Directions

For views of architecture and other site-specific works, use terms that indicate the direction of the view relative to the compass points.

Example

[for a skyscraper]

View Description (display):
oblique view facing northwest

View Type (controlled):
oblique view

If retrieval on the cardinal directions (for example, *north, south, east, west, southeast*) is required, this information should be indexed in View Type.

Example

[for a burial mound]

View Description (display):
partial view facing southeast

View Types (controlled):
partial view • southeast view

Time-Based Works

For images of performance art and other time-based works, describe the view and place it within the context of the whole, if possible.

Example

[for an image from a performance video]

View Description (display):
one still (frame) from the beginning of the performance video showing a woman, folding laundry

View Types (controlled):
partial view • frame

9.2.2   Rules for View Subject

9.2.2.1   Brief Rules for View Subject

Record the subject as depicted in the view distinct from general subject information recorded for the work.

Singular vs. Plural

Generally use the singular, including the proper names of iconographical themes, mythological events, persons, places, and so forth. When the singular is inappropriate, use the plural, as warranted by the subject being cataloged. See the discussion in Chapter 6: Subject.

Example

[for a detail of a still life]

View Subjects: bird's nest • urn • knife • apple • lilies

Capitalization and Abbreviations

Capitalize proper names; for other terms, use lowercase. Avoid abbreviations.

Examples

[for a detail in a group portrait]

View Subjects: Allan Pinkerton (American Secret Service agent, detective, 1819-1884)
• chair • table

[for a detail in a cityscape]

View Subject: Santa Maria del Fiore (Florence, Italy)

Language of the Terms

Use terms in the language of the catalog record (English in the United States), except in cases where no exact English-language equivalent exists. Use diacritics as appropriate.

Examples

[for a detail in a still life]

View Subjects: façon de Venise

[for a partial view of an office building]

View Subjects: outdoor café

9.2.2.2   *Additional Recommendations for View Subject*

9.2.2.2.1   VARIOUS TYPES OF IMAGES

The subjects recorded for the image views will vary depending upon the view and content of the image. The examples below illustrate one possible way that several view information fields for the image and subject fields for the work could display together.

Portion or Extent

If a view includes a portion of the entire work, describe the subject of the part that is captured in the view (for example, the west façade of a cathedral). Note the significant details captured by the image, particularly when the image contains subject matter prominent in the detail but not prominent in the work as a whole. It is not necessary to repeat subject information that is in the Work Record, unless it applies specifically to the image view at hand.

Examples

[for Reims Cathedral]

Work: Free-Text Subject field:
cathedral dedicated to Notre-Dame

Work: Controlled Subject fields:
cathedral • worship • Notre-Dame

Image: View Description (display):
west façade, partial view of the area from the rose window to the ground

Image: View Types (controlled):
partial view • east view

Image: Controlled View Subject fields:
west façade • rose window • portal • jamb statues

[for a painting]

Work: Free-Text Subject field:
Shah Jahan on horseback dressed for the hunt

Work: Controlled Subject fields (repeatable):
portrait • Shah Jahan • horse • hunt

Image: View Description (display):
detail of the face of the horse

Image: View Type (controlled):
detail view

Image: Controlled View Subject fields:
horse • face

Objects Not Part of the Work

If the image view contains persons or objects that are not a part of the work, such as lampposts in the example below, but are a significant part of the image, record this.

Examples

[for Tweed Courthouse, New York City]

Work: Description field:
formerly served as the New York County Courthouse, now houses Department of Education and an educational center

Work: Controlled Subject fields:
courthouse • office building • educational center

Image: View Description (display):
oblique view of the columned portico, facing south

Image: View Types (controlled):
partial view • oblique view • south view

Image: Controlled View Subject fields:
portico • Corinthian columns • lampposts

9.2.2.2.2 VIEW SUBJECT NOTE FIELD

If required by your institution, further describe the View Subject in a note, either in one reserved specifically for View Subject (see View Subject Note in the example below) or in a general note in the Image Record.

[for Growth House]

Work: Free-Text Subject field:

experimental dwelling, temporary construction that changes with the seasons

Work: Controlled Subject fields:

dwelling • experimental building • temporary construction • seasons • change

Image: View Description (display):

exterior view of the façade in October 1975, vegetables sprouting from the wall

Image: View Types (controlled):

exterior view • partial view

Image: Controlled View Subject fields:

façade • vegetables

Image: View Subject Note: The work changes with the seasons. This view captures the house in the fall when the seed walls have sprouted, bloomed, and developed vegetables growing from the walls.

9.2.3 Rules for View Date

9.2.3.1 *Brief Rules for View Date*

Record the year, or the day, month, and year when the view depicted in the image was captured. For Display Date, use natural language. For Earliest and Latest Dates, use the format YYYY-MM-DD or another format prescribed in either ISO 8061 or *W3C XML Schema Part 2*.

Example

Display Date:

30 October 1953

Controlled Date fields:

Earliest: 1953-10-30; **Latest**: 1953-10-30

For general information about recording dates, follow the recommendations in Chapter 4.

9.2.3.2 *Additional Recommendations for View Date*

9.2.3.2.1 SPECIFICITY OF DATES

Record the day, month, and year of the image. If the day and month are unknown, record the year.

Examples

[for a Maya pot]

View Description (display):

detail of anthropomorphic jaguars

Display Date:

photographed 21 September 1985, following the earthquake of 19 September

Controlled Date fields:
Earliest: 1985-09-21; **Latest**: 1985-09-21

[for the Ceiling of the Sistine Chapel, the Vatican]

View Description (display):
interior view, partial view, of the hands in the Creation of Adam

Display Date:
photographed in 1989, after restoration

Controlled Date fields:
Earliest: 1989; **Latest**: 1989

Record the hours and minutes, if significant and if known.

Example

[for a scene from performance art]

View Description (display):
oblique view of the stage, opening of performance

Display Date:
photographed 30 May 1998, 6:15 am

Controlled Date fields:
Earliest: 1998-05-30 06:15:00; **Latest**: 1998-05-30 06:15:00

9.2.3.2.2 APPROXIMATE DATES

Indicate uncertainty or approximate dates in the Display Date. Estimate Earliest and Latest Dates to facilitate retrieval. See Chapter 4 for general recommendations regarding approximate dates.

Example

[for the Great Pyramids, Giza, Egypt]

View Description (display):
distant view, facing west

Display Date:
photographed in the 1930s

Controlled Date fields:
Earliest: 1930; **Latest**: 1939

9.2.3.2.3 VARIOUS TYPES OF IMAGES

Record dates appropriate for the image view, as outlined below.

Phase of the Work

If the image documents a phase or aspect of the production or creation of the work, include the date. If the image documents an event that altered the work (for example, before or after restoration, before or after damage occurred), include the date.

> *Examples*
>
> [for the East Building, National Gallery of Art, Washington, DC]
>> **View Description (display)**:
>> interior view, Mezzanine level facing east
>>
>> **Display Date**:
>> during final construction, Spring 1977
>>
>> **Controlled Date fields**:
>> **Earliest**: 1977-03-01; **Latest**: 1977-06-30
>
> [for a panel painting after restoration]
>> **View Description (display)**:
>> detail of Athena's face
>>
>> **Display Date**:
>> after restoration, photograph taken on July 11, 2001
>>
>> **Controlled Date fields**:
>> **Earliest**: 2001-07-11; **Latest**: 2001-07-01

Historic Views

Include the date for historic views.

> *Example*
>
> [for the Berlin Wall]
>> **View Description (display)**:
>> oblique view facing east
>>
>> **Display Date**:
>> photographed in 1969
>>
>> **Controlled Date fields**:
>> **Earliest**: 1969; **Latest**: 1969

Conceptual Art

Include the date or range of dates for views of conceptual works, particularly when the concept involves impermanence.

Example

[for Christo's Surrounded Islands, Miami]

View Description (display):
aerial view, at sunset

Display Date:
photographed in 1981

Controlled Date fields:
Earliest: 1981; **Latest**: 1981

9.3   PRESENTATION OF THE DATA

9.3.1   Display and Indexing

9.3.1.1 *Free-Text vs. Controlled Fields*

For a discussion of when and why separate free-text and controlled fields are recommended, see Part 1: Database Design and Relationships: Display and Indexing.

9.3.1.2 *Fields in Authority File and Work Record*

Controlled Fields for View Description

Information in the free-text View Description should be indexed for retrieval in the controlled fields. If including a free-text View Description is not possible, a rudimentary display may be constructed by concatenating data from controlled fields.

The View Description may repeat the View Type, integrating it in the free-text field for easy comprehension by the end user. It may also omit View Type, in which case View Type may be concatenated with View Description in display.

Controlled Fields for View Type

View type should be a repeatable controlled field.

Controlled Fields for View Subject

View Subject should be displayed in a way that ensures that the end user can also see the subject of the work, which may have both free-text and controlled components. The subject of the image may be described in the free-text View Description. Any subject information in the View Description (display) that is required for retrieval of the image should be indexed in View Subject.

The View Subject element is a repeatable controlled field intended to allow retrieval and should ideally be linked to an authority file or controlled list. It may be linked to the same authority that controls terminology for the subject of the work. See Chapter 6: Subject for further discussion of how to record subject matter.

Controlled Fields for View Date

View Date is ideally a set of three fields: a display field to express nuances of the date to the end user, and two indexed fields representing the earliest and latest dates implied in the display date. The date fields for retrieval should contain dates formatted properly to allow retrieval. For general information about recording dates, follow the recommendations in Chapter 4.

9.3.2 Examples

Examples of Work and linked Image Records are included below. For additional examples, see the end of Part 1, the end of each chapter, and the CCO Web site. In the examples, *controlled* refers to values controlled by an authority file, controlled list, or other rules (for example, rules for recording dates). *Link* refers to a relationship between a Work Record and an Authority Record or between Work and Image Records. All links are controlled fields. In the examples that follow, Related Work Records are abbreviated for the sake of brevity. All Work Records should be as complete as possible. See the various chapters for discussions of individual metadata elements, whether they should be controlled, and the respective advantages of an authority file or a controlled list. In all examples in this manual, both within and at the end of each chapter, data values for repeatable fields are separated by bullet characters.

Figure 42

Image Record Linked to Work and Authority Records: Modern Building

Required and recommended elements are marked with an asterisk.

Image Record

- ■ **Image Number**: 200347
- ■ ***View Description***: interior view, atrium with staircase
- ■ ***View Type*** *[link]*: interior view
- ■ ***View Subject*** *[link to authorities]*: atrium • staircase
- ■ ***View Date*** *[controlled]*: 1969
- ■ **Related Work** *[link to Work Record]*: *Munson-Williams-Proctor Institute*; art center; Philip Johnson (American, 1906-2005); designed in 1957, completed in 1960; Utica (New York, United States)

Authority Record

- ■ ***Term***:
  - interior view
- ■ ***Note***: Refers to photographs or other representations of the inside of a building or other structure or object that has interior and exterior space.
- ■ ***Source*** *[link to Source Record]*: *Art & Architecture Thesaurus* (1988-).

Work Record

- ■ **Class** *[controlled]*: architecture • Modern art
- ■ ***Work Type*** *[link to authority]*: art center
- ■ ***Title***: Munson-Williams-Proctor Institute I **Title Type**: preferred
- ■ ***Creator display***: Philip Johnson (American,1906-2005)
  - ***Role*** *[link]*: architect I *[link]*: Johnson, Philip
- ■ ***Creation Date***: designed in 1957; completed in 1960
  - *[controlled]*: **Earliest**: 1957; **Latest**: 1960
- ■ ***Subject*** *[link to authorities]*: architecture • art center
- ■ ***Current Location*** *[link to authority]*: Utica (New York, United States)
- ■ ***Materials and Techniques***: steel frame construction, granite faced, bronze girders
  - **Material** *[link]*: granite • bronze I **Technique** *[link]*: steel frame
- ■ **Description**: The Institute illustrates Johnson's appreciation of Mies van der Rohe's single-span structures. It is a granite-clad cube supported by monumental bronze girders. The ground level is recessed, glazed, and hidden in a surrounding moat. The central atrium is the focus for the interior.
- ■ **Description Source** *[link to authority]*: Philip Johnson - Alan Ritchie, Architects. [online] http://www.pjar.com (accessed July 14, 2004).
- ■ **Related Images** *[link to Image Records]*: 200347

Figure 43

Image Record Linked to Work and Authority Records: Egyptian Monument

Required and recommended elements are marked with an asterisk.

Image Record

- ■ **Image Number**: 1234
- ■ ***View Description**: the Great Sphinx with the Great Pyramid in the background
    - *[link]*: Great Sphinx • Great Pyramid
- ■ ***View Type** *[link]*: exterior view • <u>oblique view</u> • partial view
- ■ ***View Date** *[controlled]*: 1950
- ■ **Related Work** *[link to Work Record]*: *Great Sphinx*; colossus; unknown Egyptian; Fourth Dynasty; Giza (Egypt)

Authority Record

- ■ ***Terms**:
    - <u>oblique view</u> (preferred)
    - diagonal view
- ■ ***Note**: Refers to depictions from a vantage point at an angle to the perpendiculars of the subject.
- ■ ***Source** *[link to Source Record]*: *Art & Architecture Thesaurus* (1988-).

Work Record

- ■ **Class** *[controlled]*: sculpture • architecture • Egyptian art
- ■ ***Work Type** *[link to authority]*: colossus
- ■ ***Title**: Great Sphinx | **Title Type**: preferred
    - **Title**: Abu al-Hawl | **Title Type**: alternate
- ■ ***Creator display**: unknown Egyptian
    - ***Role** *[link]*: artists | *[link]*: unknown Egyptian
- ■ ***Creation Date**: Fourth Dynasty, reign of King Khafre (ca. 2575-ca. 2465 BCE)
    - *[controlled]*: **Earliest**: -2585; **Latest**: -2555
- ■ ***Subject** *[link to authorities]*: religion and mythology • portrait • sphinx (Egyptian iconograph) • King Khafre (Egyptian king, ca. 2575-ca. 2465 BCE) • Pharaonic power • Sun God (Egyptian deity)
- ■ **Culture**: Egyptian (ancient)
- ■ ***Current Location** *[link to authority]*: Giza (Egypt)
- ■ ***Measurements**: 20 m (height) (66 feet); 73 m (length) (240 feet)
    - *[controlled]*: **Value**: 20; **Unit**: m; **Type**: height | **Value**: 73; **Unit**: m; **Type**: length
- ■ ***Materials and Techniques**: limestone, carved from live rock
    - **Material** *[link]*: limestone | **Technique** *[link]*: rock-cut architecture
- ■ **Description**: The sphinx is an embodiment of kingship, placed to the south of the Great Pyramid at Giza. It is probably intended to represent King Khafre, although later generations believed that it was the Sun God.
- ■ **Description Source** *[link to authority]*: Janson, H. W., *History of Art.* 3rd ed. New York: Harry N. Abrams, Inc., 1986; **Page**: 60 ff.
- ■ **Related Image** *[link to Image Record]*: 1234

Figure 44
Image Record Linked to Work and Authority Records: German Desk

Required and recommended elements are marked with an asterisk.

Image Record

■ **Image Number**: 98077
■ ***View Description**: detail of the desktop with inlaid coat of arms
■ ***View Type** *[link]*: detail view • overhead view
■ ***View Subject** *[link to authorities]*: coat of arms • electoral bonnet • lions
  [link]: lions • electoral bonnet • coat of arms
■ ***View Date** *[controlled]*: 2001-03-01
■ **Related Work** *[link to work]: Reading and Writing Stand*; table; Abraham Roentgen (German, 1711-1793); ca. 1760; J. Paul Getty Museum (Los Angeles, California, United States); 85.DA.216

Authority Record

■ ***Term**:
  detail view (preferred)
■ ***Note**: Refers to depictions containing a partial view that focuses on a particular detail of the whole.
■ ***Source** *[link to Source Record]: Art & Architecture Thesaurus* (1988-).

Work Record

■ **Class** *[controlled]*: furniture • decorative arts
■ ***Work Type** *[link to authority]*: table • reading desk
■ ***Title**: Reading and Writing Stand | **Title Type**: preferred
■ ***Creator display**: Abraham Roentgen (German, 1711-1793)
    ***Role** *[link]*: cabinetmaker | *[link]*: Roentgen, Abraham
■ ***Creation Date**: ca. 1760
    [controlled]: **Earliest**: 1755; **Latest**: 1765
■ ***Subject** *[link to authorities]*: study • reading • writing • coat of arms • Johann Philipp von Walderdorff
■ ***Current Location** *[link to authority]*: J. Paul Getty Museum (Los Angeles, Calilfornia, United States) | **ID**: 85.DA.216
■ ***Measurements**: 77.47 x 71.75 x 48.19 cm (30 1/2 x 28 1/4 x 19 1/4 inches)
    [controlled]: **Value**: 77.47; **Unit**: cm; **Type**: height | **Value**: 71.75; **Unit**: cm; **Type**: length | **Value**: 48.19; **Unit**: cm; **Type**: depth
■ ***Materials and Techniques**: oak veneered with palisander, alder, rosewood, ivory, and mother-of-pearl; parquetry decoration
    Material *[link]*: oak • alder • rosewood • ivory • mother-of-pearl | **Technique** *[link]*: cabinetmaking • parquetry • veneering
■ **Description**: When closed, this stand appears to be in the form of a table, yet it extends and opens in a complex manner to serve several functions. In the center of the writing surface is the coat-of-arms of Johann Philipp von Walderdorff, Elector and Archbishop of Trier.
■ **Description Source** *[link to authority]*: J. Paul Getty Museum. *Handbook of the Collections*. Los Angeles: J. Paul Getty Museum, 1991; **Page**: 102.
■ **Related Image** *[link to Image Record]*: 98077

Note

1. The ISO standard recognizes year zero. Humanities databases, however, will generally disregard it in calculations of earliest and latest dates.

Part THREE

Authorities

A.1 Personal and Corporate Name Authority

A.1.1 ABOUT THE NAME AUTHORITY

A.1.1.1 Discussion

The Personal and Corporate Name Authority contains names and other information about artists, architects, studios, architectural firms, and others responsible for the design and production of cultural works. This authority file will also contain information about patrons, repositories, and other persons or corporate bodies related to particular works. This authority file includes records for individuals (persons) and for organizations or any other two or more persons working together (corporate bodies).

Person

Persons include individuals whose biographies are well known, such as *Rembrandt van Rijn (Dutch painter and printmaker, 1606-1669)*, and creators with identified oeuvres but whose names are unknown and whose biography is estimated or surmised, such as *Master of Alkmaar (North Netherlandish painter, active ca. 1490-ca. 1510)*. The name authority is limited to real, historical persons. Fictional persons are recorded in the Subject Authority.

Corporate Body

A corporate body may be a legally incorporated entity, such as a modern architectural firm, but does not necessarily have to be legally incorporated; for example, a 16th-century sculptors' studio or family of artists may be recorded as a corporate body. Corporate bodies should be organized, identifiable groups of individuals working together in a particular place and within a defined period of time. A work-

279

shop may be included in the Personal and Corporate Name Authority if the work-shop itself is a distinct group of individuals, collectively responsible for fostering the creation of art (for example, the 13th-century group of French illuminators, Soissons Atelier). Museums and most other repositories are also corporate bodies. Certain events, such as conferences, are typically treated as corporate bodies and recorded in this authority (for historical events, see A4: Subject Authority).[1]

Persons and Corporate Bodies That Are Not Creators

The discussion in this chapter focuses on creators and repositories. However, institutions may use a single authority file to record all nonfictional persons and corporate bodies associated with the work; for example, the Personal and Corporate Name Authority should include records for art academies, merchants, rulers, manufacturers, patrons, and any person depicted in works.

Unknown Creators

Note that a designation such as *workshop of Raphael* is outside the scope of this kind of authority file. In this example, the concept *workshop of* is considered a qualifier of the attribution to *Raphael* (whose record would be in this authority file). This qualifier belongs in the Work Record. Qualifiers may be used in Work Records when the identity of a creator is unknown but he has worked closely with a known creator; in such cases, it is common to associate the work with the name of a known creator whose oeuvre is stylistically similar or otherwise related to the work at hand. In such cases, you should link the Work Record to the Authority Record for the known creator, but the known creator's name needs to be qualified in the Work Record with a phrase such as *workshop of, follower of, attributed to*, or *studio of*. For definitions of these qualifiers and further discussion of this issue, see Chapter 2: Creator Information: Suggested Terminology for Qualifier and Extent.

Other examples of unknown creators include unidentified artistic personalities with unestablished oeuvres, referred to by designations such as *Florentine* or *unknown 16th-century Florentine*, and may be included in this authority.

In this approach, separate Authority Records are maintained for cultures and ethnic groups in the Personal and Corporate Name Authority that can be linked to all Work Records for which this heading applies (illustrated in Figure 46). In such cases, the generic identification does not refer to one identified, if anonymous, individual; but instead the same heading refers to any number of anonymous, unidentified artistic personalities linked in various Work Records. The heading may or may not include the word *unknown*, provided that it is done consistently.

Another approach for cases in which the identity of a hand and its oeuvre is not established is to devise a generic identification for display in the Work Record by concatenating terms from the culture element (see Chapter 4: Stylistic, Cultural, and Chronological Information), with or without a word such as *unknown* (but be consistent). In the example in Figure 45, the word *unknown* has been added to the culture term to create a heading for the Creator display.

Figure 45
Unknown Artist's Appellation Constructed for End Users

Work Record

- **Class**: sculpture
- ***Work Type**: statue
- ***Title**: Dancing Devata | **Title Type**: preferred
- ***Creator display**: unknown Indian
- ***Role**: sculptor
- ***Creation Date**: 12th century
- **Culture**: Indian
- ***Subject**: Devata • movement • dance
- ***Current Location**: Metropolitan Museum (New York, New York, United States)
- **Creation Location**: Uttar Pradesh (India)
- ***Measurements**: height: 85.1 cm (33 1/3 inches)
- ***Materials and Techniques**: stone
- **Description**: This celestial dancing figure displays sinuous contours and richly ornamented surfaces that exemplify a shift in style ...

Figure 46
Unknown Artist's Appellation Stored in Authority File

Work Record

- **Class**: sculpture
- ***Work Type**: statue
- ***Title**: Dancing Devata | **Title Type**: preferred
- ***Creator display**: unknown Indian
  - ***Role**: sculptor
  - ***Name** *[link to authority]*: unknown Indian
- ***Creation Date**: 12th century
- ***Subject**: Devata • movement • dance
- ***Current Location**: Metropolitan Museum (New York, New York, United States)
- **Creation Location**: Uttar Pradesh (India)
- ***Measurements**: height: 85.1 cm (33 1/3 inches)
- ***Materials and Techniques**: stone
- **Description**: This celestial dancing figure displays sinuous contours and richly ornamented surfaces that exemplify a shift in style ...

Personal and Corporate Name Authority Record

- ***Name**:
  - unknown Indian
- ***Display Biography**: Indian artist

About Repositories

The location of a work (recorded in the Work Record) may be a repository. Administrative repositories (for example, museums and other institutions) should be controlled by corporate body authority records in this authority file; the record for the museum should in turn contain the geographic location of the repository, ideally through a link to the Geographic Place Authority. Other locations for works are buildings (not administrative repositories) and geographic locations; see Chapter 5: Location and Geography, A2: Geographic Place Authority, and A4: Subject Authority.

For repositories and other corporate bodies in this authority file, some cataloging institutions may also need to record the buildings that house the corporate bodies as architectural works in their own right. Both the corporate body and the building as a work may have the same name, but they are separate entities. Records for these buildings as architectural works should be separately recorded with other Work Records, even if this requires some redundancy. For example, the *National Gallery of Art* in Washington is a corporate body that has a board of directors and other related people; it acquires art works and cares for the objects under its protection. In a hierarchical data model, its parts would be the departments in the National Gallery, such as the *Department of Prints, Drawings, and Photographs, Index of American Design*, and so forth. The corporate body would likely still exist if the art collection were moved to new buildings. The buildings that currently house this corporate body and its art works are collectively also called the *National Gallery of Art*, but that work of architecture has different characteristics from the institution and is recorded in different database fields; it therefore should be recorded as a work in its own right, if such information is pertinent for the cataloging institution. As a work of architecture, the National Gallery has building materials, dates of design and construction, styles, and creators (the architects John Russell Pope and I. M. Pei). In a hierarchical data model, its parts would be the *West Building* and the *East Building*. Of course, in such a data structure, the record for the National Gallery of Art as an institution would be linked to the record for the National Gallery of Art as an architectural work.

Ambiguity and Uncertainty

When creating an Authority Record, if information about a person or corporate body is ambiguous or uncertain, the cataloger should state only what is known. When information is uncertain, it may still be recorded, but with an indication of uncertainty or approximation—such as *ca.* or *probably*—in the Note or Display Biography fields. Important information in these free-text fields should be indexed in controlled fields. Rules should be in place to ensure consistency in recording uncertain data. If biographical information is uncertain or ambiguous, this should be indicated in the Display Biography. Such uncertainty may require that the multiple possibilities be indexed in the controlled fields. For example, if it is uncertain whether a creator was Flemish or French, this should be explained in the Display Biography (for example, *Flemish or French painter, 14th century*), and both nationalities should be indexed in the controlled fields for retrieval. If a cataloger is uncertain whether one artist is the same person as another person with a similar name, rather than mistakenly linking the two names in one record, separate records should be made for each person until the issue is resolved through additional research.

Organization of the Data

The creator's names, nationality, life roles, and life dates are critical access points and are required.

Some fields in this authority file are intended for display. Others should be formatted and used for indexing and retrieval (see Display and Indexing below). The only required free-text field discussed in this section is the Display Biography for the creator. It is assumed that key data values must be separately formatted and linked to controlled vocabularies to allow for retrieval, which this manual refers to as *indexing*.

Ideally, this authority file should be in the form of a thesaurus to allow for equivalence, associative, and occasionally whole-part relationships (see *Controlled Vocabulary: Thesaurus*).

Although names and biographical information about creators are stored in this authority file separately from the Work Records, in retrieval such information should be accessible in combination with fields in the Work Record. For example, a user may request *tapestries* (work type in the Work Records) by *Italian artists* (artist nationality in the Personal and Corporate Name Authority Records). The relationships between the Work Record and the authority file should also permit, when referring to the creator in the Work Record, the preferred name of the creator and a Display Biography—generally the nationality, life roles, and life dates—to be displayed through a link to an Authority Record.

Display Biography, Birth Date, Death Date, Note, and Gender should not be repeatable elements. All other elements should be repeatable. One of the names should be flagged as preferred. A brief discussion of the elements or fields recommended for this authority file is included in this section. For further discussion of the relationships between this authority file and the Work Record, see Chapter 2: Creator Information. For further discussion of this authority file and additional fields, see *Categories for the Description of Works of Art: Creator Identification*. For a fuller set of editorial rules for personal and corporate body names, see the *Union List of Artist Names Editorial Guidelines*.[2]

Recommended Elements

A list of the elements discussed in this chapter appears below. Required elements are noted. Display may be a free-text field or concatenated from controlled fields. Note that the same elements are used for persons and corporate bodies.

> Names (preferred, alternates, and variants) (required)
> Note
> Display Biography (required)
> Birth Date (required) (Start Date for corporate bodies)
> Death Date (required) (End Date for corporate bodies)
> Nationality (required) (National Affiliation for corporate bodies)
> Life Roles (required) (Functions for corporate bodies)
> Gender (not applicable for corporate bodies)
> Date of Earliest Activity
> Date of Latest Activity
> Place/Location
> Related People and Corporate Bodies
> Relationship Type
> Events
> Sources (required)
> [Record Type (Person or Corporate Body) (controlled list)]

About the Examples

The examples throughout this section are for illustration only. Local practice may vary. The examples tend to show the fullest possible use of display and indexing fields, which may not be necessary for all institutions.

A.1.1.2 Terminology

A.1.1.2.1 *Sources for Terminology*

A.1.1.2.1.1 NAMES OF PERSONS AND CORPORATE BODIES

Published sources of names of individual creators, firms, and repositories include the following:

> Getty Vocabulary Program. *Union List of Artist Names* (ULAN). Los Angeles: J. Paul Getty Trust, 1988-. http://www.getty.edu/research/conducting_research/vocabularies/ulan/.

> Library of Congress Authorities. Washington, DC: Library of Congress, 2002. http://authorities.loc.gov/.

> *Grove Dictionary of Art Online.* New York: Grove's Dictionaries, 2003. http://www.groveart.com/.

> Thieme, Ulrich, and Felix Becker, eds. *Allgemeines Lexikon der bildenden Künstler von der Antike bis zur Gegenwart.* 37 vols. 1907. Reprint, Leipzig: Veb E. A. Seemann Verlag, 1980-1986.

> Bénézit, Emmanuel, ed. *Dictionnaire critique et documentaire des peintres, sculpteurs, dessinateurs et graveurs.* 1911-1923. Reprint, Paris: Librairie Gründ, 1976.

> Meissner, Günter, ed. *Allgemeines Künstlerlexikon: die bildenden Künstler aller Zeiten und Völker.* Munich: K. G. Saur, 1992-.

> *Macmillan Encyclopedia of Architects.* Edited by Adolf K. Placzek. New York: Free Press; London: Collier Macmillan, 1982.

> *Official Museum Directory.* Washington, DC: American Association of Museums, 2004.

Additional general encyclopedias and dictionaries of creators may be used. In addition, standard textbooks for art history and Web sites or catalogs for art museums can serve as sources for names and biographical information about creators and repositories. You may also refer to more specialized sources of creator names, including national sources such as Bolaffi's *Dizionario dei pittori italiani* (1972-1976) for Italian artists or Snodgrass's *American Indian Painters* for Native American artists.[3]

A.1.1.2.1.2 NATIONALITY AND PLACES

Nationality and places of birth, death, and activity may be controlled by the *Getty Thesaurus of Geographic Names* (TGN) or another source of geographic names or nationality terms (and recorded in the geographic authority file; see A2: Geographic Place Authority). The nationality field may also record culture, race, or ethnicity, which may be controlled by the *Art & Architecture Thesaurus* (AAT) or another appropriate source (and recorded in the Concept Authority). The Nationality file for the *Union List of Artist Names* contains terms for nationality and for culture, race, and ethnicity.

> Getty Vocabulary Program. *Art & Architecture Thesaurus.* Los Angeles: J. Paul Getty Trust, 1988-. http://www.getty.edu/research/ conducting_research/vocabularies/aat/. (Especially the Styles and Periods facet, where culture names are sometimes included).

> Getty Vocabulary Program. *Getty Thesaurus of Geographic Names.* Los Angeles: J. Paul Getty Trust, 1988-. http://www.getty.edu/ research/conducting_research/vocabularies/tgn/. (Includes noun forms of geographic names as well as adjectival forms, which are nationalities).

> Getty Vocabulary Program. *Union List of Artist Names: Editorial Guidelines: Appendix G: Nationality and Places.* 2000-. http://www.getty .edu/research/conducting_research/vocabularies/guidelines/ulan_4 _7_appendix_g_nationality_place.html. (Terms in this list are derived from the TGN and the AAT).

> Library of Congress Authorities. *Library of Congress Subject Headings.* Washington, DC: Library of Congress, http://authorities.loc.gov/.

A.1.1.2.1.3 LIFE ROLES AND FUNCTIONS

Life roles for persons or terms for function for corporate bodies may be controlled by the AAT, especially the People hierarchy.

A.1.1.2.1.4 BIRTH/START DATES AND DEATH/END DATES

Date information must be formatted consistently to enable retrieval on dates. Local formatting rules should be in place; suggested formats are available in the ISO standard and *W3C XML Schema Part 2.*

> ISO 8601:2004 Numeric representation of Dates and Time. *Data elements and interchange formats. Information interchange. Representation of dates and times.* Geneva, Switzerland: International Organization for Standardization, 2004.

> *XML Schema Part 2: Datatypes, 2001.* http://www.w3.org/TR/ xmlschema-2/.

A.1.1.2.1.5 OTHER ELEMENTS

Display Biography is a free-text field; controlled vocabulary is advised, but not required. Gender should be controlled with values such as *male, female, unknown.* Related people and corporate bodies may be controlled by linking to other records in this authority file.

A.1.2 EDITORIAL RULES

A.1.2.1 Rules for Names

A.1.2.1.1 *Brief Rules for Names*

Record one or more proper names, appellations, pseudonyms, nicknames, or other identifying phrases for the person or corporate body. It is required to record at least one name—the preferred name, which is the name used most often in scholarly literature to refer to the person or corporate body.

Capitalization and Abbreviations

Capitalize proper names. For the preferred name, capitalize surnames, initials, forenames, and honorifics consistently. Avoid abbreviations, except for the abbreviations for numbers (such as *3rd*) and for abbreviations that are part of a corporate body's official name (such as the ampersand, &).

> *Examples*
>
> **Name**: Warhol, Andy
>
> **Name**: López, José Antonio
>
> **Name**: Sullivan, Louis H.
>
> **Name**: Boyle, Richard, 3rd Earl of Burlington
>
> **Name**: El Greco
>
> **Name**: Gobelins Tapestry Manufactory
>
> **Name**: Richard Meier & Partners

For the preferred name, if a name includes an article or preposition used as a prefix (such as *de, des, le, la, l', della, van, von, von der*), generally use lowercase (for example, Loo, Abraham Louis van). If the inverted form of the name is indexed with the prefix as the first word, however, the prefix should generally be capitalized (for example, *Le Gros, Jean*).

Language of the Names

For the preferred name, for persons and corporate bodies, use the name in the language of the catalog record, if applicable: for example, *Raphael* in English, *Raffaelo* in Italian; *National Museum* in English, *Národní Muzeum* in Czech. Use diacritics as appropriate.

In brief, for the preferred name for English-language records, use the commonly used English name if warranted by authoritative sources. If an English name does not exist or is not warranted by sources, use the vernacular name as the preferred name.

PERSONAL NAMES

Most non-English-language personal names do not have an English equivalent. In such instances, use authorized sources and do not invent English translations of names when they are not found in the sources.

CORPORATE BODY NAMES

Most major institutions in non-English-speaking places, however, do have an English equivalent for their name. If the English name appears in an authoritative source, including catalogs and Web sites published by the institution, use the English name as the preferred name. If you cannot find an English name in an authoritative source, however, do not invent one. Instead, use the vernacular name.

VERNACULAR AS VARIANT NAME

If an English name is the preferred name, that is, when English is not the vernacular name for this person or corporate body, include the vernacular name as a variant name.

Examples

[for a museum in Prague, Czech Republic, the preferred name is English because the English name appears most often in English-language sources and on the English page of the official Web site of the Museum]

Names: National Museum (preferred) • Národní Muzeum

[for a museum in Mexico City, the preferred name is English as warranted by English-language sources]

Names: National Museum of Anthropology (preferred) • Museo Nacional de Antropología

[for a French architectural studio, preferred name is French because the French name is most often used in English-language sources]

Names: Atelier Le Corbusier (preferred) • Le Corbusier Studio

ENGLISH AS VARIANT NAME

If the English name is used only in minor sources, that is, when the vernacular name is preferred in authoritative sources, include the English name as a variant name.

Example

[for a museum in Bologna, Italy, preferred name is Italian because the Italian name is generally used in authoritative English-language sources, including English translations of catalogs published by the institution itself; the English name appears only occasionally in minor and antiquated sources]

Names: Pinacoteca Nazionale (preferred) • National Picture Gallery

A.1.2.1.2 *Additional Recommendations for Names*

A.1.2.1.2.1 PREFERRED NAME

For each person and corporate body, label one name or appellation as preferred. Choose the name used most often in authoritative sources and scholarly literature.

Examples

> **Name**: O'Keeffe, Georgia (preferred)
>
> **Name**: Arakawa, Shusaku (preferred)
>
> **Name**: Sullivan, Louis H. (preferred)
>
> **Name**: Leonardo da Vinci (preferred)
>
> **Name**: Master of the Zurich Adoration (preferred)
>
> **Name**: I. M. Pei & Partners (preferred)

In choosing the preferred name, for each person or corporate body record, label one name as preferred. To select a preferred name, consult the recommended sources for terminology. If the name is not in these sources, use the name preferred in general reference sources and standard textbooks in art history in the language of the catalog record (English in the United States). For non-artists, choose the name most commonly used in appropriate standard sources, such as a general encyclopedia or biographical dictionary.

If sources disagree, go down the list of preferred sources and use the name in the first-listed source. If the ULAN and Library of Congress authorities or subject headings disagree on the form of the name for a given person or corporate body, choose one of the two as the preferred name, and always include the other as a variant. Your institution should have a rule denoting the preferred source.

For names that are not found in standard sources, consult journal articles or other published sources; you may also consult the signature on the work at hand. In the rare case when a name cannot be found in a published source, construct a preferred name based on *Anglo-American Cataloguing Rules*: 22 (Headings for Persons), 24 (Corporate Bodies), or the *Chicago Manual of Style*: (Personal Names), (Names of Organizations).[4]

A.1.2.1.2.2 ADDITIONAL NAMES

Include alternate and variant names that appear in published sources and represent significant differences in form or spelling. Include names in multiple languages, variants that differ in diacritics and punctuation, name inversions, translations, and variant transliterations. Include married names, pseudonyms, and nicknames, if appropriate.

Examples

> **Names**: Šiškin, Ivan Ivanoviè (preferred) • Schischkin, Iwan Iwanowitsch • Chichkin, Ivan Ivanovitch
>
> **Names**: Zinkeisen, Anna Katrina (preferred) • Heseltine, Anna Katrina, Mrs.

A.1.2.1.2.3 NATURAL AND INVERTED ORDER

Names may be in natural order (for example, *Christopher Wren*, used for display) or in inverted order (for example, *Wren, Christopher*, used for indexing). Record the preferred name in both natural and inverted order; if possible, flag them so they may be used in different situations (for example, natural order for wall labels; inverted order for lists and reports).

Syntax

For the inverted order form of the name, record the name in the following order: last name, comma, first name, comma, followed by middle names or initials and title, if any.

For the natural order form of the name, record the name in the following order: first name, middle names or initials (if applicable), and last name. If there is a title, separate it from the name with a comma. For *the Elder* or *the Younger*, do not use a comma. For *Jr.* or *Sr.*, use a comma.

Use periods with initials; if there are multiple initials, include a space between them. Exceptions are for initials that are part of an official name of a corporate body (for example, the acronym *MoMA*, which would be an alternate name, not the preferred name).

Examples

Names: Harpignies, Henri-Joseph (preferred) • Henri-Joseph Harpignies (display name)

Names: Lücke, Carl August, the Younger (preferred) • Carl August Lücke the Younger (display name)

Names: Alexander, R. M. (preferred) • R. M. Alexander (display name)

No Last Name

If there is no last name for a person, as for early artists or corporate bodies, flag the natural order form of the name as the preferred name.

Example

Names: Bartolo di Fredi (preferred) • Bartolo di Fredi Cini • Bartholus Magistri Fredis de Senis

A.1.2.1.2.4 VARIOUS KINDS OF NAMES

Include names as outlined below.

Fullness of the Name

Include significant differences in the fullness of the name. The preferred name should not necessarily be the fullest name, but rather the most commonly used name in authoritative sources and scholarly literature.

Example

Names: Meier, Richard (preferred) • Meier, Richard Alan

Abbreviations

Include commonly used abbreviations and initials among the alternate names. Put the abbreviation and a corresponding full name in separate instances of the Name element, as in the example below; do not append the abbreviated name in parentheses after the preferred name.[5] In general, avoid abbreviations in the preferred name, unless the official, commonly used name contains initials or abbreviations.

Example

> **Names**: Skidmore, Owings and Merrill (preferred) • SOM

Pseudonyms and Nicknames

Include pseudonyms and nicknames if these are found in standard sources. If a pseudonym or nickname is the preferred name, do not invert it if it is not inverted in authoritative sources.

Examples

> **Names**: Man Ray (preferred) • Radnitzky, Emmanuel • Rudnitsky, Emmanuel
>
> **Names**: El Greco (preferred) • Theotokopolous, Domenikos
>
> **Names**: Pontormo (preferred) • Carrucci, Jacopo • Giacomo da Pontormo

Distinguishing Members of the Same Family

Include designations that distinguish two or more members of the same family bearing the same name (for example, *the Elder* or *Jr.*).

Examples

> **Names**: Breughel, Pieter, the Elder (preferred) • Pieter Bruegel the Elder • Brueghel, Pieter, I
>
> **Names**: Hartray, John F., Jr. (preferred) • John F. Hartray, Jr. • Hartray, J. F., Jr.

Titles

Include honorifics and titles, as appropriate. For the preferred name, use the name most commonly used in standard sources (which may omit the title).

Examples

> **Names**: Rubens, Peter Paul (preferred) • Peter Paul Rubens (display) • Rubens, Sir Peter Paul • Sir Peter Paul Rubens
>
> **Names**: Leo X, Pope (preferred) • Pope Leo X (display) • Medici, Giovanni de'

Names in Different Languages

If there are commonly used variants in various languages, include them as alternate names.

Examples

[in English and Native American language]

> **Names**: Kicking Bear (preferred) • Mato Wanartaka

[in Italian and French]

    Names: Giambologna (preferred) • Bologna, Giovanni • Bologna, Giovanni da • Bologne, Jean de • Boulogne, Jean de

Early Creators

For Western creators dating from the 16th century and before, do not invert the preferred name if it is not inverted in authoritative sources. Such names are often a combination of a given name plus a patronymic, place name, or other descriptive phrase, and are thus not inverted. You may include an inverted version of the name as an alternate name. These same rules may occasionally apply to artists living after the 16th century as well.

    Example

    Names: Leonardo da Vinci (preferred) • Vinci, Leonardo da

Non-Western Creators

For non-Western creators, do not invert the preferred name if it is not inverted in authoritative sources. In such cases, the name may already be listed in inverted order or may otherwise be inappropriate for inversion.

    Example

    Names: Zhang Xu (preferred) • Chang Hsü • Zhang Chengshi

Corporate Bodies

For corporate bodies, do not invert the preferred name. Use abbreviations (for example, ampersand or initials), if found in authoritative sources.

    Examples

    Name: Adler and Sullivan (preferred)

    Names: Eero Saarinen & Associates (preferred) • Saarinen & Associates, Eero

Former Names

Include former names and name changes as variants.

FOR PERSONS

If a person's name has changed over time, include the former names. Examples include legal name changes (for example, a married name) and any other instance of former appellations. The preferred name should be the one most often found in authoritative sources.

    Example

[for married and maiden names]

    Names: Alma-Tadema, Laura Theresa (preferred) • Laura Theresa Alma-Tadema • Alma-Tadema, Laura Theresa Epps • Alma-Tadema, Mrs. Laurence • Epps, Laura Theresa

FOR ANONYMOUS ARTISTS

For creators whose identity has changed over time through scholarship, include their previous appellations as alternate names.

Example

[it is generally accepted that Robert Campin is the formerly anonymous Master of Flémalle]

Names: Campin, Robert (preferred) • Robert Campin • Master of Flémalle

If the identity of a creator is uncertain, do not record the additional names together in the same record. If scholarly opinion is divided about whether or not the anonymous creator is the same person as a named creator, make two separate records and link them as Related People (see Related People and Corporate Bodies below).

FOR CORPORATE BODIES

Generally, include the former names as historical names in one record rather than two if the corporate body is a historical studio or institution (for example, *Manufacture Royale des Gobelins* and *Manufacture Nationale des Gobelins* are two names in the same record), or if the primary partners have remained the same for a modern firm. Make two separate records if the function or location of the historical corporate body changed with the name change, or if the question involves a modern firm and legal incorporation, the primary partners have changed, and the firm apparently prefers to clearly distinguish its separate incarnations. Link the related corporate bodies (see Related People and Corporate Bodies below).

Anonymous Creators

For anonymous creators, use an appellation provided by an authoritative source or devised by scholars. In the context of this manual, an *anonymous creator* is defined as a creator whose hand is identified and oeuvre is established, but whose name is not known (for example, *Master of the Morgan Leaf*). This type of creator is distinguished from *unknown creators*, discussed below. Generally, do not invert appellations for anonymous creators.

Examples

Name: Monogrammist A. D. L.

Name: Borden Limner

Unknown Creators

Some institutions may choose to create appellations for unknown generic groups to which works with unknown attributions may be linked.[6] Make a generic appellation that includes the word *unknown* and the culture or nationality (for example, *unknown Korean*). Alternatively, include broad dates (for example, *unknown 18th-century Korean*). Whichever method is used, be consistent. See also Chapter 2: Creator Information.

Examples

>   **Name**: unknown 16th-century Italian
>
>   **Name**: unknown Sioux
>
>   **Name**: unknown
>
>   **Name**: 18th-century French
>
>   **Name**: Anasazi
>
>   **Name**: anonymous
>
>   **Name**: anonymous German

A.1.2.2   Rules for Other Elements

A.1.2.2.1 *Rules for Display Biography*

A.1.2.2.1.1 RECORDING DISPLAY BIOGRAPHY

Record a concise phrase noting the following biographical details for a person: nationality, life roles, and birth and death dates. Record a concise phrase noting the following pertinent characteristics of a corporate body: national affiliation, function, and dates of establishment and dissolution. Display biography is used to create labels or headings in the Work Record and in lists (see also Chapter 2: Creator Information: Listing Biographical Information).

Capitalization and Abbreviation

Capitalize nationality, culture, place names, period names, or other proper nouns. Use lowercase for all other words. Avoid abbreviations, except for the word *circa* (*ca.*), the numbers in century or dynasty designations (for example, *17th century*), and *BCE* and *CE*.

>   *Examples*
>
>   **Display Biography**: Russian painter, 1893-1936
>
>   **Display Biography**: American miniaturist, active 1860s
>
>   **Display Biography**: French porcelain manufactory, flourished ca. 1731-1794
>
>   **Display Biography**: Roman sculptor, 1st century BCE

Syntax

List information in the following order for a person: nationality, space, life role or roles, comma, birth and death dates.[7] For a corporate body, list analogous information in the same order: national affiliation, term indicating function, and dates of establishment and dissolution. In a span of dates, list birth date (start date), dash, death date (end date). Include all digits for both years in a span (for example, *1831-1890*, not *1831-90*). Do not use an apostrophe (for example, *1350s* or *1900s*, not *1350's* or *1900's*). If *ca.* applies to both years in a date span, repeat it with the second year for clarity (for example, *ca. 1720-ca. 1785*).

Examples

Display Biography: Indian sculptor, 1923-1982

Display Biography: British architectural firm, 1910-1944

Display Biography: Flemish sculptor and architect, ca. 1529-1608, active in Italy

Display Biography: Kenyan craftsman, ca. 1865-ca. 1905

Display Biography: American photography studio, flourished 1850s

Display Biography: Maya vase painter, 10th century

If the word *probably* or other indications of uncertainty are included, change the order and syntax as necessary for clarity.

Examples

Display Biography: sculptor, probably Polynesian, 19th century

Display Biography: English photography studio, probably established before 1888

Include place of activity if nationality is unknown or if place of activity is different than nationality. Use natural word order.

Examples

Display Biography: Mexican mosaicist, active ca. 1820-ca. 1840

Display Biography: Flemish sculptor and architect, 1529-1608, active in Italy

Display Biography: Greek architect, active 4th century in southern Italy

Display Biography: British publishing house, 19th century, active primarily in India

Gregorian Calendar

List dates as years in the proleptic Gregorian calendar, which includes dates before the Gregorian was officially introduced. If another calendar is referenced, include the date in the Gregorian calendar. Use *BCE* (Before Current Era) and *CE* (Current Era) if the year alone would be confusing or ambiguous to the end user. Do not use *BC* and *AD*.

Example

Display Biography: Italian pietra dura workshop, active 1588 to the present

Display Biography: Roman emperor and patron, 63 BCE-14 CE

Display Biography: Persian weaver, died 946 anno Hegirae (1540 CE)

Display Biography: Sienese painter, active by 1353, died 1410 (1409 Sienese calendar)

A.1.2.2.1.2 AMBIGUITY AND UNCERTAINTY

Avoid phrasing the text in a way that can be confusing or ambiguous. Clearly indicate uncertain or ambiguous information, including approximate dates, by using *circa* (*ca.*) and qualifiers such as *probably*.

Examples

Display Biography: Netherlandish painter, ca. 1564-after 1612

Display Biography: French or Flemish draftsman, active by 1423, died 1464

Display Biography: Russian illuminator and designer, probably 1862-before 1910

Display Biography: Attic vase painters, active ca. 585-ca. 570 BCE

If only either the birth or start date or the death or end date is known, or for living artists or extant corporate bodies for whom a death or end date is not applicable, clearly indicate the meaning of the single date known by using *born* or *died* for persons, or other terms appropriate to corporate bodies.

Examples

Display Biography: African sculptor, died 1978

Display Biography: Japanese photographer, born 1963

Display Biography: Canadian architectural firm, established 1931

Alternatively, some local practice requires catalogers to list the birth date or start date followed by a dash (for example, *Japanese sculptor, 1963-*, or *Canadian architectural firm, 1931-*). Whichever method is used, be consistent.

For the Display Biography, use dates of activity when life dates are unknown for persons; use dates of flourishing when dates of establishment and dissolution are unknown for corporate bodies. Do not include your own guesses regarding life dates in the Display Biography. However, for the controlled dates for retrieval, estimate birth and death dates when necessary; see Rules for Birth/Start Dates and Death/End Dates.

Examples

Display Biography: Italian sculptor, ca. 1230-ca. 1275

Display Biography: Persian weaver, active mid-18th century

Display Biography: Chinese calligrapher, active 1730s

Display Biography: German printmaking studio, flourished 1930s

A.1.2.2.1.3 ANONYMOUS PERSONS

Some institutions prefer to keep name authority records for every anonymous circumstance. If that is the practice, then, for an anonymous person, or for any other person or corporate body where biographical information is unknown or incomplete, record the deduced nationality or locus of activity and approximate dates of activity.

Examples

> **Display Biography**: Italian painter, active 1330s-1340s
>
> **Display Biography**: sculptor, probably Spanish, active 18th century in California
>
> **Display Biography**: group of vase painters, probably Greek, active in Campania in mid-4th century BCE

A.1.2.2.1.4 INDEX BIOGRAPHICAL INFORMATION

Use controlled fields to index important biographical information, including nationality, life roles, and birth and death dates for persons. Index the analogous elements for corporate bodies.

Example

> **Display Biography**: French architect and designer, 1871-1922
> **Controlled fields**:
> > **Nationality**: French
> > **Life Roles**: architect • designer
> > **Birth Date**: 1871
> > **Death Date**: 1922

A.1.2.2.2 *Rules for Nationality*

Record a term referring to the national, geopolitical, cultural, or ethnic origins or affiliation of the person or corporate body. This element does not refer only to nationality in a modern, legal sense. Record the adjectival name form of a nation, place name, culture, or ethnic group. Terms should be controlled by Nationality and Culture element terms from the Concept Authority and Geographic Place Authority.

Examples

> **Nationality**: English
>
> **Nationality**: Nigerian
>
> **Nationality**: Vietnamese
>
> **Nationality**: Italian
>
> **Nationality**: Sienese
>
> **Nationality**: Berber
>
> **Nationality**: Celtic
>
> **Nationality**: Native American
>
> **Nationality**: ancient Roman

Specificity

Record a designation at the level of nation (for example, *Italian*) or a broad culture (for example, *Native American*). If known, for broad culture, also include a more specific designation (for example, *Sioux* or *Lakota* in addition to *Native American*, and *Florentine* in addition to *Italian*).

Historical Nationalities

Include a historical nationality when warranted (for example, for a 14th-century artist from Brussels, it is common practice in the discipline of medieval art history to list the nationality as *Flemish* rather than *Belgian*, because Belgium was not a nation until the 19th century). If appropriate for a specific discipline, include a more specific designation in addition to the modern nation (for example, both *Sienese* and *Italian* for a 14th-century artist).

Multiple Nationalities

If the person was active in two nations, or if the nationality is uncertain and two nationalities are possible, include both.

> *Examples*
>
> [person had two nationalities over a lifetime]
>
> > **Display Biography**: Chinese architect, 1898-1967, naturalized American
> > **Nationalities**: Chinese • American
>
> [nationality is uncertain]
>
> > **Display Biography**: Dutch or German printmaker, 16th century
> > **Nationalities**: Dutch • German
>
> [national affiliation is uncertain]
>
> > **Display Biography**: American or Canadian photography studio, early 19th century
> > **Nationalities**: American • Canadian
>
> [both the specific and more general culture terms are indexed]
>
> > **Display Biography**: Native American painter, ca. 1846-1904
> > **Nationalities**: Native American • Sioux

A.1.2.2.3 *Rules for Birth/Start Dates and Death/End Dates*

Record the year when the person was born, or when a corporate body was established or came into existence, and the year when the person died, or when the corporate body was dissolved.

> *Examples*
>
> > **Display Biography**: British printmaker, 1876-1934
> > > **Birth Date**: 1876
> > > **Death Date**: 1934
> >
> > **Display Biography**: Dutch art gallery, 1841-1928
> > > **Start Date**: 1841
> > > **End Date**: 1928

Syntax

Record the year of birth and death (or of founding and dissolution) using the pro-leptic Gregorian calendar. For indexing dates BCE, use negative numbers. Use four digits for most years. If possible, for years that require fewer than four digits, follow the ISO and W3C standards, which suggest inserting leading zeroes (for example, *0350*).

> *Example*
>
> **Display Biography**: Greek vase painter, ca. 340-ca. 265 BCE
> > **Birth Date**: -0350
> > **Death Date**: -0275

If your institution records month and day, use the following syntax: *YYYY-MM-DD* (year, month, day, separated by dashes). Alternatively, use another syntax allowed by the standards listed in Sources for Terminology above.

> *Example*
>
> **Display Biography**: American sculptor, 1787-1852
> > **Birth Date**: 1787-01-24
> > **Death Date**: 1852-03-02

Uncertainty and Estimating Dates

Record uncertainty and ambiguity related to life dates or dates of existence (for corporate bodies) in the Display Biography. For every case where the exact birth and death date are not known with certainty, estimate dates for retrieval. However, do not include estimated dates in the Display Biography, because this would be misleading to the end user.

For birth and death dates for retrieval, estimate years by adding or subtracting years for expressions such as *ca.* or *possibly*. If only dates of activity are known, or if the dates of birth or death are uncertain or approximate, record birth and death dates that are the earliest and latest possible delimiters of lifespan of a person or of the existence of a corporate body. Estimations are appropriate because these dates are controlled for search and retrieval, and should not be displayed to the end user.

> *Examples*
>
> **Display Biography**: Armenian monk and copyist, active ca. 1065
> > **Birth Date**: 1020
> > **Death Date**: 1120
>
> **Display Biography**: Canadian engineering firm, established 1857, dissolved ca. 1864
> > **Start Date**: 1857
> > **End Date**: 1869

For *ca.*, estimate the birth or start date or the death or end date by adding or sub-tracting ten years, or more or fewer, as appropriate, based on your source. For example, if the display biography states born *ca. 1620* or established *ca. 1620*, the controlled birth or start date for retrieval could be estimated by subtracting ten years, 1610. If no better information is available, estimate the greatest likely life span as 100 or 120 years for the life of a person, or as the beginning and end dates of centuries.

Examples

Display Biography: German painter, ca. 1620-1654
  Birth Date: 1610
  Death Date: 1654

Display Biography: French miniaturist, 14th century
  Birth Date: 1300
  Death Date:1399

Display Biography: American sculptor, died 1831
  Birth Date: 1731
  Death Date:1831

Display Biography: French painting studio, 17th century
  Start Date: 1600
  End Date: 1699

Birth and death dates for a person, or start and end dates for a corporate body, are required. Do not leave the death or end date blank for living artists or extant corporate bodies, or those records will not be available for retrieval by date spans. Fill in the elements with an appropriate estimated value to allow efficient retrieval. Remember that these elements are intended for retrieval, not display; thus end users should never see these values. When in doubt, it is better to estimate dates that are too broad rather than too narrow. The examples include a death date that allows a 100-year life span for the person and uses *9999* for the corporate body. As you maintain the authority file over time, replace estimated values with the actual death dates based on death notices or updates from a published vocabulary, such as the ULAN.

Examples

[only birth date is known, death date is estimated for retrieval]

Display Biography: Sri Lankan architect, born 1921
  Birth Date: 1921
  Death Date: 2021

Display Biography: American art museum, founded 1923
  Start Date: 1923
  End Date: 9999

Estimate dates for other situations as necessary. For example, if you know only the death date, subtract 100 to 120 years for an estimated birth date for retrieval. For additional general information about dates, see Chapter 4: Stylistic, Cultural, and Chronological Information.

Example

[only death date is known, birth date is estimated for retrieval]

Display Biography: American illustrator, died 1896
  Birth Date: 1796
  Death Date: 1896

A.1.2.2.4 *Rules for Life Roles or Function Roles*

Record the major professional roles played by the individual throughout his or her lifetime, or the major functions or roles that define the activities or purpose of the corporate body.[8]

Examples

[for persons]

Life Role: painter

Life Role: sculptor

Life Role: goldsmith

Life Role: printmaker

Life Role: illuminator

Life Role: architect

Life Role: author

Life Role: pope

Life Role: publisher

[for corporate bodies]

Function/Role: architectural firm

Function/Role: art academy

Function/Role: religious order

Function/Role: museum

Function/Role: archive

Specificity

Use the most specific life role or function applicable. For example, use *painter* rather than *artist*, and *art museum* rather than *institution*, if it is known. A single artist may have multiple roles, including some that are very specific. Roles for an artist, for example, could include *painter, watercolorist,* and *portraitist*.

Multiple Roles

If an artist has multiple professional roles, or if a corporate body had multiple primary functions, include them all.

Example

Display Biography: Egyptian architect, urban planner, and engineer, born 1965
Life Roles: architect • engineer • urban planner

Display Biography: South African art museum and art gallery, established 1978
Functions/Roles: art museum • art gallery

A.1.2.2.5 *Rules for Sources*

Include citations for the vocabulary resource or other work, published or nonpublished, that was the source of names, note, or other information in the authority record. Using a Source Authority is recommended (see *Categories for the*

Description of Works of Art: Related Textual References). Whether or not a Source Authority is used, record citations consistently, using the rules in the *Chicago Manual of Style*.

A.1.2.2.6 *Additional Elements*

A.1.2.2.6.1 INCLUDE ADDITIONAL ELEMENTS AS NECESSARY

Additional elements may be included if necessary. For more information regarding elements in an authority record for creators and other persons or corporate bodies, consult the creator identification authority in *Categories for the Description of Works of Art*, the *Union List of Artist Names Editorial Guidelines, MARC21 Concise Format for Authority Data*, and *MADS: Metadata Authority Description Schema*.[9]

A.1.2.2.6.2 RECORD TYPE

CCO recommends using a Record Type element, although this is administrative rather than a descriptive metadata element and therefore outside of the scope of this manual. Record Type should be used to distinguish records for persons from those for corporate bodies. See the discussion in *Categories for the Description of Works of Art: Person/Corporate Body Authority*.

A.1.2.2.6.3 GENDER

Record the gender of the person, which refers to the sex of the individual. This is a controlled field with terminology such as *male, female,* and *unknown*. Gender is generally not applicable for corporate bodies, although exceptions may be made in the case, for example, of modern artists' collectives that are all male or all female.

A.1.2.2.6.4 DATES OF ACTIVITY

Include Earliest Active Date and Latest Active Date to delimit the known period of artistic activity of an individual or flourishing of a corporate body. Indexing dates of activity may be helpful for creators who were active as artists during only part of their adult lives (for example, for Grandma Moses, who became a painter late in life).

Example

[for Grandma Moses]

Display Biography: American painter, 1860-1961, active from 1930s
Birth Date: 1860
Death Date: 1961
Earliest Active: 1930
Latest Active: 1961

If only dates of activity or flourishing are known, birth and death dates and dates of establishment and dissolution should be estimated and recorded in Birth Date and Death Date, as described.

A.1.2.2.6.5 PLACE/LOCATION

Record the noun form of place names indicating where a person was born, died, or was active, or the location of a corporate body. This name should be displayed with its broader contexts, including the nation, for example, *Siena (Tuscany, Italy)*.

Examples

[for Andrea Schiavone]

Display Biography: Italian painter and printmaker, ca. 1500-1563, born in Dalmatia
Birth Date: 1490
Death Date: 1563
Birth Place/Location: Zadar (Dalmatia)
Death Place/Location: Venice (Italy)
Active Place/Location: Italy

[for the National Gallery of Art]

Display Biography: American art museum, established in 1937
Start Date: 1937
End Date: 9999
Place/Location: Washington (DC, United States)

A.1.2.2.6.6 RELATED PEOPLE AND CORPORATE BODIES

Link to records for related people and corporate bodies as necessary, including student-teacher relationships, relationships between family members who are creators, or relationships between a firm or studio and its members. These relationships are called associative relationships. See Part 1: Authority Files and Controlled Vocabularies.

Relationship Type

Record the type of relationship between two persons or corporate bodies. Examples include *student of, teacher of, sibling of, son of, partner of,* and *member of.* Note that relationships must be reciprocal and the phrases used to describe them must make sense from both records' points of view (for example, the reciprocal Relationship Type for *teacher of* would be *student of*).

Related Person's Name

Record (or link to) the name of the related person or corporate body. It should be a link to the Authority Record for the related person or corporate body.

Examples

[for Gao Jianfu]

Display Biography: Chinese painter, 1879-1952
Related Person:
Relationship Type: sibling of
Related Person label: Gao Qifeng (Chinese painter, 1889-1935)

[for Frank Lloyd Wright]

> **Display Biography**: American architect, 1867-1959
> **Related Corporate Body**:
>> **Relationship Type**: founder of
>> **Related Corporate Body label**: Oak Park Studio (American architectural firm, established ca. 1896, dissolved 1909)

Broader Contexts

Record broader contexts (hierarchical, whole-part relationships) between a corporate body and its divisions, such as divisions in an architectural firm, manufactory, or museum, as necessary. Ideally this should be done by using a hierarchy. An example is the French Gobelins manufactory, which had different divisions that produced tapestries (*Gobelins Tapestry Manufactory*), furniture (*Gobelins Furniture Manufactory*), and other types of works.

> *Example*

[for Gobelins]

> **Display Biography**: French craftsmen's factory, established in 1662 in Paris
> **Hierarchical relationships**:
> Gobelins
> ..... Gobelins Furniture Manufactory
> .... Gobelins Marquetry Studio
> .... Gobelins Pietra Dura Studio
> ..... Gobelins Metalwork Studio
> .... Gobelins Engraving Studio
> .... Gobelins Silversmiths' Studio
> ..... Gobelins Painting Studio
> ..... Gobelins Sculpture Studio
> ..... Gobelins Tapestry Manufactory
> .... Gobelins Dye Works

To organize a large authority file, hierarchical relationships may be used to divide records into facets, for example, for artists-persons, artists-corporate bodies, unknown creator designations, and non-artists.

A.1.2.2.6.7 NOTE

Record a free-text descriptive note to explain biographical information, such as current scholarly opinion regarding an ambiguous birth date or the possible identification of an anonymous artist, or to describe important aspects of the artist's career or the corporate body's activities.

> *Examples*

[for the 14th-century Sienese painter, Bartolommeo Bulgarini]

> **Note**: Phases of Bartolommeo's career were formerly attributed to anonymous masters known as Ugolino Lorenzetti and the Master of the Ovile Madonna. Bartolommeo's early works were heavily influenced by Pietro Lorenzetti and Ugolino di Nerio. During the 1350s, he followed the fashion in Siena by returning to the two dimensionality, fluid lines, and decorative details of Simone Martini. He worked primarily in Tuscany, painting

extensively for various Sienese churches, including five panels for Santa Maria della Scala, where he and his wife were lay members of its charitable society. He held minor public offices in Siena. He died on 4 September 1378.

[for the Gobelins manufactory]

Note: Established in 1662 in Paris, closed in 1694; the tapestry works reopened in 1699 and worked into the 20th century. Gobelins was established by Louis XIV for the production of furnishings for the royal household. The factory was formed largely from an amalgamation of existing workshops. The Gobelins specialized in tapestries, paintings, sculptures, metalwork, engraving, and furniture making. Each workshop operated semi-independently, and the head of each workshop was responsible for his own accounts.

A.1.2.2.6.8 EVENTS

Record events including activity, baptism (for example, when the birth date is unknown), or participation in competitions.

A.1.2.2.6.9 OTHER DATES

Record dates for various elements throughout the record, such as dates of a relationship between related people and corporate bodies (for example, between a student and teacher, or between an architectural firm and its members).

A.1.3 PRESENTATION OF THE DATA

A.1.3.1 Display and Indexing

A.1.3.1.1 *Free-Text vs. Controlled Fields*

For a discussion of when and why separate free-text and controlled fields are recommended, see Part 1: Database Design and Relationships: Display and Indexing.

A.1.3.1.2 *Fields in the Authorities and Work Record*

A.1.3.1.2.1 INDEXING AUTHORITY INFORMATION

Repeatable fields should be used for names, nationality, life roles, and places. Birth date, death date, and gender should not be repeatable. Linking to multiple related people and corporate bodies should be possible. Ideally, the biographical information should be recorded in a free-text display biography; important details of the biography should be indexed in controlled fields. If it is not possible to have a free-text field, a rudimentary display biography can be created by concatenating data from controlled fields.

Example

Names:
Le Corbusier (preferred)
Jeanneret, Charles Édouard
Charles Édouard Jeanneret
Jeanneret-Gris, Charles Édouard

Display Biography: Swiss architect, painter, and theorist, 1887-1965, active in France

    [Birth Date: 1887]

    [Death Date: 1965]

Nationality: Swiss • French

Life Roles:

    architect • urban planner • painter • draftsman • theorist • author • designer

Places of Birth, Death, Activity:

    Born: La Chaux-de-Fonds (Neuchchatel Canton, Switzerland)

    Died: Roquebrune (Alpes-Maritimes, Provence-Alpes-Côte d'Azur, France)

    Active: France (Europe) (from 1917)

Gender: male

Related People and Corporate Bodies:

    director of: Atelier Le Corbusier (French architectural studio, established in first quarter of 20th century)

Source: *Union List of Artist Names* (1988-).

A.1.3.1.2.2 MINIMUM CONTROLLED FIELDS

Nationality or National Affiliation

Nationality should be a repeatable controlled field. If the controlled terminology for this element does not have a hierarchical structure in your system, catalogers will need to enter both the most specific and a more general term to allow efficient retrieval (for example, *Nigerian* and *African*).

Some institutions may wish to record nationality, culture, and race-ethnicity as three separate fields rather than a single field. However, given that it is often difficult for catalogers to draw the boundaries between these concepts and that end users are likely to blur these distinctions when searching (thus the distinction is not important in retrieval), most institutions will find it convenient to record them together, thus saving time and labor and avoiding the possibility of errors. In any case, all should be accessible together for retrieval.

Dates

Birth and Death Dates are controlled fields intended to provide consistently formatted data that will be used in retrieval. They index the dates expressed in the Display Biography.

Birth and Death Dates should be controlled by rules in ISO or W3C standards (see Chapter 4: Stylistic, Cultural, and Chronological Information). Practical considerations, such as the limitations of the institution's computer system, may require departure from the standards, however. For example, some systems do not allow storing leading zeroes with numbers.

Life Roles and Functions

Use a repeatable controlled field for life roles and functions. If the controlled terminology for this element does not have a hierarchical structure, catalogers may need to enter both the most specific and a more general term (that is, *artist* and *painter*) to allow good retrieval.

Sources

To control terminology for citations, use controlled lists or a separate authority file for sources, if possible.

A.1.3.1.3 *For Display in the Work or Image Record*

Creator names in the Personal and Corporate Name Authority will need to be appropriately displayed in the Work or Image Record—for example, in the Work Record in Creator display (Chapter 2). For display, the element names may be altered depending on whether the information refers to a person or a corporate body. For example, displaying the element tag Birth Date is appropriate for a person, but the element tag Start Date is more appropriate for a corporate body.

How to Create a Label for Display

To create a label to identify the person or corporate body in a display in the Work or Image Record, it is recommended to combine the preferred name and Display Biography (for example *Tenkamenin (King of Ghana, 1037-1075)*. Ideally, this may be done automatically by concatenating elements; alternatively, use a free-text field and construct the label by hand. A label display should be created for all persons and corporate bodies that are used in any field of the Work or Image Record.

Some institutions may wish to omit the life roles in the Work Record display because in that context the role specific to the work being cataloged will be displayed instead (see Chapter 2: Creator Information). Similarly, certain institutions may prefer to use the inverted indexing form of the name rather than the natural order in some situations (in alphabetized results lists, for example).

Syntax

In the examples, for the sake of clarity, the Display Biography is placed in parentheses. However, using no parentheses or another method of punctuation is also acceptable, provided it is applied consistently.

Examples

[displays with preferred name in natural order followed by Display Biography]

Vincent van Gogh (Dutch painter and draftsman, 1853-1890)

Kicking Bear (Native American painter, ca. 1846-1904)

María Luisa Fernanda de Borbón (Spanish painter, 1832-1897)

Pieter Bruegel the Elder (Flemish painter, ca. 1525-1569)

Oak Park Studio (American architectural firm, established ca. 1896, dissolved 1909)

[displays with inverted form of preferred name followed by Display Biography; note that not all names can be inverted]

Gogh, Vincent van (Dutch painter and draftsman, 1853-1890)

Kicking Bear (Native American painter, ca. 1846-1904)

Borbón, María Luisa Fernanda de (Spanish painter, 1832-1897)

Bruegel, Pieter, the elder (Flemish painter, ca. 1525-1569)

Oak Park Studio (American architectural firm, established ca. 1896, dissolved 1909)

[displays with preferred name in natural order followed by Display Biography, minus life roles]

Vincent van Gogh (Dutch, 1853-1890)

Kicking Bear (Native American, ca. 1846-1904)

María Luisa Fernanda de Borbón (Spanish, 1832-1897)

Pieter Bruegel the Elder (Flemish, ca. 1525-1569)

Oak Park Studio (American, established ca. 1896, dissolved 1909)

Syntax in Displays for Repositories

Label displays for repositories in Work Records typically differ from those for other corporate bodies. Repositories generally should be displayed with the preferred name and the geographic location rather than with the Display Biography. See Chapter 5: Location and Geography.

Examples

The Louvre (Paris, France)

National Gallery of Art (London, England)

Gallerie degli Uffizi (Florence, Italy)

Capital Museum (Beijing, China)

A.1.3.2 Examples

Examples of Authority Records are included below. For additional examples, see the end of Part 1, the end of each chapter in Part 2, and the CCO Web site. In the examples, *controlled* refers to values controlled by an authority file, controlled list, or other rules (for example, rules for recording dates). *Link* refers to a relationship between two Authority Records. All links are controlled fields. In all examples in this manual, both within and at the end of each chapter, data values for repeatable fields are separated by bullet characters.

Figure 47
Authority Record for a Person

*This is a full record; not all records require information in all these fields.
Required and recommended elements are marked with an asterisk.*

Personal and Corporate Name Authority Record

■ ***Names**:

    Gentileschi, Artemisia (preferred, inverted)

    Artemisia Gentileschi (preferred, natural order)

    Gentileschi, Artemesia (variant)

    Schiattesi, Artemesia (variant)

    Lomi, Artemisia (variant)

■ ***Display Biography**: Italian painter, 1593-1651/1653

■ ***Nationalities** *[controlled]*:

    Italian

    Roman

■ ***Birth Date** *[controlled]*: 1593; **Death Date** *[controlled]*: 1653

■ ***Life Roles** *[controlled]*:

    painter

    draftsman

■ **Gender** *[controlled]*: female

■ **Place of Birth** *[link]*: Rome (Lazio, Italy)

■ **Place of Death** *[link]*: Naples (Campania, Italy)

■ **Places and Dates of Activity** *[link]*:

    Florence (Tuscany, Italy) I **Date**: 1612-1620

    Rome (Lazio, Italy) I **Date**: 1620-1630

    Naples (Campania, Italy) I **Date**: 1630-1638

    London (England, United Kingdom) I **Date**: 1638-1641

■ **Related People**:

    Relationship Type *[controlled]*: child of

    [link to related person]: Gentileschi, Orazio (Italian painter, 1563-1639)

    Relationship Type *[controlled]*: student of

    [link to related person]: Tassi, Agostino (Italian painter, ca. 1579-1644)

    Relationship Type *[controlled]*: spouse of; **Date**: married in 1612

    [link to related person]: Stiattesi, Pietro (Italian painter, active 17th century)

■ **Note**: Artemisia Gentileschi was the most ambitious and influential female painter of her time. She spread the Caravaggesque style throughout Italy and expanded the narrow possibilities for female artists. Artemisia was taught to paint by her father, Orazio Gentileschi, who painted directly on the canvas and used live models. Her paint-handling in her early works reflects her father's influence, yet she also departed from him by choosing to paint dramatic narratives starring female heroines. In 1612, Artemisia left Rome for Florence, after taking part in a trial against her art teacher, Agostino Tassi, who allegedly raped her. She then worked in Rome, Genoa, Venice, and Naples. In 1638 she was in London caring for her ailing father. She died between 1651 and 1653.

■ ***Sources** *[links to Source Records]*:

    Union List of Artist Names (1988-).

    Thieme-Becker, *Allgemeines Lexikon der Künstler* (1980-1986).

    Bolaffi, *Dizionario dei pittori italiani* (1972-1976).

Figure 48
Authority Record for a Corporate Body

Record for a repository. Required and recommended elements are marked with an asterisk.

Personal and Corporate Name Authority Record

- ***Names**:
  Sterling and Francine Clark Art Institute (preferred)
  Clark Art Institute (variant)
- ***Display Biography**: American Art Institute, founded 1950
- ***Nationality** *[controlled]*: American
- ***Start Date** *[controlled]*: 1950; **End Date** *[controlled]*: 9999
- ***Roles** *[controlled]*:
  art institute
  museum
  research center
- **Place/Location** *[link]*: Williamstown (Massachusetts, United States)
- **Related Corporate Bodies**:
  Relationship Type *[controlled]*: associated with
  [link to related corporate body]: Williams College
  Relationship Type *[controlled]*: broader context for
  [link to related corporate body]: Sterling and Francine Clark Art Institute Library
- **Note**: The Sterling and Francine Clark Art Institute is an art museum and a center for research and higher education. Williams College, in cooperation with the Sterling and Francine Clark Art Institute, offers a two-year course of study leading to the degree of Master of Arts in the history of art.
- ***Sources** *[link to Source Records]*:
  Official Museum Directory 2004 (2004).
  Sterling and Francine Clark Art Institute online (2003-).

Figure 49
Authority Record for an Anonymous Creator with a Known Oeuvre

Record for an ancient Greek vase painter. Required and recommended elements are marked with an asterisk.

Personal and Corporate Name Authority Record

▧ ***Names**:
   Painter of the Wedding Procession (preferred)
   Wedding Procession Painter (variant)
   Der Maler des Hochzeitszugs (variant)
▧ ***Display Biography**: Greek vase painter, active ca. 360s BCE
▧ ***Nationality** *[controlled]*: Ancient Greek
▧ ***Start Date** *[controlled]*: -0390; **End Date** *[controlled]*: -0330
▧ ***Roles** *[controlled]*:
   artist
   vase painter
▧ **Place of Activity** *[link]*: Athens (Periféreia Protevoúsis, Greece)
▧ **Note**: Working in Athens in the 300s BCE, the Painter of the Wedding Procession decorated pottery primarily in the red-figure technique. As with most vase-painters, his real name is unknown, and he is identified only by the style of his work. He decorated mostly large vases, such as hydriai and lebetes. He was also one of the many vase-painters who received a commission for Panathenaic amphorai, which were always decorated in the old-fashioned black-figure technique. The Painter of the Wedding Procession was among the last vase-painters working in Athens before the tradition of painted ceramics died out in Greece. He produced vases in the Kerch style, named for a city on the Black Sea in southern Russia where many vases in this style have been found.
▧ ***Sources** *[link to Source Records]*:
   J. Paul Getty Museum, collections online (2000-) (accessed January 21, 2005).
   Schefold, Karl. *Kertscher Vasen.* Berlin: 1930.

Notes

1. Included in the Personal and Corporate Name Authority are events that are formally convened, directed toward a common goal, capable of being reconvened, and have formal names, locations, dates, and durations that can be determined in advance of the event (for example, *Society of Architectural Historians Annual Meeting*). See the Library of Congress Name Authority file and AACR for formulating names for such events. See also *PCC Task Group on Name Versus Subject Authorities Final Report*, at http://www.loc.gov/catdir/pcc/archive/divworld.html.

2. The *Union List of Artist Names Editorial Guidelines* can be found at http://www.getty.edu/research/conducting_research/vocabularies/editorial_guidelines.html.

3. *Dizionario enciclopedico Bolaffi dei pittori e degli incisori italiani dall'XI al XX secolo.* Turin: Giulio Bolaffi, 1972-1976. Snodgrass, Jeanne O. *American Indian Painters; A Biographical Directory.* New York: Museum of the American Indian, Heye Foundation, 1968.

4. Keep in mind that AACR is describing how to make headings, not how to fill in the name field of an authority file or database. In the Personal and Corporate Name Authority, you can add the Display Biography to the name to form a heading, but do not put the biographical information in the Name element.

5. If the preferred name is an abbreviation, you may put the full name in parentheses for heading displays, but do not put both values in one name element, as this would have a negative effect on indexing and retrieval. See Presentation of the Data: Display and Indexing.

6. Because it is recommended to always display a value in the Creator field in the Work Record, in order to control values for unknown attributions, unknown creators may be recorded in the Personal and Corporate Name Authority for local use. Alternatively, if the value for unknown creators is not recorded in the Creator element of the Work Record, it should be displayed and retrievable in this field for end users by concatenating values from other fields. See Chapter 2 for additional discussion.

7. For display in the Work Record, institutions may wish to omit the roles in the Display Biography because they could be confused with the role pertinent to the work being cataloged. See Chapter 2: Creator Information.

8. Note that Life Roles (Functions for a corporate body) are different from roles in the Work Record. The Life Roles are all the roles the artist had over a lifetime (or that a corporate body had over its existence); these roles are recorded in the Authority Record. Life roles or functions are distinguished from the element roles is in the Work Record, which refers only to the artist's roles regarding that particular work.

9. The *Union List of Artist Names Editorial Guidelines* can be found at http://www.getty.edu/research/conducting_research/vocabularies/editorial_guidelines.html; *MARC21 Concise Format for Authority Data*, at http://www.loc.gov/marc/authority/ecadhome.html; *MADS: Metadata Authority Description Schema*, at http://www.loc.gov/standards/mads/mads-outline.html.

A.2 Geographic Place Authority

A.2.1   ABOUT THE GEOGRAPHIC PLACE AUTHORITY

A.2.1.1   Discussion

The Geographic Place Authority contains information about geographic places important to the cultural works and creators. The places noted in this authority include both physical features and administrative entities.

Physical Features

Physical features include entities that are part of the natural physical condition of the planet, such as continents, rivers, and mountains. Surface features as well as underground and submarine features may be included, as necessary. Former features, such as submerged islands and lost coastlines, may also be included, as necessary.

Places on planet Earth, other planets, and other celestial bodies may be included. Mythological, legendary, and imaginary places (for example, *Atlantis, Garden of Eden, Wonderland*) should be recorded in the Subject Authority.

Administrative Geographic Entities

Administrative geographic entities include man-made or cultural entities typically defined by political and administrative boundaries, such as empires, nations, states, districts, townships, and cities. Entities set up by ecclesiastical or tribal governing bodies may also be included, as necessary. Both current and historical places, such as deserted settlements and former nations, may be included. Most records in this authority will probably represent nations and the administrative subdivisions and inhabited places belonging to them.

The Geographic Place Authority may contain names for archaeological sites (for example, *trench A66 (Flag Fen, Essex, England)*) and street addresses. This authority may also include what are called *general regions*, that is, recognized, named areas with undefined, controversial, or ambiguous borders. An example is the Middle East, which refers to an area in southwestern Asia and northeastern Africa that has no defined borders and is variously interpreted to mean different sets of nations.

Terminology for generic cultural and political groups is outside the scope of this authority file, and should generally be recorded in the Concept Authority. However, the political state of a cultural or political group, and the territory within its boundaries, are within the geographic authority scope. For example, the *Ottoman Turks* are outside the scope, though the *Ottoman Empire* could be included.

Built works are generally outside of the scope and should be recorded as works or in the Subject Authority, depending on local practice (see A4: Subject Authority).

Geographic Places and Locations of Works

Geographic place terms are used primarily in describing the location of works. In the case of built works (such as the *Arch of Constantine*), monumental sculpture, and certain other works, this may be a city, such as *Rome (Italy)*, or other geographic place controlled by the authority file. For other works, such as a painting, the locations are often administrative repositories, such as museums and other institutions, which should be controlled by corporate name authority records, which in turn would have a location field in which the link to the geographic place would be maintained (see Chapter 5: Location and Geography and A1: Personal and Corporate Name Authority).

When cataloging a work located in a building such as a church, for example, *Santa Croce (Florence, Italy)*, or another building that does not house a museum, building names should generally be recorded in the Subject authority. These records may be linked to the location fields of works as necessary (see A4: Subject Authority and Chapter 5: Location and Geography).[1] Alternatively, buildings may be cataloged as built works in their own Work Records, and linked to other Work Records as necessary.[2]

Ambiguity and Uncertainty

When creating an authority record, the cataloger should state only what is known about a geographic place. When information is uncertain, it may still be recorded, but with an indication of uncertainty or approximation—such as *ca.* or *probably*—in the Note field. Important information in the Note field should be indexed in controlled fields. Rules should be in place to ensure consistency in recording uncertain data. For example, if it is uncertain whether an ancient town has a modern equivalent, rather than mistakenly linking the ancient name with the modern town in the same record, a separate record should be made for the ancient town until such time that the question is resolved through additional research.

Organization of the Data

The various names that might apply to a place are critical access points and therefore required. The place type, which describes the kind of place represented (*nation*, *city*, or *mountain*, for example), is also required.

Ideally, this authority should be in the form of a thesaurus to allow for equivalence, associative, and whole-part relationships (see Part 1: Authority Files and Controlled Vocabulary: Thesaurus). An indication of the broader context of the place is also required (for example, the broader context for *Ethiopia* is *Africa*). Having a hierarchical structure that allows for the place name to be displayed within its broader contexts, either indented in vertical displays or concatenated in horizontal strings, is recommended.

Some fields in this authority may be used for display. Others are intended for retrieval. If the horizontal parent string is constructed by hand (in the absence of a hierarchical structure, from which it could be concatenated), broader context display would be a display field. In the absence of a hierarchical structure, a broader context display field could be constructed by hand (for example, *Dunhuang, Gansu, China*). If date fields are included, they may include fields intended for display and others for indexing and retrieval.

Coordinates should be recorded in appropriate sets (such as latitude and longitude), but the sets need not be repeatable. The note need not be repeatable. All other elements should be repeatable. The hierarchical structure should allow polyhierarchical relationships (a place may have two broader contexts, for example). One of the names should be flagged as preferred. A brief discussion of the elements or fields recommended for this authority file is included in this section. For further discussion of this authority file and additional fields, see the *Categories for the Description of Works of Art: Place/Location Identification* authority. For a fuller set of editorial rules for geographic names, see the *Getty Thesaurus of Geographic Names Editorial Guidelines*.[3] For further discussion of the relationships between this authority and the Work Record, see Chapter 5: Location and Geography.

Recommended Elements

A list of the elements discussed in this chapter appears below. Required elements are noted. Display may be a free-text field or concatenated from controlled fields.

> Names (preferred, alternates, and variants) (required)
> Broader Context (required)
> Place Type (required)
> Coordinates
> Note
> Related Places
> Relationship Type
> Dates
> Sources (required)

About the Examples

The examples throughout this section are for illustration only. Local practice may vary. The examples tend to show the fullest possible use of display and indexing fields, which may not be necessary for all institutions.

A.2.1.2 Terminology

A.2.1.2.1 *Names*

Published sources of geographic information include the following:

Getty Vocabulary Program. *Getty Thesaurus of Geographic Names* (TGN). Los Angeles: J. Paul Getty Trust, 1988-. http://www.getty.edu/ research/conducting_research/vocabularies/tgn/.

National Geospatial Intelligence Agency (NGA), formerly United States National Imagery and Mapping Agency (NIMA). (Advised by the US Board on Geographic Names USBGN). *GEOnet Names Server* (GNS). http://earth-info.nga.mil/gns/html/ [foreign names].

United States Geological Survey (USGS). *Geographic Names Information System* (GNIS) [online database]. Washington: U.S. Geological Survey, 1998-. http://geonames.usgs.gov (January 7, 2004).

Library of Congress Authorities. *Library of Congress Subject Headings*. Washington, DC: Library of Congress, 2005. http://authorities .loc.gov/.

Times Atlas of the World. 10th comprehensive ed. New York: Times Books, 1999.

New International Atlas. 25th anniversary ed. Reprinted, Chicago: Rand McNally, 1994.

Princeton Encyclopedia of Classical Sites. 2nd ed. Princeton, NJ: Princeton University Press, 1979.

Cohen, Saul B., ed. *Columbia Gazetteer of the World*. New York: Columbia University Press, 1998.

Merriam-Webster's Geographical Dictionary. 3rd ed. Springfield, MA: Merriam-Webster, 1997.

Additional encyclopedias and dictionaries of geographic information may be used as sources for geographic names.

A.2.1.2.2 *Place Types*

Place types may be controlled by the place type values in the *Getty Thesaurus of Geographic Names* or, for many terms, by using the *Getty Art & Architecture Thesaurus* (AAT).

Getty Vocabulary Program. *Getty Thesaurus of Geographic Names* (TGN). Los Angeles: J. Paul Getty Trust, 1988-. http://www.getty.edu/ research/conducting_research/vocabularies/tgn/.

Getty Vocabulary Program. *Art & Architecture Thesaurus*. Los Angeles:
J. Paul Getty Trust, 1988-. http://www.getty.edu/research/
conducting_research/vocabularies/aat/. (Especially the Settlements
and Landscapes hierarchy).

National Geospatial Intelligence Agency (NGA), formerly United States
National Imagery and Mapping Agency (NIMA). (Advised by the U.S.
Board on Geographic Names USBGN). *GEOnet Names Server* (GNS).
http://earth-info.nga.mil/gns/html/ [foreign names].

A.2.1.2.3 *Coordinates*

Coordinate information must be formatted consistently to allow retrieval. Local
rules should be in place. The format is described in the ISO standard. The other
sources named provide the coordinate values.

The ISO standards for geographic information are still in the process of being
written. In the meantime, many of the issues the ISO committees are discussing
are addressed in Wolfgang Kresse and Kian Fadaie's *ISO Standards for Geographic
Information* (Berlin: Springer, 2004).

Getty Vocabulary Program. *Getty Thesaurus of Geographic Names* (TGN).
Los Angeles: J. Paul Getty Trust, 1988-. http://www.getty.edu/
research/conducting_research/vocabularies/tgn/.

National Geospatial Intelligence Agency (NGA), formerly United States
National Imagery and Mapping Agency (NIMA). (Advised by the U.S.
Board on Geographic Names USBGN). *GEOnet Names Server* (GNS).
http://earth-info.nga.mil/gns/html/ [foreign names].

United States Geological Survey (USGS). *Geographic Names Information
System* (GNIS) . Washington: U.S. Geological Survey, 1998-.
http://geonames.usgs.gov (accessed January 7, 2004).

A.2.1.2.4 *Dates*

Date information must be formatted consistently to allow retrieval. Local formatting rules should be in place; suggested formats are available in the ISO standard
and *W3C XML Schema Part 2*.

ISO 8601:2004 Numeric representation of Dates and Time. *Data
elements and interchange formats. Information interchange. Representation of dates and times.* Geneva, Switzerland: International
Organization for Standardization, 2004.

XML Schema Part 2: Datatypes, 2001. http://www.w3.org/TR/
xmlschema-2/.

A.2.1.2.5 *Other Elements*

Related places may be controlled by linking to other records in this authority file.

A.2.2 EDITORIAL RULES

A.2.2.1 Rules for Place Names

A.2.2.1.1 *Brief Rules for Place Names*

Record one or more proper names, appellations, nicknames, or other identifying phrases for the place. It is required to record at least one name—the preferred name, that is, the one used most often in standard sources.

Capitalization and Abbreviations

Capitalize proper names.

> *Examples*
>
> > **Name**: Siena
> >
> > **Name**: Beijing
> >
> > **Name**: Flanders
> >
> > **Name**: Nile River
> >
> > **Name**: Northern Sporades Islands

Generally, if the preferred name includes an article or preposition (such as *los*, *il*, *la*, *l'*, *de*, *des*, *della*), use lowercase. If an article or preposition is the first element in the name, however, spell it with an initial capital letter. Consult standard reference sources for guidance on the capitalization of articles and prepositions for each name (see Terminology above).

> *Examples*
>
> [for an Olmec site, *de los* is in lowercase]
> > **Name**: Laguna de los Cerros
>
> [for a city, *los* is capitalized]
> > **Name**: Los Angeles

Avoid abbreviations for the preferred name. Include common abbreviations in alternate names to provide additional access points (for example, *Mt. Etna, St. Louis, USA*).

Language of the Names

For the preferred name, use the name in the language of the catalog record, if applicable. For example, in English use *Venice*, rather than the Italian *Venezia*. This will apply to the names of nations, certain internationally known cities, and major physical features. Other than these, place names generally do not have an English equivalent. In such cases, prefer the local (vernacular) name as found in authoritative English-language sources. Do not translate place names into English unless an English-language equivalent is found in a standard source.

A.2.2.1.2 *Additional Recommendations for Names*

A.2.2.1.2.1 PREFERRED NAME

For each place, label one name or appellation as preferred. Choose the name used most often in standard authoritative sources in the language of the catalog record (for example, in the United States, the English *Morocco* should typically be the name preferred over the transliterated Arabic *Al-Magreb*).

> *Examples*
>
> > **Name**: Greece (preferred)
> >
> > **Name**: Italy (preferred)
> >
> > **Name**: Mongolia (preferred)
> >
> > **Name**: Mexico City (preferred)

For each geographic place record, label one name as preferred. To select a preferred name, consult the recommended sources for terminology. For names that are not found in standard sources, consult maps and other published sources. If sources disagree, go down the list of preferred sources and use the name in the first-listed source. In the rare case when a name cannot be found in a published source, construct a preferred name based on *Anglo-American Cataloguing Rules*: 23 (Geographic Names) or the *Chicago Manual of Style* (Place Names).

A.2.2.1.2.2 ADDITIONAL NAMES

Include alternate and variant names that appear in published sources and represent significant differences in form or spelling. Include names in multiple languages, variants that differ in diacritics and punctuation, name inversions, translations, variant transliterations, and historical names. Include common abbreviations and nicknames, if appropriate.

> *Examples*
>
> > **Names**: Lisbon (preferred) • Lisboa • Lisbonne • Felicitas Julia (historical)
> >
> > **Names**: Tokyo (preferred) • Tōkyō • Tokio • Edo • Yeddo
> >
> > **Names**: Philadelphia (preferred) • City of Brotherly Love

A.2.2.1.2.3 NATURAL AND INVERTED ORDER

In most cases, record preferred names for administrative places, such as cities and nations, in natural order (for example, *Los Angeles*, not *Angeles, Los*). Rare exceptions may be found in standard sources (for example, *Hague, The*). Record the preferred names for physical features and certain other types of places in inverted order (for example, *McLaughlin, Mount*, for indexing and alphabetical lists), but include the natural order form of the name as an alternate name (for example, *Mount McLaughlin*, for displays). Use the indexes of standard sources to determine when names should be inverted.

For the natural order form of the name, record the full name in natural word order (for example, *United States of America*).

For the inverted order form of the name, record the trunk or core of the name first, comma, and the word or words describing its place type (which will be in the language of the name).

Examples

[for a lake]

Names: La-Croix, Lake (preferred, inverted) • Lake La-Croix (display name)

[for a creek, *arroyo* means small river or creek]

Names: Abuelos, Arroyo de los (preferred, inverted) • Arroyo de los Abuelos (display name)

A.2.2.1.2.4 VARIOUS KINDS OF NAMES

Include names as outlined below.

Fullness of the Name

Include significant differences in the fullness of the name, particularly when they help to distinguish between two places that could be confused (for example, with the two nations called *Congo*). Given that the purpose of the preferred name is to identify the place in displays, the preferred name will not necessarily be the fullest official name, but may instead be a shorter and commonly used name (as found in authoritative sources).

Examples

[for the former Zaire]

Names: Congo (preferred) • Democratic Republic of the Congo • Zaire (historical)

[for the former Congo Brazzaville]

Names: Congo Republic (preferred) • Republic of the Congo • Congo • Congo Brazzaville (historical)

Abbreviations

Include commonly used abbreviations and initials as variant names. Include ISO codes, U.S. postal codes, or other commonly used standard codes. In general, avoid abbreviations in the preferred name, unless the official, commonly used name contains initials or abbreviations.

Examples

Names: Saint Vincent (preferred) • St. Vincent

Names: United Kingdom (preferred) • UK • GBR (ISO 3-letter code)

Names: California (preferred) • CA (U.S. Postal code)

Names in Different Languages

If the place is known by variant names in different languages, include them as variant names.

Examples

> **Names**: Strasbourg (preferred) • Strassburg • Estrasburgo
>
> **Names**: Egypt (preferred) • Miṣr • Jumhuriyah Misr al-'Arabiyah • Arab Republic of Egypt • Égypte • Agypten

A.2.2.2 Rules for Other Elements

A.2.2.2.1 *Rules for Place Type*

Record one or more words or phrases that characterize significant aspects of the place, including its role, function, political anatomy, size, or physical characteristics.

Examples

> **Place Type**: nation
>
> **Place Type**: province
>
> **Place Type**: inhabited place
>
> **Place Type**: archaeological site
>
> **Place Type**: valley

Specificity

Use the most specific place type applicable (that is, *archaeological site* rather than *site*), if known.

Capitalization and Abbreviation

Use lowercase for place types unless the term includes a proper name of a period, culture, or the like.

Example

> [for Cissbury Ring, West Sussex, England]
>
> **Place Types**: deserted settlement • Iron Age center

A.2.2.2.2 *Rules for Hierarchical Placement*

Record the hierarchical (whole-part) relationships between a place and another place, such as between cities and the nations to which they belong by placing the record in a hierarchy.

Example

> Africa (continent)
> .... Benin (nation)
> .... Atakora (province)
> .... Bassila (inhabited place)

Levels of Parents

Be consistent in how many levels of subdivisions will be used within each nation. For all nations, include one level of subdivision, if possible. For large nations with large subdivisions, include both first-level and second-level subdivisions, if possible (for example, include both the first-level subdivision states and the second-level counties in the United States, such as *Corinth, Knox County, Tennessee, United States*).

If the authority file includes extraterrestrial places, include the level of planet.

Example

Mars (planet)
.... Planum Australe (plain)

Multiple Parents

If possible, use a polyhierarchy to link a place to multiple parents, as necessary. Examples include linking a disputed territory to multiple nations or a city to both its current and historical parents. In the example, the inhabited places linked to the historical parent Etruria would also be linked to the appropriate administrative region in modern Italy (some are in Tuscany, others in other regions).

Examples

[for the ancient confederation of Etruria]

Europe (continent)
..... Italian Peninsula (peninsula)
.... Etruria (former group of nations, states, cities)
.... Arezzo (inhabited place)
.... Bologna (inhabited place)
.... Cerveteri (inhabited place)
.... Chianciano Terme (inhabited place)
.... Chiusi (inhabited place)
.... Cortona (inhabited place)
.... Fiesole (inhabited place)
.... [and so on]

[for the modern region of Tuscany; Arezzo, Chiusi, and others appear in both views of the hierarchy]

Europe (continent)
... Italy (nation)
.... Tuscany (region)
.... Arezzo (inhabited place)
.... Chiusi (inhabited place)
.... Cortona (inhabited place)
.... Fiesole (inhabited place)
.... Florence (inhabited place)
.... Lucca (inhabited place)
.... Pisa (inhabited place)
.... San Gimignano (inhabited place)
.... Siena (inhabited place)
.... Volterra (inhabited place)

A.2.2.2.3 *Rules for Sources*

Include citations for the vocabulary resource or other published or unpublished work that was the source of names, note, or other information in the Authority Record. Using a Source Authority is recommended (see in *Categories for the Description of Works of Art: Related Textual References*). Whether or not a Source Authority is used, record citations consistently, using the rules in the *Chicago Manual of Style*.

A.2.2.2.4 *Additional Elements*

A.2.2.2.4.1 INCLUDE ADDITIONAL ELEMENTS AS NECESSARY

Additional elements may be included if necessary. For more information regarding elements in an Authority Record for geographic places, consult the place/location identification authority in *Categories for the Description of Works of Art* and the *Getty Thesaurus of Geographic Names Editorial Guidelines*, *MARC21 Concise Format for Authority Data*, and *MADS: Metadata Authority Description Schema*.[4]

A.2.2.2.4.2 RECORD TYPE

CCO recommends using a Record Type element, though it is an administrative rather than a descriptive metadata element and therefore outside of the scope of this manual. Record Type should be used to distinguish records for physical features and administrative entities. See the discussion in *Categories for the Description of Works of Art: Place/Location Authority*.

A.2.2.2.4.3 COORDINATES

Record a set of numbers to define points on the earth's surface that correspond to the physical location of the place. Use an authoritative source for coordinates. Latitude is the angular distance north or south of the equator, measured along a meridian. Longitude is the angular distance east or west of the Prime Meridian at Greenwich, England.

In atlases and many other sources, latitude and longitude are expressed as degrees, minutes, and seconds with a directional indicator (east, west, north, or south). In some sources, latitude and longitude may be expressed as decimal degrees (used by GIS and other systems). For decimal degrees, the minutes of latitude and longitude are converted to decimal fractions of degrees; coordinates south of the equator and west of the prime meridian are expressed as negative numbers. In the examples below, both degrees-minutes-seconds and decimal degrees are displayed for each point.[5]

The minimum requirement for geographic coordinates would be a representation of a single point for each place, corresponding to a point in or near the center of the inhabited place, political entity, or physical feature. For linear features such as rivers, record the point representing the source of the feature.

Example

[for the Great Zimbabwe ruins]

Coordinates:
    Lat: 20 16 00 S degrees minutes seconds
    Long: 030 54 00 E degrees minutes seconds
    (**Lat**: -20.2667 decimal degrees)
    (**Long**: 30.9000 decimal degrees)

In addition to the coordinates representing the center, a set of four bounding coordinates may be used to roughly encompass the area of a geographic feature or administrative entity.

Example

[for the Great Lakes Region]

Coordinates:
    Lat: 45 00 00 N degrees minutes seconds
    Long: 085 00 00 W degrees minutes seconds
    (**Lat**: 45.0000 decimal degrees)
    (**Long**: -85.0000 decimal degrees)

Bounding Coordinates:
    South Bounding Lat: 43 09 25 N degrees minutes seconds
    North Bounding Lat: 48 48 46 N degrees minutes seconds
    East Bounding Long: 082 29 53 W degrees minutes seconds
    West Bounding Long: 092 01 17 W degrees minutes seconds
    (**South Bounding Lat**: 43.1560 decimal degrees)
    (**North Bounding Lat**: 48.8120 decimal degrees)
    (**East Bounding Long**: -82.4910 decimal degrees)
    (**West Bounding Long**: -92.0160 decimal degrees)

A.2.2.2.4.4 RELATED PLACES

Link to records for related places as necessary, similar to a *see also* reference. These relationships are called associative relationships. See Part 1: Authority Files and Controlled Vocabularies.

Relationship Type

Record the type of relationship between two places. Examples include *ally of, predecessor of, successor of, related to, distinguished from.*

Related Place Name

Record (or link to) the name of the related place. It should be a link to the Authority Record for the related place.

Examples

[for the South Sea Islands, which are often confused with Oceania]

Related Place:
    Relationship Type: distinguished from
    Related Place: Oceania

> [for Orvieto and its Guelf allies]
> > **Related Place**:
> > > **Relationship Type**: ally of
> > > **Related Place**: Bologna (Emilia-Romagna, Italy)

A.2.2.2.4.5 NOTE

Record a free-text descriptive note to explain pertinent information about the place, such as a brief history, why it is important to art history, or how it is distinct from another nearby place with the same or a similar name.

> *Example*

> [Luxor (Upper Egypt region, Egypt)]
> > **Note**: With the village of Karnak, Luxor is located on the site of ancient Thebes (capital of the New Kingdom). It is noted for having ruins of many temples and burial grounds. When Thebes declined, Luxor remained the more heavily populated part of the ancient city and grew into a modern market town.

A.2.2.2.4.6 DATES

Record dates for various elements throughout the record, such as dates when a place was inhabited, when a particular name was used, or when a relationship between two places was extant.

A.2.3 PRESENTATION OF THE DATA

A.2.3.1 Display and Indexing

A.2.3.1.1 *Free-Text vs. Controlled Fields*

For a discussion of when and why separate free-text and controlled fields are recommended, see Part 1: Database Design and Relationships: Display and Indexing.

A.2.3.1.1.1 INDEXING AUTHORITY INFORMATION

A repeatable field should be used for names. Place types should be a repeatable controlled field. Sets of coordinates need not be repeatable. Dates should be controlled and consistently formatted. To control terminology for sources, use controlled lists or a separate authority file for sources. Linking to multiple related places and polyhierarchical relationships should be possible (for further discussion, see Part 1: Authority Files and Controlled Vocabularies: Thesaurus).

A.2.3.1.1.2 CONCATENATING AUTHORITY INFORMATION

If this element does not have a hierarchical structure, catalogers may need to enter both the most specific and a more general term. Where appropriate for the sake of clarity, it should be possible to display the place name with its broader contexts in horizontal strings, in the Location element of the Work Record, for example. This is ideally done by concatenating data from the controlled fields and linked broader contexts. If this is not possible, a free-text broader context display field may be used instead. The example below illustrates both the hierarchical relationships and a free-text broader context display in the same record. Hierarchical displays are recommended, where pertinent, and should use indentation to indicate broader-narrower contexts.

Example

Names:

Mexico City (preferred)

Ciudad de México

Mexiko, Ciudad de

Tenochtitlán (historical)

Broader Context display: Distrito Federal, Mexico

Hierarchical Position:

North and Central America (continent)

.... Mexico (nation)

.... Distrito Federal (national district)

.... Mexico City (inhabited place)

Place Type: inhabited place

Coordinates:

Lat: 19 24 00 N degrees minutes

Long: 099 09 00 W degrees minutes

(**Lat**: 19.4000 decimal degrees)

(**Long**: -99.1500 decimal degrees)

Source: *Getty Thesaurus of Geographic Names* (1988-).

A.2.3.1.2 *For Display in the Work or Image Record*

Names in the Geographic Place Authority will need to be appropriately displayed in the Work or Image Record (as illustrated in Chapter 5: Location and Geography).

How to Create a Label for Display

To create a label to identify the place in a display in the Work or Image Record, combine the preferred name with enough parents (broader contexts) to identify the place unambiguously. Ideally, broader contexts for display will be constructed automatically through hierarchical relationships. If this is not possible, a free-text broader context display string may be constructed by hand. In the example below, both the broader context display (constructed by hand) and the hierarchical relationships are indicated.[6]

Example

[for the town of Balmaceda (Aisén, Chile)]

Broader Context display: Aisén, Chile

Hierarchical Relationships:

South America (continent)

..... Chile (nation)

.... Aisén (region)

.... Balmaceda (inhabited place)

Syntax

Display the natural order form of the preferred name with sufficient broader contexts to identify it unambiguously. Place type may be added to clarify the type of place in the Work or Image Record. In the examples below, for the sake of clarity, the broader contexts are placed in parentheses. However, using no parentheses or another method of punctuation is also acceptable, provided it is applied consistently.

Examples

[displays with preferred name and parents]

> Machupicchu (Cuzco department, Peru)
>
> Luxor (Upper Egypt region, Egypt)
>
> Durham (England, United Kingdom)
>
> Basai Darapur (Delhi, India)
>
> Fan Si Pan (Vietnam)

[displays with preferred name, parents, and place type]

> Machupicchu (Cuzco department, Peru) (deserted settlement)
>
> Luxor (Upper Egypt region, Egypt) (inhabited place)
>
> Durham (England, United Kingdom) (county)
>
> Basai Darapur (Delhi, India) (neighborhood)
>
> Fan Si Pan (Vietnam) (peak)

Hierarchical Displays

Hierarchical displays should use indentation to indicate broader-narrower contexts. It should be possible to display the place name with its broader contexts and place type in horizontal strings, as discussed.

A.2.3.2 Examples

Examples of Authority Records are included below. For additional examples, see the end of Part 1, the end of each chapter in Part 2, and the CCO Web site. In the examples, *controlled* refers to values controlled by an authority file, controlled list, or other rules (for example, rules for recording dates). *Link* refers to a relationship between two Authority Records. All links are controlled fields. In all examples in this manual, both within and at the end of each chapter, data values for repeatable fields are separated by bullet characters.

Geographic Place Authority Record

▦ ***Names**:

Alexandria (preferred, English)

Al-Iskandariyah (preferred, vernacular)

Alexandrie (variant)

Alejandría (variant)

Alessandria (variant)

Alexandria Aegypti (variant)

Rhakotis (variant, historical)

▦ **Broader Context display**: Urban region, Egypt

▦ ***Hierarchical position** *[link]*:

Africa (continent)

.... Egypt (nation)

.... Urban (region)

.... Alexandria (inhabited place)

▦ ***Place Type** *[controlled]*:

inhabited place

city

regional capital

port

▦ **Coordinates** *[controlled]*:

Lat: 31 12 00 N degrees minutes

Long: 029 54 00 E degrees minutes

(**Lat**: 31.2000 decimal degrees)

(**Long**: 29.9000 decimal degrees)

▦ **Note**: The city is located on a narrow strip of land between the Mediterranean Sea and Lake Mariut; it is now partially submerged. Alexandria was built by the Greek architect Dinocrates for Alexander the Great, and was the renowned capital of the Ptolemies when they ruled Egypt. It was noted for its library and a great lighthouse on the island of Pharos. It was captured by Caesar in 48 BCE, taken by Arabs in 640 and by Turks in 1517. The city was famed for being the site of convergence of Greek, Arab and Jewish ideas. Occupied by the French 1798-1801, by the British in 1892; evacuated by the British in 1946.

▦ ***Sources** *[link to Source Records]*:

Getty Thesaurus of Geographic Names (1988-).

Princeton Encyclopedia (1979); **Page**: 36.

NIMA, GEOnet Names Server (2000-) (accessed April 18, 2003).

Figure 51
Authority Record for a Physical Feature

Required and recommended elements are marked with an asterisk.

Geographic Place Authority Record

■ ***Names**:

  Ötztaler Alps (preferred)

  Ötztal Alps (variant)

  Oetztaler Alps (variant)

  Venoste, Alpi (variant)

  Ötztaler Alpen (variant)

■ **Broader Context display**: Alps • Europe

■ ***Hierarchical position** *[link]*:

  Europe (continent)

  .... Alps (mountain system)

  .... Ötztaler Alps (mountain range)

■ ***Place Type** *[controlled]*: mountain range

■ **Coordinates** *[controlled]*:

  Lat: 46 45 00 N degrees minutes

  Long: 010 55 00 E degrees minutes

  (**Lat**: 46.7500 decimal degrees)

  (**Long**: 10.9167 decimal degrees)

■ **Note**: Located in the eastern Alps on the border of South Tirol, Austria, and Trentino-Alto Adige, Italy.

■ ***Sources** *[link to Source Records]*:

  Getty Thesaurus of Geographic Names (1988-).

  Webster's Geographical Dictionary (1988); **Page**: 906.

  NIMA, GEOnet Names Server (2000-) (accessed April 18, 2003).

Geographic Place Authority Record

■ ***Names**:
    Burgundy (preferred, English)
    Bourgogne (preferred, vernacular)
    Burgund (variant)
    Bourgogne, duché de (variant)
    Burgundy, duchy of (variant)
    Duchy of Burgundy (variant)

■ **Broader Context display**: Europe

■ ***Hierarchical position** *[link]*:
    Europe (continent)
    .... France (nation)
    .... Burgundy (historical region)

■ ***Place Type** *[controlled]*:
    historical region
    kingdom
    duchy

■ **Coordinates** *[controlled]*:
    Lat: 47 00 00 N degrees minutes
    Long: 004 30 00 E degrees minutes
    (**Lat**: 47.0000 decimal degrees)
    (**Long**: 4.5000 decimal degrees)

■ **Note**: Historic region that included a kingdom founded by Germanic people in the 5th century CE. It was conquered by the Merovingians and incorporated into the Frankish Empire in the 6th century. It was divided in the 9th century, and united as the Kingdom of Burgundy or Arles in 933. The area flourished culturally during the 14th and 15th centuries.

■ ***Sources** *[link to Source Records]*:
    Getty Thesaurus of Geographic Names (1988-).
    Cambridge World Gazetteer (1990); **Page**: 211.
    Webster's Geographical Dictionary (1988); **Page**: 191.

Notes

1. Given that built works may be both subjects and locations of works, it is more efficient to store the information in only one authority rather than in both the Subject and Geographic Place Authorities. The built work may in addition be stored as a work in its own right in a Work Record, which will typically have a full set of fields to record the architect, date of construction, materials, dimensions, and other information that cannot typically be captured in a subject Authority Record. For institutions whose emphasis is on cataloging architectural drawings, a separate Architectural Subject Authority may be created, which would contain the same fields as a Work Record for built works. See the full description of this authority in the *Guide to the Description of Architectural Drawings*.

2. In the library community, there have recently been discussions regarding whether to treat building names as corporate body names or as subject headings. Currently, in some records, a heading such as *Empire State Building* is given in the USMARC 110 field, which is for corporate bodies. But at the same time the Library of Congress lists *Empire State Building* in its subject authority file, not its name authority file.

3. The *Getty Thesaurus of Geographic Names Editorial Guidelines* can be found at http://www.getty.edu/research/conducting _research/vocabularies/editorial_guidelines.html.

4. The *Getty Thesaurus of Geographic Names Editorial Guidelines* can be found at http://www.getty.edu/research/conducting _research/vocabularies/editorial_guidelines .html; *MARC21 Concise Format for Authority Data*, at http://www.loc.gov/marc/authority/ecadhome.html; *MADS: Metadata Authority Description Schema*, at http://www.loc.gov/standards/mads/mads-outline.html.

5. To allow retrieval on the coordinates, the data should be fielded following ISO standards and using a published authority such as the *Getty Thesaurus of Geographic Names*; the examples below show a display of the data (an alternate display could use standard symbols rather than spelling out degrees, minutes, and seconds).

6. The broader contexts in the Work Record may be displayed through the link to the Geographic Place Authority by using the broader context display field in the authority (see the discussion in Chapter 5: Location and Geography). Alternatively, the broader contexts may be concatenated by algorithm from the hierarchical parents for the place in the authority. If the broader contexts are thus added by algorithm rather than constructed by hand, develop a formula to consistently include the English name (if any) for the first-level administrative level and nation to display as parents with the city name. For example, *Lazio, Italy* displayed with *Rome* would be noted as *Rome (Lazio, Italy)*. Suitable algorithms may also be developed for broader context display for physical features, regions, and other types of geographic entities. The only advantage of including a broader context display (constructed by hand) in addition to the hierarchy is that you may thus create parent strings that are custom designed and relevant to particular situations. For example, you may not want to display *Lazio* with *Rome*, because it is not needed to identify the famous city, *Rome, Italy*. In general, however, you will require the region level for less well-known places in Italy (for example, *San Gimignano, Tuscany, Italy*) and to disambiguate homographs. If you are creating the broader contexts by algorithm, you will have to use a consistent formula that allows the most obscure place to be identified, thus using some levels of broader context that are unnecessary for the most well-known places.

A.3 Concept Authority

A.3.1 ABOUT THE CONCEPT AUTHORITY

A.3.1.1 Discussion

The Concept Authority contains most of the terminology needed for the Work or Image Records, excluding proper names; thus it can be described as containing information about generic concepts as opposed to proper nouns or names. This authority file may include terminology to describe the type of work (for example, *sculpture*), its material (for example, *bronze*), activities associated with the work (for example, *casting*), its style (for example, *Art Nouveau*), the role of the creator or other persons (for example, *sculptor, doctor*), and other attributes or various abstract concepts (for example, *symmetry*). It may include the generic names of plants and animals (for example, *dog* or *Canis familiaris*, but not *Lassie*). It should not include proper names of persons, organizations, geographic places, named subjects, or named events.

The scope of the Concept Authority will vary according to local requirements; institutions must analyze their own needs and structure this authority file accordingly. See also Part 1: Authority Files and Controlled Vocabularies. Some institutions may wish to create separate authorities for various elements, such as Work Type and Materials. However, given the overlap in terminology needed for various elements, it is typically more efficient to include all such terminology in a single, faceted Concept Authority, because it avoids redundant entry of a given term in multiple authorities. The following discussion is presented from the point of view of a single generic Concept Authority, which exists in a system along with four separate authorities for personal and corporate names (A1), geographic places (A2), subjects (A4), and sources (see Part 1: Authority Files and Controlled Vocabularies: Source Authority).

Divisions of the Authority

In the Concept Authority, dividing terms into various logical categories (called *facets* in the jargon of thesaurus construction) will make the authority file more useful and easier to maintain. Terminology could fall into the following categories, which are derived from the facets of the *Art & Architecture Thesaurus*.

OBJECTS

The objects facet includes all discrete tangible or visible things that are inanimate and produced by human endeavor; that is, that are either fabricated or given form by human activity. These include built works, visual works, various types of other objects, furnishings, images, and written documents. They range in purpose from utilitarian to the aesthetic (for example, *façades, cathedral, garden, painting, sculpture, albumen print, amphora,* chaises longues, *Battenberg lace*). The objects facet may also include some natural objects or animate objects, such as landforms and plants (for example, *mountains, cliff, flowers, daffodil, Narcissus pseudonarcissus*). Terminology from this category is used in the Work or Image Record in Work Type (Chapter 1), Subject (Chapter 6), Class (Chapter 7), and View Type and View Subject (Chapter 9) elements.

MATERIALS

Materials include physical substances, whether naturally or synthetically derived, including specific materials and types of materials. They may be either raw materials or materials designed for a specific function (for example, *oil paint, tempera, sandstone, iron, clay, adhesive, emulsifier, lumber, Japanese beech*). Terminology from this category is used in the Work or Image Record in Materials (Chapter 3), Subject (Chapter 6), and View Subject (Chapter 9) elements.

ACTIVITIES

Activities may include areas of endeavor, physical and mental actions, discrete occurrences, systematic sequences of actions, methods employed toward a certain end, and processes occurring with materials or objects. Activities may range from branches of learning and professional fields to specific life events, from mentally executed tasks to processes performed on or with materials and objects, from single physical actions to complex games (for example, *archaeology, engineering, analyzing, contests, exhibitions, running, drawing (image-making), sintering, corrosion*). Terminology from this category is used in the Work or Image Record in Techniques (Chapter 3), Subject (Chapter 6), and View Subject (Chapter 9) elements.

AGENTS

Agents can include generic designations of persons, groups of persons, and organizations identified by occupation or activity, by physical or mental characteristics, or by social role or condition (for example, *printmaker, architect, landscape architect, donor, doctor, corporation, religious order*). Generic names of animals are included as well (for example, *wolf* or *Canis lupus*). Terminology from this category is used in the Work or Image Record in Creator Role (Chapter 2), Subject (Chapter 6), View Subject (Chapter 9), and Life Role (in the Personal and Corporate Name Authority) elements.

STYLES, PERIODS, AND CULTURES

Styles, periods and cultures can include stylistic groupings, distinct chronological periods, cultures, peoples, and nationalities that are relevant to cultural works (for example, *French*, *Louis XIV*, *Xia*, *Black-figure*, *Abstract Expressionist*, *Renaissance*, *Chumash*). Terminology from this category is used in the Work or Image Record in Style and Culture (Chapter 4), Subject (Chapter 6), View Subject (Chapter 9), and Nationality/Culture (in the Personal and Corporate Name Authority) elements.

PHYSICAL ATTRIBUTES

Physical attributes can include perceptible or measurable characteristics of materials and artifacts as well as features of materials and artifacts that are not separable as components. Included are characteristics such as size and shape, chemical properties of materials, qualities of texture and hardness, and features such as surface ornament and color (for example, *strapwork*, *borders*, *round*, *water-logged*, *brittleness*, *vivid blue*). Terminology from this category is used in the Work or Image Record in the physical characteristics (Chapter 3), Subject (Chapter 6), and View Subject (Chapter 9) elements.

ASSOCIATED CONCEPTS

Associated concepts can include abstract concepts and phenomena that relate to the study and execution of a wide range of human thought and activity. Also covered here are theoretical and critical concerns, ideologies, attitudes, and social or cultural movements (for example, *beauty*, *balance*, *connoisseurship*, *metaphor*, *freedom*, *socialism*). Terminology from this category can be used in Subject (Chapter 6) and View Subject (Chapter 9) elements.

Discrete Concepts

A concept in the context of this authority file is a discrete entity or idea. Records in this authority file generally should represent discrete concepts, not subject headings. In contrast to a discrete concept, a subject heading typically concatenates multiple terms or concepts together in a string. For example, *Pre-Columbian sculptures* is a heading composed of terms representing two discrete concepts: Pre-Columbian (a style and period) and sculpture (a type of work). *Pre-Columbian* as a style and period term may be combined with many other terms and retain its meaning; *sculpture* may also be combined with many other style or period terms and still retain its meaning. See Part 1: Authority Files and Controlled Vocabularies for a further discussion of the distinction.

A term for a concept is not necessarily a single word; terms can also be a phrase, such as *rose windows*, *flying buttresses*, *book of hours*, *High Renaissance*, and *lantern slides*. Maintaining discrete concepts, as opposed to headings or compound terms, in the structure of the authority file will make it more versatile in cataloging and more powerful in retrieval.

Compound Terms

In cataloging, it may be necessary to combine discrete terms into compound terms. Combining compound terms in free-text fields for display in the Work and

Image Record is recommended. In the example below, the material red silk is displayed in the free-text field and indexed in controlled fields. The material and color are indexed in separate fields that are controlled by the Concept Authority.

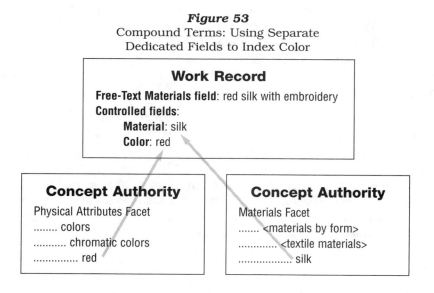

Figure 53
Compound Terms: Using Separate
Dedicated Fields to Index Color

Some institutions may not have free-text fields, and thus may need to combine the discrete concepts from the Concept Authority into compound terms in the controlled fields in the Work Record. If so, ideally each part of the phrase, such as red silk in the materials field, should retain its original links to the discrete parts of the Concept Authority.

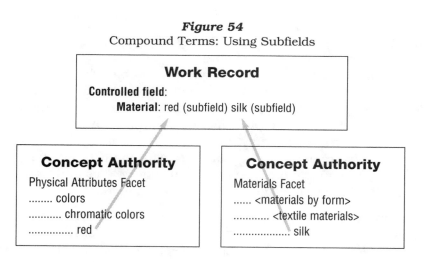

Figure 54
Compound Terms: Using Subfields

Another way to include compound terms in the Work Record is to add compound terms to the Concept Authority. This may be appropriate or even necessary for institutions building specialized authorities for local use. In the example, each color of silk is listed as a separate compound term in the local Concept Authority. If this method is used, the institution must decide how to most effectively flag such terms that are no longer compatible with standard sources of vocabulary, such as the AAT.

Figure 55
Compound Terms: Using Local
Precoordinated Terms

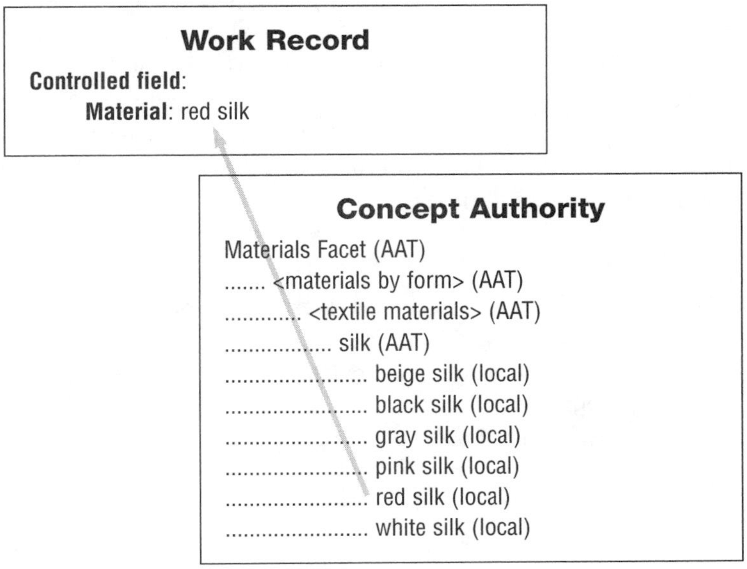

Work Record

Controlled field:
    Material: red silk

Concept Authority

Materials Facet (AAT)
.... <materials by form> (AAT)
.... <textile materials> (AAT)
.... silk (AAT)
.... beige silk (local)
.... black silk (local)
.... gray silk (local)
.... pink silk (local)
.... red silk (local)
.... white silk (local)

Ambiguity and Uncertainty

When creating an Authority Record, the cataloger should state only what is known about a concept in relation to a work. When information is uncertain, it may still be recorded, but with an indication of uncertainty or approximation—such as *ca.* (for dates) or *probably*—in the Note (Scope Note) field. Rules should be in place to ensure consistency in recording uncertain data. For example, if a cataloger finds a materials term in a journal article and is uncertain if it is exactly the same as another material with a similar name, rather than mistakenly linking the two terms in one record, a separate record should be made for each term until the question is resolved through additional research.

Organization of the Data

Terms that are synonyms for each concept are critical access points and are therefore required. A Note (sometimes called a Scope Note) describing the scope and meaning of the concept within the authority file is recommended.

Ideally, this authority file should be in the form of a thesaurus, allowing for equivalence, associative, and broader-narrower relationships (see Part 1: Authority Files and Controlled Vocabulary: Thesaurus). An indication of the broader context of the concept is also required. Having a hierarchical structure that allows for the term to be displayed within its broader contexts, either indented in vertical displays or concatenated in horizontal strings, is recommended.

Some fields in this authority file may be used for display. Others are intended for retrieval. The Note field is intended for display. If the horizontal parent string is constructed by hand (in the absence of a hierarchical structure, from which it could be concatenated), broader context would be a display field. If date fields are included, they may include fields intended for display and others that are formatted and used for indexing and retrieval.

A brief discussion of the elements or fields recommended for a concept term authority is included in this section. For further discussion of this authority file and additional fields, see the *Categories for the Description of Works of Art: Generic Concept Identification* authority. For a fuller set of editorial rules for creating terminology, see the *Art & Architecture Thesaurus Editorial Guidelines*.[1] For further discussion of the relationships between this authority and the Work Record, see various chapters in Part 2, especially Chapter 1: Object Naming and Chapter 3: Physical Characteristics.

Recommended Elements

A list of the elements discussed in this authority follows. Required elements are noted.

> Terms (preferred, alternates, and variants) (required)
> Qualifier
> Broader Context (required)
> Note (required)
> Dates
> Related Concepts
> Relationship Type
> Sources (required)

About the Examples

The examples throughout this section are for illustration only. Local practice may vary. The examples tend to show the fullest possible use of display and indexing fields, which may not be necessary for all institutions.

A.3.1.2 Terminology

A.3.1.2.1 *Sources for Terminology*

A.3.1.2.1.1 TERMS

Published sources of information for concepts in this authority file include the following:

> Getty Vocabulary Program. *Art & Architecture Thesaurus* (AAT). Los Angeles: J. Paul Getty Trust, 1988-. http://www.getty.edu/research/conducting_research/vocabularies/aat/.

> Library of Congress Authorities. *Library of Congress Subject Headings.* Washington, DC: Library of Congress. http://authorities.loc.gov/.

> Library of Congress. *Thesaurus for Graphic Materials 2, Genre and Physical Characteristics.* Washington, DC: Library of Congress, Cataloging Distribution Service. http://lcweb.loc.gov/rr/print/tgm2/.

Chenhall, Robert G. *Revised Nomenclature for Museum Cataloging: Revised and Expanded Version of Robert G. Chenhall's System for Classifying Man-Made Works.* Edited by James R. Blackaby, Patricia Greeno, and The Nomenclature Committee. Nashville, TN: AASLH Press, 1988.

Genre Terms: Thesaurus for Use in Rare Book and Special Collections Cataloging. 2nd ed. Prepared by the Bibliographic Standards Committee of the Rare Books and Manuscripts Section (ACRL/ALA). Chicago: Association of College and Research Libraries, 1991.

Paper Terms: Thesaurus for Use in Rare Book and Special Collections Cataloging. Prepared by the Bibliographic Standards Committee of the Rare Book and Manuscripts Section (ACRL/ALA). Chicago: Association of College and Research Libraries, 1990.

Mayer, Ralph. *Artist's Handbook of Materials and Techniques.* 5th ed. Revised and updated by Steven Sheehan. New York: Viking, 1991.

Oxford Companion to Art. 17th impression. Edited by Harold Osborne. Oxford: Clarendon Press, 1996.

Oxford English Dictionary. 2nd ed. Edited by J. A. Simpson and J. C. Weider. New York: Oxford University Press, 1989.

There are numerous other thesauri, vocabularies, encyclopedias, and dictionaries that can provide terminology for a generic concept authority file.

A.3.1.2.1.2 DATES

Date information must be formatted consistently to allow retrieval. Local formatting rules should be in place; suggested formats are available in the ISO standard and *W3C XML Schema Part 2*.

ISO 8601:2004 Numeric representation of Dates and Time. *Data elements and interchange formats. Information interchange. Representation of dates and times.* Geneva, Switzerland: International Organization for Standardization, 2004.

XML Schema Part 2: Datatypes, 2001. http://www.w3.org/TR/xmlschema-2/.

A.3.1.2.1.3 OTHER ELEMENTS

Related concepts may be controlled by linking to other records in this authority file.

A.3.2 EDITORIAL RULES

A.3.2.1 Rules for Terms

A.3.2.1.1 *Brief Rules for Terms*

Record one or more words or identifying phrase used for the concept. Proper names of persons, organizations, geographic places, named subjects, or named events are excluded. Recording at least one term is required—the preferred term, which is the one used most often in scholarly literature to refer to the concept (see Part 1: Authority Files and Controlled Vocabularies: How to Create Authority Records).

Capitalization and Abbreviations

For most terms, use lowercase. Exceptions include the names of styles and periods and terms that include a brand name or a proper name of a person or geographic place. Avoid abbreviations.

> *Examples*
>
> **Term**: tempera
>
> **Term**: stained glass
>
> **Term**: decorative arts
>
> **Term**: painter
>
> **Term**: watercolorist
>
> **Term**: Angevin Gothic
>
> **Term**: Fome-Cor™
>
> **Term**: Brussels lace
>
> **Term**: Tudor roses

Language of the Terms

For the preferred term, record a term in the language of the catalog record, which is American English in the United States. For records in American English, include variant terms (synonyms) in British English when the spelling differs. Synonyms in other languages may also be included.

> *Examples*
>
> **Terms**: elevators (preferred) • lifts (British English)
>
> **Terms**: artists' colormen (preferred) • artists' colour-men (British English)
>
> **Terms**: amphitheater (preferred) • amphiteatre (British English) • anfiteatro (Italian)

For terms where no exact English-language equivalent exists or where the foreign-language term is more commonly used than the English term, use the term commonly used in English publications. Use diacritics as required.

> *Examples*
>
> **Term**: papier-mâché
>
> **Term**: Schnitzaltars
>
> **Term**: santos

A.3.2.1.2 *Additional Recommendations for Terms*

A.3.2.1.2.1 PREFERRED TERM

For each concept, label one term as preferred (the descriptor). This should be the term used most often in standard authoritative sources in the language of the catalog record (for example, in the United States, the American English *still life* should be the preferred term rather than the French *nature morte* or the British English *still-life*).

Examples

Term: steel

Term: encaustic paint

Term: embroidery

Term: cathedrals

Term: landscape architects

Term: High Renaissance

To determine which term is preferred, consult the recommended Sources for Terminology above. When sources do not agree, go down the list of preferred sources and use the term in the first-listed source.

A.3.2.1.2.2 SINGULAR VS. PLURAL

Include singular or plural as outlined below.

For Objects

Include both singular and plural forms of a term for objects. Catalogers may need to have both forms available for use in various fields of the Work Record. For example, if one chair is being cataloged, use the singular form *chair* in the Work Type field. Alternately, if a watercolor painting depicting several chairs is being cataloged, use the plural form *chairs* in the Subject field of the Work Record.

Example

Terms: chairs (preferred, plural) • chair (preferred, singular)

If the term is a loan word or otherwise derived from a foreign language, the preferred plural term should be the plural form most often found in standard sources in the language of the cataloging institution (for example, for American English, *gymnasiums* is preferred, not *gymnasia*; *violoncellos* is preferred, not *violoncelli*; but *rhyta* is preferred, not *rhytons*). However, if the Anglicized plural is used as a preferred term, the plural form in the vernacular language should be recorded as a variant term (that is, *gymnasia* and *violoncelli* should be variant terms for the concepts).

Example

Terms: violoncellos (preferred, plural) • violoncello (preferred, singular) • violoncelli

For Materials

Use the singular noun form for the preferred term for materials.

Examples

Term: bronze

Term: leather

Term: mother of pearl

Term: wicker

For Processes

Use the noun or gerund form for the preferred term for processes, techniques, and functions.

Examples

Term: decoration

Term: urbanization

Term: lacquering

Term: sketching

A.3.2.1.2.3 ADDITIONAL TERMS

Include any additional terms by which the concept is known. Include all important terms that may provide access: alternate terms, variant spellings, synonyms, historical terms, terms in inverted and natural order, singular and plural forms, and terms in various parts of speech (for example, noun, adjective, and gerund).

Examples

Terms:
  flying buttresses (preferred, plural)
  flying buttress (preferred, singular)
  arch buttresses
  arched buttresses
  flyers
  buttresses, flying

Terms:
  watercolorists (preferred, plural)
  watercolorist (preferred, singular)
  water-colourists (British English)
  watercolor painters
  watercolorist's
  watercolorists'
  painters, watercolor

Synonyms

For alternate terms, add only terms that have true synonymity or an identical meaning with all other terms in the record (for example, *kettle stitch*, *catch stitch*, and *ketch stitch* are synonyms referring to the same stitch used in bookbinding).

Do not include terms that have only *near-synonymity* or that are merely related and not necessarily synonyms (for example, *Viking* and *Norse*). Exceptions may be made for various parts of speech (for example, the noun and adjectival form of the same term may be included in the same concept record).

Terms in Different Languages

Include terms in various languages, if necessary. The language of the term may be flagged. See also Language of the Terms above.

Example

Terms:
    still lifes (preferred, plural, English)
    still life (preferred, singular, English)
    still-lifes (English)
    still lives (English)
    nature morte (French)
    natura morta (Italian)
    naturaleza muerta (Spanish)
    stilleven (Dutch)
    Stilleben (German)

A.3.2.1.2.4 NATURAL AND INVERTED ORDER

Generally, record terms in natural order. Include variants in inverted order to provide access or to use in alphabetical lists (for example, natural order, *onion domes*, and inverted, *domes, onion*).

Example

Terms:
    onion domes (preferred, plural)
    onion dome (preferred, singular)
    bulbous domes
    Turkish domes
    domes, bulbous
    domes, onion
    domes, Turkish

A.3.2.1.2.5 QUALIFIERS FOR HOMOGRAPHS

For homographs, terms with the same spelling but different meanings, add a qualifier to distinguish between the terms (in the examples, notes are included to explain the differences in meaning). Qualifiers may refer to the broader context of the term or to another significant distinguishing characteristic.

Example

Term: drums (walls)
    Note: The vertical walls, circular or polygonal in plan, that carry a dome.

Term: drums (column components)
    Note: Cylinders of stone that form the shaft of a column.

Term: drums (membranophones)

> **Note**: Membranophones with a resonating cavity covered at one or both ends by a membrane, which is sounded by striking, rubbing, or plucking.

Homographs may occur as preferred or alternate terms.

> *Example*
>
> [for the homographs *trumeaux*, which include distinguishing qualifiers]
>
> **Terms**:
>> pier glasses (preferred, plural)
>> pier glass
>> pier-glasses
>> pier-glass
>> glasses, pier
>> mirrors, pier
>> pier mirrors
>> trumeaux (pier glasses)
>> trumeau (pier glass)
>
> **Terms**:
>> trumeaux (doorway components) (preferred, plural)
>> trumeau (doorway component)

A.3.2.2 Rules for Other Elements

A.3.2.2.1 *Rules for Hierarchical Placement*

Record the hierarchical (genus-species) relationships between a concept and its parent by placing it in a hierarchy. Concepts may be arranged according to defined characteristics, from broader class to specific items. Discrete areas of the hierarchy may be devised (called *facets*), if necessary. See Discussion.

> *Example*
>
> Objects Facet
> ...... Visual Works
> .... funerary sculpture
> .... brasses (memorials)
> .... effigies
> .... gisants
> .... haniwa
> .... mintadi
> .... bitumba
> .... mma
> .... niombo
> .... tomb slabs
> .... ushabti

If appropriate and possible, link a concept to multiple parents in cases where the same concept may logically belong in two or more sections of the authority file. When a concept does have two parents, the authority file is *polyhierarchical* (that is, a particular concept can have two or more broader concepts) rather than *mono-hierarchical* (where each concept can have only one broader concept). In the example, the concept chapels may denote both a stand-alone single built work or a component of a building and therefore has two broader concepts.

Example

Objects Facet	Objects Facet
.... Built Environment	.... Components
.... Single Built Works	.... <rooms and spaces>
.... religious buildings	.... chapels
.... chapels	

A.3.2.2.2 *Rules for the Note*

Include a note explaining the meaning of the concept within the context of this authority file and how it should be used. Notes should be objective, specific, prescriptive, and based on authorized sources and the intended use of the concept in the local system.

Examples

[for rhyta (vessels for serving and consuming food)]

Note: Refers to vessels from Ancient Greece, eastern Europe, or the Middle East that typically have a closed form with two openings, one at the top for filling and one at the base so that liquid could stream out. They are often in the shape of a horn or an animal's head, and were typically used as a drinking cup or for pouring wine into another vessel.

[for padstones (wall components)]

Note: Refers to blocks of stone placed in masonry walls under girders or other beams or trusses in order to distribute the load; for shaped stones placed on sloping walls to support the copings of gables, use "kneelers (gable components)."

[for Sukkot (Jewish holiday)]

Note: The Jewish autumn festival celebrated in September or October (15-21 Tishri) as a festival of thanksgiving. Sukkot is one of three Jewish pilgrim festivals. In biblical times the festival was associated with the agricultural year. Following the tradition established in Leviticus (23: 42), "booths" or temporary shelters are built in homes, gardens, and synagogues in memory of the huts used by the Israelites after leaving Egypt.

A.3.2.2.3 *Rules for Sources*

Include citations for the vocabulary resource or other published or nonpublished work that was the source of names, note, or other information in the Authority Record. Using a Source Authority is recommended (see *Categories for the Description of Works of Art: Related Textual References*). Whether or not a Source Authority is used, record citations consistently, using the rules in the *Chicago Manual of Style*.

A.3.2.2.4 *Additional Elements*

A.3.2.2.4.1 INCLUDE ADDITIONAL ELEMENTS AS NECESSARY

Additional elements may be included if necessary. For more information about elements in an authority record for generic concepts, consult the generic concept identification authority in *Categories for the Description of Works of Art*, the *Art & Architecture Thesaurus Editorial Guidelines*, the *MARC21 Concise Format for Authority Data*, and *MADS: Metadata Authority Description Schema*.[2]

A.3.2.2.4.2 RECORD TYPE

CCO recommends using a Record Type element, though this is an administrative rather than a descriptive metadata element and therefore outside of the scope of this manual. Record Type should be used to distinguish records for concepts from Authority Records intended to supply organizing levels of the hierarchy (for example, *guide terms*). See the discussion in *Categories for the Description of Works of Art: Generic Concept Authority*.

A.3.2.2.4.3 RELATED CONCEPTS

Link to records for related concepts as necessary, similar to a *see also* reference. These are called associative relationships. See Part 1: Authority Files and Controlled Vocabularies.

Relationship Type

Record the type of relationship between two concepts. Examples include related to, distinguished from, and other more specific phrases to describe relationships between processes, materials, events, and agents in the authority file. Note that relationships must be reciprocal and the phrases used to describe them must make sense from the perspectives of both records.

Related Term

This field records the preferred term for the related concept. It should be a link to the authority record for the related concept, if possible.

> *Examples*
>
> [for frescoes (paintings)]
>
> **Related Concept**:
> > **Relationship Type**: materials used
> > **Related Concept**: arriccio (plaster)
> >
> > **Relationship Type**: materials used
> > **Related Concept**: intonaco (plaster)
> >
> > **Relationship Type**: materials used
> > **Related Concept**: sinopie (underdrawings)

[for watercolor (paint)]

> **Related Concept**:
>> **Relationship Type**: objects using
>> **Related Concept**: watercolors (paintings)
>>
>> **Relationship Type**: users
>> **Related Concept**: watercolorists (painters)

A.3.2.2.4.4 DATES

Record dates for various elements throughout the record, such as the date or range of dates during which the concept is relevant or was used or the date when a term first came into use.

A.3.3 PRESENTATION OF THE DATA

A.3.3.1 Display and Indexing

A.3.3.1.1 *Free-Text vs. Controlled Fields*

For a discussion of when and why separate free-text and controlled fields are recommended, see Part 1: Database Design and Relationships: Display and Indexing.

In indexing authority information, a repeatable field should be used for the term. Most other fields in the authority file should be controlled repeatable fields. Dates should be controlled and consistently formatted to permit efficient retrieval. To control terminology for sources, use controlled lists or a separate authority file for sources, if possible. Linking to multiple related concepts and polyhierarchical relationships should be possible (for further discussion, see Part 1: Authority Files and Controlled Vocabularies: Thesaurus).

Broader contexts for display should be constructed through hierarchical relationships. If this is not possible, a free-text broader context display text string may be written.

> *Example*
>
> **Terms**:
>> basilicas (preferred, plural)
>> basilica (preferred, singular)
>
> **Broader Context display**: Single Built Works
> **Hierarchical position**:
>> Objects Facet
>> .... Built Environment
>> .... Single Built Works
>> .... basilicas
>
> **Note**: Refers to religious or secular buildings characterized by an oblong plan divided into a nave with two or more side aisles, the former higher and wider than the latter and lit by clerestory windows; usually terminated by an apse.
> **Related Concepts**:
> related to: basilican plan (<building plan attributes>, Physical Attributes)
> **Source**: *Art & Architecture Thesaurus* (1988-).

A.3.3.1.2 *For Display in the Work or Image Record*

Terms in the Concept Authority will need to be appropriately displayed in the work or image record, as illustrated in Chapter 1: Object Naming and Chapter 3: Physical Characteristics.

How to Create a Label for Display

To create a label to identify the concept in a display in the Work or Image Record, display the term and qualifier (if any) or a fuller label to identify the concept in a display. The label may combine the preferred term and one or more parents (broader contexts); choose the number of parents based on how many are necessary to identify the concept unambiguously and provide context. If such a label is constructed, the qualifier is typically unnecessary because it would be redundant. Ideally, the label may be constructed automatically; alternatively, use a free-text field to construct it by hand.

> *Examples*
>
> [displays comprising the terms, with the qualifier, if any]
>
> > eben
> > stained glass (material)
> > rhyton
> > Late Edo
>
> [label displays, comprising the terms with broader contexts]
>
> > eben (ceremonial sword)
> > stained glass (inorganic material)
> > rhyton (culinary container)
> > Late Edo (Japanese period)
> > Sakya (Tibetan Buddhism)

Syntax

Display the natural order form of the preferred term with broader contexts in parentheses. Using no parentheses or another method of punctuation is also acceptable, provided it is applied consistently.

Hierarchical Displays

Hierarchical displays should use indentation to indicate broader-narrower contexts. It should be possible to display the term with its broader contexts in horizontal strings, as discussed.

A.3.3.2 Examples

Examples of Authority Records are included below. For additional examples, see the end of Part 1, the end of each chapter in Part 2, and the CCO Web site. In the examples, *controlled* refers to values controlled by an authority file, controlled list, or other rules (for example, rules for recording dates). *Link* refers to a relationship between two Authority Records. All links are controlled fields. In all examples in this manual, both within and at the end of each chapter, data values for repeatable fields are separated by bullet characters.

Figure 56
Authority Record for a Material

Required and recommended elements are marked with an asterisk.

Concept Authority Record

- ***Terms**:
  - travertine (preferred)
  - travertino
  - lapis tiburtinus
  - travertine marble
  - roachstone
- **Broader Context display**: sinter, limestone
- ***Hierarchical position** *[link]*:
  - Materials
  - .... rock
  - .... sedimentary rock
  - .... limestone
  - .... sinter
  - .... travertine
- ***Note**: A dense, crystalline or microcrystalline limestone that was formed by the evaporation of river or spring waters. It is named after Tivoli, Italy (Tibur in Latin), where large deposits occur, and is characterized by a light color and the ability to take a good polish. It is typically banded, due to the presence of iron compounds or other organic impurities. It is often used for walls and interior decorations in public buildings. It is distinguished from tufa by being harder and stronger.
- **Related Concepts**:
  - **Relationship Type** *[controlled]*: distinguished from
  - *[link to related concept]*: tufa (sinter, limestone)
- ***Source** *[link to Source Record]*:
  - *Art & Architecture Thesaurus* (1988-).

Figure 57
Authority Record for a Work Type

Required and recommended elements are marked with an asterisk.

Concept Authority Record

■ ***Terms**:
> reredoses (preferred, plural)
> reredos (preferred, singular)
> retablos (reredos)

■ **Broader Context display**: altarpiece

■ ***Hierarchical position** *[link]*:
> Objects
> .... Visual Works
> .... <religious visual works>
> .... altarpieces
> .... reredoses

■ ***Note**: Refers to relatively large ornamented walls, screens, or other structures located above and behind the high altar of a Christian church. A reredos may be placed against the apse wall or directly behind the altar, or may form part an altar screen. The term was in common use by the 15th century, and was derived from an Anglo-French word meaning rear or behind. In Spanish churches, the reredos grew to be as wide as the nave and reaching to the vaulting of the roof. It is distinct from a retable; Where the reredos typically rises from ground level behind the altar, the retable is smaller, standing either on the back of the altar itself or on a pedestal behind it. Many altars have both a reredos and a retable. In architecture the term reredos may also refer to a screen or partition wall in other contexts, for example, to the wall forming the back of a fireplace or open hearth in ancient halls.

■ **Related Concepts**:
> **Relationship Type** *[controlled]*: distinguished from
> *[link to related concept]*: choir screens
> **Relationship Type** *[controlled]*: distinguished from
> *[link to related concept]*: retables (altarpieces)
> **Relationship Type** *[controlled]*: distinguished from
> *[link to related concept]*: retablos (panel paintings)

■ ***Source** *[link to Source Record]*:
> *Art & Architecture Thesaurus* (1988-).

Figure 58

Figure 58
Authority Record for a Style

Required and recommended elements are marked with an asterisk.

Concept Authority Record

▪ ***Terms**:
    Mannerist (preferred, English)
    Mannerism (alternate)
    Maniera (Italian)

▪ **Broader Context display**: Renaissance-Baroque style

▪ ***Hierarchical position** *[link]*:
    Styles and Periods
    .... <styles and periods by region>
    .... European
    .... <Renaissance-Baroque styles and periods>
    .... Mannerist

▪ ***Note**: Refers to a style and a period in evidence approximately from the 1520s to 1590, developing chiefly in Rome and spreading elsewhere in Europe. The style is characterized by a distancing from the Classical ideal of the Renaissance to create a sense of fantasy, experimentation with color and materials, and a new human form of elongated, pallid, exaggerated elegance.

▪ **Related Concept**:
    Relationship Type *[controlled]*: related to
    [link to related concept]: Late Renaissance

▪ ***Source** *[link to Source Record]*:
    Art & Architecture Thesaurus (1988-).

Figure 59

Authority Record for an Animal

Required and recommended elements are marked with an asterisk.

Concept Authority Record

■ ***Terms**:

    Canis lupus (preferred, species name)

    gray wolf (preferred, common name)

    timber wolf

    grey wolf

■ ***Hierarchical position** *[link]*:

    Animal Kingdom

    .... Vertebrates (subphylum)

    .... Mammalia (class)

    .... Carnivora (order)

    .... Canidae (family)

    .... Canis lupus

■ ***Note**: The best-known of the three species of wild doglike carnivores known as wolves. It is the largest nondomestic member of the dog family (Canidae) and inhabits vast areas of the northern hemisphere. It once ranged over all of North America from Alaska and Arctic Canada southward to central Mexico and throughout Europe and Asia above 20 degrees N latitude. There are at least five subspecies of gray wolf. Most domestic dogs are probably descended from gray wolves. Pervasive in human mythology, folklore, and language, the gray wolf has had an impact on the human imagination in mythology, legends, literature, and art.

■ ***Sources** *[link to Source Records]*:

    "Wolf." *Encyclopaedia Britannica* online (accessed May 25, 2005).

    Animal Diversity Web. University of Michigan Museum of Zoology, 1995-2002. http://animaldiversity.ummz.umich.edu/ (accessed May 25, 2005).

Notes

1. The *Art & Architecture Thesaurus Editorial Guidelines* can be found at http://www.getty .edu/research/conducting_research/ vocabularies/editorial_guidelines.html.

2. The *Art & Architecture Thesaurus Editorial Guidelines* can be found at http://www.getty .edu/research/conducting_research/ vocabularies/editorial_guidelines.html; *MARC21 Concise Format for Authority Data*, at http:// www.loc.gov/marc/authority/ecadhome.html; *MADS: Metadata Authority Description Schema*, at http://www.loc.gov/standards/mads/ mads-outline.html.

A.4 Subject Authority

A.4.1 ABOUT THE SUBJECT AUTHORITY

A.4.1.1 Discussion

The Subject Authority contains terminology related to subjects depicted in a work or image (see Chapter 6: Subject and Chapter 9: View Information: View Subject). The authority should be reserved for iconographical terminology, including proper names of literary, mythological, or religious characters or themes, historical events and themes, and any other terminology needed for subjects that fall outside the scope of the other three authorities.

Given the wide range of subject matter of works, the Subject Authority must necessarily be built and maintained in a way best suited to the individual requirements of the collection being cataloged. Unlike with the Personal and Corporate Name Authority or the Geographic Place Authority, there is no single published authority file that can serve as a model source in building a subject authority file. Institutions must analyze the characteristics of their collections and the requirements of their users, and organize categories (or facets) and subcategories of subjects that make sense for their individual situation (for example, *Christian Iconography, Hindu Iconography, Historical Events, Literature,* and the like).

Named Iconographic Subjects, Literature, and Events

Iconography is the narrative content of a figurative work depicted in terms of characters, situations, and images that are related to a specific religious, social, or historical context. The subject authority should contain the proper names or titles of iconographic subjects. Themes from religion, such as *Ganesha* or *Life of Jesus Christ,* and mythology, such as *Herakles* or *Quetzalcóatl (Maya deity),* are iconography. Themes from literature, such as *Jane Eyre* or *Lohengrin*, and historical events, such as *Coronation of Charlemagne* or *United States Westward Expansion*, are also included.[1]

Buildings and Other Works as Subjects

The proper names of buildings may be used in the Subject and Location fields of a Work Record. For example, if you are cataloging a 19th-century watercolor of the Parthenon, you will want to record the subject *Parthenon* in that Work Record. There are two approaches for maintaining an authority file for building names. Names of buildings can be recorded as subject terms in the Subject Authority. Note, however, that if the cataloging institution wishes to retrieve information on the buildings as works in their own right, the buildings should be recorded also (or instead) as separate Work Records, where the names of architects, dates, construction materials, and the like can be recorded together with the building names. The record for the built work would then be linked as a Related Work to the records for drawings, photographs, paintings, and other works in which it is depicted. Similar decisions should be made for paintings, sculptures, and other types of works that are depicted in art works. See Part 1: Related Works and Chapter 6: Subject for further discussion.

Subject Terminology in the Other Authorities

In cataloging a work or image, subject terms may be drawn from the Personal and Corporate Name Authority, Geographic Place Authority, and Concept Authority files as well as from the Subject Authority (see Chapter 6: Subject). It is more efficient to use the terms already included in the other authorities rather than to create duplicate Authority Records.

PEOPLE AND CORPORATE BODIES AS SUBJECTS

Personal and corporate body names that are subjects of works or images should be recorded in the Personal and Corporate Name Authority. CCO recommends that records for all actual persons be maintained in the Personal and Corporate Name Authority; an institution that diverges from this practice needs to establish clear criteria, first, for when the proper names of persons who are subjects of art works will be included in the Subject Authority and, second, when they will be included instead in the Personal and Corporate Name Authority. The boundary between actual historical persons and mythological, religious, or legendary persons may sometimes be unclear. For example, Napoleon Bonaparte would universally be recognized as a historical person, but the placement of Saint John the Baptist in the Subject Authority or the Personal and Corporate Name Authority may be decided differently by different institutions. Note that certain events, such as conferences, are typically treated as corporate bodies and recorded in the Personal and Corporate Name Authority.[2]

GEOGRAPHIC PLACES AS SUBJECTS

CCO recommends that geographic places that are subjects should be recorded in the Geographic Place Authority. Institutions should make decisions on mythological and legendary places to be included in the Subject or the

Geographic Place Authority because the distinction between real and legendary places is not always easy to determine.

GENERIC SUBJECT TERMS

CCO recommends that genre terms such as *still life* or *landscape* be maintained in the Concept Authority. The Concept Authority will also contain terms for certain objects and general concepts: objects depicted as subjects (*flowers, vase, table, tablecloth, hillfort, cathedral, trees*), materials in subjects (*satin, water, bread*), activities (*marriage, baptism, funeral, battle, coronation, Christmas*), agents (*king, bishop, peasants, guild, woman, housewife, prostitute, Felis domesticus, horses*), physical attributes (*yellow, zodiac symbols, Maltese cross, sunburst*), associated concepts (*pastoral, erotica, propaganda, grandeur, ugliness, Lutheran*), and styles and periods as they are depicted in subjects (*Roman ruins, African, punk costume*).

Ambiguity and Uncertainty

When creating an Authority Record, the cataloger should state only what is known about the subject. When information is uncertain, it may still be recorded, but with an indication of uncertainty or approximation—such as *ca.* or *probably*—in the Note field. If specific information is unknown, more general data may be recorded. For example, for the subject *Hannibal crossing the Alps*, the cataloger may be uncertain in what Alpine chain Hannibal made his crossing; it would be better to name the larger mountain system *Alps*, rather than mistakenly naming an incorrect mountain pass or range. Important information in the note field should be indexed in controlled fields. Rules should be in place to ensure consistency in recording uncertain data.

Organization of the Data

As with all authority terminology, each subject may be known by various synonyms. These name variations for subjects are critical access points and are therefore required. Related keywords, described below, are recommended.

CCO recommends that the Subject Authority be in the form of a thesaurus to allow for equivalence, associative, and whole-part or genus-species relationships (see Part 1: Authority Files and Controlled Vocabulary: Thesaurus). When subjects are displayed in a Work or Image Record, an indication of the broader context of the subject is recommended where appropriate. Having a hierarchical structure that allows for the subject name to be displayed within its broader contexts, either indented in vertical displays or concatenated in horizontal strings, is recommended. Examples include *Hannibal crossing the Alps (Punic Wars)*, *Bastet (Egyptian goddess)*, and *Aesop's Fables (Fables, Literature)*. In the absence of a hierarchical structure, from which it could be concatenated, a broader context display field could be constructed by hand.

Some fields in the Subject Authority may be used for display. Others are intended for retrieval. In the absence of a hierarchical structure, a broader context display field could be included. If date fields are included (*the Spanish Civil War (1936-1939)*, for example), they may comprise fields intended for display and others that are formatted and used for indexing and retrieval.

Some institutions may wish to make links from this authority file to the other three authorities. For example, to make a complete record for an event in the Subject Authority, it may be necessary to link to records for persons or geographic places in other authorities.

The Note need not be repeating. All other elements should be repeating. One of the names should be flagged as preferred. A brief discussion of the elements or fields recommended for this authority file follows later in this section. For further discussion of this authority file and additional fields, see *Categories for the Description of Works of Art: Subject Identification*. For further discussion of the relationships between this authority file and the Work Record, see Chapter 6: Subject.

Recommended Elements

A list of the elements discussed in this section appears below. Required elements are noted.

> Subject Names (preferred, alternates, and variants) (required)
> Broader Context (required, if applicable)
> Related Keywords (required, if applicable)
> Note
> Dates
> Related Subjects (required, if applicable)
> Related Geographic Places
> Related People or Corporate Bodies
> Related Concepts
> Relationship Type
> Sources (required)

About the Examples

The examples throughout this section are for illustration only. Local practice may vary. The examples tend to show the fullest possible use of display and indexing fields, which may not be necessary for all institutions.

A.4.1.2 Terminology

A.4.1.2.1 *Sources for Terminology*

A.4.1.2.1.1 SUBJECT NAMES

Sources for subject names and terms appear below.

Iconographic Themes

> Library of Congress Authorities. *Library of Congress Subject Headings.* Washington, DC: Library of Congress. http://authorities.loc.gov/.
>
> *ICONCLASS* (Most useful for Western religious and mythological subjects) http://www.iconclass.nl/.
>
> Garnier, François. *Thesaurus iconographique: système descriptif des représentations.* Paris: Léopard d'or, 1984.
>
> Roberts, Helene E., ed. *Encyclopedia of Comparative Iconography: Themes Depicted in Works of Art.* 2 vols. Chicago: Fitzroy Dearborn, 1998.

Stutley, Margaret. *Illustrated Dictionary of Hindu Iconography*. London: Routledge and Kegan Paul, 1985.

Narkiss, Bezalel, et al. *Index of Jewish Art: Iconographical Index of Hebrew Illuminated Manuscripts*. Jerusalem: Israel Academy of Sciences and Humanities; Paris: Institut de recherche et d'histoire des textes, 1976-1988.

Fictional Characters

Magill, Frank N. *Cyclopedia of Literary Characters*. Rev. ed. Edited by A. J. Sobczak. Pasadena, CA: Salem Press, 1990-1998.

Seymour-Smith, Martin. *Dent Dictionary of Fictional Characters*. London: Orion Publishing, 1991.

Names of Buildings

Avery Architectural & Fine Arts Library. *Avery Index to Architectural Periodicals at Columbia University*. Los Angeles: J. Paul Getty Trust, 1994-. Online by subscription at http://www.getty.edu/research/conducting_research/avery_index/.

Macmillan Encyclopedia of Architects. Edited by Adolf K. Placzek. New York: Free Press; London: Collier Macmillan, 1982.

America Preserved: Checklist of Historic Buildings, Structures, and Sites. 60th ed. Washington, DC: Library of Congress, Cataloging Distribution Service, 1995.

Fletcher, Sir Banister. *History of Architecture*. 20th ed. Oxford; Boston: Architectural Press, 1996.

Grove Dictionary of Art Online. New York: Grove's Dictionaries, 2003. http://www.groveart.com/.

Library of Congress Authorities. *Library of Congress Subject Headings*. Washington, DC: Library of Congress. http://authorities.loc.gov/.

Events

Library of Congress Authorities. *Library of Congress Subject Headings*. Washington, DC: Library of Congress. http://authorities.loc.gov/.

Mellersh, H. E. L., and Neville Williams. *Chronology of World History*. 4 vols. Santa Barbara, CA: ABC-CLIO, 1999.

Grun, Bernard. *Timetables of History: Horizontal Linkage of People and Events*. 3rd ed. New York: Simon and Schuster, 1991.

Thompson, Sue Ellen, and Helene Henderson, comps. *Holidays, Festivals, and Celebrations of the World Dictionary*. 2nd ed. Detroit, MI: Omnigraphics, 1997.

Kohn, George Childs. *Dictionary of Wars*. Revised ed. New York: Facts on File, 2000.

Given the wide range of potential subject matter, local terminology will probably also have to be developed based on encyclopedias, dictionaries, and other sources. Additional subject terminology may be stored in the Personal and Corporate Name Authority, Geographic Place Authority, and the Concept Authority, as well as in a dedicated Subject Authority. For a fuller listing of sources for subject terminology, see Chapter 6: Subject.

A.4.1.2.1.2 RELATED KEYWORDS

Related keywords for subjects should come from controlled lists.

A.4.1.2.1.3 DATES

If dates are used, date information must be formatted consistently to allow retrieval. Local rules should be in place. Suggested formats are available in the ISO standard and *W3C XML Schema Part 2*.

> ISO 8601:2004 Numeric representation of Dates and Time. *Data elements and interchange formats. Information interchange. Representation of dates and times.* Geneva, Switzerland: International Organization for Standardization, 2004.
>
> *XML Schema Part 2: Datatypes, 2001.* http://www.w3.org/TR/ xmlschema-2/.

A.4.1.2.1.4 OTHER ELEMENTS

Related subjects may be controlled by linking to other records in this authority file.

A.4.2 EDITORIAL RULES

A.4.2.1 Rules for Subject Names

A.4.2.1.1 *Brief Rules for Subject Names*

Record one or more terms, names, appellations, or other identifying phrases for the subject. Recording at least one name is required—the preferred name, which is the one used most often in scholarly literature to refer to the subject.

Capitalization and Abbreviations

Capitalize the proper names of events (real or fictional), fictional characters, and titles of literature, songs, and so on.

> *Examples*
>
> **Name**: Coronation of Queen Elizabeth II
>
> **Name**: Venus (Roman goddess)
>
> **Name**: Saint John the Apostle Cathedral

Avoid abbreviations for the preferred name. Include common abbreviations in alternate names to provide additional access points (for example, *St. John the Apostle Cathedral*).

Language

For the preferred name or term, use a name or term in the language of the catalog record, if applicable (for example, *Adoration of the Magi* in an English record, rather than the Italian *Adorazione dei Magi*). If there is no English equivalent for a subject, use a name in the appropriate language. Use diacritics as appropriate.

Examples

> **Name**: Adoration of the Magi (Life of Jesus)
>
> **Name**: Noli me tangere (Life of Jesus)
>
> **Name**: Quetzalcóatl (Maya god)

A.4.2.1.2 *Additional Recommendations for Subject Names*

A.4.2.1.2.1 PREFERRED NAME

For each subject, label one name as preferred. To select a preferred name, consult the recommended sources for terminology. If the term does not appear in authoritative or scholarly literature, choose the name or term used most often in the literature of art history or other professional literature in the language of the catalog record (English in the United States).

Examples

> **Name**: Coronation of Napoleon Bonaparte (preferred)
>
> **Name**: American Civil War (preferred)
>
> **Name**: Hercules (preferred)
>
> **Name**: Olouaipipilele (preferred)
>
> **Name**: Virgin Hodegetria (preferred)
>
> **Name**: Death and the Miser (preferred)
>
> **Name**: Snow White and the Seven Dwarfs (preferred)

To determine which subject name is used most often in publications, consult the preferred names in the sources for terminology listed above. If sources disagree, go down the list of preferred sources and use the name in the first-listed source. For names that are not found in standard sources, construct a preferred name based on the *Anglo-American Cataloguing Rules* or the *Chicago Manual of Style*.

A.4.2.1.2.2 ADDITIONAL NAMES

Include any additional names or terms by which the subject is known. Record all variant names that appear in published sources and represent significant differences in form or spelling, including variant names, names in multiple languages, variants that differ in diacritics and punctuation, name inversions, and other variations.

Examples

> [names as derived from Latin and Greek, and in Italian]
>
> **Names**: Hercules (preferred) • Herakles • Heracles • Ercole
>
> **Names**: American Civil War (preferred) • War Between the States

A.4.2.2 Rules for Other Elements

A.4.2.2.1 *Rules for Sources*

Include citations for the vocabulary resource or other published or unpublished work that was the source of names, note, or other information in the Authority Record. Using a Source Authority is recommended (see *Categories for the Description of Works of Art: Related Textual References*). Whether or not a Source Authority is used, record citations consistently, using the rules in the *Chicago Manual of Style*.

A.4.2.2.2 *Rules for Hierarchical Placement*

Record the hierarchical (whole-part or genus-species) relationships between a subject and another subject, such as between a general theme and the individual episodes in a particular saga. This should ideally be achieved by placing the Authority Record in a hierarchy.

Examples

[hierarchy for iconographical themes]

Christian iconography
..... Life of Jesus
.... Nativity
.... Adoration of the Shepherds
.... Adoration of the Magi
.... Presentation in the Temple
.... Miracle at Cana
.... Passion of Christ

[example based on ICONCLASS][3]

Classical Mythology and Ancient History
...... the Greek heroic legends
.... story of Hercules
.... early life, prime youth of Hercules
.... love-affairs of Hercules
.... most important deeds of Hercules: the Twelve Labours
.... preliminaries to the Twelve Labours of Hercules
.... Twelve Labors: first series
.... Hercules chokes the Nemean lion with his arms
.... Hydra of Lerna is killed by Hercules
.... Ceryneian hind of Arcadia is captured by Hercules
.... Erymanthian boar is captured by Hercules
.... Hercules cleanses the stables of Augeas
.... Stymphalian birds are shot by Hercules
.... Cretan bull is captured by Hercules
.... four mares of King Diomedes are captured
.... Hippolyte, the Amazon, offers her girdle to Hercules
.... Twelve Labors of Hercules: second series
.... [and so on]

If appropriate and possible, link a concept to multiple parents in cases where the same subject may logically belong in two or more sections of the authority file. Links to multiple parents are called polyhierarchical. For example, it may be necessary to link an event such as *Hannibal crossing the Alps* to the broader context *Punic Wars* as well as to the *life of Hannibal* through polyhierarchical relationships.

A.4.2.2.3 *Rules for Related Keywords*

Attributes are proper names and terms that characterize significant aspects of a subject in general. In other words, they are keywords or additional indexing terms related to a subject that can greatly enhance searching and retrieval. These are not characteristics of only one particular depiction of the subject, but instead general characteristics that will aid retrieval of all works that portray a given subject, no matter the particular depiction in any given single work. List roles, significant characters, events, and other characteristics of the subject.

Examples

[for Baby Jaguar]

Related Keywords: deity • jaguar (Panthera onca)

[for Cloelia]

Related Keywords: maiden • hostage

A.4.2.2.4 *Rules for the Note*

Include a note to explain the subject and how it is portrayed in visual culture.

Examples

[for the *Virgin Hodegetria (type of Virgin Mary)*]

Note: Meaning "Showing the Way Virgin," the iconography typically shows the Virgin Mary, half- or full-length, holding the Christ Child in one arm (generally her left) and pointing to him with her other hand. The Christ Child typically has one hand raised in blessing. It is most common in Eastern Christian art.

[for the *Feast of Sada (episode of Shahnama, Persian Epic)*]

Note: It is a feast that was held in celebration of mankind's discovery of how to strike sparks by hitting two stones together. Hushang tried to throw a stone at a dragon lurking behind some rocks; he missed the dragon, but sparks were created when his stone missile hit the rocks. He built a large fire and held a feast to celebrate his discovery.

[for the *Adoration of the Magi (Life of Jesus)*]

Note: Magi venerate the Christ Child, typically in the cave or stable where he was born. They often offer gifts of gold, frankincense, and myrrh, representing Christ's kingship, divinity, and future death. In early representations, they comprise three or four bearded men, who are astrologers with pointed Phrygian caps. By the Renaissance, they were generally three men portrayed as kings with crowns. They may be of three different races and represent the three ages of man (youthful, middle-aged, and elderly). They typically stand or kneel before the Holy Family, offering their gifts.

A.4.2.2.5 *Additional Elements*

A.4.2.2.5.1 INCLUDE ADDITIONAL ELEMENTS AS NECESSARY

Additional elements may be included if necessary. For more information about elements in an Authority Record for subjects, consult the subject identification authority in *Categories for the Description of Works of Art.*

A.4.2.2.5.2 RECORD TYPE

CCO recommends using a Record Type element, although this is administrative rather than a descriptive metadata element and therefore outside of the scope of this manual. Record Type should be used to distinguish between various types of records, for example, religion and mythology, literature, person (a character, for example, *Zeus*), animal (a character, for example, *Peter Rabbit*), event (whether real or fictional, for example, *Vietnam War*, *Judgment of Paris*), place (legendary or imaginary, for example, *Garden of Eden*). See the discussion in *Categories for the Description of Works of Art: Subject Authority.*

A.4.2.2.5.3 RELATED SUBJECTS

Make nonhierarchical links between records for different subjects in this authority file, as necessary. These are similar to a *see also* reference.

Relationship Type

Record the type of relationship between the two subjects. Use controlled terminology developed locally.

Related Subject Name

Record the name of the related subject. This should be a link to the Authority Record for the related subject, if possible.

Examples

[for *Hathor (Egyptian goddess)*]

Related Subject:
> **Relationship Type:** identified with
> **Related Subject:** Aphrodite (Greek goddess)

[for *Brynhild (Valkyries, Norse mythology)*]

Related Subject:
> **Relationship Type:** protagonist in
> **Related Subject:** Song of the Nibelungs (epic poem)

> **Relationship Type:** child of
> **Related Subject:** Odin (Norse god)

A.4.2.2.5.4 LINKS TO OTHER AUTHORITIES

Link to records for related people, geographic places, and concepts as necessary, that is, to the Personal and Corporate Name Authority, Geographic Place Authority, and Concept Authority.

Example

> **Subject Name**: Hannibal crossing the Alps
> **Relationship Type**: protagonist
> **Related People** *[link to Personal and Corporate Name Authority]*:
> Hannibal Barca (Carthaginian general, 247 BCE-ca. 183/181 BCE)
>
> **Relationship Type**: location of event
> **Related Geographic Place** *[link to Geographic Place Authority]*:
> Cottian Alps (Alps, Europe) (mountain range)

A.4.3   PRESENTATION OF THE DATA

A.4.3.1   Display and Indexing

A.4.3.1.1 *Free-Text vs. Controlled Fields*

For a discussion of when and why separate free-text and controlled fields are recommended, see Part 1: Database Design and Relationships: Display and Indexing.

A.4.3.1.1.1 INDEXING AUTHORITY INFORMATION

The Names field should be repeating. Most other fields in the Subject Authority should be controlled repeating fields. Ideally, linking to multiple related subjects and polyhierarchical relationships should be possible (for discussion, see Part 1: Authority Files and Controlled Vocabularies: Thesaurus). To control terminology for citations, use controlled lists or a separate authority file for sources, if possible.

A.4.3.1.1.2 CONCATENATING AUTHORITY INFORMATION

Where appropriate for the sake of clarity, it should be possible to display the subject name with its broader contexts in horizontal strings, in the Subject element of the Work Record, for example. This is ideally done by concatenating data from the controlled fields and linked broader contexts. If this is not possible, a free-text broader context display field may be used instead. The example below illustrates both the hierarchical relationships and a free-text broader context display in the same record. Hierarchical displays are recommended, where pertinent, and should use indentation to indicate broader-narrower contexts.

Example

Subject Names:
Magi (preferred)
Three Kings
Three Wise Men
Broader Context display: Biblical characters
Hierarchical position:
Christian iconography
...... Biblical characters
.... Magi
Related Keywords: kings • astronomers • travelers
Related Subjects:
Journey of the Magi (Life of Jesus)
Adoration of the Magi (Life of Jesus)
Magi become bishops (Acts of Thomas)
Sources:
Catholic University of America. *New Catholic Encyclopedia*. New York: Publishers Guild in association with McGraw-Hill Book Co., 1967-1979.
ICONCLASS. http://www.iconclass.nl/.

A.4.3.1.2 *For Display in the Work or Image Record*

Names in the Subject Authority will need to be appropriately displayed in the Work or Image Record (as illustrated in Chapter 6: Subject).

How to Create a Label for Display

To create a label to identify the subject in a display in the Work or Image Record, display the preferred name of the subject and one or more parents (broader contexts), as necessary. Ideally, the label may be constructed automatically or by hand using a free-text field.

Examples

Hun-Camé (Maya demons)

Cloelia (Plutarch's Life of Publicola)

Krishna Battles the Armies of the Demon Naraka (Stories of Lord Vishnu)

In the examples above, for the sake of clarity, broader contexts are placed in parentheses. However, using no parentheses or another method of punctuation is also acceptable, provided it is applied consistently.

Hierarchical Displays

Hierarchical displays should use indentation to indicate broader-narrower contexts. Displaying the subject with its broader contexts in horizontal strings, as discussed, should be an option.

A.4.3.2 Examples

Examples of Authority Records are included below. For additional examples, see the end of Part 1 and each chapter in Part 2. In the examples, *controlled* refers to values controlled by an authority file, controlled list, or other rules (for example, rules for recording dates). *Link* refers to a relationship between two Authority Records. All links are controlled fields. In all examples in this manual, both within and at the end of each chapter, data values for repeatable fields are separated by bullet characters.

Figure 60

Authority Record for a Religious Figure

Required and recommended elements are marked with an asterisk.

Subject Authority Record

▨ ***Names**:
Shiva (preferred)
Siva
Siwa
Sambhu
Sankara
Pasupati
Mahesa
Mahadeva
Auspicious One

▨ **Broader Context display**: Hindu god

▨ ***Hierarchical position** *[link]*:
Hindu Iconography
.... Hindu gods
.... Shiva

▨ ***Related Keywords** *[link]*: androgynous • dancer • mendicant • yogin • herdsman • destroyer • restorer • ascetic • sensuality • avenger

▨ **Note**: One of the primary deities of Hinduism. He is the paramount lord of the Shaivite sects of India. Shiva means auspicious one in Sanskrit. He is one of the most complex gods of India, embodying contradictory qualities: both the destroyer and the restorer, the great ascetic and the symbol of sensuality, the benevolent herdsman of souls and the wrathful avenger. He is usually depicted as a graceful male. In painting, he is typically white or ash-colored with a blue neck, hair represented as coil of matted locks, adorned with the crescent moon and the Ganges. He may have three eyes and a garland of skulls. He may have two or four arms and carry skulls, a serpent, a deerskin, trident, a small drum, or a club with a skull on it. He is depicted in art in various manifestations, often with one of his consorts.

▨ **Related Subjects**:
Relationship Type *[controlled]*: focus of | *[link to related subject]*: Saivism
Relationship Type *[controlled]*: manifestation is | *[link to related subject]*: Ardhanarisvara
Relationship Type *[controlled]*: manifestation is | *[link to related subject]*: Nataraja
Relationship Type *[controlled]*: manifestation is | *[link to related subject]*: lingus
Relationship Type *[controlled]*: consort is | *[link to related subject]*: Parvat
Relationship Type *[controlled]*: consort is | *[link to related subject]*: Uma
Relationship Type *[controlled]*: consort is | *[link to related subject]*: Sati
Relationship Type *[controlled]*: consort is | *[link to related subject]*: Durga
Relationship Type *[controlled]*: consort is | *[link to related subject]*: Kali
Relationship Type *[controlled]*: consort is | *[link to related subject]*: Sakti
Relationship Type *[controlled]*: parent of | *[link to related subject]*: Ganesha
Relationship Type *[controlled]*: parent of | *[link to related subject]*: Skanda
Relationship Type *[controlled]*: animal image is | *[link to related subject]*: Nandi the Bull

▨ **Related Geographic Place**:
Relationship Type *[controlled]*: developed in | *[link to related geographic place]*: India (Asia)

▨ ***Sources** *[link to Source Records]*:
Besset, L. *Divine Shiva*. New York: Edmonds, 1997.
"Siva," *Encyclopaedia Britannica* online (accessed February 4, 2004).
Toffy, M., ed. *Gods and Myths: Hinduism*. New Delhi: Garnier, 1976.

Figure 61
Authority Record for a Named Event
Required and recommended elements are marked with an asterisk.

Subject Authority Record

■ ***Names**:

First Battle of Bull Run (preferred)

First Battle of Manassas

■ **Broader Context display**: Civil War

■ ***Hierarchical position** *[link]*:

Historical Events

.... American Civil War

.... Battles

.... First Battle of Bull Run

■ ***Related Keywords** *[controlled]*: battle • invasion • casualties

■ **Note**: One of two battles fought a few miles north of the crucial railroad junction of Manassas, Virginia. The First Battle of Bull Run (called First Manassas by the South) was fought on July 21, 1861, at a very early stage of the war. Both armies were ill-prepared, but political pressures forced the Northern General Irvin McDowell to advance to a small stream named Bull Run near Manassas in northern Virginia, southwest of Washington; this was a move against the Southern city of Richmond, Virginia.

■ **Related Subject**:

Relationship Type *[controlled]*: predecessor was

[link to related subject]: First Shenandoah Valley Campaign

■ **Related People or Corporate Bodies**:

Relationship Type *[controlled]*: participant

[link to related person]: General Irvin McDowell (American Union general, 1818-1885)

Relationship Type *[controlled]*: participant

[link to related person]: General P.G.T. Beauregard (American Confederate general, 1818-1893)

■ **Related Geographic Place**:

Relationship Type *[controlled]*: location

[controlled, link]: Manassas (Virginia, United States)

■ **Date**: July 21, 1861

[controlled]: **Earliest**: 1861; **Latest**: 1861

■ ***Sources** *[link to Source Records]*:

Antietam National Battlefield [online]. Washington, DC: National Park Service. http://www.nps.gov/anti/home.htm (accessed February 5, 2004).

Kohn, George Childs. *Dictionary of Wars*. Rev. ed. Facts on File, 2000.

Figure 62
Authority Record for an Iconographic Episode
Required and recommended elements are marked with an asterisk.

Subject Authority Record

■ ***Names**:
> Marriage of the Virgin (preferred)
> Sposalizio
> Betrothal of the Virgin
> Marriage of Mary and Joseph

■ **Broader Context display**: Life of the Virgin Mary

■ ***Hierarchical position** *[link]*:
> Christian iconography
> ...... New Testament
> .... Life of the Virgin Mary
> .... Marriage of the Virgin

■ ***Related Keywords** *[controlled]*: betrothal • high priest • marriage • temple

■ **Note**: Mary and Joseph are married by the high priest (ICONCLASS). The story is not in the canonical Bible; it comes from the apocryphal Book of James (or Protoevangelium, Infancy Gospel 8-9) and the Golden Legend by Jacobus de Voragine. The "marriage" scene is technically a betrothal. It generally takes place in or outside the temple. Mary and Joseph typically stand to either side of the priest, who joins their hands in betrothal. Joseph may be seen as an older man. He has been chosen from a group of suitors, all of whom had been asked by the high priest to bring a rod (a branch or twig) to the altar; the rod of Joseph bloomed miraculously by intervention of the Holy Spirit, thus designating him as the man chosen by God to be the spouse of Mary.

■ **Related Subject**:
> **Relationship Type** *[controlled]*: actor is | *[link to related subject]*: Mary
> **Relationship Type** *[controlled]*: actor is | *[link to related subject]*: Joseph

■ ***Sources** *[link to Source Records]*:
> ICONCLASS http://www.iconclass.nl/. Notation: 73A42: Bible--New Testament--(scenes from the life of) John the Baptist and Mary--Mary and Joseph--marriage of Mary and Joseph, 'Sposalizio'
> Jacobus de Voragine. *Golden Legend of Jacobus de Voragine*. Translated and adapted from the Latin by Granger Ryan and Helmut Ripperger. New York: Arno Press, 1969.
> Osborne, Harold, ed. *Oxford Companion to Art*. 17th impression. Oxford: Clarendon Press, 1996; **Page**: 1195 ff.
> Testuz, Michel. *Protoevangelium Jacobi: Apocryphal books*. Facsimile of the Papyrus Bodmer V Manuscript. Cologne and Geneva: Bibliotheca Bodmeriana, 1958.

Figure 63
Authority Record for a Fictional Place

Required and recommended elements are marked with an asterisk.

Subject Authority Record

■ ***Names**:
  Niflheim (preferred)
  Niflheimr
  House of Mists

■ **Broader Context display**: Norse mythology

■ ***Hierarchical position** *[link]*:
  Norse mythology
  ...... Creation story
  .... Niflheim

■ ***Related Keywords** *[controlled]*: underworld • creation • death • mist • cold • dark

■ **Note**: In the Norse creation story, Niflheim was the misty region north of the void (Ginnungagap) in which the world was created. It was also the cold, dark, misty world of the dead, ruled by the goddess Hel. In some accounts it was the last of nine worlds, a place into which evil men passed after reaching the region of death (Hel). It was situated below one of the roots of the world tree (Yggdrasill). Niflheim contained a well (Hvergelmir) from which many rivers flowed.

■ **Related Subject**:
  Relationship Type *[controlled]*: ruled by
  [link to Related Subject]: Hel (Norse goddess)

■ ***Sources** *[link to Source Record]*:
  "Niflheim." *Encyclopaedia Britannica* online (accessed June 13, 2005).

Notes

1. Named recurring events, such as conferences, are recorded in the Personal and Corporate Name Authority. See A1: note 1.

2. Included in the Personal and Corporate Name Authority are events that are formally convened, directed toward a common goal, capable of being reconvened, and have formal names, locations, dates, and durations that can be determined in advance of the event. See the Library of Congress Name Authority file and AACR for formulating names for these events.

3. The string of ICONCLASS headings for 94L322, one of the subjects in this hierarchy, would be the following: *Classical Mythology and Ancient History—the Greek heroic legends (I)—(story of) Hercules (Heracles)—most important deeds of Hercules: the Twelve Labours—the Twelve Labours: first series—the Hydra of Lerna is killed by Hercules.*

Selected Bibliography

American Library Association. *Anglo-American Cataloguing Rules*. 2nd ed., 2002 revision. Chicago: American Library Association, 2002. Note: AACR is due to be rewritten and published in 2008. The working title of the new rules is *RDA: Resource Description and Access*, as of this writing. For the status of the new publication, see "Current Activities: Joint Steering Committee for the Revision of Anglo-American Cataloguing Rules." http://www.collectionscanada.ca/jsc/current.html.

Avery Architecture & Fine Arts Library, Columbia University. *Avery Index to Architectural Periodicals*. Los Angeles: J. Paul Getty Trust, 1994. Available online by subscription.

Baca, Murtha. "A Picture Is Worth a Thousand Words: Metadata for Art Objects and Their Visual Surrogates." In *Cataloging the Web: Metadata, AACR, and Marc21*, edited by Wayne Jones et al. Lanham, MD: Scarecrow Press, 2001.

——. "Practical Issues in Applying Metadata Schemas and Controlled Vocabularies to Cultural Heritage Information." *Electronic Cataloging: AACR2 and Metadata for Serials and Monographs, Cataloging & Classification Quarterly* 36, no. 3-4 (2003): 47-55.

——, ed. *Introduction to Art Image Access: Issues, Tools, Standards, Strategies*. Los Angeles: Getty Research Institute, 2002.

——, ed. *Introduction to Metadata: Pathways to Digital Information*. Los Angeles: Getty Information Institute, 1998. Newer version is available online at http://www.getty.edu/research/conducting_research/standards/intrometadata/.

Baca, Murtha, and Patricia Harpring, eds. *Categories for the Description of Works of Art*. [online]. Los Angeles: J. Paul Getty Trust and the College Art Association, 2000. http://www.getty.edu/research/conducting_research/standards/cdwa/ (accessed April 22, 2006).

Bates, Marcia J. "Indexing and Access for Digital Libraries and the Internet: Human, Database, and Domain Factors." *Journal of the American Society for Information Science* 49, no. 13 (1998): 1185-1205.

Beebe, Caroline. "Image Indexing for Multiple Needs." *Art Documentation* 19, no. 2 (2000): 16-21.

Bell, Lesley Ann. "Gaining Access to Visual Information: Theory, Analysis and Practice of Determining Subjects—A Review of the

Literature with Descriptive Abstracts." *Art Documentation* 13, no. 2 (Summer 1994): 89-94.

Bénézit, Emmanuel, ed. *Dictionnaire critique et documentaire des peintres, sculpteurs, dessinateurs et graveurs*. Originally published 1911-1923. Paris: Librairie Gründ, 1976.

BHA: Bibliography of the History of Art/ Bibliographie d'histoire de l'art. Los Angeles, California: J. Paul Getty Trust; Vandoeuvre-lès-Nancy, France: Centre national de la recherche scientifique, Institut de l'information scientifique et technique; 1991-. Online by subscription.

CDWA Lite: XML Schema Content for Contributing Records via the OAI Harvesting Protocol. Los Angeles: J. Paul Getty Trust, 2005. http://www.getty.edu/research/conducting_research/standards/cdwa/cdwalite/cdwalite.html (accessed April 22, 2006).

Chenhall, Robert G., *Revised Nomenclature for Museum Cataloging: Revised and Expanded Version of Robert G. Chenhall's System for Classifying Man-Made Works*. Edited by James R. Blackaby, Patricia Greeno, and The Nomenclature Committee. Nashville, TN: AASLH Press, 1988.

CHIN. *Data Dictionary: Humanities*. Gatineau, Quebec: Canadian Heritage Information Network (CHIN). http://daryl.chin.gc.ca:8000/BASIS/chindd/user/wwwhe/SF.

Fletcher, Banister. *History of Architecture*. 20th ed. Oxford; Boston: Architectural Press, 1996.

Getty Vocabulary Program. *Art & Architecture Thesaurus* (AAT). Los Angeles: J. Paul Getty Trust, 1988. http://www.getty.edu/research/conducting_research/vocabularies/aat/ (accessed April 22, 2006).

———. *Editorial Guidelines*. Los Angeles: J. Paul Getty Trust, 2003. http://www.getty.edu/research/conducting_research/vocabularies/editorial_guidelines.html (accessed April 22, 2006).

———. *Getty Thesaurus of Geographic Names* (TGN). Los Angeles: J. Paul Getty Trust, 1988-. http://www.getty.edu/research/conducting_research/vocabularies/tgn/ (accessed April 22, 2006).

———. *Union List of Artist Names* (ULAN). Los Angeles: J. Paul Getty Trust, 1988-. http://www.getty.edu/research/conducting_research/vocabularies/ulan/ (accessed April 22, 2006).

Grove Dictionary of Art Online. New York: Grove's Dictionaries, 2003. http://www.groveart.com.

Harpring, Patricia. "Can Flexibility and Consistency Coexist? Issues in Indexing, Mapping, and Displaying Museum Information." *Spectra* 26, no. 1 (Spring 1999): 33-35.

———. "Cataloging Architectural Drawings: The Architectural Subject Authority of the Foundation for Documents of Architecture." *Visual Resources* 7, no. 1 (1990): 55-63.

———. "Resistance Is Futile: Inaccessible Networked Information Made Accessible Using the Getty Vocabularies." In *Annual Conference Proceedings*. Silver Spring, MD: American Society for Information Science, 1999.

———. "The Role of Metadata Standards in Mapping Art Information: The Visual Resources Perspective." *VRA Bulletin* 27, no. 4 (Winter 2000): 71-76.

Hensen, Steven L., comp. *Archives, Personal Papers, and Manuscripts*. 2nd ed. Washington, DC: Society of American Archivists, 1989.

Hourihane, Colum. "Subject Classification for Visual Collections: An Inventory of Some of the Principal Systems Applied to Content Description in Images." *VRA Special Bulletin no. 12* (1999).

Hutchins, W. J. "The Concept of 'Aboutness' in Subject Indexing." In *Readings in Information Retrieval*, edited by Karen Sparck Jones and Peter Willett. San Francisco: Morgan Kaufmann, 1997.

Jörgensen, Corinne, ed. "Perspectives on Image Access: Bridging Multiple Needs and Multiple Perspectives." Special section of the *Journal of the American Society for Information Science and Technology* 52, no. 11 (September 2001): 905-979.

Lancaster, F. Wilfrid. *Vocabulary Control for Information Retrieval*. 2nd ed. Arlington, VA: Information Resources Press, 1986.

Lanzi, Elisa, ed. *Introduction to Vocabularies: Enhancing Access to Cultural Heritage Information*. Los Angeles: The J. Paul Getty

Trust, 1998. Updated version edited by Patricia Harpring at http://www.getty.edu/research/conducting_research/vocabularies/introvocabs/ (accessed April 22, 2006).

Lewis, Elizabeth Matthew. "Visual Indexing of Graphic Material." *Special Libraries* 67 (November 1976): 518-527.

Library of Congress Authorities. *Library of Congress Name Authorities.* Washington, DC: Library of Congress, 2005. http://authorities.loc.gov/ (accessed April 22, 2006).

———. *Library of Congress Subject Headings.* Washington, DC: Library of Congress, 2005. http://authorities.loc.gov/ (accessed April 22, 2006).

McRae, Linda, and Lynda White, eds. *ArtMARC Sourcebook: Cataloging Art, Architecture, and Their Images.* Chicago: American Library Association, 1998.

Panofsky, Erwin. *Meaning in the Visual Arts: Papers In and On Art History.* Garden City, NY: Doubleday Books, 1955.

Pass, Gregory. *Descriptive Cataloging of Ancient, Medieval, Renaissance, and Early Modern Manuscripts.* Chicago: Association of College and Research Libraries, 2003.

Porter, Vicki, and Robin Thornes. *Guide to the Description of Architectural Drawings.* New York: G. K. Hall, 1994. Updated version available at http://www.getty.edu/research/conducting_research/standards/fda/ (accessed April 22, 2006).

Rhyne, Charles S. "Images as Evidence in Art History and Related Disciplines," *VRA Bulletin* 25, no. 1 (1998): 58-66.

Roberts, Helene E. "Do You Have Any Pictures of—?: Subject Access to Works of Art in Visual Collections and Book Reproductions," *Art Documentation* 7, no. 3 (Fall 1988): 87-90.

———, ed. *Encyclopedia of Comparative Iconography: Themes Depicted in Works of Art.* Chicago: Fitzroy Dearborn, 1998.

———. "A Picture Is Worth a Thousand Words: Art Indexing in Electronic Databases." *Journal of the American Society for Informa-tion Science and Technology* 52, no. 11 (September 2001): 911-916.

Rowley, Jennifer and John Farrow. *Organizing Knowledge: An Introduction to Managing Access to Information.* 3rd ed. Burlington, VT: Gower, 2000.

Schmitt, Marilyn, ed. *Object, Image, Inquiry: The Art Historian at Work.* Santa Monica, CA: Getty Art History Information Program, 1988.

Simard, Françoise, and France Desmarais. *Documenting Your Collections, Info-Muse Network Documentation Guide.* 2nd ed. Translated by Terry Knowles and Pamela Ireland. Montreal: Société des musées quebécois, 2002.

Society of American Archivists. *Describing Archives: A Content Standard.* Chicago: Society of American Archivists, 2004.

SPECTRUM: The UK Museum Documentation Standard. 2nd ed. Revised and edited by Jeff Cowton. Cambridge: The Museum Documentation Association, 1997.

Straten, Roelof van. *Introduction to Iconography.* Rev. English ed. Translated from the German by Patricia de Man. Yverdon, Switzerland: Gordon and Breach, 1994. Reissued, Overseas Publishers Association, 2000.

Thieme, Ulrich, and Felix Becker, eds. *Allgemeines Lexikon der bildenden Künstler von der Antike bis zur Gegenwart.* 37 vols. 1907. Reprint, Leipzig: Veb E.A. Seemann Verlag, 1980-1986.

Turner, James M. "Subject Access to Pictures: Considerations in the Surrogation and Indexing of Visual Documents for Storage and Retrieval." *Visual Resources* 9, no. 3 (1993): 241-271.

Will, Leonard D. *Thesaurus Principles and Practice.* http://www.willpower.demon.co.uk/thesprin.htm (accessed April 22, 2006).

Glossary

architectural works   Also referred to as *built works* and the *built environment*; structures or parts of structures that were made by human beings; the term is typically reserved for structures that are large enough for human beings to enter, are of practical use, and are relatively stable and permanent.

art works   Visual arts that are of the type collected by art museums; CCO deals with cultural works, which include art works and other works.

associative relationship   A relationship in a thesaurus, namely the relationship between concepts that are closely related conceptually, but the relationship is not hierarchical because it is not whole-part or genus-species. *See also* **equivalence relationship** and **hierarchical relationship**.

authority   A source of standardized forms of terms. Should include references from the variant forms to the preferred form.

authority file   A file, typically electronic, containing Authority Records.

cataloger   In the context of CCO, the person who records information in the Work or Image Record. *See also* **end user**.

cataloging   In the context of CCO, the compilation of information by systematically describing the works and images in a collection.

cataloging tool   In the context of CCO, a type of system that focuses on content description and labeling output (for example, slide labels or wall labels), often part of a more complex collection management system.

classification   In the context of CCO, the systematic categorization of works in categories according to established criteria.

collection   In the context of the cataloging levels discussed in CCO, multiple items that are conceptually or physically arranged together for the purpose of cataloging or retrieval. *See also* **item**, **group**, **volume**, **series**, **set**, and **component**. In a broader sense, typically plural (*collections*), the holdings of a given museum or other repository.

collection management system (CMS)   In the context of museum and special collections cataloging, a type of database system that allows an institution to control various aspects of its collections, including acquisitions, loans, and conservation.

component   A part of a larger item. A component differs from an item in that the item can stand alone as an independent work but the component typically cannot or does not stand alone (for example, a panel of an intact polyptych, an architectural component). *See also* **item**, **group**, **volume**, **collection**, **series**, and **set**.

controlled fields   In the context of CCO, **fields** in a record that are specially formatted and often linked to controlled vocabularies (authorities) or controlled lists to allow for successful retrieval. *See also* **indexing**.

controlled list   A simple list of terms used to control terminology. In a well-constructed controlled list, the following should be true: each term must be unique; terms should all be members of the same class; terms should not be overlapping in meaning; terms should be equal in granularity-specificity; and terms should be arranged alphabetically or in another logical order. A type of controlled vocabulary.

controlled vocabulary   An organized arrangement of words and phrases that are used to index content or to retrieve content through navigation or searching, or both; typically a vocabulary that includes preferred terms and has a limited scope or describes a specific domain.

core elements   In the context of CCO, the set of metadata elements representing the fundamental or most important information required for a **minimal description** of a work or image.

cultural works   In the context of CCO, art and architectural works, and other artifacts of cultural significance, including both physical objects and performance art.

database   A structured set of data held in computer storage, especially one that incorporates software to make it accessible in a variety of ways.

data content   In the context of CCO, the organization and formatting of the words or terms that form the **data values**.

data elements   The specific items or types of information that are collected and aggregated in a **database**.

data structure   A given organization of data, particularly the **data elements** combined with specific, defined links.

data values   In the context of CCO, the terms, words, or numbers used to fill in **fields** in a Work or Image Record.

descriptive metadata   In the context of CCO, data intended to describe and identify cultural works and images.

digital asset management (DAM) tool   A type of **system** for organizing digital media assets for storage and retrieval. Digital asset management tools sometimes incorporate a descriptive cataloging component, but they tend to focus on managing workflow for creating digital assets (for example, digital images, audio clips) and managing rights and permissions.

display fields   In the context of CCO, showing data in natural language that is easily read and understood by users and can convey nuance and ambiguity. Display information may in some cases be concatenated from controlled fields; in other cases, this information is best recorded manually in free-text display fields.

end user   In the context of CCO, the client or patron who retrieves, views, and uses the data compiled by the museum, other repository, or visual resources collection. *See also* **cataloger** and **user**.

equivalence relationship   A relationship in a **thesaurus**, namely the relationship between synonymous terms or names for the same concept, typically distinguishing preferred terms (descriptors) and nonpreferred terms (variants). *See also* **associative relationship** and **hierarchical relationship**.

exhaustivity   In the context of CCO, the degree of depth and breadth that the cataloger uses in description. *See also* **specificity**.

field   A discrete unit of information. In the context of CCO, often used to denote an area (often mapping to a metadata element in a metadata element set) in the user interface of a system where information is displayed or the cataloger can enter information. In this context, **field** is not necessarily equivalent to a database field, which is a placeholder for a set of one or more adjacent characters comprising a unit of information in a database, forming one of the searchable items in a database.

free-text field   A **field** that contains data that may be entered without any formal or system-defined structure, typically allowing the **cataloger** free use of grammar and punctuation.

group   In the context of the cataloging levels of works or images discussed in CCO, an archival group (or record group), which is an aggregate of items that share a common provenance. *See also* **item**, **volume**, **collection**, **series**, **set**, and **component**.

guidelines   A set of statements or other indication of policy or procedure by which a course of action may be determined. *See also* **rules**.

hierarchical relationship   A relationship in a **thesaurus**, namely one of the broader and narrower (parent-child) relationships between two entities, either whole-part or genus-species. *See also* **whole-part relationship**.

image   In the context of CCO (sometimes capitalized), a visual representation of a work, typically existing in photomechanical, photographic, or digital format. In a typical visual resources collection, an image is a slide, photograph, or digital file. *See also* **work**.

indexing   In the context of CCO, the process of evaluating information and creating indexing terms with controlled vocabulary that will aid end users in finding and accessing the Work or Image Record. Refers to indexing done by human labor, not to the automatic parsing of data into a data index, which is used by a system to speed up search and retrieval.

item   An individual object or work. *See also* **group**, **volume**, **collection**, **series**, **set**, and **component**.

link   In the context of CCO, a relationship between two works, a work and an image, or a work or image and an authority; not the same thing as a hypertext link.

metadata   Broadly, "data about data," but in practice, a structured set of descriptive elements used to describe a definable entity. This data may include one or more pieces of information, which can exist as separate physical forms. In the context of CCO, it includes data associated with an information object for purposes of description of a cultural work or associated entity, administration, legal requirements, technical functionality, use and usage, or preservation.

minimal description   In the context of CCO, a **record** containing the minimum amount of information in the minimum number of fields or metadata elements.

online catalog   A type of **system** end users access to search for and view data and images. In the context of CCO, one produced by a museum or other repository, or representing a consolidated collection from several institutions.

polyhierarchical relationships   **Hierarchical relationships** in which each child record may be linked to multiple parent records.

preferred name/preferred term   When discussing authority files or links to authorities in the context of CCO, the name flagged to represent a given concept, person, or place in a given situation (for example, for display in the Work Record). An Authority Record may have more than one name flagged as *preferred* for use in various situations. For example, one name may be in inverted order and flagged as *preferred indexing name* while another may be in natural order and flagged as *preferred display name*.

record   Or **catalog record**; in the context of CCO, a conceptual arrangement of fields referring to a work or image; not the same thing as a database record, which is one row in a database table or another set of related, contiguous data.

related works   In the context of CCO, works that have an important conceptual relationship to each other.

relational database   A **database** that organizes data into related rows and columns as specified by a given relational model in which various relationships are defined.

relationship   A link between two data sets, or, more generally, any association, linkage, or connection between two entities of the same or different types in a system or network. *See also* **link**.

rules   A set of authoritative, prescribed directions for conduct. *See also* **guidelines**.

series   In the context of CCO, a number of works that were created in temporal succession by the same artist or studio and intended by the creator or creators to be seen together or in succession as a cycle. *See also* **item**, **group**, **volume**, **collection**, **set**, and **component**.

set   An assembly of items that the creator intended to be together (for example, a tea set, a desk set, a pair of terrestrial and celestial globes). A set differs from a collection in that it is typically smaller and was intended by the creator to be grouped together. *See also* **item**, **group**, **volume**, **collection**, **series**, and **component**.

specificity   In the context of CCO, the degree of precision or granularity used in description. *See also* **exhaustivity**.

standard   A practice (for example, a set of **rules**) or a product (for example, a vocabulary resource) that is widely recognized or employed as an authoritative or recognized exemplar of correctness or best practice.

subject headings   Words or phrases used to describe the content of a work. *Precoordination of terminology* is a characteristic of subject headings, meaning that they combine several unique concepts together in a string. A type of **controlled vocabulary**.

synonym ring   A set of terms that are considered equivalent.

system   Or **computer system**; a number of interrelated hardware and software components that work together to store and convert data into information by using electronic processing. Within the context of CCO, typi-cally refers to cataloging tools, collection management systems, presentation tools, and digital asset management tools. *See also* **database**.

taxonomy   An orderly classification for a defined domain. A type of **controlled vocabulary**.

thesaurus   A semantic network of unique concepts, including relationships between synonyms, broader and narrower contexts, and other related concepts. Thesauri may be monolingual or multilingual. A type of **controlled vocabulary**.

user   In the context of CCO, any person who uses the CCO guide or a computer system. *See also* **cataloger**, **end user**.

volume   Sheets of paper, vellum, papyrus, or another material that are bound together. Volumes may include printed books, manuscripts, sketchbooks, or albums. *See also* **item**, **group**, **collection**, **series**, **set**, and **component**.

whole-part relationship   A relationship between a larger entity and a part or component. In the context of CCO, typically a relationship between two Work Records or two records in an authority (in which case the relationship occurs in a **thesaurus**). *See also* **hierarchical relationship**.

work   In the context of CCO (sometimes capitalized), a creative product, including architecture, art works such as paintings, drawings, graphic arts, sculpture, decorative arts, photographs that are considered to be art, and other cultural artifacts. A work may be a single item or it may be made up of many physical parts. *See also* **image**.

Contributors

Murtha Baca

Murtha Baca is head of the Getty Vocabulary Program and the Digital Resource Management Department at the Getty Research Institute in Los Angeles. She holds a PhD in art history and Italian language and literature from UCLA. Murtha has published extensively on data standards and controlled vocabularies for indexing and accessing cultural heritage information and enhancing end-user access to images and related data online. In 2002 she edited *Introduction to Art Image Access: Issues, Tools, Standards Strategies* (Los Angeles: Getty Research Institute). Murtha has taught many workshops and seminars on metadata, visual resources cataloging, and thesaurus construction at museums, universities, and other organizations in North and South America and in Europe; she teaches a graduate seminar on metadata in the Department of Information Studies at UCLA.

Patricia Harpring

Patricia Harpring is the managing editor of the Getty Vocabulary Program in Los Angeles, which produces the *Getty Thesaurus of Geographic Names*, the *Union List of Artist Names*, and the *Art & Architecture Thesaurus*. With Murtha Baca, she co-edited *Categories for the Description of Works of Art*. She has worked on and written about data standards and controlled vocabularies for architecture and art-historical materials for more than a decade, including work with ISO (International Organization for Standardization) and NISO (National Information Standards Organization). She holds a PhD in art history.

Elisa Lanzi

Elisa Lanzi is director of the Imaging Center at Smith College, where she builds digital collections and tools for teaching and learning. Prior to this position, Lanzi was a founding partner of Lanzi/Warren Associates, a consultancy that helped clients develop information management practices for improved access to their collections. Lanzi also was manager of the Getty *Art & Architecture Thesaurus*, where she initiated training programs for cultural heritage documentation. She is the author of *Introduction to Vocabularies: Enhancing Access to Cultural Heritage Information*. As chair of the Visual Resources Association Data Standards Committee she helped initiate the VISION project, a collaborative demonstration database for visual resources material, and the *VRA Core Categories*, a metadata standard for cataloging images. Lanzi is a past president of the Visual Resources Association and is active in numerous other professional organizations. She holds a degree in English and art history and has a master's degree in Library and Information Science from the University at Albany (SUNY).

Linda McRae

Linda McRae is university librarian and director of the College of Visual and Performing Arts Visual Resources Library at the University of South Florida. Her research and publications have focused on descriptive standards for cultural objects and images. She has served as the Documentation Standards editor for the *Visual Resources Association Bulletin*. She contributed to the development of the *Visual Resources Association Core Categories, Version 3.0 (VRA Core 3.0)* and *Categories for the Description of Works of Art* (CDWA), two widely referenced standards for the description of works of art. She has published numerous articles and co-authored two books: *African Ethnonyms: Index to Art Producing Peoples of Africa* (1996, G.K. Hall) and *ArtMARC Sourcebook: Cataloging Art, Architecture, and Their Visual Images* (1998, American Library Association).

Ann Whiteside

Ann Whiteside is Head, Rotch Library of Architecture and Planning at MIT. She has wide experience in descriptive metadata and the cataloging of images. Her experience includes developing metadata element sets and guidelines both nationally and at individual institutions, planning for production and delivery of digital images, and overseeing and managing image collections. Ms. Whiteside has participated in the development of image cataloging databases, union catalogs for image collections, and writing cataloging guidelines for local use. She has chaired the Visual Resources Association Data Standards Committee and is a current member. She conducts workshops on image cataloging, and presents papers regarding cataloging issues. She is also a consultant for digital image projects and an advisory committee member for projects related to digital imaging and image management. She is past president of the Visual Resources Association and current president (2006-2007) of the Art Libraries Society of North America.

Index

Names for elements in the Work Record and Authority Records are capitalized. Examples of cataloging practice for works given in the text are shown in italics in the index (e.g., *painting* examples). The examples may be helpful in cataloging a similar work, but for full information and for rules where examples for a particular type are not available, look under the element being cataloged (e.g., Title) or the issue under consideration (e.g., capitalization and abbreviations). "Fig" after a page number indicates examples of complete Work Records, often including links to Authority Records. Page numbers followed by "n" indicate a note on that page.

anonymous creators with a known oeuvre (*cont.*)
  Authority Record, 310 fig 49
  biographical information, 84, 296
  See also unknown creators
apartment building example, Title, 64
appearance, style terms referring to, 161-162
approximate dates of creation, 158
approximate dates of views, 271
approximate measurements, 106, 120
approximations. *See* uncertainty
apron example, Materials and Techniques, 130
arch example
  Date, 169
  Measurements, 110
  View Description and View Type, 265
archaeological site example, Discovery Location, 197
archaeological sites
  Geographic Place Authority, 313
  location, 197
  titles for, 50, 63
archaeological terms, sources of terminology, 213-214
architectural complex example, Title, 67, 68
architectural details
  Materials and Techniques, 128
  Physical Description, 149
architectural drawing example
  Creators, 86, 90
  Date, 176
  Description, 250
  Measurements, 116
  Title, 63
architectural drawings
  creators, 87
  scale, 115-116
  work types for, 56
architectural firm as creator, 87
architectural records example, Measurement, 119
architectural works
  dates of creation, 157
  dates in display, 171
  definition, 375
  form in Work Type, 55
  Location, 194
  Materials and Techniques, 129-130
  Measurements, 119-120
  repositories as, 282
  sources for, 211
  Subject, 207, 223
  titles for, 63, 64
  views, cardinal directions, 266-267

views, interior or exterior, 265
views, subjects of, 210
views of, 7
whole-part relationships in, 16-17
See also buildings and built works
archival group, 377
area, measurement of, 113
armor example, Style, 163
arrowhead example
  Discovery Location, 198
  Measurement, 119
art center example
  View Description and View Type, 264
  Work Record, 275 fig 42
art works, definition, 375
articles (initial) in title, 59
artist. *See* Creator
artistic periods. *See* periods, artistic or historical
artist's books, Materials and Techniques, 127-128
artist's proofs, State, 105, 136
"assistant to," or "associate of," use of, 95
associative relationships
  Concept Authority, 344
  definition, 29-30, 375
  Geographic Place Authority, 323-324
  See also equivalence relationships; reciprocal relationships; related works
astronomy, sources of terminology, 214
"atelier of," use of, 95
Attribution Qualifier
  definition, 78
  organization of data, 44, 79, 99, 107
  terminology, 94-95
attribution types for creator, 84-93
authority, definition, 375
authority files
  definition, 28, 375
  list of links to, 44-47
  overview, 27-34
  relationships in, 21-22 fig 2
  See also Concept Authority; Geographic Place Authority; Personal and Corporate Name Authority; Source Authority; Subject Authority
Authority Records, creation of, 31-32
Authority Records, examples of
  animal, 350 fig 59
  anonymous creator with a known oeuvre, 310 fig 49
  city (administrative place), 327 fig 50

corporate body, 309 fig 48
fictional place, 368 fig 63
historical region (administrative place), 329 fig 52
iconographic episode, 367 fig 62
material, 347 fig 56
named event, 366 fig 61
person, 308 fig 47
physical feature, 328 fig 51
religious figure, 365 fig 60
style, 349 fig 58
work type, 348 fig 57

B

banner example, Materials and Techniques, 125
bannerstone example
  Date, 174
  Description, 250
basilica example
  whole-part relationship, 17, 38-39 fig 7
  Work Record, 38 fig 7, 75 fig 13, 154 fig 21, 243 fig 38
  Work Type, 54, 55
basket example, Current Location, 195
bas-relief (low-relief) sculpture example
  Conservation and Treatment History, 145
  Description, 253
  Discovery Location, 197
  Title, 68
BC and AD in dates, 169
BCE and CE in dates, 168, 169, 294
"before" and "after" in date of the work, 173
"before present" in dates, 169-170
binding method, 127
biographical information
  anonymous creators, 84
  display of, 83, 293-304
  uncertain, 282
  in Work Record, 78-79
Birth Date (Personal and Corporate Name Authority)
  organization of data, 283, 305
  rules, 297-298
  sources for, 285
bon à tirer, State, 136
book example
  Edition, 139
  Inscription, 143
  Work Record, 232 fig 35
books
  Edition, 105, 138-139
  Materials and Techniques, 127-128
  Measurements, 118
  Work Type referring to content, 56

medium and support (*cont.*)
   in Work Types, 56
   See also Materials and Techniques; supports (backing)
memorial building example
   Description, 250
   whole-part relationships in, 17
metadata, definition, 377
metadata standards in key principles, 2
method of application of materials. *See* techniques
method of representation, descriptive note, 250
minimal descriptions, 7-11, 377. *See also* required elements
mixed media. *See* multiple media
mobile example, Title, 61
model example, Materials and Techniques, 127
mola (clothing) example, Materials and Techniques, 130
monastery example
   whole-part relationships in, 16-17
   Work Type, 54
monumental works, location of, 194
mosaic example
   Date, 173
   View Description and View Type, 264
   Work Type, 56
mosque example
   Title, 65
   Work Type, 57
mosque lamp example, Work Type, 56
motifs and patterns, 144
motion pictures, running time, 115
movable works, location of, 193-194
movements as style terms, 156, 163
multiple broader contexts. *See* polyhierarchical relationships
multiple class designations, 240
multiple creators
   attribution to, 78, 85-86
   groups of works, 90
   See also Attribution Qualifier
multiple dates for work. *See* Date Qualifier (creation date)
multiple media
   in different parts of works, 132
   priority of, 126-127
   syntax, 122-123
multiple nationalities, 297
multiple objects in one view, 266
multiple parent-child relationships. *See* polyhierarchical relationships

multiple roles, 78, 97. *See also* Life Role
multiple subjects in a work, 223
multiple titles for works, 65
multiple-part works. *See* components of multiple-part works
mural example
   Location, 195
   Materials and Techniques, 125
museum collections
   creator information, 78
   database design in, 25
   and Physical Characteristics, 106
   use of Class, 235
museum example
   view information, 265, 266
   Work Record, 180 fig 23
   Work Type, 57
musical instrument example, Date, 176
mythological figures, in Title, 62
mythological places. *See* legendary or fictional places

N

Name (Geographic Place Authority), 314
Name (Personal and Corporate Name Authority), 283
Name (Subject Authority), 357-358
names
   fullness of (*see* fullness of names)
   of persons, in Subject, 212, 217, 353
   preferred (*see* preferred names)
   See also Term; terminology
narrative subjects, 218
Nationality (Personal and Corporate Name Authority)
   in biographical information, 83, 157
   organization of data, 283, 305
   rules, 296-297
   sources for, 284-285
   See also Culture
natural and inverted order. *See* inverted or natural order of names and terms
necklace example, Materials and Techniques, 129
neighborhoods, in Location, 197
new media. *See* computer art; digital media; electronic media
nicknames, 81, 290
no date available for date of work, 175
non-artists as creators, 88-90
nonrepresentational works, 221 fig 31
   Subject, 207, 221
   See also abstract works

non-Western art, titles for, 50, 63
non-Western creators, inversion of names, 291
normalizing queries, 32, 41n4
Note (Concept Authority), 341, 343
Note (Geographic Place Authority), 314, 324
Note (Personal and Corporate Name Authority), 283, 303-304
Note (Subject Authority), 355, 360
notes, descriptive. *See* Description; Other Descriptive Notes
notes, display of, 254
notes, scope (Concept Authority), 335
nuance of location, 186, 192
nuance of subject, 216
numbered titles, 64
numerals
   in dates, 167
   in edition, 138
numeric ID. *See* Repository's Unique ID
numerical indicators (State), 136. *See also* State Identification
numerical values. *See* Value (numerical)

O

obelisk example, Location, 194
obi example, Work Type, 55
object type. *See* Work Type
objects facet in Concept Authority, 332, 339
objects not part of the work, in view information, 269
oblique projection example, groups of works, 58
observation tower example, Work Record, 153 fig 19
"office of," use of, 95
of-ness, 207-208, 234n5
ongoing works, dates for, 171
online catalog, 27, 377
"or" in date of the work, 171-172
order of topics in descriptive note, 248
original objects vs. visual surrogates
   description of, xii
   measurement of unavailable objects, 120
ornament (jewelry) example, Style, 162
Other Descriptive Notes
   organization of data, 45, 246
   rules, 252-253
other location information, 187
other title types, 69
owners' names in titles, 64
owner's title, 60-61
ownership history, 200

P

preferred terms
    Concept Authority, 339, 344-
        345
    definition, 377
preferred titles, 58, 69, 70
pre-iconographical description, 208
preparatory works in extrinsic rela-
    tionship, 17-18
presentation databases, 26-27
presentation drawing example
    groups of works, 58
    Work Type, 56
presentation of the data. *See* dis-
    play and indexing
president's dwelling example, Work
    Record, 181 fig 24
previous subjects. *See* former iden-
    tifications of subjects
print example
    Date, 170
    Edition, 139, 140
    Edition Size, 138
    Facture, 143
    Inscription, 141
    Mark, 134
    Materials and Techniques, 126
    Measurements, 116
    multiple creators, 86
    Subject, 220 fig 30, 224
    Title, 61, 65, 66, 67, 68
    Work Record, 74 fig 12
printer's proof, State, 105, 136
prints
    Edition, syntax of, 138
    Materials and Techniques, 126
    State, 105, 106, 135-140
private collections, in Location, 196
"probably" in date of the work, 171
process (technique). *See* Materials
    and Techniques
proper names. *See* Names
provenance (ownership history),
    200
pseudonyms and nicknames, 81,
    290
publishers as creators, 88
punctuation in Work Type, 55
"pupil of," use of, 95
pyramid example
    Facture, 143
    view information, 265, 271

Q

qualifiers
    attribution (*see* Attribution
        Qualifier)
    for dates, 83-84, 158, 159, 176-
        177
    decades and centuries, 174
    homographs, 341-342
    little-known places, 198
    Materials and Techniques, 44-
        45, 107, 111, 147

Measurements, 44, 107, 111
    for Style or Period, 164
    term, 336

R

radiocarbon dating, 182n3
radiograph example, Work Type, 55
range or position, in View
    Description, 264
ranges of years. *See* spans of years
rare book example
    Materials and Techniques, 127
    Measurements, 118
reading desk example, Work
    Record, 277 fig 44
reciprocal relationships, 22-23 fig
    3, 302
recommended elements. *See*
    required elements
record, definition, 377
Record Type
    Concept Authority, 46, 283, 344
    Geographic Place Authority, 46,
        314, 322
    Personal and Corporate Name
        Authority, 46, 301, 366
    Subject Authority, 46, 355, 361
    use of, 13, 58
references (citations), Source
    Authority, 33-34. *See also*
    sources of terminology
regions as geographic places, 313
Related Concepts, 336, 344
Related Geographic Places, 314,
    316, 323-324, 355
Related Keywords, 355-357, 360
Related People and Corporate
    Bodies, 283, 302-303, 355
Related Subjects, 355, 361
related terms (Concept Authority),
    336, 344
related works, 13-19
    cataloging decisions about, 3
    conceptual relationships among
        works, 18
    definition, 377
    descriptive note, 251
    displays of, 18-19, 22, 67, 225
    in Subject display, 224
    in Work Records, 19, 37 fig 6,
        38-39 fig 7
    vs. Work-Images, 5
relational databases, 20, 377
Relationship Type (Concept
    Authority), 46, 336, 344
Relationship Type (Geographic
    Place Authority), 46, 314,
    323
Relationship Type (Personal and
    Corporate Name Authority),
    46, 283, 302
Relationship Type (Subject
    Authority), 47, 355, 361

relationships
    Concept Authority, 342-344
    and database design, 20-27
    definition, 377
    entity relationship diagram, 23
        fig 1
    equivalence, 29, 376
    extrinsic, 17-18
    intrinsic, 13-17
    in key principles, 3
    type and reciprocity, 22-23 fig 3
    whole-part between works, 51
    See also associative relation-
        ships; hierarchical relation-
        ships; links; related works
relator terms. *See* Creator Role
religious subjects
    Authority Record for, 365 fig 60
    titles for, 62
repeatable fields, 23. *See also*
    "organization of data" under
    specific elements, e.g.,
    Creator
repositories
    in authority, 281-282 (*see also*
        Personal and Corporate
        Name Authority)
    display of names, 307
    language of name, 192
    as location, 184, 195-196, 313
    sources of terminology for
        names, 188-189
    syntax of names, 193
Repository's Unique ID, 45, 50,
    184, 187
representational subjects
    narrative, 218
    non-narrative, 219
required elements
    Class, 236
    Concept Authority, 336
    Creator, 79
    definition, 43
    Geographic Place Authority, 314
    Location, 187
    notes, 246
    Personal and Corporate Name
        Authority, 283
    Physical Characteristics, 107
    Style, Culture, and Date, 158-
        159
    Subject, 211
    Subject Authority, 355
    Title, 51
    view information, 261
    Work Records, 11-12
    Work Type, 51
restoration history. *See*
    Conservation and Treatment
    History
retrieval issues
    considerations, 32-33
    and database design, 26

retrieval issues (*cont.*)
    images of works, 261
    normalizing queries, 41n4
    vocabularies for, 30, 31
ring (jewelry) example, Materials
    and Techniques, 132
rock carving example, Date, 169
rock painting example, Current
    Location, 198
roles. *See* Creator Role; function of
    corporate bodies; Life Role
room example, Title, 68
round painting example,
    Measurements, 112
round works, measurement of,
    111-112
rounding of measurements, 120
rulers' names
    as date of work, 175
    style terms referring to, 163
rules, definition, 378
running time measurements, 115

S
sacramentary example
    Description, 248
    Work Record, 179 fig 22
sampler (textile) example, Work
    Type, 57
Scale
    organization of data, 44, 107,
        146
    terminology, 115-116
"school of"
    in Style, 156
    use of, 95
science, general, sources of termi-
    nology, 214
scope note, Concept Authority,
    335. *See also* Description
screen example
    Class, 240
    Materials and Techniques, 128
    Measurements, 117
    Title, 63
    Work Record, 151 fig 18
scroll example
    Measurements, 114
    Work Type, 55
scroll painting example, Work Type,
    54
sculpture
    form in Work Type, 55
    Materials and Techniques, 126-
        127
sculpture example
    Creator Role, 96
    Date, 169, 171, 176
    Description, 249, 251
    Edition, 140
    Location, 193, 199, 200
    Materials and Techniques, 122,
        126, 127

Title, 61, 62, 64
    View Description and View
        Type, 265, 266
    Work Type, 57
search and retrieval. *See* retrieval
    issues
senior and junior in names, 289,
    290
series of works
    definition, 378
    in subject display, 224
series records
    elements for, 12
    relationships in, 15-16
set, definition, 378
sex. *See* gender
Shape
    organization of data, 44, 107,
        146
    terminology, 112-113
shared cataloging environments
    and use of Class, 236. *See
        also* consortial environments
shield strap example, Work Type, 56
shrine example, Date, 172
signatures. *See* Inscription
simple attributions, 85
singular vs. plural terms
    Class, 238
    Concept Authority, 339-340
    and Library of Congress Subject
        Headings, 234n3
    Materials and Techniques, 121
    in retrieval, 32-33
    Subject, 215
    View Subject, 267
    Work Type, 54
sinopia (drawing) example, Work
    Type, 55
size and requirements of the collec-
    tion, 8
size measurements, 113, 114
size of edition. *See* Edition Size
sketch example
    Current Location, 196
    Materials and Techniques, 123
    Title, 63
skyscraper example
    Date, 170
    Title, 64
    View Description and View
        Type, 267
    Work Type, 55
slashes, use of in dates, 174
snuff box example, Materials and
    Techniques, 129
sofa example
    Date, 177
    Materials and Techniques, 128
Source (Concept Authority), 336,
    343
Source (Description), organization
    of data, 45, 246

Source (Geographic Place
    Authority), 314
Source (Other Descriptive Notes),
    246
Source (Personal and Corporate
    Name Authority), 283
Source (State), 44, 107, 137
Source (Subject Authority), 355
Source (Title), 49, 51
Source Authority
    definition, 33-34
    links to notes, 254
    organization of data, 44, 107
sources, and notes, 246, 253
sources of information for State,
    137
sources of information for Title, 69
sources of terminology
    Class, 236-237
    Concept Authority, 336-337
    Creator, 79-80
    Creator Role, 80
    Date, 159, 167, 262, 270, 285,
        305, 316, 337, 357
    Geographic Place Authority,
        315-316, 322
    Location, 187-189
    notes, 246-247
    Personal and Corporate Name
        Authority, 283, 285, 300-
        301, 306
    Physical Characteristics, 108
    Style and Culture, 159
    Subject, 211-214
    Subject Authority, 355-357, 359
    Title, 52-53
    view information, 261-262
    Work Type, 52
spans of years
    date of the work, 157, 158, 166-
        167
    groups of works, 175
    indicating uncertainty, 83, 171-
        173
    year of completion, 170
    and years BCE, 183
    See also Birth Date; dates of
        activity; Death Date
spatial relationships among works,
    18
specificity or granularity
    Class, 236, 239
    Creator Role, 96
    Culture, 158
    Date, 158, 171-175
    definition, 8, 378
    in general, 31
    Location, 185, 195-200
    Nationality, 297
    notes, 246
    Physical Characteristics, 106
    Place Type, 320
    roles, life or function, 300